THE PROLETARIAN GAMBLE

ASIA-PACIFIC: CULTURE, POLITICS, AND SOCIETY

....

Editors: Rey Chow, H. D. Harootunian, and Masao Miyoshi

THE PROLETARIAN GAMBLE

Korean Workers in Interwar Japan

Ken C. Kawashima

DUKE UNIVERSITY PRESS   DURHAM AND LONDON   2009

Printed in the United States
of America on acid-free paper ∞
Designed by Amy Ruth Buchanan
Typeset in Quadraat by
Achorn International, Inc.
Library of Congress Cataloging-in-
Publication Data appear on the last
printed page of this book.

Duke University Press gratefully
acknowledges the support of the
Department of East Asian Studies
at the University of Toronto, which
provided funds towards the production of this book, and also The
Academy of Korean Studies Grant,
which is funded by the Korean
Government (MEST, Basic
Research Promotion Fund).

This book is dedicated to Fujiya and Joung-ja Kawashima

CONTENTS

....

ACKNOWLEDGMENTS

I'd like to thank my family for all their inspiration and support over the years: Joung-ja Kawashima, my loving mother; and Kimi Kawashima, my Supreme Sistah. Most of all, I would like to dedicate this book to the memory of my father, Fujiya Kawashima, who taught me a great deal about Japan, Korea, history, and art.

I count myself as one of the lucky ones to have known and worked with historian Harry Harootunian for such a long time. He's been an intellectual inspiration since my undergraduate days at the University of Chicago, and he has guided my studies, research, and thinking in a thousand and one ways ever since. This book simply could not have been written had it not been for his tireless support and intellectual companionship.

Katsuhiko Mariano Endo has saved my life more than once in addition to enlightening me with the finer points of Uno Kōzō's methodology; and Rebecca Karl has been a one-in-a-million teacher and friend since my days at NYU. I'd like to also thank Hyun Ok Park, Bill Haver, Louise Young, Sabu Kohso, Bruce Cumings, Tets Najita, Tak Fujitanti, Matsumoto Takenori, Nagahara Yutaka, Higuchi Yuichi, Oki Kosuke, Sato Takashi, Adachi Mariko, Jesook Song, Andre Schmid, Ritu Birla, Kanishka Goonewardena, Gavin Smith, Atsuko Sakaki, Eric Cazdyn, Janice Kim, Robert Albritton, Shivrang Setlur, C-Murda Vernon, Olga Fedorenko, and Sun-young Yang. Lastly, Sugar Brown expresses musical thanks to Rockin' Johnny Burgin, Taildragger, Dave Waldman, Sho'nuff Sho, Suzuki Sue, Watanabe Satoshi, Noma Ichiro, Samm Bennett, Haruna Ito, Paul Dutton, Dr. Feelgood, The Wolf of Nitouk, and Bob Vespaziani.

I originally completed the archival research for this project between 1998 and 2000 at the Ohara Institute for Social Problems (Hōsei University), where Suzuki Akira, Sadamori-san, and Iida-san were especially kind and helpful to me. Generous research grants from the Fulbright Foundation and Hōsei University's International Fellowship made that research possible.

Last but not least, I'd like to thank Reynolds Smith, Neal McTighe, Emily Bliss, Sharon Torian, and Celia Braves of Duke University Press for their enthusiasm and cooperation in publishing this book.

INTRODUCTION

....

Instead of thinking contingency as a modality of necessity, or [as] an exception to it, we must think necessity as the becoming-necessary of the encounter of contingencies.

—Louis Althusser, 1982

One morning in 1930, in the Japanese industrial city of Osaka, Korean worker Koh Joon-sok woke up in his single room in a Korean-managed rooming house for day workers (*doboku beya*), ate his breakfast, and then left the house, pretending to hunt for a job. He felt compelled to at least appear to be looking for a job; he had been unemployed for over a month, and he owed money to two fellow Koreans who managed rooming houses for Korean day workers in Osaka. Koh's original dream was to work in Japan and study at the same time (kugaku), and he had borrowed some money from his Korean acquaintances and friends, primarily to purchase books and other study-related supplies.[1]

Koh had come to Osaka in 1925 from his native Cheju Island in Korea, where his family had struggled to make ends meet since the implementation in 1920 of the Japanese *sammai zōshoku keikaku*, or the program to increase rice production. Koh left Cheju Island in search of work to earn much-needed cash, a portion of which he planned to send back to his family in Korea. But Koh had been fired from his first job in Japan, had quit his second job after one too many racist comments and a fistfight over a bicycle, and had been fired from his third job for a minor, honest mistake. Now, not only was he unable to subsidize his family in Korea, but he also owed money to the rooming house managers, men whose generosity, help, and social connections to factory bosses and sub-contractors had helped Koh secure his jobs in Japan. Koh was painfully aware that his debts represented a reduction in the rooming managers' monthly incomes.

Finding work as a Korean during an industrial recession in Osaka hadn't been easy, but Koh was able to land his first job at a small, family-operated factory that packaged electrical light bulbs. For 65 sen a day, and from 7:30 in the morning to 6:30 in the evening, Koh worked the machines that manufactured paper containers. His wages were significantly less than those of the Japanese workers there, and he earned only 15 sen above the daily cost—50 sen—of his rooming house. Out of his remaining 15 sen, 8 went to train fare to get to and from the factory, leaving him 7 sen a day to get by—not enough to both cover his daily necessities and subsidize his family. Then, one day, he was asked to deliver a large supply of light bulbs on a bicycle. Koh had little experience riding bicycles, let alone riding them with a large and heavy load to carry, and he crashed the bike and broke all the light bulbs. The boss's last words to Koh were, "You stupid Korean! Damn Fool! Get outta here!" (Chōsenjinme ga! Aho dara! Deteke!).[2]

Koh began searching for another job, but quickly realized that almost all factories were unwilling to employ Koreans. For a month Koh went jobless, and he soon owed his rooming house manager 20 yen in rent. Koh felt lucky, therefore, when he was presented with a new job prospect, as an apprentice to a blacksmith at the Morita Ironworks factory. There, he could live on the site and earn 3 yen a month, an amount Koh hoped would allow him to start night classes. He took the job, which mostly entailed work around the shop floor that the two other employees, both Japanese, did not do, such as cleaning and sweeping, drawing water from the street water pipes to use in the factory, and keeping the fires in the large ovens burning all day. The monthly wage of 3 yen, however, was not enough to send him to night classes. After paying for a toothbrush, toothpaste, towels, public baths, train fare, haircuts, shirts, work pants, shoes, and socks, Koh had little left over. He decided to skip baths to save money, and his body was continually caked in coal residue and machine grease. On top of this, the boss, determined to make Koh work hard all day long, castigated Koh for occasionally reading a newspaper, which Koh did to improve his Japanese. His boss told him to forget about studying and to just work hard. Maybe one day, his boss said, he could go back to Korea and begin his own business in ironworks or machine manufacturing. Koh endured the terrible pay, the demoralizing colonial work ethic, and his boss's demeaning disciplinary tactics for nearly three years, but after the boss's wife told Koh that his "Korean shit" was stinking up the shared bathroom in the factory, and after one of the Japanese workers punched Koh in the face after Koh used his bicycle without permission to run a small errand for the boss, Koh had finally had enough. He quit, returned to the rooming house, and began a search for a new job.

Another month passed without finding work. Finally, Koh's friend at the rooming house introduced him to a job opening at a small printing press, owned by a Japanese couple, in the Higashi ward of Osaka. Koh's job included cleaning parts of the press after the day's work was completed, including the stone tablets that were inked daily to meet the day's printing orders. One morning, Koh discovered one of the stone tablets in the factory that had not yet been cleaned. Surely the boss did a late night printing job, Koh speculated, and was too tired to clean the stone tablet before going to sleep. Koh scrubbed and washed down the stone—but it so happened that the boss had received an order for a printing job late in the night, and had deliberately left the stone tablet inked because he intended to use it first thing in the morning. When the boss and his wife discovered that Koh had mistakenly cleaned the stone, they exploded in anger, calling him a fool. Even though it was an honest mistake, and even though Koh apologized, he was fired.

Once again, Koh was unemployed, and with each passing day, thoughts of the accumulating debts from his unpaid housing costs outweighed any hopes of attending night school or sending money back home to Korea. Koh, full of despair and frustration, was tired of searching for job after job amidst oppressive uncertainty, tired of enduring repeated racist incidents both on and off the job, and tired of the predictability of unpredictable firings. In short, he was sick of these proletarian dice-box blues. In his autobiography, *Border Crossings*, Koh writes:

> Falling into unemployment again, I left the rooming house after eating breakfast, but only pretended to leave the house to look for a job. With no idea where to go or what to do, I kicked around town aimlessly, and my entire daily routine consisted of going to Nakanojima Park and sleeping on a bench. If I had any money, I'd have gone to the movies, but I had none. The Nakanojima public library was nearby, but I didn't even feel like reading a book. I didn't feel like doing anything. I only prayed that someone would find me a job.[3]

The situation in which Koh Joon-sok repeatedly found himself was common to Korean workers in interwar Japan in a number of ways. Discrimination and racism against Korean workers in Japan existed not only in terms of the kinds of jobs that were available—and, more often, unavailable—to Korean workers, but also in the pervasive discriminatory practices of employers, who would habitually suddenly fire or refuse to hire Korean workers, especially in factories between the two World Wars. Koh's living situation was also commonplace for Korean workers, insofar as he was often compelled to reside with fellow Korean workers in rooming houses managed by Koreans. These circumstances reflect the pervasive racism in the housing markets of Japan. Racism here took the form of Japanese landlords refusing to lease to Korean tenants and of mass evictions of Korean tenants from rooming houses. At the same time, Koh's housing situation shows the extent to which Korean workers depended on Korean rooming house managers as social liaisons to sites of employment. The Korean housing situation thus contained within it a social network that facilitated the process of finding work; it was part of the larger commodification of labor power. However, there was a limit to this social network, partially because of frequent evictions, which threatened the existence of these social connections between housing and work, but also because factory doors were increasingly closed to Koreans during the economic recession of the 1920s and early 1930s. Extremely few Korean workers were hired in large-scale factories, and when Korean workers found employment in small, family-owned factories, employment usually did not last more than six months. Koh's three-year tenure at the printing press factory was, in this regard, relatively long. For most Korean workers, three years at a fixed site of work was extremely rare.

As the agricultural immiseration of the Korean countryside worsened over the span of the 1920s and 1930s, the number of Korean workers migrating to Japan steadily increased, but they consistently found few opportunities to work in factories. An increasingly chronic and large reserve of Korean workers was therefore compelled to find employment outside of the factory system, and to search for work on a daily basis in the day labor market, where employment was not guaranteed. Daily employment was by its very nature temporary, and workers were often regarded as disposable labor on construction sites for public works. Worse, employment in the day labor market was necessarily vulnerable to chance: one had to rise early in the morning, stand on designated corners of the city as a so-called tachinbō or ankō, and hope to encounter familiar sub-contractors or their labor brokers (often called tehaishi, 手配師) seeking cheap and temporary labor for the day. Day labor was thus contingent in at least two senses, first in the sense of being vulnerable to chance, but also in the sense of being dependent upon social, institutional, or semi-institutional connections. In addition, day laborers lived at the whim of uncontrollable matters such as the weather. A well-known adage among day workers was, "You don't have to kill a day worker with a knife; the rain will do just the same."

Koh's situation not only reveals a common plight among Korean workers in Japan, but also the unique proletarian condition of being caught between the acute necessity of working to survive, and the equally acute contingencies associated with finding and maintaining a job in a capitalist commodity economy. What begs further historical, theoretical, and political analysis is the way the proletariat is compelled to experience the shaking of the dice-box of chance on the road to work. Koh's precarious situation in Nakanojima Park tells us that we need to think about how the proletariat is bound to work out of necessity, yet amidst conditions that are necessarily contingent. How are workers compelled to work for wages out of necessity, but with no guarantees that work can be gotten? How and why is the process of finding work in a capitalist commodity economy contingent—but necessarily so? What is contingent about the commodification of labor power, and how are workers compelled to become dependent on a wide array of social and institutional networks of power to find work?

The Ideology of Capitalist Chance

These are important and germane questions to ask in our contemporary capitalist conjuncture, for they are commonly obscured by a prevailing ideology that announces that today's capitalism operates like a huge casino, where winners and losers are determined by the invisible hand of luck, and by the aleatory throw of the dice. For example, Susan Strange famously writes in *Casino Capitalism* that the international financial system has become "so much like a gambling hall . . . [that it] has made inveterate, and largely involuntary, gamblers of us all."[4] The problem with the casino simile, however, is that it treats the appearance of chance and contingency in capitalism as inevitable and natural phenomena. This analysis disavows and conceals the fact that the appearance of chance in capitalism follows a trajectory of necessity that is bound to the workings of capitalist production based on the commodification of labor power and the process of exchange between owners of money and labor power. Therefore, in opposition to the blind acceptance of the metaphysics of speculation and the ideology of pure chance in texts such as *Casino Capitalism*, what we need to think about today is the materialism of what Louis Althusser called the becoming-necessary of contingency in capitalism, a problem acutely perceivable in the process of transforming labor power into a commodity, and in the aleatory encounter between owners of money and owners of labor power.[5]

Althusser's rethinking of the concept of materialism from the perspective of the becoming-necessary of contingency in the encounter between owners of money and owners of labor power is crucial to understanding the problem of labor in our transnational, post-Fordist situation. Many have already pointed out that in America and Europe since the oil shock of 1973, the condition of the working class has become much more precarious and contingent as the result of flexible modes of capitalist accumulation, neoliberal deregulation, and the privatization of social welfare. For example, recent scholars have drawn attention to what has been called contingent work and contingent labor, especially in the case of chronic temp workers in contemporary America.[6] Grace Chang has referred to the contingencies of immigrant labor in post-Fordist America when she describes "disposable domestics."[7] And who today can deny the importance of the problem of contingent labor in America, especially in light of recent immigration policy proposals in America which, according to Martin Kopple, are designed to "allow some immigrants to eventually obtain permanent residence while keeping millions in a vulnerable status in order to maintain a permanent pool of super-exploited labor"?[8] In Europe, too, it is common today to refer to contingent employment to describe the unpredictable social conditions in which the immigrant *travailleur precaire* struggles to find even part-time work.[9] The burning of suburban Paris by unemployed youth last year is testament to the severity and urgency of this situation. In post-Mao China, the so-called socialist market economy has produced the world's largest floating population, whose precarious existence hangs in the balance as many leave the vast countryside to find non-guaranteed work in China's industrial cities.[10] And in post-bubble, post-Koizumi, privatization-wild Japan, and under the ultranationalist flag waving of pro–militarist fascist hacks like Tokyo mayor Ishihara Shintaro, who today can deny the now chronic existence of the *fureeta*, that mass of workers—young and old, foreign and non-foreign, educated and non-educated—who are maintained and exploited as a contingent and, in euphemistic terms, flexible labor pool to meet the post-Fordist (and perhaps post-Toyota-ist) demands and fluctuations of industrial, commercial, and finance capital?[11] In short, if an analysis of labor today is to be carried out, it cannot be done without considering the way workers are bound to work in a milieu of contingencies with no guarantees of subsistence.

A Short Genealogy of Capitalist Contingency

It would be wrong, however, to approach the problem of contingent labor as if it were simply an effect of the transformation of capitalism after 1973. The contemporary proliferation, maintenance, and exploitation of contingent labor should not blind us to the fact that contingent labor and the inexorable contingency inherent to the commodification of labor power are endemic to capitalist commodity economies, and that that has been true since the inception of industrial capital. Writing in 1819, for example, John Charles-Leonard de Sismondi described an entirely new social situation in early industrial France, one in which workers were first separated from their communal properties in the countryside and then compelled to work in the cities, but with no guarantees of subsistence. Sismondi writes:

> We are, and it has not been sufficiently emphasized, in an entirely new social situation, of which we have as yet very little experience. There is a trend towards the separation of all forms of property from all forms of labour, towards the dissolution of all the ties between master and servant, and towards the elimination of any involvement of the latter in the profits of the former. . . . The condition into which we are now entering is entirely new; the labouring population is free; but it has no guarantee of its subsistence. It must live from its work; but it never sees and never knows who will consume the product of its labour. It has no means of measuring its efforts in relation to the rewards it might expect.[12]

In a similar vein, historian and philosopher Jacques Rancière has shown in his book *Nights of Labor* how the misfortune of the worker's condition in France in the 1830s was strikingly similar to today's *travailleur precaire*. That condition in the 1830s, Rancière argues, did not lie so much "in the unbridled fury of poverty as in the Brownian movements that constantly affect[ed] precarious and transitory forms of existence."[13] Rancière thus identified an aleatory population, a population of workers that had been thrown into a capitalist commodity economy like a throw of the dice, and that experienced "the aleatory character of a situation daily put into question." This aleatory population, Rancière continues:

> Represents less the army of the marginal or declassed than the proletariat in its very essence that is concealed under the wretched or glorious images of the factory damned. . . . They represent very accurately the

aleatory history and geography that bring together those individuals who live, each and every one, in the absolute precariousness of having no trump to play but the availability of their arms and suffering from the day-to-day uncertainty of their employment more than from the exploitation of their product.[14]

It was Karl Marx, however, who was perhaps the first to argue and demonstrate fully how the poverty of the free worker was tied fundamentally to the worker's agony of having to work in order to live, but with no guarantees for the exchange of labor power as a commodity. As he wrote in the *Grundrisse*, the free worker has "[n]ecessity on all sides, [but does not have] . . . the objectivities necessary to realize himself as labor capacity."[15] The free worker—who is free in a double sense, of being free to sell his or her labor power as a commodity, but also free of all means of production to provide for self-subsistence—is forced to necessarily confront all kinds of contingencies in the process of the sale and purchase of labor power, all kinds of accidents and uncontrollable risks that prevent the worker from realizing his labor potential. On the hard road to work through commodification, the free worker is offered only the thought of realizing his labor capacity or potential through exchange, but with no attendant, practical guarantees to do so. This insight leads Marx to write these words: "It is already contained in the concept of the 'free worker' that he is a pauper: *virtual pauper*. . . . He can live as a worker only insofar as he exchanges his labor capacity for that part of capital which forms the labor fund. *This exchange is tied to conditions which are accidental for him, and indifferent to his organic presence. He is thus a virtual pauper.*"[16]

Marx's insight on the virtual pauper, which is inextricably bound to the concept of the free worker, is premised on the problem of "conditions which are accidental" or contingent for the seller of labor power. This insight is just as important to understanding the historical conditions of contingent labor in our contemporary neoliberal, capitalist economy as it is to understanding the Korean colonial working class in interwar Japan, their forms of destitution, as well as their various political and social struggles involving labor and urban tenant unions. Korean workers were not simply oppressed in Japan by the fury of poverty, but by the anguish of never knowing whether they would earn wages to subsist. The analysis of this chronic sense of anticipation and anxiety has yet to be fully accounted for in historical studies or by government surveys. For example, interwar Japanese government surveys on the conditions of Korean workers in Japan completely failed to capture, let alone question, this sense of anticipation and uncertainty; instead surveys merely documented, primarily through statistics, the most outwardly visible aspects of poverty, such as low income levels, cheap wages, expenses for means of subsistence, run-down housing conditions, tattered clothing, and lack of hygiene. These empirical findings obfuscated the practices and processes that, if analyzed, would have disclosed the extent to which Korean free workers were poor because they were compelled to confront, on a daily basis, a wide range of contingencies and uncertainties within the process of exchange. These contingencies were the root cause of the poverty experienced by the Korean working class and by masses of Korean proletarians. This was particularly true when these contingencies were combined with institutionalized forms and practices of racism.

Rethinking the Proletariat through the Surplus Population

Here the reader may ask, "But are you really talking about Korean proletarians? Can you really think of Mr. Koh—chronically unemployed, pretending to look for a job, and sleeping on a bench in Nakanojima Park as a daily routine—as a proletarian? Has he not more accurately fallen into the ranks of the lumpenproletariat?" Other readers may ask, "Aren't you confusing 'proletarian' for 'immigrant,' and aren't you really talking about the radical alterity of the colonial other in the cosmopolitan belly of the beast?" And a much less sympathetic reader may even ask, "Isn't the very concept of the proletariat simply passé? Didn't it die out with the end of history and the fall of the Soviets, and with the rampant de-industrialization of the 1980s and 1990s in the Free World? Moreover, hasn't Lou Dobbs proven that everyone is part of the middle class?"

The differences between these questions and their attendant political and theoretical positions are fairly obvious, but the problem is that they all secretly hold to—and perhaps even secretly wish for—an ideal image of what the proletariat is or used to be. The ideal image is (still) one that is defined largely through occupations, usually those in factories. This is particularly true for many Marxist approaches to labor. The common Marxist conceptualization of the proletariat focuses almost exclusively on the problem of exploitation in terms of fixed occupations within sites of capitalist production. At the same time, however, it has also been shown that the conceptualization of the proletariat, especially in the text of Marx, is fundamentally ambivalent.[17] On the one hand, Marx emphasized the proletariat in terms of its experience within capitalist production, where the unpaid labor of workers is exploited in the process of transforming surplus labor time into surplus value. In this approach, Marx especially conceptualized the proletariat in terms of the most mature forms and methods of capitalist exploitation of his time, or what he called the "real subsumption of labor" and the "production of relative surplus value." An important methodological dimension to this approach is that, to analyze the exploitation of the proletariat within capitalist production, one must assume theoretically the completion of the commodification of labor power.

On the other hand, and in a different but related approach to the proletariat, Marx did not or could not assume the completion of the commodification of labor power. Here, Marx approached the notion of the proletariat in terms of the insecurity and contingency, experienced by the owner of labor power, in the process of exchange. This insecurity stemmed from the process of so-called primitive accumulation, the process in which direct producers were dispossessed of their means of production and subsistence, and were subsequently compelled to sell their only remaining commodity, their labor power, but with no guarantees of an exchange. This was the Marx who promoted a notion of the proletariat that resonated with his conception of the virtual pauper mentioned above. The only problem with this approach is that Marx generally relegated this conceptualization of the proletariat to the contingencies of commodification in the transition from pre-capitalist to capitalist societies.[18] Korean workers, Korean surplus populations, and especially Korean day workers in interwar Japan, show us that this process was not simply a matter of the transition to capitalism, but was endemic to capitalism itself. Moreover, unlike the former approach, the commodification of labor power is here incomplete, continually discontinuous in contingent ways, chronically interrupted, disrupted, suspended, deferred, delayed, and prolonged, often agonizingly so. The majority of Korean working class struggles in Japan took place precisely amidst this contingent, insecure, and "continually discontinuous" process of commodification, particularly in the day labor market.

In this book, and without nullifying or rejecting the approach to the proletariat as a working population whose surplus labor time is exploited in capitalist production, I am seeking to revitalize and give equal importance to the latter approach to the proletariat mentioned above, the virtual pauper approach (if you will). I argue that Korean workers in Japan were proletarians even though the majority of them were not factory workers, but rather chronically unemployed, immigrant day workers in the public works industry. The essence of the Korean proletariat in Japan, however, did not lie in the fact that they were day workers per se. The important point is that they were expropriated from their land in Korea, and were compelled to find work in Japan—but with no guarantees of finding it. That the majority of Korean workers in Japan were day workers reveals the extreme existential form of their proletarian condition.

This approach to the proletariat requires that we emphasize two points. The first point is that the formation of the proletariat, and its experience of contingency and exploitation, is premised on the problem of so-called primitive accumulation, or the violent separation of producers from their means of production and subsistence. In the case of Korean proletarians, this was apparent after the Japanese created a system of private property in colonial Korea, and especially after tens of thousands of Korean peasants were expropriated during the program to increase rice production in Korea. This program effected a process of expropriation that lasted throughout most of the colonial period (1910–45), and contributed just as much to the maintenance of capitalism in Japan as it did to the emergence of capitalism in Korea. Primitive accumulation in Korea, obviously, should not be separated conceptually from the ongoing development of capitalism in Japan, or from the expansion of Japanese imperialism and colonialism. Nor should it be understood simply as a past moment in the transition to capitalism, but as an ongoing and recurring problem of capitalist commodity economy itself. The key point about primitive accumulation, as an ongoing problem of the capitalist commodity economies, is that it produces workers who have nothing to sell as a commodity except their labor power, but with no guarantees for a sale. On the one hand, this precarious position is an effect of primitive accumulation; on the other hand, however, it is the fundamental condition for capitalist exploitation.[19]

The second point is that the conception of the proletariat cannot be understood properly without taking into consideration how the working class also exists as a surplus population, or as what Marx called the "relative surplus population." The surplus population is a relative surplus population because it is produced as a superfluous population in relation to capital's laboring process (or what Marx called the "organic composition of capital," which is divided between variable and fixed capital, with the former representing funds for wages). This population is formed when the capitalist laboring process is reorganized and rationalized, particularly during times of economic recession and depression. In this book, this problem is particularly visible with the proliferation of unemployed workers after the manufacturing boom during the First World War in Japan came to an abrupt end between 1918 and 1920. This population is therefore a relative surplus population because it is produced as an excess or remainder of capitalist production itself. As such, however, it reproduces the basic relationship of separation, between owners of money and owners of labor power, that is indispensable for the reproduction of capitalist social relations.[20]

In sum, therefore, the conception of the proletariat that I am taking up here requires that we broaden the common, more restricted conceptualization of the proletariat in terms of exploitation within production, and expand it to encompass the contingent terrain of passage that mediates, connects, and disconnects surplus populations of workers to the laboring process. The concept of the proletariat must therefore be loosened from the prevailing identification of the true or archetypical proletarian existence defined in terms of fixed occupations or fixed sites of production, such as the factory. The experiences of Korean day workers in interwar Japan teach us that the proletariat is less about a particular occupation than about the compulsions to occupy a social and economic position in which one has to sell labor power as commodity in order to live, and this, amidst conditions that do not guarantee the realization of one's labor power. Moreover, the proletariat is not simply a working population toiling and becoming exploited within production (as so-called productive labor); it is also, fundamentally, a surplus population that is exploited and maintained in limbo, in conditions of extreme contingency and precariousness, and therefore in destitution, on the exterior cusp of production, in a relation of separation and mediated distance from capital.

A Proletarian History of the Search for Work

How, then, is one to describe these proletarian lives that hang on the contingent search for work and housing amidst forms of racism, on the anticipation of work just as much as the experience of working itself? How is one to describe the traces of anxiety and rage buried beneath the countless footsteps imprinted along these precarious paths to work and housing, paths that were in fact often detours and dead ends? Labor and social histories of the interwar period in Japan have especially ignored these questions. More often than not, the predominant historiography focuses on the expansion of the Japanese factory system, the rise of labor movements found therein, and the development of managing practices that were implemented in response to these movements. It has been common in histories of Japanese heavy industries, for example, to analyze the salient changes in the Japanese factory system during the interwar period as a way to explain the phenomenon, pervasive in Japan until the end of the economic bubble of the early 1990s, of the so-called lifetime employment system (nenkin seidō). These studies offer important ways to understand how capitalism in Japan developed and expanded rapidly after the overthrow of the Tokugawa shogunate in 1868, and how this rapid development was part and parcel of the way capitalist practices in Japan were reproduced through specific mechanisms of power that exploited the working classes in Japan. Nonetheless, these histories generally look only at factories' oppressive work conditions and their internal relations of social domination. In this way historians have often assumed that the search for work, by countless masses of workers, was completed.[21] By and large, these histories of work and labor in Japan begin where the search for work ends. As a result, they remain silent on the historical process of searching for work.

More specifically, how can a history of the search for work change the way we think about categories like commodification and exploitation? This book narrates a history of the search for work itself, and does so by analyzing the ways in which Korean peasants in colonial Korea were compelled to search for wage-work in Japan amidst precarious and racist conditions that threatened secure housing, and that cast them out of the factory system and into the day labor market. It was here in the Japanese day labor market, where employment was by definition erratic and irregular, that Korean workers found temporary wage-work as construction workers on large public works projects. When work on these projects was secured, Korean workers fought the sun, rain, and snow to pave long stretches of roads, toiled in deep gravel pits, risked serious injuries in laying miles and miles of railway lines, exploded mountainsides to build tunnels, and waded in water and mud to build river embankments and underground water works pipelines.

Moreover, it was here in the day labor market that Korean day workers, along with Japanese day workers, experienced forms of economic exploitation that differed significantly from forms of exploitation in the factory system. As I discuss in detail in chapter 3, it was on the road to work that Korean day workers especially experienced, identified, and fought against a particular form of exploitation—chūkan sakushu (中間搾取), or intermediary exploitation, a wage system in which commission fees for labor introductions were subtracted from the nominal wages of Korean day workers by social and institutional agents mediating the sale and purchase of Korean labor power in the day labor market. The subtraction of these fees from workers' wages left little, and often nothing, in terms of actual or real wages, and was commonly referred to, by workers and sub-contractors alike, as the practice of *pinhane*, literally a decapitated head (頭刎ね or ピンハネ). To sub-contractors, pinhane was a means to reduce expenditures on wages. To day workers, however, it was an exploitative system that took advantage of their insecurity of employment and their dependence on social intermediaries for connections to sites of work. It was a form of exploitation that did not take place within production only, but rather in the insecure passage between the labor market and sites of production.

How the majority of Korean workers, throughout the entire interwar period in Japan, continually and consistently found themselves searching for work in the day labor market is the broad topic of this book. Unlike histories of factory work that generally presuppose the completion of the sale and purchase of labor power as a commodity, this book instead presents a history in which the sale and purchase of labor power was constantly incomplete, interrupted, and maintained in agonizing suspense. In this way, this book presents a narrative of Korean workers in Japan that is often overlooked and neglected within a tradition of historical studies of labor in modern Japan that privileges the factory floor as the primary site to understand the nature of capitalist work and exploitation.[22]

A Network of Commodification and Forms of State Power

Crossing the straits from Korea to Japan, or else finding themselves stranded in Japan in chronic unemployment, Korean proletarians had severely limited options in finding work and housing. Racist Japanese landlords, as well as landlord federations, consistently and persistently refused to lease rooms or homes to Korean worker-tenants, leading to various strategies and tactics to secure housing. Yet even then Korean worker-tenants faced persistent evictions on a mass level, and, pushed into the streets, they constructed handmade barracks. Urban planning expansion into the fringes of the cities, however, provoked clashes between urban land developers, the police, and homeless Korean populations, leading to city-ordered evacuations of Korean squatters and barrack residents (chapter 4). Paralleling the exclusions from the housing markets, factory doors were increasingly closed to Korean workers, especially after the manufacturing boom during the First World War, compelling Korean workers to find erratic work in the day labor market. Here, Korean workers entered into wage regimes through specific social and institutional mediations that exploited their insecurity of employment as much as their products of labor.

These social and institutional mediations formed a specific milieu in which Korean proletarians and surplus populations tried to secure both temporary housing and temporary work. However, while these mediations alleviated some of the most dire contingencies experienced by Korean workers, they did not, and could not, eliminate the risks facing the vast majority of Korean workers on a daily basis. Quite the contrary, they tended, on the one hand, to displace or defer these risks onto other institutional practices, thereby creating social and institutional divisions among Korean communities. On the other hand, insofar as there were few or no other means to alleviate the insecurities and pressures of the labor and housing markets for Korean proletarians, Korean workers were compelled to become partially, if not wholly, dependent on these mediations for subsistence. The dependence on these mediations emerged out of the contingencies of the labor and housing markets, and was an ongoing precondition for the exploitation of Korean labor power in Japan. The commodification of Korean labor power, therefore, was not simply contingent in the sense of the unpredictable or the aleatory; it was also contingent upon a social and institutional network that created dependencies as the basis for exploitation. In this sense, therefore, the social milieu was more accurately a network of commodification of Korean labor power.

This network of commodification involved various state apparatuses and state power. A good portion of this book, therefore, analyzes the relationship between Korean surplus populations and the forms and practices of state power that attempted—and often failed—to manage, politically repress, and commodify Korean labor power. What has to be analyzed closely, therefore, are the precise mechanisms of state power, the forms they took, and their interrelating networks. In chapter 1, state power is analyzed in terms of its close relationship to industrial capital. I look, therefore, at how Japanese industries during the First World War manufacturing boom relied on government intervention to actively recruit Korean peasants from the Korean peninsula, and to commodify their labor power as a lever against organized Japanese trade unions and their attendant high wages. In chapter 4, the problem of state power appears in the form of the juridical courts that protected the system of urban private property in Japan, that intervened in struggles between Korean tenants and urban Japanese landlords, and that ultimately took the side of racist Japanese landlords, thereby accelerating the evictions and expulsions of Korean tenants out of the urban Japanese housing markets. In chapter 6,

I look at how state power took the form of the Unemployment Emergency Relief Programs (UERP). The UERP, I argue, did not provide unemployment relief to Korean workers. Rather, it maintained the insecurity of employment for thousands of Korean workers as the ground for exploiting their labor. This was done institutionally by codifying Korean workers as individual subjects through a discriminating, Kafkaesque bureaucracy and registration process, and by institutionally separating registered Korean workers from registered Japanese workers as the basis for exploiting Korean day workers through UERP practices—practices that ultimately proved no different from those practices found in the wider day labor market. All of these forms and functions of state power were constantly concerned with commodifying the labor power of Korean surplus populations. At the same time, for thousands of Korean proletarians in Japan, finding even erratic work and temporary housing were contingent upon these forms and functions of state power. This dependence formed the crucible in which Korean worker struggles against state power emerged.

It would be historically and theoretically inaccurate to argue, however, that state power stood undivided in relation to Korean surplus populations. State power was not a monolithic force, nor did it simply marginalize Korean workers in Japan. In chapter 5 state power itself is considered as split internally, between a public face, and a disavowed, supplementary and violent underside on which public state power nonetheless relies. This is particularly visible in the way the Sōaikai, a Korean welfare organization, was established institutionally, largely as a so-called preventive police organization (or yobō keisatsu, 予防警察). The concept of the preventive police was introduced in Japan around 1917, shortly after the Russian Revolution, when it became clear to the Japanese Home Ministry that the juridical police force in Japan was overwhelmed by a proliferation of urban crimes connected to the intensity of organized labor struggles during the economic recession. Welfare organizations such as the Sōaikai were thus integrated into the ranks of the preventive police system, and increasingly functioned as a (publicly disavowed) front line of police work. Existing as a para-police force, these organizations were the clearest institutional manifestation of a new police slogan in Japan: the massification of the police, and the policification of the masses (警察の民衆化と民衆の警察化). As a preventive police organization, however, the Sōaikai's institutional status was ambiguous. Though defined as a private welfare organization specializing in Korean day workers, it was financially supported by the police, various government ministries, the army, and even transnational corporations such as Mitsubishi and Mitsui. This ambiguous status created a gray zone of institutional practices that allowed the Sōaikai to arrogate police power unto itself in the name of protecting so-called Japanese–Korean harmony and to use organized violence with impunity, particularly against Korean communist labor unions in Japan such as Rōsō, as well as against peasant protests in southern Korea.

State power thus has to be considered in light of its own internal splitting, and not simply as a unified force in direct opposition to Korean populations toiling in the margins of Japanese society. A crucial ideological dimension to the way state power was split internally was in representing and making abject "unruly Koreans" (or what the media called *futei senjin*), while simultaneously idealizing notions of Korean identity and ethnic difference. Here again the Sōaikai is the best example of this problem. The Sōaikai was not only a manifestation of the preventive police; it was also an effect of the shift in 1919, by the colonial government in Korea, the Sōtokufu, from military rule (*budan seiji*) to cultural rule (*bunka seiji*). Under cultural rule, Korean populations were no longer targeted for repression as a homogeneous population. Instead, repression became selective and involved a precarious balancing act of supporting and promoting ethnic Korean identity as a way to eliminate class consciousness—but only up to a certain point. When ethnic identity threatened to coalesce into a national liberation movement, or into a clear anti-colonial movement, the police and the Sōaikai relied on violence, again in the name of Japanese–Korean harmony and supposedly protecting homeless and unemployed Korean workers. In this capacity, what has to be emphasized is that these purportedly multicultural discourses of the Sōaikai existed in the same continuum as Sōaikai violence—violence, moreover, that was connected to other nodal points in the institutional and social network of commodification that discriminated against Korean workers on the basis of ethnicity.

Anti-Sōaikai movements by Korean workers, tenants, and peasants countered this violence, but it was precisely at the height of these movements and protests that the co-founder and vice president of the Sōaikai, Pak Ch'um-gum, became the first Korean or colonial subject to be elected into the Japanese diet in 1932. Pak Ch'um-gum became a public figure that represented an idealized Korean minority in Japan. At the same time, however, his meteoric ascent from the mud and blood of the day labor market to the shimmering gold of parliament represented precisely a disavowal of the Sōaikai's dirty work as a preventive police organization. And while the Sōaikai and Pak Ch'um-gum often spoke of "all Koreans in the Japanese empire," as if

Koreans were a unified ethnic lot, the reality was that the Sōaikai was both a cause and a symptom of the political and economic divisions that fragmented Korean surplus populations in Japan. What is at stake in the analysis of the internal splitting of state power, therefore, is not the problem of the Korean margin, but rather what I have called the divided margin. As such, it has much to do with a rethinking of the notion of the Korean minority in Japan.

Questioning the Korean Minority and the Korean Problem

This study does not present a narrative of what might be called the Korean minority in Japan. While past studies on a unified Korean minority in interwar Japan have informed this study greatly, this book differs from these studies in a number of ways. First, this book argues that the problems of ethnic discrimination and racism must be shown and revealed in their proper historical situations before any conclusions are made about a putatively coherent and unified Korean minority that can be said to experience racism. While the best of these studies correctly identify the problem of discrimination and racism as a fundamental aspect of the everyday life of Koreans in Japan, the experience of discrimination (sabetsu) is more often than not announced than actually shown in its precise historical situations, practices, and social relations.[23] It has been common, for example, to state that racism prevented Koreans from having secure housing in Japan. This is true, but it does not explain how racism existed and operated through specific practices and social relations within the housing markets, as well as in the legal court systems that mediated housing disputes involving Korean tenants. It is also commonly announced that racism existed in differences between wage levels of Korean and Japanese workers. This, however, does not explain how specific practices and methods of distributing and paying wages to Korean workers mediated and even institutionalized the problem of unequal wages according to ethnicity. This book thus argues that the problem of ethnic discrimination has to be explained and shown historically, and not simply stated or assumed as a problem experienced by a putatively unified Korean minority in Japan.[24]

Second, by analyzing how racism operated historically through specific forms and practices, especially in the housing and labor markets of Japan, I argue that it is impossible to assume a coherent and unified Korean minority—not simply because certain Koreans experienced racism more or less than other Koreans, but because certain strata of the Korean population in Japan were engaged in practices, both socially and institutionally, that had discriminating and racist effects on fellow Korean workers in Japan. The problem therefore is not simply a monolothic Korean minority toiling in a singular margin of Japanese society, but rather the problem of a divided margin. This divided margin was part and parcel of specific practices—endemic, for example, to the day labor market—that divided Korean surplus populations in Japan, often for political reasons, and that produced Korean minorities within Korean populations themselves. The crucial question here is under what historical circumstances did these practices themselves emerge and become reproduced in Japan. The question, therefore, is not, What is the Korean minority? Rather, it is, How were Koreans becoming minor in Japan, even within Korean populations and communities, and as a result of practices that divided Korean surplus populations?

Third, the reason for posing these questions is not simply that the historiography of Koreans in Japan overlooks them. The real problem is that the historiography of Koreans in Japan often overlooks these questions because they fall into a positivist, empiricist, and sociologizing trap that stems from the government and state documents upon which studies rely for historical data. One could call this trap the ethnic-epistemological reduction. The problem, in other words, is not that prewar government sources did not think or conceptualize or know about a Korean minority; the problem is that that is only what government sources could conceptualize and know. On this basis, countless surveys, commissioned and conducted on the assumption of a pregiven Korean minority, undertook the daunting and endless task of producing all kinds of knowledge about Koreans: where they came from in Korea, where they lived in Japan, whether they were married or single, how many children they had, when they came to Japan and why, what kinds of jobs they worked, how much they earned in Korea and in Japan, what organizations they participated in and when they joined them, what they wrote and published, what they wore, what their accents were like when they spoke Japanese, what they ate, where they drank, what the physiological shape of their faces, their craniums, and their feet were like, and so on. This vast production of knowledge was predominantly statistical, and quintessentially the effect of the policeman's gaze in Japan. Behind the mountains of statistics and empirical data, however, lay concealed a positivist method that reduced—often by a methodological sleight of hand—various social and economic problems experienced by Koreans in Japan, to a problem of Koreans. This knowledge was then shared, disseminated, and reproduced by various non-police government agencies, such as regional labor exchange bureaus and city municipal offices. Collectively, this knowledge gained a formal name: the Korean problem (*chōsenjin mondai*).

This ethnic-epistemological reduction of prewar government surveys can be seen in the vast proliferation of government surveys that had "The Korean Problem" or "The Problem of Korean Workers" (*chōsenjin rōdōsha mondai*) in their titles.[25] For example, in an important survey from 1931, "The Problem of Korean Workers," the author, Sakai Toshio of the Osaka Metropolitan Government, appropriates the language of Marxism to identify Korean workers in Japan as a surplus population (*kajō jinkō*), and goes on to describe how miserable the lives of Koreans were because they had no secure employment or housing in Japan. Yet for Sakai, the identification of the insecurities of Korean surplus populations in Japan was reduced to Koreans only, largely in order to propose various institutional ways to contain, confine, control, and regulate social and political movements of Korean surplus populations. In this sense, Sakai revealed a similar position to other social policy makers—progressive, liberal, and conservative alike. What they all concluded was more or less the same: *Develop Korean industry to absorb Korean surplus populations! Send them to Manchuria or Siberia instead! Suspend unrestricted migration from Korea to Japan! Get them out of the unemployment system in Japan! Create more welfare organizations, just for Koreans! Police them more!* These were typical and common policy-related mantras and bromides, repeated obsessively and compulsively throughout the 1920s and 1930s. The significance of this repetition, however, is that they represented the limits of how Korean surplus populations, and the contingencies that they experienced on a daily basis, were conceptualized. To the authors of these surveys, these were all considered matters reducible to the Korean problem. In short, prewar government and police surveys racialized or ethnicized social problems experienced by Korean workers, and reduced them to a problem of being Korean itself, to problems of Koreans. In this way, these surveys were unable to think beyond the positivity of Koreans in Japan.[26] In this regard, it has to be said that much of contemporary scholarship on Koreans in Japan, despite various critiques of the political positions represented by these government surveys, has often unwittingly echoed and reproduced this ethnic-epistemological reduction found in prewar government surveys.[27] Contemporary scholars, in their approaches to the Korean minority or to Korean ethnicity, have not done enough to critically distinguish their research methodologies from those that underlie the prewar state discourse of the Korean problem. In this way, these studies have not been able to elucidate how the essential problems, experienced by Koreans in Japan, offer a way to think about a much broader problem that is not reducible simply to Koreans in Japan. If anywhere, a new, broadly applicable analysis might come from the study of divisions internal to the particularity of Koreans in Japan, and of the way Korean political subjectivity in Japan was split between ethnic particularity, on the one hand, and a capacity to stand for something universal, namely the proletariat and class struggle, on the other.

The Proletarian Gamble and Class Struggle

The unifying thread of this book is that Korean worker struggles emerge out of the search for work and out of the process of transforming the labor power of Korean surplus populations into the basic cell of capitalism: the commodity. The search for work in Japan first began in Korea, with the immiseration and expropriation of Korean peasants under colonial agrarian policies led by Japanese finance capital, and then began in earnest once Korean surplus populations arrived on Japanese soil. The road to work and housing in Japan, however, was not straight, but instead a continuous detour of unpredictable changes in direction, sudden obstacles, and surprise trap doors. Becoming a worker in Japan for Korean surplus populations, therefore, always involved the shaking of the dice-box of chance, not in the Nietzschean sense of the way history is made, but in the way Marx described how the free worker was always already a virtual pauper because of the inherent contingency of exchange. How Korean surplus populations became actual paupers out of this condition of virtual pauperization; how Korean workers fought against the racist and necessarily contingent conditions of exchange; and how Korean workers struggled against certain notions of what it meant to be Korean that were represented in various multiethnic discourses of Japan's multinational colonial regime—all of these struggles lead us to scrutinize carefully the particular situations and conditions in which the labor power of Korean surplus populations in Japan was commodified.

In the following chapters, many different struggles can be seen at work: struggles against recruitment practices (chapter 1), unfair and discriminatory wages (chapters 2 and 3), sudden firings (chapter 3), racist housing practices (chapter 4), divide and conquer tactics of Korean workers that seized hold of anti-discrimination rhetoric (chapter 5), and Kafkaesque bureaucratic red-tape (chapter 6). Not all of these struggles were necessarily coordinated with each other; many were just flashes in the night, sparks for a unified movement to come. Between the two wars, arguably the most challenging aspect of Korean working class politics in Japan was that the terrain of struggle, while in one way or another related to the commodification of labor power, created extremely diverse forms of protest and struggle. If, in this book, however, I have given particular attention to Korean workers involved in Rōsō (the largest Korean communist labor union in Japan, established in 1925), and in Zenkyō (the Japanese communist labor union), it is because they succeeded, albeit often in limited and restricted ways, in giving a common focus to these diverse struggles, and in elevating particular Korean struggles to a universal level of class struggle.

This is precisely what the Japanese state could not tolerate, and it is this political act—of creating a politicized Korean proletarian subjectivity, through these labor unions and political parties, that was split between its particular ethnic struggles and its capacity to stand in for the universal problem of the proletariat in class struggle—that posed the greatest obstacles to the intensification and extension of capitalist exploitation in interwar Japan. This political act, moreover, was not reducible to a political call for Japanese-Korean harmony (naisen yūwa), mutual love (sōai), or co-prosperity (kyōei), or to what we would today call multicultural tolerance or ethnic diversity. This political act rather offered a critique of these sugar-coated concepts when it became clear that these concepts were invoked strategically in colonial discourses and practices under the banner of liberal humanism, and when it was clear that these concepts were commonly implicated in economic exploitation and racist violence. This political act thus cut through and expressed a refusal to tolerate the liberal bromides and policies that were justifying, upholding, and celebrating the greater East Asian co-prosperity sphere as a viable alternative to the contradictions of capitalism, the experience of modernity, and the violent, racist forms of European and American imperialism at the time. It is with this political act in mind, finally, that this book hopes to bring to light the revolutionary possibilities and chances of the proletarian gamble.

Structure of the Book and Archival Matters

Each chapter in this book addresses a particular experience of contingency on the road to commodification—the sudden chances, the social and institutional dependencies, and the infuriating problems that emerged in the process of selling labor power as a commodity. All the chapters address the interwar years, with the exception of chapter 1, which focuses on the war years (1914–18). I have also tried consciously to make a steady progression, from chapter to chapter, in discussing several forms and functions of the capitalist state, and their specific relation(s) with, and against, Korean surplus populations in Japan. The discussion of the state first arises in this book in chapter 1 with a discussion of war-time labor recruitments; in chapter 2, in a discussion of primitive accumulation in Korea and industrial recession in Japan; in chapter 4 on housing and private property; and especially in chapters 5 and 6, which deal with the police, welfare, and the unemployment system in Japan. I decided to discuss the Unemployment Emergency Relief Program (UERP) in the last chapter because it seemed to be the clearest and most unambiguous state apparatus discussed in the book. The boundaries of the state apparatuses were much less clear in the case of the police and welfare, for reasons I explore in detail in chapter 5. For this reason, I have put the chapter on policing and welfare prior to the discussion of the UERP.

By and large, the archival material that was used in this book came from the pre–Second World War archives from the Ohara Shakai Mondai Kenkyūjō, located on the western campus of Hosei University in Tokyo. I thank Professor Yutaka Nagahara for introducing me to the archive at Ohara. In many ways, my immediate archival strategy, if one could call it that, was to find and collect materials that were not already included in Pak Kyung-shik's indispensable collection of primary documents relating to Koreans in prewar Japan, but that could be used in combination with Pak's materials.[28] Throughout this book, I have referred to Pak's collection of primary documents as ZCKSS (five volumes), an abbreviation for *Zainichi Chōsenjin Kankei Shiryō Shūsei*. Pak's documents, therefore, formed the basic pivot for the entire archival process. Most of the materials on strikes, union pamphlets, flyers, surveys of working conditions, and some police-related issues came from the Ohara archives.[29] Materials on unemployment, welfare, the police, housing, and housing disputes were found mostly at Tokyo University's main library, the Tōdai Shaken library, the economics library, and the law school library. Newspaper sources were found at Tōdai and the Diet Library, and materials authored by city governments were found in all of the above libraries, as well as in the Tokyo Metropolitan Library in Hirō. I thank Professor Takenori Matsumoto of Tokyo University for helping me around Tōdai in 2003. Lastly, I obtained some other helpful materials in Pak Kyung-shik's privately collected documents, currently catalogued in Saga Kenritsu University's main library. Here, one realizes that the materials, published in Pak's collection of primary prewar documents, represent just a tiny fraction of the total materials Pak collected over the course of his life.

1

THE BIRTH OF THE UNCONTROLLABLE COLONIAL SURPLUS

....

A Prehistory of the Korean Problem

One of the abiding insights made by Marx in *Capital* is that in the colonies of capitalist nation-states the illusions of the capitalist law of the supply and demand of labor are shattered. In the home country, the great beauty of capitalist production consists in being able to reproduce the wage worker by periodically setting him free, i.e., firing him, and by producing a surplus population that stands in relative exteriority to capitalist production as the precondition for the commodification of labor power. Periodically treating labor power as a disposable commodity is thus the way capitalist production can ensure that its most indispensable commodity—labor power—is always already there when capitalist production experiences so-called labor shortages during times of industrial expansion. It is this reproductive mechanism that allows for the smug deceitfulness of the political economist, not to mention the Japanese colonial policy maker, to think, and to formalize into naturalized axioms of economic movement, that owners of labor power—who are in fact compelled to enter into a relation of dependence with the wage form—can enter into a free contract between sellers and buyers, between owners of the commodity labor power, on one side, and owners of capital, on the other. In the colonies, however, "this beautiful illusion is torn aside"[1] because the conditions for the appearance of owners of labor power on the stage of the capitalist market do not originally exist there. The dependence on wages must therefore be "created by artificial means," and until that happens, the law of the supply and demand of labor is torn aside. In this way, this artificial and historical process in the colonies represents that which originally took place in the home country, but which has long since been repressed and disavowed there. The political and economic unconscious of the home country dwells in the artificial processes in the colonies.

The year 1910, when the Japanese imperial army transformed Korea into Japan's most prized colony, marks the beginning of precisely this kind of artificial process. The social effect of this process took the form of a colonial surplus population that came, and was brought, to Japan as sellers of the indispensable commodity of labor power. At the same time, however, the flow of colonial surplus populations into Japan repeatedly reminded the colonial metropole and its various guardians of the limits to the imperial process of repression on which the political unconscious of the home country was based. The precondition for producing artificially a colonial reserve army of workers was the transformation of Korean peasants into independent producers based on the system of private property. The cadastral survey, carried out by the Sōtokufu from 1910 to 1918 at a cost of 20.4 million yen, contributed to this end by implementing a new land registration system (in Korean, *tochi daichō*; *t'oji taejang*) that expedited the privatization of public land, land previously owned by Korean *yangban* (the landed aristocracy) and other classes of the feudal bureaucracy. The two other basic objectives of the survey were to recalculate and register land prices and to cultivate land.[2] And similar to the cadastral survey that was carried out in Japan by the Meiji state beginning in 1873, the colonial land survey in Korea served as a basic legal channel to integrate and reform the existing feudal tax system (*kyolbu*), and to replace it with a modern monetary tax system through which an accumulation of cash payments of taxes, based on newly recalculated land prices, could be appropriated by the colonial government. Compared to land taxes imposed by the Meiji state in Japan, however, taxes were kept low to promote colonial investments in the land by Japanese corporations and wealthy Korean landlords.[3] Nonetheless, Korean peasants struggled to make cash payments of increasing taxes exacted by the colonial government, and many went bankrupt. These circumstances represented an ongoing opportunity for Japanese landlords and capitalists to cooperate with preexisting Korean landlords to buy up large landholdings, reaching 40,000 multiple landholdings by the beginning of the 1920s.[4] At the same time, Korean peasants, especially in the provinces of Cholla and Kyongsang, had no choice but to become tenanted or semi-tenanted, a trend that increased exponentially after 1920, when the colonial government instituted its most significant economic policy in Korea, the program to increase rice production. With the cadastral survey completed by 1918 and the program to increase rice production underway by 1920, the Korean countryside soon transformed into a source of cheap rice exports for the domestic rice market in Japan. Social relations in Korean villages began to break down under the pressures of the new cash economy, however, and peasants increasingly became a floating, rural population with nothing but its capacity to work as its only remaining, sellable commodity.

Four years after the cadastral survey was underway in Korea, Japanese industry was about to enter into a brief but intense period of unprecedented industrial and financial growth. Taking advantage of the war overseas, Japanese manufacturers expanded and intensified production at breakneck speed, producing and exporting manufactured goods to Asian and to European countries. With the war, Japanese industry entered an industrial phase of new economic prosperity that transformed Japan from a debtor nation of 1.1 billion yen in 1914 to a creditor nation of 2.77 billion yen in early 1920.[5] With this phase of industrial prosperity that accompanied the war boom, the number of factories in Japan increased from 31,717 in 1914 to 45,806 in 1920, and the number of factory workers rose during the same years from 948,000 to 1,612,000.[6] Reflecting the demand for labor power during the war years, formal wages for factory workers also increased dramatically during these years. For example, from 1914 to 1920, wages in the textile industry rose from 0.35 yen to 1.03 yen; in metals, from 0.75 yen to 2.17 yen; in ceramics, from 0.58 yen to 1.66 yen; in chemicals, from 0.61 yen to 1.46 yen; and in public works, 1.39 yen to 3.50 yen.[7] The problem for workers, however, was that while formal wages increased, this increase did not match the rate of inflation of general prices of commodities. One index of this disparity is that while general commodity prices increased from 100 to 303 from 1914 to 1919, wages only increased from 100 to 252 during the same years.[8] This disparity led to a sharp rise in factory strikes demanding higher wages. In 1914, there were 50 strikes involving 7,904 workers; in 1919, the number of strikes increased ten-fold to 497, involving 63,137 workers.[9] With this political development especially, Japanese industry looked to Korea for fresh blood.

The conjuncture of the cadastral survey in Korea and the manufacturing boom in Japan during the war years forms the historical backdrop of this chapter. The purpose of this chapter is to look at how the dominant form of commodifying Korean labor power during and immediately following the manufacturing boom produced a very specific colonial surplus population in Japan, one that was, from the perspective of the colonial and metropolitan authorities, extremely difficult to control socially, politically, and economically. This is to say that this chapter does not begin with Korean migration to Japan per se, which began at least as far back as 1910, the year of the annexation, the year when Koreans were proclaimed to be imperial subjects of the Japanese empire, and were, as such, free to travel anywhere they pleased within the empire.[10] Indeed, beginning in 1910, Korean migration to Japan increased annually, slowly at first, then quickly and exponentially during and after the years of the First World War. Here, however, I focus on the dominant form of commodifying Korean labor power during the war years as the analytical lens through which to trace the emergence of an uncontrollable colonial surplus population in Japan, one that came from the southernmost provinces of Korea. The birth of the uncontrollable colonial surplus also forms the prehistory of what would become known in Japan in the 1920s as the Korean problem.

The Mass Recruitment of Korean Peasants as Workers during the First World War

The prehistory of the so-called Korean problem can be traced back to a specific form of commodifying Korean labor power that emerged within, and as part of, the changes taking place inside Japanese industry during the First World War. Seeking to fill shortages of labor power and to stem the tide of rising wages for an increasingly politicized and unionized Japanese work force, owners of factories and coal mines in Osaka, Kobe, Fukuoka, and Hokkaido turned their eyes to colonial Korea, where they actively recruited Korean peasants from the southernmost provinces of the Korean peninsula as cheap, temporary, and non-unionized industrial workers. The primary method of recruiting Korean workers was based on direct company recruitment (gyōsha chokusetsu boshū), in which factories dispatched their own company recruiters (boshū jūjisha) directly to the Korean countryside, where peasants were contracted as unskilled, short-term workers in small- and medium-sized factories in Osaka, Kobe, and Fukuoka, as well as in coal mines in Hokkaido. Initiated by Japanese companies and their employed recruiters, administered bureaucratically by the police bureau of the Korean government through a process of recruitment approval (boshū kyoka), and aided and monitored by port authorities in the southern provinces of Korea as well as in the major sea ports in Japan, these mass recruitments were the dominant form of commodifying Korean labor power during the war years.

While these practices can be traced back to 1913 with the recruitment of female Korean workers for the Setsuritsu cotton factory in Kobe, the historical essence of the mass recruitments was that it was a war-economy phenomenon that was not clearly discernible as a general practice until the peak war years. The year 1917 marked the height of recruiting Korean workers, with 80 recruitment outings bringing in 28,737 Korean workers to Japan. As table 1 shows, the majority of recruited Korean workers during this time were hired as workers in coal mines in Fukuoka and Hokkaido, and in cotton factories in Osaka, Okayama, and Hyogo prefectures. According to a survey that covered January to August of 1917, 16,590 workers were recruited, 11,875 of whom were men. Of the remaining 4,715 female workers, all except 200 were recruited into cotton factories.[11] Korean men in factories and coal mines worked primarily as unskilled assistants (but not apprentices) on temporary contracts that usually lasted 2 to 3 years. Korean female workers, mostly in cotton factories (and some in glass factories), were also hired on temporary contracts of the same duration. An important characteristic of the recruitment of Korean workers during the war period, therefore, is that the majority of Korean workers were employed as temporary or short-term contract workers in factories, coal mines, and cotton factories, and only secondarily as construction workers in public works construction sites. This trend would change dramatically after the end of the war boom in 1918 and especially after the 1920 economic crisis.

Broadly speaking, the recruitment of Korean workers was an extension of existing recruitment practices that had accompanied the rapid development of capitalism in Japan since the Meiji period. As is well known, the most extensive use and abuse of recruiting practices were in textile factories, which significantly expanded in the 1880s and 1890s. Incapable of meeting the increasing demand for labor power of textile factories in the cities, and eager to keep down costs of labor as much as possible, Japanese textile factories competed against each other to recruit and contract young, female workers by dispatching large groups of recruiters to distant Japanese villages in the countryside. The recruitment of female workers during the Meiji period generally did not take place through direct company recruitments, but rather through advertising agencies, family intermediaries, and independent labor brokers who connected employer and employee. Especially during the interwar period, direct recruitments increased (despite various legal movements against them), largely as a direct response to the intense competition between textile factories during the war boom.[12] As a result, recruiters, many of whom received cash per worker recruited, competed with each other, double-crossed employers by recruiting the same individual for multiple factories at once,

TABLE 1. Distribution of Recruited Korean Workers, 1917

	Mining	Long-shoremen	Construc-tion	Shipping	Glass	Cotton	Other	Total
Fukuoka	3,900	300	—	—	200	—	—	4,400
Hiroshima	—	—	—	1,000	—	—	950	3,450
Okayama	—	—	—	—	—	1,750	250	200
Hokkaido	1,210	—	600	—	—	—	—	1,810
Hyogo	—	—	—	300	—	640	500	1,440
Osaka	—	30	—	200	30	1,150	—	1,410
Tokyo	—	—	550	—	—	—	—	550
Akita	500	—	—	—	—	—	—	500
Yamaguchi	—	300	—	—	—	—	—	300
Gifu	250	—	—	—	—	—	—	250
Karafuto	250	—	—	—	—	—	—	250
Wakayama	—	—	100	—	—	100	—	200
Aichi	—	—	—	—	—	30	—	30
Total	6,110	630	1,250	1,500	230	5,170	1,700	16,590

Source: Chōsen Ihō, October 1917.
Note: Out of 16,590 workers, 11,875 were male and 4,715 female. "Other" contains 700 sawyers, 500 rope and nail workers, and 500 wood burners. Finally, the total figures for "cotton" do not add up correctly in the original.

and concealed or exaggerated working conditions as they canvassed for workers in the countryside.

During the Meiji period, work agreements were often not formalized in contracts, but instead secured through verbal promises. Later, however, formal contracts were drawn between the recruiter and the worker (or, in cases when the worker was a legal minor, the legal guardian of the worker). Escorted by recruiters to the city, the workers soon found themselves far away from home, living in poorly ventilated and crowded factory dormitories, and working long hours in labor-intensive production lines. They fell into poverty from reduced wages stemming from mandatory dormitory fees, and they could not quit their jobs because of either physical coercion or dire economic consequences, many of which stemmed from mandatory savings plans that workers could not cash in on until their work contract concluded, typically after three years. The recruited factory women also quickly realized that the brutal working conditions in which they toiled in the cities all too frequently contradicted the working conditions promoted and promised by the recruiters in the villages back home.[13]

Recruitment practices also took place within the heavy industries dating back to the 1910s, but unlike textile factories' recruitment practices, they generally had a double purpose. On the one hand, factories in the heavy industries deployed factory recruiters to increase the number of regular workers (jōyō-kō rōdōsha) as a means to deepen factory paternalism and to reduce high labor turn-over of skilled workers. On the other hand, however, recruiters were also used to increase the use of temporary (rinjikō rōdōsha) and day labor workers (hiyatoi rōdōsha) as a way to provide factory management with greater labor flexibility in the face of fluctuating business cycles and an increasingly vociferous trade union movement.[14]

The practice of recruiting Korean workers stemmed out of preexisting practices of labor recruitment in Japan. At the same time, there were specific characteristics to the recruitment of Korean workers that suggest differences from past forms of labor recruitment in Japan. First, common to recruitment practices of the twentieth century in Japan, the recruitment of Korean workers took place on the basis of contracts. Though female factory workers were generally recruited on an individual basis, the predominant method of recruiting Korean workers took place on a group basis, typically with groups of Korean peasants from the same village or hometown. Shūdan boshū, or mass recruitment, thus seems to have been the standard practice for factory and other company recruitments in Korea, and while it is unclear who the recruited party's signatory was in cases of mass recruitment, it is probable that the signatory was an individual selected by the group as its representative. This is corroborated by police notifications (tsūchō), distributed to recruiters and published in Sōtokufu publications such as the Chōsen Ihō, which emphasized the importance of having the recruited group (kumi) select one of its own members to take care of the group's collective concerns while in Japan, and to maintain communications with the hometown or village in Korea.[15]

Second, Korean workers were generally not hired as regular workers but rather as temporary and supplementary workers whose employment was only intended to meet a brief labor shortage stemming from the war-time manufacturing boom. Newspaper articles as well as government dossiers such as the Kokka Gakkai Zasshi often referred to Korean workers as marginal or limit workers (genkai rōdōsha) to specify the temporary use of Korean workers whose wages, for reasons to be discussed below, were consistently 30 to 50 percent lower than wages of Japanese workers in the same occupation.[16] More common, however, was the description of Korean workers as supplementary labor or hojoteki rōdō. As one police report stated, Korean workers were recruited by factories in Osaka, Kobe, and Fukuoka, as well as in coal mines in Hokkaido and Fukuoka, only as a supplementary labor force, one that did not exist apart from the brief and sudden boom in the war-time manufacturing industries.[17] A report from the Hokkaido Tankō Kisen corporation similarly noted that Koreans were employed on a temporary and experimental (shikenteki rōdō) basis at the Yubari coal mine in Hokkaido.[18]

The most significant difference, however, was the extent to which the colonial government in Korea, the Sōtokufu, actively took part in the process of recruiting Korean workers. Its standard involvement in recruitment practices can be gleaned from several Sōtokufu police notices from April 1913, September 1917, and October 1917.[19] These notices, as well as their summaries in publications such as the Chōsen Ihō, outline the standard procedures. In cases when recruiters sought more than ten workers, the recruiting company was required first to apply to the Sōtokufu's police to state its intention to recruit in Korea. According to the Sōtokufu police guidelines, the application letter had to include the type of industry; the factory name; its location in Japan; the types of labor is used in the factory; the ratio of male to female workers; the length of time the recruiters intended to stay in Korea for recruitment; information on employees other than recruiters who intended to accompany the recruitment trip; and finally, data pertaining to the conditions listed on the required contract for recruitment.[20] The contract had to stipulate: (a) the type of work and the period of the contract; (b) working hours, including break time length; (c) methods of wage payment; (d) methods of savings; (e) costs for everyday items that would not be covered by the company; (f) methods of payment for travel fees for returnees in the cases of death or injury; (g) information on medical fees not covered by the company; and (h) approval of a guardian for workers between the ages of 14 and 20.[21] Once the police in Seoul approved the applications, the recruiters were generally required to pay a nominal recruitment fee of 11 to 15 yen.[22] Recruitment data as well as future advertisements for recruitments were also posted every November in the Sōtokufu-issued journal, Chōsen Ihō.

Police participation was a standard and absolute condition for recruiting Korean workers. Police were used as mediating agents to ensure a smooth exchange between Korean peasants and the company recruiter. In no cases were Japanese company recruiters permitted to canvas potential workers in rural villages unaccompanied by the police. In cases where recruiting took place in just one province in Korea, an approved police chief (Ninka Keimu Buchō) was required to accompany the recruiters; in cases where recruiting took place in multiple provinces, the head police chief (Keimu Sōchō) was required to accompany the recruiters. With the police overseeing the negotiations between the parties, recruiters explained the conditions stipulated on the contract and then the workers, after signing the contract, were given a departure date as well as a date to file their recruitment with the port authorities. The police had the right to deny recruitment applications from companies in Japan, and they could also fine recruiters up to 200 yen, especially in cases in which false information was printed on the contracts.[23] For recruitments that succeeded in bringing Korean workers to Japan, the police in Korea then "wrote reports on the conditions of workers in Korea for submission to the police in Tokyo and Osaka," with whom "strict communications were to be maintained."[24]

Arguably the most important aspect of the Sōtokufu's involvement in recruitments, however, was its role in setting the wages of recruited Koreans. This was done by providing wage guidelines to Japanese companies, factories, and coal mines wishing to recruit and employ Korean workers. Typically, guidelines involved a three-tiered wage chart that was given to all recruiters and their employers. For example, the Osaka Mainichi Shimbun reported in 1917 that the Sōtokufu's three-tiered wage chart was distributed to recruiters for the Chūgoku iron foundry for calculating the wages for 500 Koreans employed under the miscellaneous jobs category within the steel factory. The three tiers represented high, middle, and low wages, with the highest wages fixed at 0.45 yen (or 45 sen), middle wages at 0.40 yen, and the lowest wages at 0.35 yen. Moreover, the article showed that these wages were all 30 percent less than those of unskilled Japanese workers.[25] Similar wage levels were found in the Dairi glass factory in Fukuoka the same year, where the highest wages for Korean workers were 0.45 yen. By comparison, the highest wages for Japanese were 1.00 yen.[26] In July 1917, the Manshū Nichi Nichi newspaper reported that wages for Korean workers in coal mining, cotton spinning, rubber manufacturing, steel factories, hydroelectric plants, and public works construction were all between 0.35 yen and 0.55 yen.[27] And in August 1917, the Keijō Nippō reported that wages for Korean male factory workers in Japanese factories were all found to be between 0.35 and 0.60 yen, and between 0.18 and 0.24 yen for Korean female cotton factory workers.[28]

What begs overall emphasis, therefore, is the way the colonial government artificially created a labor market in Korea in response to changes in Japanese industry. This was done through institutional means that involved fundamentally the state repressive apparatus of the police, the work of which stratified unskilled labor in Japan's industrial labor market along wages that differed according to ethnicity. The determination of wages for recruited Korean workers was not left, however, to the invisible hand of the so-called competitive labor market. Rather, in setting and standardizing wages for Korean workers at prices 30 percent below Japanese wages, the Sōtokufu's interventions in the recruitment process exposed its readiness to violate the sacred laws of supply and demand that had come to characterize labor markets in industrial Japan, and to historically and artificially create a competitive labor market in colonial Korea, for Japanese industry, out of whole cloth. Indeed, the Sōtokufu's violation of the law of supply and demand took place in response to the intense desire by Japanese industry to eliminate its most problematic effects: rising wages and a politicized labor force. As it was reported on August 12, 1917, in the Fukuoka Nichi Nichi Shimbun, "The importation of Korean workers to Japan holds great promise for capitalists insofar as they reduce production costs and increase profits; moreover, unlike Japanese workers, they are not unionized."[29] The Japanese higher police offered a similar assessment: "Because Korean workers do not fiercely confront their bosses with the same tenacity of purpose as Japanese workers, Korean workers have been employed experimentally [shikenteki] as a supplementary [hojoteki] work force."[30]

The Decline of Mass Recruitments

After 1917, however, the practice of recruiting Korean workers decreased rapidly for several reasons. Table 2 shows this clear decline in recruitments from 1917 to 1923. While 80 recruitment outings in 1917 brought nearly 30,000 Korean workers to Japan, mostly male workers in coal mining, factory, and public work construction jobs, there were only four recruitments in 1923 of 600 workers, all female cotton workers.

The decline in recruitments stemmed from the confluence of three general factors. First, recruitments decreased due to the anticipation, felt by industrial leaders in Japan, of the imminent end of the war in Europe and the manufacturing boom that accompanied it in Japan. Factories initiated new austerity measures, the foremost of which were cutting back on the labor force and halting new recruitments. Temporary workers from Korea, while briefly considered indispensable as a supplementary labor force, were now deemed disposable, and they became the first target for factory cut backs in production. Just how many workers—Korean or Japanese—were fired during this initial stage of production constriction is difficult to guess with any precision. Government statistics on unemployment, for example, began to be gathered in 1919 with the establishment of the Kyōchōkai, a quasi-government organization that documented labor disputes in large-scale factories. More statistics on unemployment were gathered after 1921, when the Labor Exchange Law was put into effect, but labor exchange offices at this time did not statistically differentiate workers as Japanese or Korean. This would not happen until the winter season of 1925, when the UERP was implemented in the six major cities. This suggests two things. On the one hand, it took the state apparatus in Japan over seven years to implement institutional means to begin the process of registering workers for unemployment relief, and to produce statistical knowledge of these workers. On the other hand, the fact that the UERP statistically differentiated registered workers as Japanese and Korean is evidence of the extent to which the policy makers of the state unemployment system had, over the course of these seven years, become aware of the extent of Korean unemployment, and felt a need to categorize and divide the mass of unemployed workers according to ethnicity.[31]

Thus, while precise statistics on Korean unemployment are unavailable during the period immediately following the war, glimpses of an increasingly chronic problem of Korean unemployment can be gleaned from various newspaper articles and government reports, especially those from Osaka. An

TABLE 2. Recruitment of Korean Workers, 1917–1923

Year	Recruitment Outings	Men	Women	Total
1917	80	18,715	10,022	28,737
1918	57	14,376	6,888	21,264
1919	27	5,060	5,055	10,115
1920	23	4,178	1,214	5,392
1921	5	4,519	2,950	7,469
1922	21	3,511	1,615	5,126
1923	4	0	600	600

Source: Chōsen Sōtokufu Keimukyoku Tokyo Shuchōin, "Chōsen Keisatsu Gaiyō."

Osaka Asahi Shimbun article from December 1918, "Need for Relief for Unemployed Korean Workers," describes the impact of the new factory austerity measures on recently recruited Korean workers: "Among those workers to be laid off from these streamlining measures, Korean workers are said to be the most numerous. . . . Alas, the time is nigh for their fate."[32] And if the end of the war boom did not clarify and accelerate this problem of excess workers, the Tokyo stock market crash of March 15, 1920, which almost overnight led to falling prices in stocks and commodities, a series of bank runs, factory and mine closings, and Japan's first taste of mass unemployment, did. Newspaper articles from 1920 in Osaka document the sudden appearance of between 4,000 and 5,000 unemployed Korean workers in Osaka in less than one year. This was half the total number of Korean workers recruited nationwide in 1919, and almost equivalent to the total number recruited nationwide in 1920.[33]

In response to the sudden appearance of unemployed Korean workers, the Sōtokufu and the metropolitan police began reassessing recruitment policy. Unemployed Korean workers were demanding severance pay, and some were also asking for travel money to return to Korea. Yet, not only were the factories rejecting their demands, leaving them without work or money in Japan, but many workers were also unwilling to return to their Korean villages, which were falling deeper and deeper into rural poverty.[34] Sōtokufu efforts to address this problem were palliative at best. Recruitment contracts were now required to stipulate that the costs of returning to Korea must be shouldered solely by the recruited worker himself or herself.[35] Factories doing the recruiting were made to provide information to Sōtokufu police authorities on company finances from the past two fiscal terms. Recruitment applications by companies that were having difficulty staying afloat during the postwar recession, or that were currently firing Korean workers, were summarily rejected.[36] The reasons for this policy were not so much that Koreans were falling into poverty due to sudden unemployment, but more that the social management of unemployed, recruited Korean workers was taking a toll on Japanese police forces. As one Sōtokufu notice reads, "Korean workers, stranded in Japan, have fallen into a life of poverty, thereby becoming a serious burden on the police."[37] Indeed, this is one way to interpret the following statement by the Asashibashi police to Osaka steel factory recruiters: "With the end of the war and the increasing problem of excess workers, the hiring of Koreans will no longer be to the employers' advantage."[38]

A second reason for decreased recruitments was that, similar to the recruiting practices in the cotton industry, problems arose from the recruiters' practices themselves. Wartime competition between factories compelled recruiters to deceive and falsely advertise working conditions in the urban factories or coal mines while canvassing potential workers in the Korean countryside. Contracts were signed in the villages where the initial encounter between recruiter and worker took place, not after the Korean worker had arrived in Japan and in the place of his or her employment. This spatial separation then became a tempting opportunity for recruiters to violate various clauses on the work contracts. These violations began on the boat, and extended into the work sites in Japan. Korean workers complained to port authorities, upon their arrival in Japan, that recruiters refused to provide meals to Koreans on the trip across the straits, revealing how recruiters tried to cut costs on travel expenses and illegally pocket funds originally advanced to them (by the factories or corporation) to cover travel expenses.[39] Common, too, were cases in which the workers arrived at the factory or coal mine and discovered that the type of work and wages differed radically from the stipulated contents of the original contract signed in Korea. In the face of this discovery, there were many cases in which Korean workers demanded repatriation at the recruiter's expense, a demand that was often unmet—often because the recruiters lacked the funds themselves—leaving the recruited Koreans stranded with no work, money, or means of returning home.[40] The problem then shifted to port authorities and the local police, but also to the factory floor or coal mine pit, where heated disputes and strikes broke out, such as the one detailed in the evening edition of the *Hokkaido-hō* on March 26, 1918:

> 150 recently recruited Korean workers confronted the Yubari-city police in a bloody showdown that began two days ago. . . . The Yubari Coal Mine has already been recruiting Koreans for some time. This time, however, after 98 Koreans were recruited and brought to the mine on the 24th, fifty of them were required to check into the company hospital for a routine health diagnosis. It was there that they could not help but see all the injured and deceased workers from the mines. Terrified by what they saw there, the Koreans decided to stop working on the afternoon of the 24th around 5 p.m., shouting angrily at the recruiter *for failing to tell them about the dangerous working conditions during the initial recruitment canvassing in Korea.* . . . The police could not quell the Koreans and . . . the Koreans could not understand what the police were instructing them to do, leading to a violent clash. Eight Koreans were seriously injured and taken to the Police Investigations Bureau in Sapporo.[41]

That the injured Korean workers were not sent back to the hospital, but rather to the police investigations bureau, is an indication of the extent to which the police were fundamentally part of the entire recruitment process, from its initial exchanges between recruiters and workers in Korea to the very process of production itself in Japan. In response to recruiting problems, the Sōtokufu police bureau tried to lessen the ill effects of corrupt recruiters—themselves structural effects of the intense competition of the factories and coal mines employing them—and warned recruiters not to exaggerate working conditions while canvassing. Moreover, recruiters were told to promote mutual surveillance (*ai-imashimu*) among groups of recruited workers as a means to prevent unionized walk-outs and strikes.[42] Police forces in Japan, however, were increasingly dispatched to coal mines to police Korean workers directly, and to prevent any such disturbances in production. The directors at the Yubari coal mine in Hokkaido, for example, organized Korean workers in groups of five to six diggers under direct supervision in the mines.[43] Moreover, not only did the police supervise worker efficiency, "promote spiritual rectification . . . and general matters of assimilation," but they also managed savings plans (*chochiku shōrei*) of Korean miners.[44] Similar to the working conditions of female cotton workers, these savings plans were mandatory and implemented to prevent premature desertions prior to the termination of contracts.[45] Police and policing measures also extended to housing conditions of recruited Korean workers. Reports from the Man-kan Tankō, also in Hokkaido, reported that Korean workers had to be housed separately from Japanese in dormitories (kishukusha) with a full-time guard to supervise and preside over "their walking, stopping, sitting and lying."[46] Similarly, in 1922, the interior ministry police bureau advised all coal mines and factories employing large numbers of Korean workers to "[s]eparate the living quarters [shukuya] of Korean workers from Japanese workers. Furthermore, the Korean quarters should be supervised and led by Korean housing bosses and supervisors, and the Japanese quarters by Japanese housing bosses."[47] Problems with recruiting, which were one of the reasons for the decline in recruitments, increasingly became synonymous with policing recruited workers. Central in their capacity to facilitate the recruitment process itself, the police were also central in supervising the segmentation of the production process along ethnicity. This was a means to prevent political alliances between workers, which leads to the third reason for the decrease in recruitments.

A political reason, or rather a political fear, lay behind the sudden decrease in recruitments of Korean workers. The Sōtokufu and police bureaus in Japan began placing severe restrictions on Koreans traveling to Japan as a measure to curb the movement of Korean students and workers involved in the Korean independence movement. Begun on March 1, 1919, the independence movement spread across the Korean peninsula with great intensity for the next year, involving two million Korean participants and some 1,500 demonstrations. Japanese military repression was brutal, killing 7,000 Koreans and arresting between 45,000 and 50,000 in the first year after March 1919.[48] As part of the colonial government's reaction to the March 1st Movement, and as early as April 1919, the home ministry issued a notice to police bureaus in all of the prefectures in Japan outlining new measures that required all Koreans traveling outside Korea to carry police-issued traveling passports, or ryokō shōmeishō. Issued by police authorities in the travelers' place of residence in Korea, the travel passports were created to identify traveling Koreans on an individual basis, and to document their place of residence in Korea and especially the names and addresses of their employers abroad.[49] Any Korean traveler with unclear travel purposes, destinations, or employers were rejected. The purpose of identifying Korean travelers, however, was clearly political; the ryoko shōmeishō system was instituted to prevent the spread of Korean independence movements outside of the Korean peninsula, and to make sure that mass-recruited Korean workers were going to Japan to work—not as activists, but as laborers.

This travel surveillance system lasted until late 1922, when the Sōtokufu believed that it had finally and adequately suppressed the most immediate effects of the independence movement. In place of the restricted travel system, a so-called free travel system (jiyū tokō) was implemented, largely as a concession to protests by Korean organizations, as well as by certain Japanese policy makers, who pointed out that restricted traveling conditions for Koreans not only was discriminatory, but also contradicted the official rhetoric of the Japanese empire, which allowed for free movement within the Japanese empire for all subjects, including colonial Koreans.[50] Jiyū tokō therefore lessened the restrictions on Korean individuals to travel between Korea and Japan, and there was a small burst of labor recruitments in late 1922. Jiyū tokō, however, lasted no more than six months, and in May 1923, the restricted travel system was reinstated, largely in reaction to the growing popularity of socialism, anarchism, and especially Bolshevism among Korean students and workers traveling to Japan. Korean socialists had already established the Korean Socialist Party in Khabarovsk, Russia, thirty kilometers from the Chinese border, in June 1918. It soon moved to Vladivostok and then to Shanghai in August 1919, where the Korean provisional government was established, and where an incipient Korean communist organization, largely under the leadership of Yi Tong-hwi, was starting up. In September 1919, another communist organization was established in Irkutsk with the aid of the Comintern, which also sent party committee member Voitinsky to Shanghai to confer with Yi Tong-hwi and others.[51] For Japanese, Chinese, and Korean revolutionaries alike, Shanghai was a hub of revolutionary action and organization, and shipping lanes between Shanghai, Pusan, Shimonoseki, Kobe, and Yokohama became extremely politicized travel routes. Especially in Shanghai, Korean socialists, communists, and anarchists were able to establish political networks with Chinese revolutionary leaders such as Sun Yat-sen, who helped Korean independence movement activists extend their movements to the United States (via Honolulu), as well as Japanese revolutionaries, including anarchists like Osugi Sakae, and the soon to be co-founder of the Japanese Communist Party, Yamakawa Hitoshi.[52]

These political connections soon found expression in the emergence of radical Korean organizations focusing on labor problems in Japan. In November 1920, Korean anarchist Pak Chun-sak, also known as Pak Yol, or, in Japanese, Boku Retsu, established the Kugakusei Dōmei for Korean student-workers in Tokyo, which promoted class struggle and direct action as vehicles for national independence. Pak would then go on to organize two other anarchist labor unions, the Kokutōkai (Black Wave Association) in the fall of 1921, and the Kokuyūkai (Black Friends Association) in November 1922. Communist labor unions also appeared on the political stage in the same month. The Hokuseikai (Northern Star Association) was formed in November in Tokyo under the banner of international communism, and in the same month, the first Korean communist labor union in Japan, the Tokyo chōsen rōdō dōmeikai (Tokyo Korean Labor Federation), was established "to advance the Korean labor movement internationally to promote the absolute victory of the world's propertyless classes; and to advance the class consciousness of Korean workers in Japan while securing stable employment."[53] A similar mission statement was made one month later by the Osaka Korean Labor Federation: "Our mission is to triumph in class struggles, to establish basic rights of survival [seizonken] of the working class. . . . And in toppling the capitalist system that exploits us to the bone, we will strive to establish a new society on the basis of workers."[54]

These political developments gave the Sōtokufu and the Japanese police many reasons to fear that large groups of recruited Korean workers, many of whom were also now falling into unemployment and poverty, would enter the ranks of anarchist, socialist, and communist movements. The home ministry began cautioning Japanese police authorities in late 1920 to intensify surveillance for supposedly lawless Koreans forming political alliances with Bolsheviks and socialists in Japan.[55] At the same time, it increased its surveillance of ships and boats coming to Japan via Shanghai and Pusan, and alerted prefectural authorities in Japan to monitor closely any Koreans without proper travel passports. Published materials that were related to the independence movement, such as political flyers or fund-raising documents, and that were hidden aboard the vessels, were now routinely confiscated.[56] After 1922, documents and police notices from the Sōtokufu and the home ministry disclosed a clear belief that the mass recruitment of Korean workers was now too risky to be allowed to continue. And so, a mere six months after the free travel system was implemented, the home ministry moved to suspend it, beginning with the following notice which it distributed to all prefectural police in Japan:

> Korean migration to Japan has gradually risen of late, especially after the Sōtokufu suspended the restricted travel system in December 1922. As a result of the economic recession in Japan, not only have countless Koreans become roving vagabonds with no work; they are increasingly involved

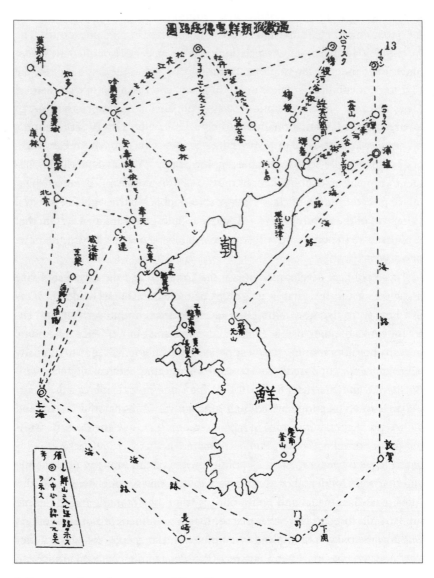

Police map of travel routes to and from Korea, 1922.
Source: Naimushō Keihōkyoku, May 1922, reproduced in Ogino, ed.,
Tokkō Keisatsu Kankei Shiryō Shūsei.

with social and labor movements in Japan, and are carrying out mass actions and demonstrations. . . . After conferring with the Sōtokufu, it has been agreed that free travel [jiyū tokō] and group recruitments [dantai boshū] should be aggressively reduced.[57]

The Birth of the Uncontrollable Colonial Surplus

The sudden proliferation of unemployed Korean workers in Japan, Korean strikes and disputes stemming from recruitment deception, and the spread of Korean political organizations that were increasingly moving towards revolutionary class struggles in addition to national liberation, all contributed to bringing an end to a first historical phase of commodifying Korean labor power in Japan. The significance of the recruitment of Korean workers is that it showed how both the colonial state, the Sōtokufu, and the metropolitan government in Japan exploited the young colony of Korea as a place to harness disposable, temporary, and supplementary labor power for Japanese industry in response to the sudden changes in the industrial business cycles. The sudden firing of recruited Korean workers immediately following the end of the war clearly showed the extent to which they were recruited strictly for temporary and supplementary purposes. Considered briefly as an indispensable labor force that was employed as a lever of accumulation to stem the rising tide of rising wages and organized Japanese trade unionism during the manufacturing boom, Korean workers in the growing recession were still deemed indispensable, but only as a disposable labor force.

What begs consideration, however, is the way the firing of Korean labor power revealed the emergence of a distinct Japanese labor market, not simply because Korean workers were generally fired before Japanese workers to protect the latter's position and security, but because Korean workers were fired first despite their relatively inexpensive wages. As a representative of the Osaka government's labor section pointed out, the decisions by Osaka factory managers to fire Korean workers first, despite their relative cheapness compared to more expensive Japanese workers, "went against the standpoint of the accountant's abacus."[58] Yet, when it came to commodifying Korean labor power during this period, this apparent violation of the law of supply and demand should not have come as such a surprise to commentators such as the one from the Osaka metropolitan government. For from the beginning of the recruitments of Korean workers, the Sōtokufu was fundamentally part of setting wage levels for recruited Korean workers through artificial means, and with the sole purpose of bringing down wage levels generally in Japan. With the end of the war, however, not only the Sōtokufu, but also Japanese police authorities had to reap just what was sown during the manufacturing boom: a growing surplus population of Korean workers in Japan that did not abide by the laws of supply and demand, and that was quickly becoming organized politically in socialist, anarchist, and communist movements. In this sense, the recruitment of Korean workers and the process of commodifying Korean labor power during the war gave birth to an uncontrollable colonial surplus, one that would persist as such in Japan throughout the chronic recession of the 1920s and early 1930s. And as Korean migration to urban Japan increased exponentially year by year—a symptom of the steadily worsening rural conditions in the southernmost provinces of Korea in the 1920s and 1930s—the uncontrollability of the colonial surplus not only intensified but morphed into different shapes and forms that frustrated, baffled, and exasperated Japanese police, factory and public works construction bosses, welfare organizations, unemployment bureaus, and urban Japanese landlords.

2

THE COLONIAL SURPLUS
AND THE VIRTUAL PAUPER

....

> Far more demoralizing than his poverty in its influence upon the . . . work-
> ing man is the insecurity of his position, the necessity of living upon wages
> from hand to mouth, that in short which makes a proletarian of him. . . . The
> proletarian, who has nothing but his two hands, who consumes today what he
> earned yesterday . . . is subject to every possible chance.
> —Friederich Engels, 1845

This passage from Engels, taken from his *Conditions of the Working Class in England*, is a fitful entryway into the situation of the colonial surplus population
coming to Japan from Korea in the 1920s and 1930s. Far more demoralizing
than the problem of poverty were the social and economic insecurities envel-
oping Korean workers in Japan. The impoverishment of Korean workers was
inseparable from specific conditions of selling their labor power, through the
form of the wage, that were consistently subject to every possible chance—including various forms of ethnic discrimination. The problem was not simply that the exchange between their labor power as a commodity and wages
brought Korean workers little cash. For the vast majority of Korean workers
in Japan, the foremost problem was that the process of exchange itself was
necessarily unpredictable, precarious, and impossible to forecast with any
certainty.

To properly grasp the quantitative problem of low wages for Koreans in
Japan, it is necessary to consider, as an introductory problem that will guide
the analysis in this chapter, how the wage form itself structurally conceals
the inherent contingency of the exchange process. The wage form conceals a
fundamental, structural asymmetry inherent to capitalist exchange, the asymmetry between the position of selling labor power as a commodity and the
position of buying it with the commodity of money. To the buyer in possession of the universally exchangeable commodity of money, these conditions

of exchange appear as something to naturally organize, stipulate, and document in the fine print of the wage contract. To the seller of labor power as a commodity, by contrast, the conditions of exchange necessarily appear beyond his or her control, accidental and contingent upon being in the right place at the right time. This asymmetry can be traced back to the very origins of capitalism. Writing in the early nineteenth century in France, for example, the political economist John Charles-Leonard de Sismondi was perhaps the first theorist of capitalist commodity economies to identify this nonguaranteed quality of the position of selling labor power. Noting the uneven rates between the dispossession of French peasants and the limited development of manufacturing in the cities, Sismondi identified how an incipient urban working population, while free from feudal ties, had no guarantee of its subsistence. "It must live from its work," he wrote, "but it never sees and never knows who will consume the product of its labour."[1]

It was Marx, however, who demonstrated systematically how the nonguaranteed position of selling was disclosed in an asymmetrical relationship of exchange that was endemic to, and constitutive of, capitalist commodity economies. Mainstream economics disavowed this asymmetry by beginning its analysis of the axiomatic motions of the economy with the result of exchange, not with its conditions. On the basis of this disavowal, classical political economy theorized—retrospectively—that the act of exchange was a symmetrical process between free and equal subjects.[2] For Marx, by contrast, the discovery of the asymmetry of exchange, and the inherent contingency of the position of selling found therein, allowed him to repose fundamentally the historical phenomenon of poverty. Poverty in a capitalist commodity economy, he argued, is not simply a condition into which a free worker falls, either before or after the process of exchange. Rather, from the perspective of the free worker, capitalist exchange itself already contains this fall into poverty—virtually. The free worker does not simply become a pauper; rather, the worker is always already a virtual pauper. He writes:

> It is already contained in the concept of the free labourer that he is a *pauper*: virtual pauper. According to his economic conditions he is merely a living labor capacity . . . Necessity on all sides, without the objectivities necessary to realize himself as labor capacity. . . . He can live as a worker only insofar as he exchanges his labor capacity for that part of capital which forms the labor fund. This exchange is tied to conditions which are accidental for him, and indifferent to his organic presence. He is thus a virtual pauper.[3]

To grasp the historical phenomenon of poverty, a close inspection of the accidental conditions of exchange and commodification is required. In the case of Korean poverty, this inspection begins with a look at a broad but particular historical conjuncture, between agrarian immiseration in Korea in the 1920s and 1930s, and industrial recession in Japan during the same decades. Not only is this conjuncture the origin of Korean poverty in Japan; it is also the historical origin of organized Korean working class movements in Japan.

The Conjuncture of Agricultural Crisis in Korea
and Industrial Recession in Japan

"Like nomads roving about in search of greener pastures, Korean workers wander the heavens and the earth in search of labor, appearing in Manchuria or in the wilderness of Siberia. Or, crossing the straits to Japan, they come as a white-robed army, a veritable Asian multitude [*gunshū*]." Thus writes Sakai Toshio, erstwhile bureaucrat and social surveyor for the Osaka metropolitan government's labor bureau, in an article from 1931, "The Korean Worker Problem."[4] The imagery of Korean workers as an army of nomads, decked out in their traditional white hemp clothing and in search of labor in Japan, was one of the most common ways to describe what had become known in Japan after 1919 as the Korean problem. Korean nomadism was especially evoked to name the phenomenon of Korean workers who had come to Japan in order to work, but who had soon fallen into chronic unemployment, as well as into political movements that demanded, through means and methods that were increasingly radical and revolutionary, the end to the colonial occupation of Korea—hence the evocation of the army of nomads. At the same time, in a kind of disavowal of this political trend of Korean workers, various Japanese government authorities also represented Koreans as aimless (*man-zenteki*) nomads who migrated and wandered to Japan with no clear purpose, as if the nomadic life was a natural predisposition of the Korean ethnos. This portrayal suggested that Koreans were bored and restless, with no clear vision of what to do with their lives, except, perhaps, to don their hemp clothing, cross the watery channels in large ships and in large masses, and frighten Japanese citizens into thinking that Korean workers were a source, rather than an effect, of various social problems and capitalist contradictions that were bursting at the seams of Japanese society.

Since the imperial annexation of Korea in 1910, the seams of Japanese society included the fertile provinces of the southern Korean peninsula. These seams were also bursting with impoverished peasants, especially after 1920, when the government-general instituted the program to increase rice production in 1920. The purpose of this program was to transform the Korean countryside into a massive colonial rice farm that could supply rice to the Japanese domestic market at cheap prices. Like most consumable commodities in Japan during the war years, the price of rice increased faster than wages, leading to mass rice riots, which lasted for 40 days and 40 nights in over 30 prefectures in the summer of 1918.[5] The Korean rice production plan, a 14-year program designed to last 30 years, was intended to supply rice to Japanese consumers at one-third the price of domestic rice. The rice increasing program could not have taken place, however, without supporting projects such as land improvement, extensive irrigation facilities, improvements in tools and seed varieties, and the development of chemical fertilizers, all of which required massive rural financing and investments. Lured by low-interest loans from the Sōtokufu and financial institutions such as the Oriental Development Company and the Industrial Bank of Korea, Japanese corporations and private financial organizations increasingly took on this role of rural financiers in Korea. They subvented land development corporations, agricultural banks, and rural credit unions, and in a profitable alliance between feudal Korean agriculture, Japanese finance capital worked closely with pre-capitalist Korean landlords toward the capitalization of Korean agriculture.[6] As a result of this conjuncture between Japanese finance capital and Korean land, Korean rice exports increased from 1,143 koku of rice in 1914 to 5,781 in 1929, accounting for 40 percent of Japan's total rice imports.[7]

The program to increase rice production was a boon for an increasing number of Japanese landlords and wealthy Korean landlords, but crippling to Korean peasants. Peasant bankruptcies stemming from high tenancy rents, high costs for fertilizers, cooperative fees, and irrigation taxes that were exacted for rural improvement projects together enabled Japanese and wealthy Korean landlords to buy up farm land. The number of Japanese landlords more than doubled between 1921 and 1930, rocketing from 44,378 to 106,298. Korean landlords, who outnumbered Japanese landlords 77 to 1 in 1921, and 35 to 1 in 1936, also increased during these years, but only by 7 percent. Landholding for Japanese landlords also increased, from 169 landlords holding more than 200 chongbol in 1921, to 181 landlords in 1936. By comparison, there were 66 Korean landlords with over 200 chongbol in 1921, and only 49 in 1936. Japanese with landholdings between 1 and 100 chongbol steadily doubled or tripled between these years. By contrast, only Korean landlords with holdings of 1 chongbol and 10 chongbol increased, by 13.2 percent and 2.3 percent respectively. Korean landlords with holdings of 5, 20, 50, 100, and 200 chongbol, however, all decreased. In short, Japanese landlords, while outnumbered by Korean landlords, owned the largest plots of land in Korea, and increased their plots on small and medium farms. By contrast, Korean landlords steadily lost land, with only small increases in farms with 1 and 10 chongbol.[8]

The peasant class also underwent dramatic changes. While owner-cultivators constituted less than 20 percent of all farm households in 1917, their numbers steadily decreased after the program to increase rice production was implemented in 1920. Semi-tenants also decreased from 40.2 percent in 1917 to 23.8 percent in 1939. By contrast, tenancy steadily increased, from 37.4 percent in 1917 to 52.4 percent in 1939, as did landless peasants, who were forced to become slash-and-burn farmers or agricultural wage workers. Clear patterns also emerged in terms of food shortages and rural destitution. According to historian Kim Yong-sop, between the years of 1930 and 1932, 18.4 percent of owner-cultivators, 37.5 percent of semi-tenants, and 68.1 percent of tenants were short of food and destitute.[9] Tenancy disputes centering around tenancy rights and rent in turn swelled as symptoms of peasant immiseration. According to Sōtokufu records, 15 disputes took place in 1920, a number that rose to 176 in 1924, and to 726 in 1930. Between 1920 and 1932, a total of 4,804 disputes were recorded involving 74,581 landlords and tenants nationwide. Interestingly, 91.5 percent of these disputes took place in the 6 southern provinces of Korea, accounting for 74.5 percent of the total participants involved in disputes nationwide. Out of the 6 southern provinces, the most numerous disputes were found in North Cholla (1,740 disputes), South Ch'ungch'ong (1,069 disputes), South Cholla (716 disputes), and South Kyongsang (642 disputes). The province with the highest numbers of participants in disputes, however, was South Cholla, with 14,188 participants between 1920 and 1932, followed by South Kyongsang (11,772 participants), and North Kyongsang (10,624 participants). In short, the provinces hardest hit by the agricultural transformation of Korea under Japanese colonial rule were in the 6 southernmost provinces, with South Cholla and South Kyongsang leading the way with the highest number of peasants involved in tenancy and rent disputes.[10]

What Japanese authorities called Korean nomadism was not a natural disposition of Koreans, but instead an effect of the steady decline in rural conditions in Korea, especially in the southernmost provinces. One of the salient effects of this rural immiseration was the migration to Japan of

Korean peasants in search of wage labor. While there was a small but consistent percentage of migrating Koreans who were former students, wage-workers, or businessmen involved in commerce, the overwhelming number of Korean workers in Japan were former peasants.[11] As various surveys from the interwar period show, farming constituted the most common prior occupation of Koreans migrating to Japan. The Osaka city government wrote in 1924 that 80 percent of Korean workers in Japan were former peasants in Korea.[12] In Kobe city in 1926, the percentage was 86.8 percent for all Korean workers in the city; for Korean longshoremen, factory workers, day workers, and construction workers in the city it was 88.7 percent, 88.9 percent, 94.7 percent, and 93.3 percent, respectively.[13] Kobe in 1935 showed nearly identical patterns, with 84 percent for single Korean workers, and 80 percent for Koreans in households. In Tokyo in 1928, 85.3 percent of all single Korean workers and 82 percent for Korean workers with households were former peasants.[14] In Osaka in 1932, nearly 90 percent of Korean workers with households were former peasants in Korea. Also in Osaka, up to 70 percent of Koreans registered in the UERP in 1932 were peasants prior to registering with the UERP. By comparison, for registered Japanese workers, only 14 percent were former peasants, the remaining percentage composed mostly of former factory workers.[15] In Kyoto in 1935, 86 percent of Korean workers cited farming as their prior occupations in Korea, and in the Amagasaki region in 1937, the percentages of former peasants for single and household Korean workers was 89.8 percent and 84.1 percent, respectively.[16]

Moreover, the two most common home provinces of Korean workers in Japan, throughout the interwar period, were those where peasant immiseration was greatest: Cholla and Kyongsang. As table 3 shows, out of the total number of Koreans migrating to Japan between 1917 and 1937, the percentage of Koreans from Cholla or Kyongsang was by far the highest, and not once during these years did it fall below 77 percent.

In analyzing various social surveys by Japanese city governments from the interwar period, historian Tonomura Masaru has also shown the salient reasons for Korean migration to Japan. The surveys introduced several categories as reasons for migration. The categories with the highest percentages were "agricultural poverty" (nōgyō fushin), "difficulty making ends meet [in Korea]" (seikatsunan), "to make money" (kane mōke), and "for work" (rōdō no tame). While the categories are rough at best, the surveys nonetheless show clearly that Korean peasants were coming to Japan primarily to earn money

TABLE 3. Birthplace of Korean Workers in Japan

Year	(A) North and South Kyongsang	(B) North and South Cholla	(C) Total Korean Population in Japan	A+B/C (%)
1917	6,988	4,293	14,501	77.8
1918	10,727	6,591	22,262	77.8
1919	13,624	8,370	28,273	77.8
1920	14,808	8,814	30,149	78.4
1921	18,396	10,725	37,271	78.1
1922	32,184	16,823	59,744	82
1923	44,655	24,315	80,015	86.2
1924	61,523	39,636	118,192	85.6
1925	66,829	44,134	129,870	85.4
1926	71,762	46,298	143,798	82.1
1927	81,992	53,823	171,275	79.3
1928	113,534	75,991	238,104	79.6
1929	134,472	85,990	275,206	80.1
1930	149,065	91,612	298,091	80.7
1931	160,217	94,552	311,247	81.9
1932	208,625	115,683	390,543	83
1933	254,186	131,932	456,217	84.6
1934	318,682	145,497	537,695	86.3
1935	371,242	173,743	625,678	87.1
1936	417,793	188,770	690,501	78.9
1937	446,926	200,800	735,689	88

Source: Tamura, "Naimushō Keihōkyoku Chōsa ni yoru chōsenjin jinkō (V)."

TABLE 4. Reasons for Migrating to Japan

Year	Prefecture/city	Survey categories for reasons for migration
1926	Kobe (Korean households)	"For work" (61.29%); "Difficulty making ends meet" (28.9%); "To make money" (2.341%); "Commerce" (2.56%)
	Kobe (single Koreans)	"For work" (61.78%); "Difficulty making ends meet" (23.98%); "To make money" (3.13%); "Work study" (8.4%)
1928	Tokyo (Korean households)	"Difficulty making ends meet" (53.25%); "Work" (20.75%); "To make money" (18.75%); "Study" (7.25%)
	Tokyo (single Koreans)	"Difficulty making ends meet" (56.25%); "Work" (12.81%); "To make money" (12.81%); "Study" (11.25%); "Technical study" (3.13%)
1932	Osaka (Korean households)	"Agricultural poverty" (55.66%); "Difficulty making ends meet" (17.21%); "To make money" (14.74%); "Employment" (2.04%); "Commercial failure" (1.93%)
1935	Tokyo (Korean households)	"To make money" (44.04%); "Difficulty making ends meet" (37.04%); "Work" (18.32%); "Study" (1.35%)
	Tokyo (single Koreans)	"To make money" (41.36%); "Difficulty making ends meet" (26.28%); "Employment" (12.29%); "Study" (11.79%); "Work" (6%)
1935	Kobe (Korean households)	"Agricultural poverty" (77.76%); "Difficulty making ends meet" (7.55%); "Commerce" (4.77%); "Employment" (2.17%); "Family circumstances" (2.17%)
1935	Kyoto	"Migrant work" (43.03%); "Difficulty making ends meet" (24.91%); "To raise standard of living" (14.29%); "To make money" (10.31%); "Brought over by invitation" (3.95%)

TABLE 4. *Continued*

Year	Prefecture/city	Survey categories for reasons for migration
1937	Amagasaki region (Korean household)	"Difficulty making ends meet" (75.65%); "To raise standard of living" (8.04%); "Migrant work" (5.66%); "For factory work" (3.44%); "Commercial accounting" (2.48%)
	Amagasaki region (single Koreans)	"Difficulty making ends meet" (75.18%); "Migrant work" (8.18%); "Raise standard of living" (5.40%); "Study" (1.75%)

Source: Tonomura, *Zainichi Chōsenjin shakai no rekishiteki Kenkyū*, 74.

through work, and as a result of economic—and primarily agricultural—hardship. As table 4 shows, for Korean workers in Osaka—the Japanese city with the highest percentage of Koreans in Japan after 1920—agricultural poverty was cited as the reason for migration for 56 percent of Korean workers in 1932. In Kobe, almost 80 percent cited agricultural poverty.

The urgent problem for Korean peasants was that, while many got out of the frying pan of agricultural immiseration in Korea by migrating to Japan, their fate was to fall into the fire of an industrial recession in Japan. Beginning in late 1918, manufacturing factories drastically reduced production in response to the end of the fighting in Europe, and heavy industries in Japan, such as shipping, chemicals, and steel, all experienced severe drops in commodity and stock prices, large-scale factory closings, and mass firings. Then, on March 15, 1920, the Tokyo stock market crashed, leading to falling commodity prices, bank runs, and factory closings on an unprecedented scale. Indeed, this is what distinguishes the economic crisis of 1920 from previous crises in Japan since the late Meiji period. The suddenness out of the crash; the expansiveness of its effects on both light and heavy industries, as well as on financial institutions; its origins in excess capital and surplus production; and the clear collision between falling profit rates and rising interest rates all have led economic historians to assert that the 1920 crisis in Japan was, at that time in the history of capitalism in Japan, unprecedented.[17] The economy that followed in the wake of the 1920 crisis, moreover, did not bounce back with any predictable periodicity, but rather proceeded from periods of recession to new periods of recession, punctuated by the financial crisis of 1922, financial disasters stemming from the 1923 earthquake in Tokyo and Yokohama, and the 1927 financial crisis (itself an effect of bank crises going back to 1923). Culminating in the depression years of 1929 and 1930, the recession after 1920 displayed something new about capitalism in Japan, namely a chronic quality. Economic commentators at the time therefore called the recession a *manseiteki fukyō*, or a chronic recession. As economic theorist Uno Kōzō has argued, and as historian Ouchi Tsutomu has shown, the chronic recession of the 1920s and early 1930s in Japan, in addition to the accelerated movements towards cartelization and *zaibatsu* power, was nothing other than one of the clearest symptoms of the extent to which industrial development in Japan, in its imperialist stage, was led—and bled—by finance capital.[18]

Colonial surplus populations coming to Japan from Korea found themselves caught between deepening immiseration in the Korean countryside, and chronic industrial recession in Japan. First and foremost, this took the form of being expelled from factories and coal mines, and being refused jobs there. A brief statistical glance at Korean employment during the interwar years gives traces of the obstacles in the labor market that Korean workers faced. While the percentage of Korean workers employed in coal mines during the war years was nearly 40, this percentage dropped steadily, from 22.9 percent in 1920 to 2.81 percent in 1935.[19] From 1922 to 1933, Korean workers employed in factories only averaged 24.3 percent, roughly half the percentage of Korean workers in factories during the war boom years.[20] As a 1923 Osaka survey, "The Korean Worker Problem," explained, this decline in the numbers of Korean workers employed in factories and coal mines stemmed from mass firings following the manufacturing boom. "During the period of economic prosperity and labor shortage [during the war], Korean workers were used as workers in small manufacturing factories. . . . In our time of economic recession, however, it is Korean workers who have been dismissed . . . and in order to save Japanese workers from falling into unemployment."[21] Four years later, a justice ministry document stated, "Small factories . . . hired Korean workers during economically prosperous times. Since then, however, Korean workers have showed a strong sense of solidarity. . . . For this reason, and also due to the economic recession, the recent tendency among small factory bosses is to restrict the number of Korean workers."[22]

After the war boom, therefore, the dominant trend among Korean workers was that they were not, for the most part, commodified in the factory system in Japan. Among the minority of Korean workers who did find work in factories, however, two salient points characterized their working conditions.

First, they did not work in capital-intensive, large-scale factories, but rather in labor-intensive, small- and medium-sized factories (chūshō kigyō) that employed fewer than 30 workers, and often in factories with fewer than 10 workers (reisai kigyō). These factories had little capital to invest in advanced technology; profits therefore stemmed from the workers' long working hours and cheap wages. As various surveys from the 1920s show, Korean wages in small- and medium-sized factories in the metals, chemicals, ceramics, and cotton industries were generally 30 to 60 percent lower than Japanese wages.[23]

Second, Korean workers were employed primarily as unskilled workers on a temporary basis. Factory work, therefore, when gotten, was not only oppressive for its cheap wages and long hours, but especially for its precariousness and instability. According to a 1923 survey from Osaka, out of 623 Korean workers surveyed in 33 factories employing more than 30 Korean workers, 28 percent lost their jobs within three months; 26 percent only worked between 6 months and 1 year; and only 3.9 percent kept factory jobs for more than 3 years. By contrast, 56 percent of Japanese workers kept factory jobs longer than 3 years, and only 9.1 percent lost jobs within 6 months.[24] In 1931, it was surveyed that only 26 percent of Korean workers maintained jobs in factories for more than two consecutive years, and 37 percent worked less than 6 months at factories before moving on to other jobs, primarily construction jobs on public works projects.[25]

Korean Free Workers and Day Workers

As conditions in the Korean countryside worsened throughout the 1920s and 1930s, and as the industrial recession deepened in Japan, the everyday life of Korean workers in the Japanese urban centers became more and more precarious. Generally expelled from the factory system during the economic recession of the 1920s and 1930s, Korean workers struggled to find secure sources of employment in Japan. Indeed, this was one of the prevailing reasons why many Koreans soon went back to the Korean countryside. A 1928 survey from South Kyongsang province in Korea showed, for example, that for 60 percent of Koreans surveyed, "lack of employment opportunities" and "unemployment" in Japan were the two leading causes for returning to Korea.[26]

Koreans who could not afford to return home, however, or those who were determined to find work in Japan outside of factories, were compelled to search for work in the day labor market (hiyatoi rōdō shijō), where "employment relationships must be renewed everyday on a temporary basis," and where labor power was sold, as the well known phrase in Kyoto went, "like fish in the summer, on a daily basis."[27] So much so was this the case for Korean workers in particular that, already in 1923, when the first thoroughgoing survey on day labor in Japan was published by the Osaka city government, it was stated, "Just as the factory system cannot be thought apart from the day labor market, the day labor market cannot be thought apart from Korean workers."[28] What this and other surveys from various city governments found—and what Korean workers in Japan knew first hand—was that the predominant form of labor for Koreans in Japan was not factory work (shokkō); rather, Koreans could mainly find jobs as free workers (jiyū rōdōsha), day laborers (hiyatoi rōdōsha), and as what was called, in Japanese, ninpu (人夫).

These three categories were the most commonly used terms to describe the majority of Korean workers in Japan. Ninpu was a broad category typically designating non-factory manual labor that had historical roots in social networks constituting the Tokugawa period day labor market, its labor suppliers, and urban public works construction sites.[29] As for the category of free workers, the Tokyo city government, for example, defined it in 1923 along three basic characteristics: (1) workers whose employment relationships are constantly changing; (2) workers whose work place is constantly changing; (3) workers who are unskilled and who work outdoors.[30] Day workers, or hiyatoi rōdōsha, were defined similarly in 1924 by the Osaka city government. The day worker, while relying on wage labor to live, did not work for a fixed employer, but rather was compelled to change employers on a daily basis; continuous employment relations therefore did not exist for the day worker. Also, like free workers, day workers were defined as those who generally worked outdoors and outside of factories and, specifically, as unskilled, manual workers. The important points for both categories, therefore, was that it was a form of employment that was inherently prone to daily changes and therefore necessarily contingent and precarious. It was not work that offered any continuity in one place or with one employer, but was constantly changing, depending on the day, the employer, and the work site. In short, it was continuously discontinuous work, and work, moreover, that was never guaranteed beyond one day. For both free workers and day workers, the immediate problem was not simply the exploitation of their labor; rather, the insecurity of employment itself was the most urgent problem. As I will discuss in more detail in the next chapter, this insecurity of employment disclosed a complex social network that on a daily

TABLE 5. Korean Employment

Year of Survey	Factory Worker (職工)		"Free Labor"; "Day Labor"; or "Non-factory Manual Labor"		Unspecified Labor (無職)		Total	
	No.	%	No.	%	No.	%	No.	%
1922	6,626	30.8	13,099	61	1,762	8.2	21,487	100
1924	16,452	18.9	61,528	70.8	8,890	10.2	86,870	100
1925	25,626	23.8	59,066	54.8	23,027	21.4	107,719	100
1926	30,028	25.3	67,234	56.7	21,288	18	118,550	100
1927	34,505	27	65,209	51.1	27,985	21.9	127,699	100
1933	65,707	19.7	124,806	37.4	143,504	43	334,017	100

Sources: Naimushō Keihōkyoku "Chōsenjin Kinjō Gaiyō," January 1922; Naimushō Keihōkyoku Hōanka, "Taisho 14 nen chu ni okeru chōsenjin no jōkyō," December 1925; Osaka-shi Shakai-bu Chōsa-ka, "Chōsenjin Rōdōsha Mondai," 1924; Tokyo-fu Shakai-ka, "Zaikyō chōsenjin rōdōsha no genjō," 1929; Chōsen Sōtokufu Keimukyoku, "Chōsenjin rōdōsha naichi tokō hogo torishimari genjō," June 1933.

basis mediated between day workers and free workers, on the one hand, and, on the other, potential employers, and that formed geographical sites within the city where large groups of day workers congregated every morning with the hopes of encountering a labor broker (rōdō burōka), a manual labor supplier (ninpu ukeōgyōsha), or some other mediating representative for large public works construction sites. Employment for the day, therefore, was contingent upon this social mediation. [31]

Table 5 above shows the extent to which the most common form of labor for Korean workers was not factory labor, but rather free labor and day labor. Korean workers in factories generally did not rise above 30 percent of the total number of Korean workers in Japan. The majority of Korean workers were rather employed as free workers, day workers, and as ninpu.

Available statistics on day labor in Japan between 1927 and 1932 additionally show that Korean day labor in the 6 major cities (Tokyo, Yokohama, Nagoya, Kyoto, Osaka, and Kobe) was generally between 10 and 20 percent, but sometimes as high as 46 percent, as was the case in Kyoto in 1927, and in Osaka in 1932. More revealing, however, is the fact that, out of the total number of working Koreans in Japan, at least 30 percent and as much as 85

TABLE 6. Korean Day Labor (I)

	Year	Estimated Total Day Workers	Estimated Korean Day Workers	Percent Korean
Tokyo	1927	47,400	8,500	17.9
	1928	70,600	10,400	14.7
	1929	99,297	13,088	13.2
	1930	104,115	17,094	16.4
	1931	129,209	12,025	9.3
	1932	132,876	11,527	8.7
Kyoto	1927	8,500	3,900	45.9
	1928	9,650	4,250	44
	1929	39,658	4,628	11.7
	1930	39,662	6,563	16.5
	1931	33,392	5,726	17.1
	1932	34,722	5,720	16.5
Osaka	1927	38,200	13,000	34
	1928	40,300	15,000	37.2
	1929	93,582	9,668	10.3
	1930	72,408	12,352	17.1
	1931	83,556	7,909	9.5
	1932	85,474	38,935	45.6
Yokohama	1927	15,500	2,550	16.5
	1928	46,050	3,250	20.2
	1929	27,048	8,336	30.8
	1930	32,453	NA	NA
	1931	34,198	NA	NA
	1932	38,281	8,202	21.4

TABLE 6. Continued

	Year	Estimated Total Day Workers	Estimated Korean Day Workers	Percent Korean
Kobe	1927	17,500	3,050	17.4
	1928	16,700	3,600	21.6
	1929	30,406	5,667	18.6
	1930	30,627	NA	NA
	1931	31,325	NA	NA
	1932	32,292	5,790	17.9
Nagoya	1927	12,200	2,550	20.9
	1928	18,200	3,550	19.5
	1929	77,401	9,853	12.7
	1930	74,143	NA	NA
	1931	71,692	NA	NA
	1932	74,443	13,309	17.9

Sources: Naimushō Shakaikyoku Shakai-bu: "Shōwa 3 nendō shitsugyo kyūsai jigyō gaiyo," October 1929; "Shitsugyō Jōkyō Suitei Geppō Gaiyō," September 1929; "Hisoka: Shitsugyo Jokyo Suitei Geppo-chu chōsenjin ni kansuru chosa," September 1929; "Shitsugyō Jōkyō Suitei Geppō Gaiyō Ji-Shōwa 4-nendō 9-gatsu tatsu Shōwa 8-nendō 8-gatsu," 1933.

percent of Korean workers were day workers. Tables 6 and 7 compare the percentage of Korean day workers with the total population of working Koreans in Japan in the cities of Tokyo, Kyoto, Osaka, and others. In Tokyo, out of 11,390 Korean workers, an estimated 8,500 were day workers, nearly 75 percent; in 1930, this increased to almost 85 percent. In Osaka and Kyoto, where factory work was more prevalent, the percentage of Korean day workers was approximately 40 percent and 30 percent, respectively.

The labor power of Korean free workers and day workers was commodified most typically in the public works industry. Unlike most of the primary industries in Japan during the recession, the public works industry, together with the electricity industry, expanded throughout the entire interwar period. This was a reflection of new urban planning policies and laws that came into existence after the war years, largely as a means to address worsening conditions in working class housing and sanitation that resulted from the enormous surge in the laboring populations in the major cities. The

TABLE 7. Korean Day Labor (II)

	Year	Employed Korean Population	Korean Day Labor	
			No.	%
Tokyo	1927	11,390	8,500	74.6
	1928	22,175	10,400	46.9
	1929	20,964	13,088	62.4
	1930	20,126	17,094	84.9
	1931	20,175	12,025	59.6
	1932	22,798	11,527	50.6
Kyoto	1927	9,538	3,900	40.9
	1928	13,188	4,250	32.2
	1929	12,066	4,628	38.4
	1930	13,099	6,563	50.1
	1931	14,875	5,726	38.5
	1932	14,598	5,720	39.2
Osaka	1927	29,857	13,000	43.5
	1928	38,728	10,400	26.9
	1929	52,157	9,668	18.5
	1930	56,058	12,352	22
	1931	58,905	7,909	13.4
	1932	77,743	38,935	50.1

Source: Tamura, "Naimushō Keihōkyoku Chōsa ni yoru chōsenjin jinko (III)."

establishment of the home ministry's city planning section in 1918 and the passage of the City Planning and Urban Buildings laws of 1919 were the clearest political expressions of this need to address what was called, throughout the interwar period, the urban problem, or toshi mondai.[32] The expansion of public works construction projects, however, was the industrial expression of this urban transformation, and construction projects literally transformed Japanese urban space and its built environment throughout the interwar period, creating thousands of new housing projects, miles and miles of new railroad tracks and paved roads, hundreds of tunnels, countless river embankments, and vast labyrinths of underground sewage systems.

Expelled from the factory system after the war and throughout the 1920s and 1930s, the majority of Korean workers were compelled to find erratic and temporary employment as unskilled construction workers on various kinds of public works construction sites. Wages for Korean construction workers, like wages for Korean factory workers, were 30 to 60 percent lower than wages for Japanese construction workers. How these wages were determined is one of the central topics of the next chapter. For now, all that needs to be emphasized is the consistent and repetitive appearance of Korean free workers and day workers in the world of the construction industry. So much so was this the case that city governments increasingly translated and naturalized this appearance of Korean workers in construction as a need and a necessity for Korean workers in the public works industry. "Especially in the areas of unskilled labor in public works construction, Koreans are an absolute necessity. Public works would be hard pressed indeed without Korean labor power," according to a Kyoto city government analysis of a survey of day workers.[33] Even the ministry of justice, which had little to do directly with the construction industry, wrote about the importance of Korean workers as a source of labor to meet a demand for cheap labor in construction. "The demand for this cheap labor stems from the recent boom in urban planning projects, one result of which is the appearance of Korean workers working the most base and dangerous jobs. . . . For this reason, in addition to the fact that the price of their labor is so cheap, Korean labor power is important indeed."[34]

Virtual Paupers, Actual Struggles: Korean Poverty and Labor Movements

The segmentation of the labor market in Japan along ethnic lines and the discrimination against Korean workers in Japan were most visible in the fact that wages for Korean workers were 30 to 60 percent lower than wages for

Japanese workers in the same occupation. Combined with statistics on Korean savings and remittances, these disparities reveal the extent to which Korean free workers, compelled to live hand to mouth amidst extremely precarious and contingent conditions of exchange, were virtual paupers in Japan.

Across the board, Korean incomes were consistently lower than Japanese incomes. The average income for Japanese worker households nationwide in 1926 was 102 yen 7 sen; in 1931 it was 83 yen 43 sen; in 1935 it was 86 yen 99 sen; and in 1938 it was 101 yen 79 sen. By contrast, the average income for Korean worker households in 1928 was 63 yen 71 sen, and, in 1935, 24 yen 93 sen in Tokyo and 46 yen 21 sen in Kyoto.[35] In Kyoto in 1930, while 40 percent of Japanese day workers earned more than 30 yen, only 13.3 percent of Korean day workers earned the same. In Osaka in 1932, 65.8 percent of Japanese construction workers had incomes between 40 and 80 yen, compared to 21.9 percent of Korean construction workers. By contrast, 73.9 percent of Korean construction workers earned between 20 and 30 yen, compared to 30.5 percent of Japanese construction workers. For day workers in Osaka, a similar pattern emerged. Of Japanese day workers, 65.1 percent earned between 40 and 80 yen, compared to 18.6 percent for Korean workers. Of Koreans, 71.8 percent earned between 20 and 30 yen, compared to 32.6 percent for Japanese workers.[36] By and large, it was extremely difficult for Korean workers and their households to break the 30 yen income line.

Remittances back to Korea were extremely limited. In Kobe in 1927, only 13.5 percent claimed to be able to send money back to Korea; in Tokyo in 1928, 7.3 percent sent remittances back home. In 1928, 40.1 percent of Koreans returning to South Kyongsang province in Korea stated they could not send money to Korea during their time in Japan; and 96.4 percent of Koreans surveyed in Osaka in 1933 said that they did not send money to Korea.[37] As for Korean savings, statistics show that large percentages of Korean workers could not afford to save much or at all. In Kobe in 1927, nearly 60 percent of Korean worker households, and 27 percent of single Korean workers, did not save or send money home. In Tokyo in 1928, 35 percent of Korean worker households could not afford to save or send remittances to Korea. A 1928 survey from South Kyongsang found that, out of 1,534 Korean workers returning to Korea after spending between 1 and 5 years in Japan, 82.6 percent of returning Koreans had no savings; 3.4 percent had savings of 10 yen; 2.6 percent had savings of 30 yen; and between 4 and 5 percent had savings between 50 and 100 yen. In Osaka in 1933, 95 percent of Korean worker households were unable to save any money.[38]

Korean poverty and ethnic discrimination, both inseparable from the continuously discontinuous and precarious periods of work for Koreans, formed
the crucible in which Korean labor and social movements on the political left
emerged in Japan. Centered in the 6 major cities of Japan, Korean communist
labor unions, in particular Rōsō, or Zai-nihon chosen rodo sōdōmei, spearheaded
Korean labor movements in the 1920s and 1930s. Established in Tokyo on
February 22, 1925, Rōsō federated 12 large Korean labor unions into a single
large organization, amassing an initial membership of 800. Concerning itself
with the complete liberation of the working class, struggles against the repression and oppression of the capitalist class, struggles against unemployment, demands for working condition reform, the right to strike, among
other causes, Rōsō had, by October of 1926, mobilized 25 other Korean labor
unions, increasing its membership to over 9,000.[39] In 1927, at its third annual
convention, Rōsō more explicitly and emphatically identified the need to combat ethnic discrimination in terms of work insecurity and low wages—what
it called ethnic wage slavery—and further stated that, because the majority of
Korean workers were not factory workers but day workers, Rōsō would have
to organize Korean workers separately from leading Japanese socialist and
communist labor unions, which based their organizations almost entirely on
factory labor.[40] After 1927, as the numbers of Korean free workers and day
workers increased, Rōsō extended its political popularity among Korean workers further, and by 1929, it had organized over 30,000 members nationwide.[41]

The development of Korean labor strikes in Japan closely followed the
development of Rōsō after 1925. A statistical overview of the flow of Korean
labor strikes between 1925 and 1935, shown in table 9, provides a glimpse
into what the leading demands of organized Korean labor unions were. While
there were only 46 strikes involving 1,075 participants in 1925, by 1930 there
were 486 strikes involving 13,803 participants. The years 1930–31 had the
most strikes and participants, with demands including the payment of wages,
dismissal compensation, higher wages, and an end to wage decreases.

The Virtual Pauper and the Uncontrollable Colonial Surplus

The historical essence of the colonial surplus populations coming to Japan
from Korea after 1920 is a population caught between agricultural immiseration in Korea, on the one hand, and an industrial recession in Japan, on
the other. In Japan, Korean surplus populations increasingly faced closed
factory doors, and even when they were open, Koreans were soon cast out

TABLE 8. Membership for *Zai-Nihon Chōsen rōdō sōdōmei* (*Rōsō*)

Year	Name	Membership
1925	1. Tokyo chōsenjin rōdō dōmei	250
	2. Chōsen rōdō sōdōmei kyōshōkai	80
	3. Kyoto senjin rōdō dōmei	70
	4. Kobe chōsenjin rōdō dōmei	90
	5. Osaka chōsenjin rōdō dōmeikai	50
	6. Sakai chōsen rōdō dōshikai	160
	7. Sakai chōsen rōdō dōshikai seinendan	50
	8. Osaka nishinari chōsen rōdō kumiai	250
	9. Osaka higashinari chōsen rōdō domei	55
	10. Tsurumachi chōsen rōdō kumiai	70
	11. Izuō chōsen rōdō kumiai	60
	12. Imafuku chōsen rōdō kumiai	55
		Total: 800
1929	1. Tokyo chōsen rōdō kumiai	3,140
	2. Kanagawa chōsen rōdō kumiai	1,500
	3. Osaka chōsen rōdō kumiai	17,000
	4. Kyoto chōsen rōdō kumiai	370
	5. Hyōgo chōsen rōdō kumiai	450
	6. Niigata chōsen rōdō kumiai	400
	7. Toyama chōsen rōdō kumiai	200
	8. Toyohashi chōsen rōdō kumiai	150
	9. Aichi chōsen rōdō kumiai	290
		Total: 23,500

Sources: Naimushō Keihōkyoku Hōanka, "Taisho 14 nen chu ni okeru chōsenjin no jōkyō," December 1925; Naimushō Keihōkyoku, *Shakai Undō no Jōkyō*, 1929; Nishinarita, *Zainichi chōsenjin no 'sekai' to 'teikoku' kokka*, 144.

TABLE 9. Labor Strikes by Koreans, 1925–1935

Demands		1925	1929	1930	1931	1932	1933	1934	1935
For wage	No. of strikes	18	79	153	103	NA	NA	NA	NA
payment	Participants	650	2,381	5,728	3,386	NA	NA	NA	NA
For rehiring	No. of strikes	2	22	43	56	NA	NA	NA	NA
	Participants	34	404	537	885	NA	NA	NA	NA
Against	No. of strikes	NA	NA	NA	NA	99	81	112	102
firing	Participants	NA	NA	NA	NA	NA	NA	NA	NA
Dismissal	No. of strikes	1	45	74	62	NA	NA	NA	NA
compensation	Participants	38	581	957	1,510	NA	NA	NA	NA
Against wage	No. of strikes	6	26	37	55	42	31	27	26
decrease	Participants	271	1,039	1,439	1,936	NA	NA	NA	NA
Wage	No. of strikes	6	37	43	65	95	102	97	94
increase	Participants	271*	2,564	2,887	3,750	NA	NA	NA	NA
Against	No. of strikes	NA	6	17	23	24	15	25	12
factory closure	Participants	NA	78	328	1,640	NA	NA	NA	NA
Other	No. of strikes	19	41	119	119	154	115	121	122
	Participants	82	614	1,927	1,972	NA	NA	NA	NA
Total	No. of strikes	46	256	486	483	414	344	382	356
	Participants	1,075	7,661	13,803	15,079	15,524	8,851	9,517	6,378

Sources: Naimushō Keihōkyoku Hōanka, "Taisho 14 nen chu ni okeru chōsenjin no jōkyō," December 1925; Naimushō Keihōkyoku, Shakai Undō no Jōkyō, 1929–35.
* In the 1925 survey, the categories for opposing decreased wages and demanding higher wages are combined into one category.

as disposable and temporary workers. The majority of Korean workers were therefore compelled to search for work as so-called free workers in the day labor market where they sought out erratic employment on public works construction sites. The precariousness of their situation, combined with wages that were consistently 30 to 60 percent lower than wages for Japanese in the same occupations, revealed how Korean free workers were, in fact, what Marx called virtual paupers. What distinguishes the Korean virtual paupers from the free workers in Marx's day, however, was the extent to which institutionalized ethnic discrimination played a fundamental role in segmenting the labor market in Japan along ethnic lines and in maintaining and reproducing contingent conditions of employment for the vast majority of Korean surplus populations in Japan. The force of organized Korean labor unions was that they identified and launched sustained critiques of precisely these contingencies in the labor markets.

3

INTERMEDIARY EXPLOITATION

Korean Workers in the Day Labor Market

Caught between the Scylla of agricultural immiseration in Korea, and the Charybdis of industrial recession in the metropolitan centers of Japan, the majority of Korean workers in interwar Japan were cast out of the factory system and compelled to find erratic and irregular employment in the day labor market. The appearance of Korean workers in the day labor market was so extensive that, as early as 1923, city governments in Japan could not write or think about the problem of day labor apart from Korean workers. Yet, while many Japanese day workers were employed as temporary workers in factories, the vast majority of Korean day workers did not toil in factories, but rather as unskilled workers on large public works construction sites. They paved roads in the cities, hauling thousands of tons of gravel; dug deep into the earth to create labyrinths of waterworks; put up embankments for rivers; laid hundreds of miles of rails for trains that connected the Japanese metropolis and its hinterlands; and handled dynamite to explode sides of mountains to create tunnels. In short, the majority of Koreans built what urban geographers now call the built environment, and it is no exaggeration to say that, without Korean construction workers, the modern infrastructure that underlay interwar Japan simply would not have materialized in the accelerated time that it did.

It will take the second half of this book to appreciate the full extent to which Korean workers did not simply appear in the day labor market, but were rather channeled into the day labor market institutionally, through the mediation of various state apparatuses and their disavowed and supplementary forms, such as Korean welfare organizations. This chapter will limit the scope of analysis to the general conditions of Korean day workers in the public works industry. At the center of this analysis is the problem of the relationship between the commodification of Korean labor power in the day labor market, and the problem of what government bureaus, sub-contractors, and day workers called intermediary exploitation, or *chūkan sakushu*. Both Japanese and Korean day workers alike knew and experienced intermediary exploitation in the day labor market, but what has to be kept in mind is that, insofar as the majority of Korean workers in Japan were day workers, the problem of intermediary exploitation in the day labor market was the predominant and prevailing form of exploitation that was experienced, identified, and critiqued by Korean workers in Japan. This was so common that even the ministry of justice, located high above the mud and blood of the day labor market, became aware of Korean critiques of intermediary exploitation, stating disparagingly in 1928, "Every time a Korean worker opens his mouth, he's always shouting 'Discrimination!' [*sabetsu*] or . . . 'Intermediary Exploitation!'."[1] As we will see later, the fact that organized Korean workers in Japan tended to focus on the problem of intermediary exploitation, and not simply on exploitation, revealed a significant difference from the political foci of unionized Japanese workers, who, for the most part, organized their politics around the shop floors of factories. The majority of Korean workers were talking about different problems of exploitation compared to the majority of Japanese workers, problems that required different forms of political organization and working class politics for Korean workers. Understanding what was at stake is critical to understanding the historicity of the problem of *chūkan sakushu*.

A Brief Introduction to the Interwar Day Labor Market and Public Works

During the recession that followed the manufacturing boom of the war years, unemployed and chronically unemployed workers swelled to form an industrial reserve army, one whose subsistence was maintained largely through a growing day labor market that supplied masses of workers, on a temporary basis, to an expanding public works industry. Unlike the heavy and light industries, the public works industry experienced a boom period following the First World War, most immediately owing to the proliferation of urban planning projects and the accompanying developments in modern, urban hygiene. In 1918, the city planning section was established in the home ministry, followed shortly by the city planning research committee, which drafted what would become the Urban Planning Law of 1919.[2] Reflecting the expansion of urban planning, the public works industry increasingly became based around sub-contracting corporations, one index being the establishment of the National Public Works Sub-Contracting Federation (*Nihon doboku kenchiku ukeyōgyōsha rengōkai*) in 1919.[3]

TABLE 10. Occupations of Day Workers prior to Unemployment Registration, Tokyo, 1928

	Japanese	Korean	Total	Percent Japanese	Percent Korean
Factory or Mine	1,380	222	1,602	86.1	13.9
Public Works	2,997	5,369	8,366	35.8	64.2
Commerce	787	159	946	83.2	16.8
Agriculture	1,763	3,743	5,506	32	68
Fishery	28	0	28	100	0
Transportation	310	16	326	95.1	4.9
Domestic	28	2	30	93.3	6.7
Miscellaneous	434	112	546	79.5	20.5

Source: Tokyo-shi Shakaikyoku, Tokyo-shi Shakaikyoku Nenpō, 1928 Nendō, 92–93.

Under the department of public works (doboku kyoku), civil engineering and construction projects expanded greatly during the interwar urban planning boom. Between 1914 and 1936, settled accounts for total road construction increased from approximately 26 million yen to 177 million yen; for river embankment projects, they rose from 28 million yen to 85 million yen; and for ports, from 3.7 million yen to 40 million yen.[4] Reflecting urban hygiene developments, total meters of underground waterworks extended from just under 2 million meters in 1912 to over 20 million meters in 1935. In Tokyo alone, total meters of sewage pipes grew from under one million in 1912 to nearly five million in 1935; in Osaka during the same years, the total rose from just 116,500 meters to 2.2 million meters.[5] Railway lines and train stations also increased, far surpassing the total mileage of rail lines laid down during the Meiji period. Between 1912 and 1937, the total kilometers of operating rail lines increased from just under 3,000 kilometers to nearly 10,000; and the number of train stations rose from 477 to 4,255.[6] Reflecting this expansion, expenditures on new national railway construction rose from 16.9 million yen in 1918 to 51.8 million in 1928;[7] expenditures on national railway improvement projects rose even more, from 54 million yen to nearly 140 million yen; and between 1913 and 1925, total spending on railroad-related subcontracting increased from 700,000 yen to nearly 3 million yen.[8]

With such a tremendous expansion of urban and transurban planning

TABLE 11. Korean Construction Workers by Prefecture

	1923	1925	1929	1930	1931	1934	1937
Tokyo	2,183	5,209	17,776	17,094	12,025	9,430	7,219
Osaka	10,471	8,742	20,533	12,352	7,909	13,401	18,952
Kyoto	2,267	2,636	5,298	6,563	5,726	6,246	9,012
Aichi	1,335	1,296	6,648	10,961	9,337	9,872	5,741
Hyogo	2,754	2,836	3,216	4,976	6,251	3,503	12,050
Kanagawa	NA	5,360	5,919	5,335	4,414	4,459	3,510

Source: Naimushō Keihōkykoku, Shakai Undō no Jōkyō.

projects underway during the 1920s and 1930s, the public works industry sought large numbers of workers, both skilled and unskilled, and looked to the swelling day labor market as its primary source of labor power. In Tokyo, day labor encompassed five areas related to either public works or general construction: (1) general (municipal) public works; (2) railway construction for the railway ministry; (3) public riverbank construction; (4) public road construction; and (5) public hydro-electric construction sites.[9] Day labor in Osaka was also fundamentally related to construction sites, namely those associated with public works, freight transport, and hygiene and waste disposal—all of which took place outdoors.[10]

With the expansion of public works rose a demand for Korean day labor within public works construction sites. The specific demand for Korean day labor in construction sites was at the intersection of two trends:

> Korean workers, alienated from general industrial factories and agriculture, have been expelled to the world of public works. This phenomenon has become undeniable the more the recruiting of construction workers has run into difficulties and high costs. . . . Due to the boom in state-led urban planning projects, an acute labor shortage has been felt in the public works labor market, especially in the fall season. . . . Korean workers are hired *en masse*, especially in times when a sudden demand for labor power is made. In this regard, Korean construction workers are a precious gem indeed.[11]

This trend became particularly acute in the earthquake-devastated city of Tokyo during its four-year reconstruction plan (1923–27), but was also common

in Yokohama, Nagoya, Osaka, Kyoto, and Kobe. In 1928, when 54.7 percent of
the total registered day workers in Tokyo were Korean, statistics showed that
out of this figure, 64.2 percent worked in public works prior to registering
within the unemployment emergency relief programs, while only 13.9 percent
worked in factories prior to registering. In contrast, only 35.8 percent of Japanese laborers worked in public works prior to unemployment registration,
while 86.1 percent previously worked in factories.[12]

While clearly a major trend in Tokyo, this was also a nationwide phenomenon. The more Korean workers entered into the world of day labor, the more
they become equated with construction work itself, so much so that the Osaka
social bureau would assert that "Korean construction workers are . . . a precious labor force."[13]

The Ethnic Division of Labor

The demand for Korean construction workers, however, was not a general
demand for cheap labor, but a specific demand for so-called unskilled construction labor. Not unlike the division of labor in factories, the distinction
between skilled and unskilled labor within the construction industry and
within public works in general was the most crucial and pervasive distinction, one that determined the nature of the employment relation as well as
the type and intensity of the labor itself. The distinction between skilled and
unskilled labor within these construction sites was generally based on levels
of efficiency, technical knowledge of machinery, and the usage of other tools.
A 1924 day labor report from Osaka defines skilled labor as a "handicraft" in
which "labor efficiency is demanded" and lists carpenters, masons, painters,
and bricklayers as examples. Tokyo's 1923 survey on day labor also listed masons, carpenters, and painters as skilled workers and noted that skilled labor
is often contracted directly by public offices.[14]

The unskilled worker, by contrast, "is usually a helper of the skilled worker,
doing miscellaneous jobs for him and requiring no specific skill or craft."[15]
In the area of Public Works construction in Osaka, for example, of 235 listed
occupations, 159, or 68 percent, of the occupations were listed as unskilled labor, dealing mostly with basic manual tasks such as digging, shoveling, hauling, and washing gravel. Unskilled labor was considered to "have no specific
training"[16] and was "usually constituted by former peasants-turned-worker or
recruited Koreans . . . who are hired en masse and on a temporary basis by sub-
contractors or sub-sub-contractors working a particular construction site."[17]

Another important distinction, which the Osaka survey makes clear, is that unskilled construction laborers changed jobs with greater frequency than skilled construction laborers. A skilled construction worker, such as a mason, working on a construction site would almost without fail be the mason on the same site the next day, the day after that, and the day after that. This kind of continuity, however, was never guaranteed for the unskilled construction laborer. "He must be able to be flexible and move from one job today to another job tomorrow. One day he may work the loading docks, haul coal the next day, and work as a construction hand the day after that."[18]

This last distinction is important to consider to understand the prevalence of injuries sustained primarily by unskilled workers. The fast turnover of unskilled workers meant that workers often did not have much time to learn how to execute the job, which often entailed highly dangerous and risky work. Injuries were a real and common problem, especially for Korean construction workers. According to a 1927 survey of the injuries and illnesses sustained by day workers who were supplied to construction sites from 19 private worker dormitories and 8 public labor exchange offices in Tokyo, unskilled construction workers experienced more injuries and illnesses from construction-related jobs than skilled construction laborers. The main factor contributing to accidents on the job, the survey states, was the continual and daily changing of jobs by unskilled workers and the lack of training for or experience with a particular job due to this itinerant schedule.[19] Out of a total of 103 reported injuries, 81 (78.6 percent) originated among unskilled labor, while 47 out of 56 (83.9 percent) of all illnesses stemming from construction sites originated in unskilled labor.[20] Especially common were accidents related to heavy soil transport and gravel cleaning (a process of washing gravel before using it for steel-enforced concrete), the highest number of which were experienced by Korean workers employed by the semi-private "assimilation" organ known as the Sōaikai.[21] The Sōaikai, whose politics and economy will be analyzed in greater detail in chapter 5, was a state-backed, Korean-led organization specializing in housing and employing (and politically repressing radical, especially communist) Korean day workers. The Sōaikai also topped all private worker dormitories in the number of injuries and illnesses stemming from construction sites in which its workers toiled. Of the 75 reported injuries from private worker dorms, the Sōaikai's Korean workers accounted for 31, or 41.3 percent, the largest single percentage of all 19 private worker dorms. The Fujigawachō worker dormitory accounted for half the number of the Sōaikai's with 15 percent.

TABLE 12. Wages of Skilled and Unskilled Construction Workers, Kyoto

	Japanese	Korean
Skilled Labor		
Carpenter	80 to 250 (sen)	NA (sen)
Mason	100 to 400	NA
Bricklayer	280	NA
Painter	250	NA
Unskilled Labor		
Construction assistant	100 to 200	100 to 130
Construction	70 to 250	60 to 160
Freight	60 to 400	120 to 180

Source: Kyoto-shi Kyōiku-bu Shakai-ka, "Kyōto-shi ni okeru hiyatoi rōdōsha ni kansuru chōsa," 45.

Unskilled, supplementary construction labor increasingly came to mean Korean labor while regular, skilled construction labor increasingly implied Japanese labor. "Especially in the area of unskilled labor in construction work, Korean workers are an absolute necessity. Public works construction sites would be hard pressed indeed without Korean workers."[22] In Kyoto, for example, the separation between skilled construction work and unskilled work was translated into ethnic difference. Table 12 demonstrates this ethnic divide while also showing significant differences in wages between Japanese and Korean unskilled workers. The point here, however, is that the skilled-unskilled division of labor was translated into an ethnic division of labor.

As we will see further in chapter 6 on the Unemployment Emergency Relief Programs, as well as in chapter 5 on Korean welfare organizations, this ethnic division of labor was an effect of the institutional channeling of day workers. The Sōaikai, for example, wrote in one of its pamphlets from 1923 that unskilled Korean construction workers "seldom, if ever, work alongside Japanese construction workers when working en masse on railway construction sites or in gravel pits."[23] In other words, the difference between skilled and unskilled labor came to be maintained as the separation between Japanese and Korean construction workers. This has to be kept in mind when one considers how city governments published surveys on the influence of Korean workers on the labor market in Japan. For example, a 1924 Osaka report on Korean workers explained how the massive flow of Korean workers into the area of public works was not adversely influencing the Japanese labor market, precisely because the division between skilled and unskilled workers was maintained through an ethnic division of labor.

> [Despite] the inexpensive price of Korean wages [in construction] and their low cost of living . . . Korean construction workers have not expelled Japanese workers from the construction worker market. The reason is that Korean construction workers work below the lowest Japanese construction workers as helpers and assistants . . . At the present moment . . . the relation between Japanese and Koreans in public works projects is one whereby the former work as skilled workers while the latter work as unskilled workers. By maintaining this distinction, the predicament of plummeting wages and lowered standards of living have been allayed somewhat.[24]

The Social Space of Intermediary Exploitation: The Hamba or Work Camp

The separation between skilled and unskilled construction workers as the separation between Japanese and Korean construction workers was maintained in the day labor market through a series of "places [bashō], institutions [kikan], and organizations [soshiki] that regulate the supply and demand of labor power."[25] The question of how this ethnic division of labor power was maintained must therefore begin with the recognition that if the day labor market revealed a market mechanism, then this mechanism did not operate by an invisible hand, but rather by (very visible) social organizations and institutions that regulated the supply and demand of labor power artificially and historically.[26] Two of the most conspicuous organizations and institutions were Korean-managed, state-funded private welfare organizations (shisetsu shakai jigyō), and the Unemployment Emergency Relief Programs. The UERP, which centered around public labor exchange offices, was established in the winter of 1925 in the six major cities. A detailed discussion of the UERP, as well as Korean welfare organizations, will be dealt with in the second half of the book, which focuses more explicitly on the role of the state in regulating Korean surplus populations in Japan.[27]

What will be given closer scrutiny here is the prevailing social form of regulating the labor power of day workers for, and on, Japanese public works construction sites. This was the *hamba* (飯場), or the work camp. As is well known among social and economic historians of Japanese industry, the hamba and its internal hierarchies of authority based on the *oyakata* system (親方制度) was the basic unit of labor organization in the mining and construction industries throughout the modern period. Its historical roots go back to the craft guilds of the Tokugawa period (1600–1868), as well as to the way casual workers, as well as criminal felons, were put to work in the feudal day labor market, known as the *ninsoku yoseba*.[28] The hamba of the interwar period in Japan carried over many of the social methods of regulating day workers that originated during the Tokugawa period, but infused them with capitalist relations of exchange based on the form of the wage. At the same time, however, wages were partially paid in kind, leading to various methods of labor remuneration that have led historians to conclude that the hamba was a pre-modern, feudal remnant in the modern era. As historian Harry Harootunian has argued persuasively, however, the true sign of modernity in Japan was precisely the co-existence of two different modes of production fused in one, historical conjuncture.[29] The hamba is perhaps an archetypical example of this sort of conjuncture. The interwar hamba was less a sign of persistent backwardness than of the coeval nature of modernity in Japan that maintained and exploited pre-capitalist social practices within, and as part of, capitalist methods of extracting surplus value through the commodification of labor power.

The hamba was a place of working and producing as well as a place of living and consuming that did not exist apart from the construction sites themselves. They were often located in geographically inaccessible places (such as coal mines), or else were shifting from place to place in accordance with the pace of work itself, as in the case of railroad or tunnel construction sites. While many hamba were constructed on the fringes of factory property and therefore had a relatively fixed quality, the real essence of the hamba is most clearly seen in the case of public works construction sites, where hamba were built, torn down, and rebuilt in accordance with constantly changing and erratic schedules of large-scale public works construction. Literally translated as a place of (consuming) food, the hamba were not a fixed form of housing, but rather camp-like places that provided transitory respite, protection, and subsistence that was inseparable from the place of work. Especially in the case of construction sites, the common form of housing within hamba took the form of barracks (*barakku*), usually made from wood or scrap tin, that were built on an extemporaneous basis.

Moreover, workers residing in hamba did not generally pay rent, which stands in contrast to the case of worker dorms. In lieu of rent, the workers had to pay a hamba-fee (hamba-ryō; hamba-dai), which covered the use of tools, the consumption of everyday necessities such as rice, sake, miso paste, vegetables, tobacco, and often clothing and shoes, and the service of introducing the day workers to construction site foremen. Hamba-dai, therefore, was less a fee for housing than the price that had to be paid for hamba services, whose costs were largely determined by the discretion of the hambagashira, meaning managers of the hamba, whose precise functions will be discussed shortly.

Not only did workers labor on the hamba, making it a place of production, but they also lived in the hamba, making it a place of consumption as well. Within the space of the hamba, day workers were both producers as well as consumers. This point cannot be underscored enough, for as consumers, the workers usually had no choice but to use the wages they earned to consume their daily necessities by purchasing these goods through privately operated commissaries within the hamba. However, workers could also request an advance on their wages in the form of tickets that could be redeemed at the commissary in exchange for staple goods. The expenses of these goods would then be taken off of the worker's wages on payday, usually at the end of the month. The bosses who organized and ran the hamba, however, took advantage of the fact that the hamba were usually nowhere near local markets where everyday goods could be purchased and typically inflated the costs of these subsistence goods, usually by ten to thirty percent, for commercial profits. Expenses associated with maintaining and accounting for the transactions at the commissaries partially justified this price inflation.

The hamba commissaries operated along principles that were almost identical to those of the British truck system (or Tommy system) that was predominant in coal mines in South Wales and the west of Scotland as early as the late fifteenth century and that continued into the nineteenth century, until it was finally outlawed with the Truck Act of 1831.[30] Like in the truck system in England, the commissaries on Japanese hamba were at the center of an arrangement on the work camp whereby some form of consumption was tied to employment and remuneration. Inflated prices for staple goods that were sold or advanced to the workers enabled labor bosses to recapture part of their expenditure on wages, as well as to reduce actual expenditures on wages. From the workers' perspective, however, it meant that their real incomes invariably fell well below their nominal levels. In many cases, moreover, advances on wages to consume daily necessities led to a condition of worker debt. While this often prevented bosses from prematurely firing workers, it also often tied workers to the labor bosses in a condition of semi-indenture.[31]

The hamba system in the public works industry was the prevailing method of organizing Korean day workers by both Japanese sub-contractors and Korean hamba managers. "The term *hamba* for the most part means Korean-managed worker dorm for Korean day workers. Hamba are simultaneously labor exchange offices for these Korean workers. . . . Japanese construction workers in the day labor market and their assistants are often found in so-called worker-rooms [*rōdō-beya*]. Korean day workers, by contrast, were found exclusively in hamba."[32] A survey from Kyoto's Social Bureau in 1937 showed that of a total of 308 households in hamba, all 308 were Korean and none Japanese.[33]

The process of recruiting Korean day workers for a hamba was carried out by three figures: hamba managers or hambagashira, labor brokers (*rōdō burōka*, often called *tehaishi*, 手配師), and local sub-bosses of work crews, known as *kumigashira* (組頭). All three figures worked for large sub-contracting labor bosses (*oyakata*), who advanced to each of them various amounts of cash to recruit and subsequently pay recruited workers their wages. A fixed percentage, typically between 10 and 20 percent, would be pinched off the top of this advanced sum as the income for the labor brokers, hambagashira and kumigashira. This process of skimming off fixed percentages from the advanced amount was called *pinhane* (ピン刎ね). Pinhane, combined with mandatory hamba-fees, formed the pillars around which intermediary exploitation existed in the day labor market. As one survey wrote, the problem of intermediary exploitation was a combination of two kinds of mandatory fees that were deducted from nominal wages and that workers—outside of striking—were helpless to determine. "The workers are exploited *twice*: once in the wages themselves [i.e., pinhane] and a second time in the form of food fees and hamba-fees."[34]

Employed by the oyakata, the hambagashira, kumigashira, and labor brokers were often one and the same person, though all of them performed similar, basic functions: recruiting day workers and introducing them to oyakata, a process which required knowing where to find the workers; paying the workers their wages after taking a fixed percentage for commission; and, especially with hambagashira and kumigashira, supervising the accounting books

on the hamba, as well as the actual process of work on the construction site.[35]
To day workers, maintaining relations with hambagashira, labor brokers,
and kumigashira was enormously important because they had direct and per-
sonal connections to sub-contracting oyakata. Hambagashira, kumigashira,
and labor brokers thus had precious knowledge of job openings at particular
construction sites, what kinds of wages were being paid, how strenuous the
working conditions were, and how far away from the city the construction site
was. Thus it was often in the interest of the day worker to maintain active relations with the labor broker; employment was often contingent upon having
and maintaining these relations.

Korean day workers were typically recruited by hambagashira or kumigashira, often directly in Korea. Moreover, kumigashira and hambagashira
were not limited to Japanese, but were often former Korean day workers with
experience in the construction industry. Having gleaned the basic conditions
and tricks of the trade, many earned the trust of Japanese sub-contractors,
and became labor brokers of Korean workers. What this meant was that Korean—not Japanese—kumigashira and hambagashira were often in charge of
managing, as well as housing, Korean workers in hamba. An Aichi prefecture
survey on Korean workers noted that, without fellow Korean kumigashira,
the Korean worker would be "like a blind man who's lost his cane."[36]

> Japanese kumigashira hire Korean workers en masse on behalf of sub-
> contractors by recruiting in Korea and then bringing them to Japan. Or
> else, a Korean worker, having worked in construction sites in Japan for a
> year or so, and having gleaned the basic conditions and tricks of the trade
> there, would cross the straits to Korea himself to publicize and recruit
> Korean [day] workers for hire in Japan.[37]

An Osaka survey further describes how the Korean kumigashira is responsible for coordinating and distributing wages through the process of
pinhane.

> Korean construction workers typically work en masse in groups of thirty or
> forty workers and are led by the crew boss who also houses the workers. . . .
> The kumigashira is also responsible for commanding and guarding over
> the workers during working hours. He himself does not work but rather
> commands. . . . the workers below him. He also distributes the funds for
> wages given to him by the primary employer to his workers, and directly
> adjusts and negotiates the amount of wages for his workers directly with

those workers. It goes without saying that he skims a percentage of these wages as part of his own income. In this way the kumigashira is essentially a labor broker.[38]

The oyakata organized kumigashira and labor brokers as part of organizing the entire hamba. The oyakata himself was hired by large contractors or sub-contractors; the latter were commissioned and employed by the state public works department (at the time known as Dobokukyoku), or else by large private corporations in the construction industry.[39] Of all of the relationships among these hierarchical tiers, only the relationship between the primary construction firm or public works government agency was formalized contractually, that is, legally and in accordance with the Japanese civil code. This contract, however, only formalized the direct relationship between the primary firm or government agency and the sub-contractors. There were no formal contractual relationships mediating the primary firm or government agency and the oyakata; the oyakata and the kumigashira; the kumigashira and the labor broker; and finally the labor broker and the day workers. Rather, these relationships were informal, usually based on verbal agreements on wages whose quantities were typically determined by the sub-contractor or oyakata himself. It was thus primarily at the sub-contractor's discretion, and not the primary firm's, to employ and pay kumigashira under his authority.

> Since day workers are hired in large groups, and since their wages are often paid on a daily basis, it is impossible for the worker to enter into a direct employment relationship with the primary employer. Rather, the worker goes through the mediating labor broker and only enters into an indirect employment relationship with the primary employer.[40]

The relationships among day workers, sub-contractors, and labor brokers rested on informal, verbal contracts, typically called a kuchi yaku, literally a verbal promise. The informal contract was often called ninpu ukeyogyōsha keiyaku (construction worker sub-contractor contract), rōryoku kyōkyū keiyaku (labor power supply contract), or rōdō kyōkyū keiyaku (labor supply contract).[41] In all of these cases, the nature of the agreements distinguished day work from so-called regular employment (jōkōyō) and its accompanying written, formal contracts between workers and factory employers. As a Tokyo regional labor exchange bureau noted, verbal contracts were especially common on two levels: between Korean construction workers, Japanese sub-contractors, and Korean hambagashira, and between Korean hambagashira and Korean day workers.[42] Thus, while "an employment relation is established between worker and labor broker, it is not an actual relation between employer and employee. There is therefore no space for negotiation between them and the working conditions are completely unclear and never fully disclosed to the worker. There isn't a trace of a formal relationship between the two."[43] The verbal promise could be broken easily, and primary employers were exculpated from taking any legal responsibility for the day workers under the supervision and leadership of the sub-contractor or labor broker. The indirect, non-legally binding relationship between day worker and primary employer had an especially enormous impact on day workers in cases of injury, illness, or death on the construction site, or else in cases where wages were not paid out to the workers. Verbal contracts thus created a space of responsibility that was ambiguous, and where the worker became the primary and sole victim. "It is impossible—outside of strikes—to negotiate with the primary employer. The latter are exempt from taking responsibility for their own construction site."[44]

Intermediary Exploitation

The prevailing method of wage distribution to day workers in public works was thus based on this social hierarchy that mediated between day workers and the managers and bosses of hamba. Known only in the vernacular as pinhane, this wage system was as extensive and multi-layered as the number of tiers of sub-contractors and labor brokers working on a particular construction site. The skimmed-off percentages, moreover, were taken off of the wages, and not from the funds relegated for construction materials, such as concrete, wood, pipes, and gravel. The reason is that the prices of the materials were strictly outlined in the contracts between primary employer and subcontractor, and between sub-contractor and sub-sub-contractor, and could not be altered without breaking the formal contracts.[45]

Pinhane thus functioned in a trickle-down manner whereby a fixed percentage of an original sum of wages would be skimmed off the top with each descending tier and pocketed by the sub-contractor or labor broker of each tier. Sub-contractor B would receive a contract from primary employer A and be given a certain amount for wages for labor, both skilled and unskilled. Sub-contractor B would then frequently sub-contract out to sub-sub-contractor C to handle the unskilled labor, but not before skimming a percentage for himself, usually 10 to 20 percent. Sub-contractor C would then take his own 20 percent before handing down the final amount for wages to the ham-bagashira, who would then allocate and distribute wages to the workers under him on the hamba, but not before taking his own 10 to 20 percent cut.

Pinhane, therefore, was a system that did not exist outside the sub-contractor and labor broker system that mediated and regulated the supply and demand of day workers for primary employers of public works construction sites. The larger the construction site—and the more differentiated the tiers of sub-contractors, sub-sub-contractors, labor brokers, hambagashira, kumigashira, and workers—the lower the real wages for the worker. While workers may not be directly employed by a sub-contractor, the sub-contractor nonetheless had the power to decide upon and fix the wages of those workers at the bottom of the tree-like structure.[46] In short, while pinhane was a source of income for sub-contractors and labor brokers, it was also the system that sucked the contents out of the nominal wages of the worker.

Moreover, the system of pinhane operated in different forms depending on the distinction between skilled and unskilled workers. For example, the amount of pinhane was generally less for skilled workers, such as masons, because these workers possessed most if not all of their own tools. Pinhane was thus partially justified on the grounds that tools were lent to workers. Unskilled workers seldom owned their own tools and were compelled to borrow the tools from the oyakata or crew boss at relatively high fixed rates (determined by the oyakata and crew boss).[47] Unskilled workers were thus hit harder in terms of pinhane "since all of the tools these workers use are borrowed from the crew bosses."[48] The differences in percentages, according to the 1924 survey on day labor in Osaka, were vast. For skilled workers, 5 to 7 percent was normally skimmed off the wages; for unskilled workers, however, 20 to 30 percent was skimmed and pocketed by the sub-contractors and crew bosses.[49]

Each sub-contractor was thus a point and a threshold through which wages would pass from a higher employer to the workers below the sub-contractor and decrease in amount by a fixed percentage that was taken and decided by the sub-contractors, labor brokers, and hambagashira. In other words, the power of pinhane stemmed from the displacement of direct employment of the workers through sub-contracting. Here the essence of intermediary exploitation can be articulated with more clarity. Intermediary exploitation showed how day workers were exploited, but not through a direct relation of contradiction to capital. Rather, this relation was diverted, distanced, deferred, segmented, and mediated by tiers and levels of sub-contractors that served as many buffers against capital. It was a social form of exploitation that increased with the distance or separation of workers from capital and that especially exploited the inherent insecurity of workers in having to occupy a position of selling labor power as a commodity with no guarantees of exchange. Intermediary exploitation did not exploit workers by exploiting the surplus labor time within production and in contradiction to capital, but rather by exploiting the social mediations that distanced workers from a direct relation of exchange with capital. Moreover, these contingent, social mediations not only supervised the process of exchange and the process of production in which workers toiled, but also guarded over the process of worker consumption and served as indirect mediators for capital. Intermediary exploitation could also be translated, therefore, as indirect exploitation, that is, exploitation based on the combination of pinhane and hamba-fees.

The problem from the workers' perspective was that it was impossible to know the precise methods by which oyakata and kumigashira calculated the percentages of pinhane. The determination of this percentage, along with hamba-fees, was made solely at the discretion of oyakata, hambagashira, and kumigashira. For "even in cases where the workers demand that the kumigashira disclose the methods and precise percentages and calculations going into the process of pinhane on the hamba, kumigashira almost always refuse to clarify these decisions and stubbornly insist upon keeping these decisions under tight wrap."[50] The 1924 Tokyo survey on day labor also states that "food fees, and more generally the hamba-fees, are determined only in the most ambiguous manner."[51] And the 1923 Osaka survey on day labor similarly states that "the problem with investigating pinhane is that kumigashira and sub-contractors are very clandestine about their methods of calculating these percentages."[52]

Furthermore, while hambagashira and kumigashira often lowered the percentages of pinhane, this was commonly compensated for by raising hamba-fees instead. High hamba-fees could easily be justified on the grounds that the hamba acted as a de facto labor introduction agency. As a Kyoto survey noted,

In these times of recession, a clear pattern has emerged whereby the rate of pinhane has declined. This depreciation, however, is more than compensated for through the extraction of exorbitant hamba fees stemming from labor exchange introductions. The reason is that, for these day work-

TABLE 13. Hamba-fees as a Proportion of Wages, Kyoto 1928–1931

Year	Hamba-fees (yen)	Wages (yen)	Hamba-fees as a proportion of wages (%)
1928	.70	2.00	35%
1929	.60	1.60	37.5%
1930	.55	1.20	45.8%
1931	.50	1.20	41.7%

Source: Kyoto-shi Kyōiku-bu Shakai-ka, "Kyoto-shi ni okeru hiyatoi rōdōsha ni kansuru chōsa," 50–51.

ers, the most urgent need is the securing of work itself. The hamba's crew bosses know this well, and in securing their hamba-fees from the workers in the name of labor exchange introductions, they secure their profits.[53]

As the postwar recession took a precipitous turn for the worse after the 1927 financial crisis, leading towards the dark descent into the Shōwa crisis of 1930, the problems of pinhane and the hamba system became increasingly urgent for Korean day workers. There were two reasons. The first was that the price of labor power often fell at a faster rate than the price of the hamba-fees. Table 13 above compares the relationship between wages of Korean day workers in Kyoto with the same workers' hamba-fees, "the workers' primary expense."[54]

The second reason was the widespread problem whereby crew bosses, both Korean and Japanese, did not pay their workers their wages, either because they were not given adequate funds for wages from the sub-contractors employing them, or because they kept the remaining funds that trickled down for themselves as their sole source of income. These two problems were not mutually exclusive, but rather coexisted and buttressed each other. It is not surprising, then, that a wave of strikes and protests by Korean day workers emerged as a result of these problems. In 1925, the problem of the non-payment of wages accounted for only 18 incidents involving Korean workers; in 1929 the figure rose to 79, and then nearly doubled to 153 in 1930.[55] Already in 1925, however, the interior ministry's police bureau was aware of the fact that wage non-payment was the predominant cause of Korean strikes: "Korean labor protests and strikes are qualitatively different from Japanese protests and strikes. For Korean strikes are predominantly strikes demanding the payment of wages. . . . The non-payment of wages to Korean construction workers is particularly evident among sub-contractors who, in these tough times of economic recession, resort to all sorts of chicanery to cut corners and evade the payment of wages to their workers."[56]

Case Example: The Sanshin Railway Strike

Nowhere were the problems of intermediary exploitation in the day labor market more clearly challenged than in the Sanshin Railway strike of 1930 in Aichi prefecture. The influence of the Sanshin Railway strike on both the Korean and Japanese labor movements is well known. In the words of historian and activist Pak Kyung-shik:

> The Sanshin Railway strike was absolutely epoch-making and revolution-ary. It was the first strike in Japan to be led by a Korean strike committee. It was the first strike to have a significant influence across Aichi prefecture and on the Japanese workers in Okazaki City in particular. [Korean] strik-ers at Sanshin received massive support from the peasants of the region. In turn, Sanshin sparked off new beginnings of the peasant movement in the region. Thus, in many important ways, Sanshin heralded a series of new political initiatives and beginnings. Following Sanshin, comrades in all regions were able to gather courage to develop and extend their own struggles.[57]

Starting in December 1927, the Sanshin Railway Corporation, at the time worth one million yen and headquartered in Tokyo,[58] began the construction of an extensive railway line in the county of Kita-Shitarachō in Aichi prefec-ture, spanning an 80-kilometer stretch across a mountainous wilderness area commonly referred to as the Hokkaido of Aichi.[59] In September 1929, the Utsunomiya-based contractor Saotome won a bid from Sanshin for 48,900 yen to complete a 10-mile segment of the railway line beginning in October of the same year.[60] Saotome in turn sub-contracted to the Meiji Construction Corporation, who in turn sub-contracted a man named Wakajima to provide unskilled day workers.[61] The amount of funds that went into the hands of Wakajima had shrunken from the 48,900 yen to 42,000 yen. Between Sao-tome and Wakajima, 6,900 yen had already been skimmed. Wakajima, armed with the 42,000, then further sub-contracted to 6 Korean hambagashira for a total of 38,000 yen, thereby taking 4,000 yen for himself. Altogether, then, the total taken out amounted to approximately 11,000 yen.[62] These 6 Korean

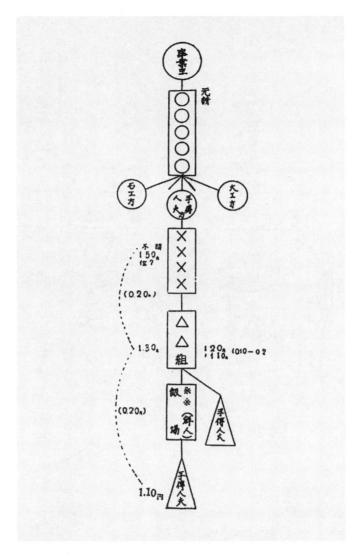

1. Wage structure of pinhane on a day labor construction site employing Korean day workers in a hamba. *Source:* Kyoto-shi Kyōiku-bu Shakai-ka, "Kyoto-shi ni okeru hiyatoi rōdōsha ni kansuru chōsa," 58.

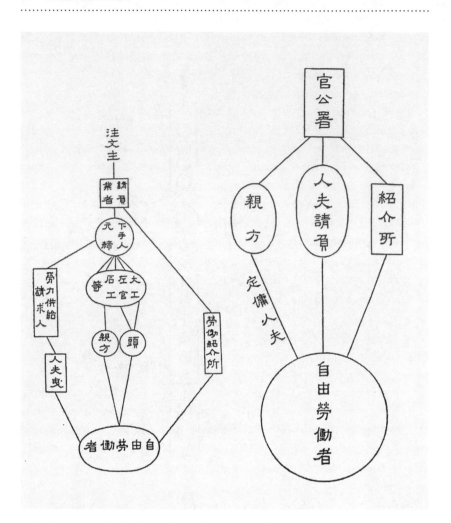

2. Institutional nodal points of day labor market in Tokyo.
Source: Shakai Jigyō, March 15, 1925, 37.

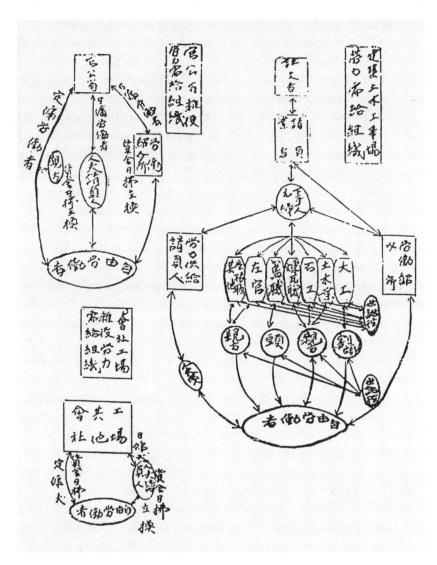

3. Institutional nodal points of day labor market in Tokyo.
Source: Tokyo-shi Shakaikyoku, "Jiyū rōdōsha ni kansuru chōsa," 77.

hambagashira constructed and managed a series of wooden barracks on the construction site and were in charge of approximately 600 Korean day workers whose daily wages ranged from 1.50 yen to 1.80 yen and who worked in groups of 20 to 50.[63] Thus, between the Sanshin corporation and the Korean day workers, there were four mediating tiers of sub-contractors.

The origins of the strike began in May, when Korean workers demanded higher wages. The demands went unaddressed for another month until the situation worsened when, after two thirds of the railway line had been completed, construction was halted due to various difficulties in the rough, mountainous terrain. Tunnel construction went badly, putting financial strains on mid-level sub-contractors. Serious injuries to large groups of unskilled workers, exacerbating the problems of the construction both financially and in terms of manpower, resulted in delays in the construction project. As the delays lengthened, however, the workers demanded payment of their wages. But while the chains of payment were successfully made from Saotome to Meiji, from Meiji to Wakajima, and finally from Wakajima to the 6 Korean hambagashira, these hambagashira did not have enough funds to pay their workers' wages. The hambagashira had to tell their workers, many of whom came from the same villages in Korea as they did, that they could not pay.

This lack of funds to pay the workers' wages then overlapped with the fact that the workers living in the hamba were made to pay a hamba-fee of 70 sen per day, which covered the use of tools, the labor exchange service, as well as costs of everyday items. Workers bought these everyday goods through commission stands on the construction sites, although the precise costs were not disclosed to the workers purchasing them since cash was not accepted at the commission stands. Instead, the undisclosed costs were subtracted from their wages at the end of the month. The journal, Kyōzai, conducted an independent investigation into the prices of these goods subsequent to the strike, and found that the prices of soy sauce, miso paste, and vegetables on the hamba were 30 percent higher than the highest market price of these commodities.[64] Large sacks of rice, normally sold for 12 yen, were said to be sold for 14 yen. Tabi, the special socks worn by construction workers in Japan, were sold on the hamba for 1.15 yen; in town they went for 0.80 yen.[65] But as long as the workers were not receiving their wages, they could not pay the hamba-fee. Moreover, they were not permitted advances on their wages. As a result, the workers organized to demand the immediate payment of their individual back wages, generally ranging from 30 yen to 50 yen per worker.[66]

Beginning late May, a strike committee was put together, organizing an action group of three hundred workers. Leaders from the Metal Workers' Union in the communist labor union, Zenkyō, helped the construction workers; they especially negotiated with the managers of the hamba commissaries to support the strike, which the latter did, eventually providing food and other groceries to workers during the strike. Zenkyō also distributed flyers to the nearby farmers to garner their support for what the strike committee anticipated to be a drawn-out, and possibly violent, strike. Two hundred workers prepared for a walk-out on the hilly area of the construction site, and several of them set up look-out posts on the hillsides and riverbanks surrounding the construction site, which they used to communicate to the strikers, through bells attached to ropes, when police and strike-breaking gangs showed up. Another one hundred gathered on the Sanri bridge, adjacent to the construction site, and, with the work of several carpenters and blacksmiths, affixed dynamite under the bridge to destroy the bridge to prevent police from crossing into the space of the construction site. Nails and spikes were scattered all around the main roads surrounding the construction site to puncture the tires of police cars.[67]

The walk-out and the strike against Sanshin and Saotome was declared on July 25, 1930, by a Korean-led strike committee formed among the workers of the Sanshin construction site. Significantly, the 6 Korean hambagashira joined the workers in mutual protest, and the workers did not target the hambagashira. Rather, the strikers targeted Sanshin and Saotome and criticized them for attempting to displace responsibility for the unpaid wages onto the Korean hambagashira.[68] Zenkyō's Central Day Workers' Union, the Toyohashi Gōdō Rōdō Kumiai, and the Niigata Korean Workers' Union joined the strike and spread the slogan: "Revolutionary Solidarity between Japanese and Korean Workers, Banzai!" They also shouted, "End intermediary exploitation now!"[69] Flyers explaining the hamba system and the workers' struggle were passed out to the peasant communities in the area, many of which in turn supported the strikers with food, shelter, and clothing.[70] On the morning of July 31, a large group of the strikers took over the office of Saotome, overpowering groups of local fire fighters and strikebreakers that were called in by Saotome to protect the office. Soon afterward, however, 29 police officers arrived by motorbike, side-cars, and buses, and they entered the office wielding sabers, which they used to slash several strikers. Workers defended the takeover of the office by pelting the police with stones and hitting them with poles and clubs. The strike committee then threatened to blow up the Sanri bridge and make the road from the bridge to the edge of the river impassable unless the police stopped the violence, and unless their demands were presented immediately to Sanshin and Saotome. Outnumbered, and fearing the destruction of the bridge, the police backed down, and this initial, bloody fight came to a halt.

The strikers demanded the immediate payment of 30,000 yen in unpaid wages from Sanshin and Saotome.[71] The Sanshin corporation itself came to the negotiations two weeks later, and only after the prefectural strike conciliator demanded Sanshin's attendance upon learning that Saotome could not afford to make the full payments. Sanshin publicly decried the strike claiming that the problem was Saotome's responsibility. A Sanshin representative was quoted as saying, "If [Saotome] didn't use those Koreans this mess wouldn't have happened in the first place."[72] Wakajima, the third sub-contractor, also denied any responsibility for the non-payment of the Korean workers, stating that he had fulfilled his role in paying the six Korean hambagashira.[73] Sanshin headquarters, Meiji Construction, Saotome-gumi, and finally Wakabayashi all claimed the same thing: It's the sole responsibility of the Korean hambagashira to pay. After one month, however, and after a series of violent battles between workers, police, and organized strike breakers, the Toyohashi city court found in favor of the strikers and ordered the immediate payment of 20,000 yen, from Sanshin and Saotome, to the strikers.[74] The victory, however, was bittersweet since by the time the court order was made, more than half of the total number of Korean strikers had been arrested and jailed. During the course of the negotiations, in fact, battalions of police did not stop attacking and arresting strikers. Many were injured; the Japanese representative from Zenkyō's Metal Workers Union, who was injured and arrested, eventually died in jail.[75]

The Sanshin strikers' victory nonetheless revealed the destruction of a hierarchical, vertical structure pitting Korean hambagashira against Korean day worker, substituting the hierarchical structure with a horizontal, transversal link between them. It also revealed a specific logic inherent to the structure and "wage decapitating" mechanism of the pinhane process, one that distanced Korean workers from the primary employer through the mediation of Korean hambagashira who hired, managed, and housed the Korean day workers. Korean hambagashira, while hired out by other sub-contractors working under the primary employer, were compelled to assume the position of sole guarantor of the Korean workers' wages. It was as if the motto of the Sanshin site was: Distance direct contact with Korean workers; make Koreans pay Korean workers; make it their problem. In other words, it was a structure that exploited Korean hambagashira to exploit Korean day workers, thereby creating a social and financial detour toward the exploitation of the Korean day workers by Sanshin. Exploitation was indirect, fragmented, displaced, and dislocated, and in the case of Sanshin, this structure failed.

The Political Significance of Korean Day Labor

On April 20, 1927, Rōsō, the largest Korean communist labor union in Japan, opened its third annual conference with a paper outlining the most salient and urgent problems facing the organization.[76] The same points were raised again and elaborated upon five months later, in an article in The Worker titled, "Recent Developments of the Labor Movement of Koreans in Japan," and written by Rōsō member Choi Un-kyo.[77] Rōsō was established in February 1925 through the federation of twelve of the largest Korean labor unions in Japan, and by identifying itself as a union that called for the freedom and liberation of Korean workers in Japan based on the contradiction between the working class and the capitalist class.[78] By early 1927, however, Rōsō's basic strategy shifted, largely in accordance with the establishment, in February 1927, of the Shinganhoe, a movement that encompassed both Korean nationalists and communists in Korea.[79] Working closely with Shinganhoe cells in Tokyo (est. May 1927), Rōsō shifted its organizational emphasis from everyday economic struggles to political and ethnic struggles within Japan. Partially reflecting the Shinganhoe's call for the immediate end of violent ethnic repression by the government-general in Korea, Rōsō also based this shift on what they identified as "particular and highly specific conditions" facing Korean workers in Japan, conditions that led Rōsō to carry out political and ethnic struggles as an independent labor organization, strategically separate from, but in solidarity with, economic struggles carried out by Japanese labor unions.[80] The rationale of this decision was that it was no longer possible for Korean workers in Japan to organize their struggles against Japanese capitalists on the economic basis of labor-capital relations alone.[81] Choi thus identified the "particular and highly specific conditions" (tokushu-teki jōken) of labor that made Korean workers in Japan "ethnic wage slave[s]" (minzokuteki chingin dorei), chained down by the double shackles of ethnic discrimination and exploitation.[82] "It is no longer possible," Choi wrote, "for our organizational activities, as well as for our union movements, to ignore these particular and highly specific conditions."[83] In other passages, the authors also referred to "particular and highly specific *social* conditions of labor," (*tokushna shakaiteki jōken*) as well as to the "particular and highly specific treatment and management" (*tokushuteki toriatsukai*) of Korean workers in Japan.[84]

The organizational stakes of understanding these "particular and highly specific" conditions for Rōsō were inseparable from two interrelated organizational problems: how to mobilize non-unionized Korean workers in Japan into the ranks of Rōsō, and how best to maintain political alliances with revolutionary Japanese labor unions. Regarding the first point, the authors of the texts noted that while the total population of Koreans in Japan in 1927 exceeded 300,000, Rōsō membership accounted for 30,312 workers—approximately 10 percent of this population. Choi argued that this figure would be higher if it were not for two obstacles that stood in the way. The first obstacle was that the vast majority of Korean workers in Japan were former peasants from the southernmost provinces of the Korean peninsula, where industrial underdevelopment was maintained throughout the colonial period. This meant that many Korean workers in Japan not only lacked formal schooling and education, but also experience and training in labor union organizations.[85]

The second reason, which is important to this discussion, reflected the fact that the majority of Korean workers in Japan were free workers who found work (when they could) in the precarious and constantly changing day labor market. As Choi points out, while Korean factory and coal mining workers each constituted 20 percent of the total Korean working population in Japan, 60 percent of Korean workers in Japan were compelled to find work outside the factory and coal mining system, and within the day labor markets of the six major urban centers of Japan (Tokyo, Yokohama, Nagoya, Kyoto, Osaka, and Kobe).

Difficulties in organizing these day workers partially stemmed from their lack of a relatively fixed place of work, such as a factory. This lack of a fixed occupational place, however, was in fact a spatial and temporal symptom of the day labor market itself. For the day labor market was largely a market for public works construction work, work, moreover, that was defined by employment irregularity, unpredictability, and contingency on a daily basis. Here in the day labor market, the low wages distributed to Korean workers on the basis of the commodification of their labor power were constantly supplemented and reproduced by the necessarily contingent nature of commodification itself, made most apparent and clear in the day labor market and in construction work specifically. It is here, too, that Korean workers felt the double shackles of low wages and ethnic discrimination in a "particular and highly specific" way compared to Japanese workers in general, as well as to Japanese day workers in particular.

The fact that the majority of Korean workers in Japan were not exploited as factory workers, but rather as free workers in the day labor market, greatly affected the organizational relationships with revolutionary Japanese trade union movements as well. While organizations such as Rōsō actively cooperated with Japanese labor unions on the level of economic and class struggles, sending Korean activists to Japanese-led factory strikes and strengthening radical trade unionism in Japan, the problem was that the organizational form of trade unionism itself, which was based in factories and along distinct industrial trade unions (sangyō betsu kumiai), effectively precluded the active participation of the majority of Korean workers in Japan.[86] Rōsō leadership thus pointed out that, from the perspective of Korean day workers, it was no longer possible to assume that the place and object of struggle (tōsō no basho; tōsō no taishō) of Japanese workers were identical (dōitsu) to the place and object of struggle of Korean workers.[87] This was true not simply because the majority of Korean workers were day workers, but also because the conditions, treatment, and management of Korean workers presented "particular and highly specific" problems compared to Japanese workers, i.e., the "double shackles" of low wages combined with the ethnic discrimination mentioned above. What has to be emphasized here is that these shackles had everything to do with the prevalence and predominance of intermediary exploitation in the everyday lives of Korean workers. The majority of Japanese factory workers did not have to confront this problem with the same frequency as Korean workers. This problem thus has to be taken into consideration when thinking about Rōsō's announcement, in 1927, that the time was not yet right for Korean workers to "directly participate in," or "maintain the same organization with," Japanese labor unions.[88] By 1929, however, and facing severe repression, Rōsō leadership announced that Rōsō would dissolve and join forces with the Japanese communist party's leading labor union, Zenkyō. And while Zenkyō made great efforts to support Korean day worker and construction workers struggles—the Sanshin strike being a case in point—Korean day worker struggles nonetheless faced great challenges in creating and maintaining a space of critique amidst the dominance of factory-based labor union movements.

4

URBAN EXPROPRIATION
AND THE THREAT OF THE OUTSIDE
....

Korean Tenant Struggles against Housing Insecurity

Every proper name is collective.
—Deleuze and Parnet, *Dialogues*

everybody wants somewhere
process and dismissal shelter and location
everybody wants somewhere
—Fugazi

After the Japanese colonization of Korea in 1910, Korean peasants throughout the 1920s and 1930s migrated to Japan in search of work, largely as the result of dire economic conditions in the Korean countryside. The Japanese institution of a system of land ownership along the principles of private property in Korea, combined with the extensive program to increase rice production from 1920 to 1934, resulted in increased tenancy and landlessness of thousands of Korean peasants. One significant result of the colonization of Korea, therefore, was the expropriation of Korean peasants who were subsequently compelled to find work in Japan in order to live. In Japan, however, pervasive racism in the housing markets continually threatened a stable and secure livelihood for Korean workers and tenants.

This chapter analyzes the vicious cycle of housing discrimination and its impact on Korean tenants in Japan. It traces how Japanese landlord practices of refusing to rent to Korean tenants compelled Korean tenants to strategically use fictive Japanese proper names on lease holding contracts to pass undetected by racist Japanese landlords. This practice, however, led to a complex micropolitics of evicting Korean tenants on the grounds that it was "fraudulent" for Koreans to use Japanese proper names on lease holding contracts. Evictions cast thousands of Korean tenants out into the streets in the late 1920s and early 1930s, and were a clear factor in the formation of Korean shantytowns and barrack communities in Japan. Urban planning projects in 1920s and 1930s Japan, however, continually threatened these homeless and barrack communities with forced evacuations led by city governments and the police. I argue, therefore, that evictions and homeless evacuations, combined with racism in Japanese cities during the interwar period, leads us to consider what I call urban expropriation. This was a process, led by legal and repressive state apparatuses, that severed tenants from lease-holding property, and that produced, as an effect, a floating mass of surplus populations whose everyday costs of subsistence were continually pushed down, and whose social existence was extremely precarious. The history of the urban expropriation of Korean tenants in Japan, however, cannot be understood properly unless the crisis of the Japanese proper name is also addressed historically.

The Housing Crisis after 1920:
Japanese Landlords and Korean Tenants

The years immediately following the cessation of the First World War marked a turning point for the housing market in the urban centers of Japan, notably in the six major cities: Tokyo, Yokohama, Nagoya, Kobe, Kyoto, and Osaka. Among these six, Osaka, the leading commercial and manufacturing metropolis in Japan, experienced the housing crisis the most acutely and was compelled to undertake the most urgent and sweeping urban policies, especially in regard to housing. In addition to being the first city (followed later by Tokyo in 1932) to expand its jurisdiction—so it officially became Greater Osaka in 1925—Osaka's city government also led the way for other cities in terms of theorizing the essence of the housing crisis during and immediately following the First World War. Prior to and during the war, the Osaka city government identified the housing problem (*jūtaku mondai*) as an "absolute and quantitative housing shortage" (*zettaiteki, ryōteki jūtaku busoku*) that stemmed from the relatively slow production and supply of housing construction in comparison with the swelling of the working population during the war.[1] Inflated prices, an effect of the manufacturing boom during the war, prevented new investments in housing construction, producing drastically low housing vacancies.[2]

After the so-called reactionary crisis of 1920, however, the fundamental problem of housing was no longer considered a matter of meeting high demand for housing with increased supply. The post-1920 housing problem was that rents continued to increase, seemingly unabated, despite falling

TABLE 14. Rent and Wage Comparison, Osaka, 1928–1938

Year	Rental Units			Wages		
	Small	Medium	Large	Cotton	Glass	Day Labor
1928	100	100	100	100	100	100
1929	99.65	99.39	99.38	103	101.94	97.47
1930	99.61	96.85	98.85	93.81	95.15	82.32
1931	98.78	95.61	98.28	78.76	87.38	70.71
1932	98.03	94.92	97.61	69.91	83.98	65.66
1933	97.28	95.61	96.4	66.37	82.52	64.65
1934	96.99	94.92	95.88	59.29	81.55	66.16
1935	96.47	94.18	95.25	60.18	81.07	67.17
1936	96.26	94.03	95.22	60.18	82.52	67.17
1937	96.07	94.07	95.16	65.49	83.5	72.22
1938	96.48	94.03	95.07	68.14	88.35	79.8

Source: Osaka-shi Shakai-bu Chōsa-ka, Hōkoku Dai 240, 21; Nihon rōdō undō shiryō i'inkai, Nihon rōdō undō shiryō, Dai-10Kan, Tōkei-Ren, 279–80.

prices, falling wages, and rising unemployment. Housing rent, despite relatively high vacancy rates, did not fall in price like other commodities during the postwar recession, producing a crisis of rental housing affordability for workers experiencing decreasing wages and rising unemployment in a time of industrial rationalization."[3]

After 1920, therefore, the essence of the housing problem was no longer a matter of an "absolute and quantitative housing shortage." As the Osaka city government pointed out, it was rather a problem of high rent. High rent, they explained, was a "purely economic class struggle" between landlords and tenants in the major cities, a struggle that itself stemmed from rampant speculations on land prices by landowners.[4] The center of the housing problem thus shifted from a housing shortage to housing affordability and high rent, from an absolute lack of housing supply to a relational problem between rent, falling wages, and increased unemployment. For this reason, Osaka officials called the housing crisis after 1920 a "relative, qualitative and economic problem" and strongly distinguished this from the pre-1920 housing shortage.[5] City officials analyzed the rise in rent by separating the problem of supply from demand and by targeting the large land companies and city landlords for clues to understanding the persistence of high rent. Many factors were cited, including high costs of construction, repair, and maintenance; rent delinquency; persistent demands by tenants for eviction remuneration (*tachinoki ryō*); the lack of state or city government rent regulation laws; high fees demanded by land and housing managers (*kanrigaisha* or *sahainin*) to manage and supervise rental units for the large land corporations; and the power of individual landlords to set rents as they pleased. The primary cause, however, was found in the frenzied speculations on ground rent (*chidai*) by landholding companies, whose numbers and competition increased dramatically after the cessation of the First World War.[6]

In 1921, the Japanese Diet passed the Law on Leased Land and Leased Buildings (*Shakuchi-shakuyahō*), which targeted lease-holding relations in the major cities of Japan and were applicable beyond the sections on lease contracts in the civil code. This couplet of laws, however, while claiming to provide all tenants with minimal lease holding security, ultimately only privileged tenants who were owners of buildings on leased land, providing them with relatively more secure, long-term lease contracts. Prior to 1921, landowners were able to exploit high rents by keeping lease terms as short as possible, thereby allowing them to increase rents with each lease renewal. After 1921, owners of leased land and buildings were given more protection with longer term leases.[7]

Significantly, however, the 1921 laws did not enforce any restrictions on either land rent (*chidai*) or building and house rent (*yachin*) directly.[8] Nor did these laws take away the power granted to landowners and landlords, according to article 617 of the civil code, to terminate leases with unspecified durations at any time and without having to supply "just reason" (*seitō no jiyū*).[9] This had an enormous impact in the residential housing market and on residential tenants in particular, since most residential leases did not specify the period of the lease. This provided landlords with the right to terminate leases at any time, demand eviction, and increase rent on new tenants.

Residential tenant unions in the urban centers of Japan fought against unrestricted rent and the power of landlords to terminate leases at any time without having to specify "just reason." Beginning in 1920, and proliferating in the late 1920s and throughout the 1930s, tenant unions, such as the Osaka Tenant Union (established in March 1920), fought for 30 percent decreases in rent and more protection for tenant security (in terms of lease continuity and renewal), as well as against seemingly arbitrary evictions of tenants.[10]

Beginning in 1928, the first Korean tenant unions emerged in Osaka. Like their Japanese counterparts, Korean tenant organizations such as the East Osaka Tenant Association (*Higashi Osaka Shakkanin Dōkōkai*, established in June 1928) and the East Osaka Tenant Union (*Higashi Osaka Shakkanin Kumiai*, established in 1929) also fought for 30 percent rent decreases and an end to forced evictions. Unlike Japanese tenant unions, however, Korean tenant unions demanded resident rights (*kyojūken*) in the face of Japanese landlords' refusals to lease homes and rooms to Koreans. In a flyer from the East Osaka Tenant Union, we find the following demand:

> We demand the establishment of Residence Rights [*ijūken*] for Koreans-in-Japan! Even if Koreans are able to pay rent, they are refused leases simply because they are Korean. When Koreans are compelled to ask Japanese to rent rooms for them, they are immediately evicted by force. First, we cry out to end ethnic discrimination of Korean tenants by Japanese landlords, and will fight to the end all those actions that take away the residence rights of Koreans in Japan.[11]

Korean tenants articulated housing demands that overlapped with those of Japanese tenants in terms of the problems of high rent and eviction, but also diverged from Japanese tenants' demands in particular ways, notably in terms of the problem of obtaining housing in the first place, a problem that stemmed from the refusals by Japanese landlords to rent to Koreans.[12] Indeed, government surveys documented that major cities were well aware of the fact that Japanese landlords were refusing to rent to Koreans, and that those refusals produced a particular housing problem amidst the general problem of high rent. In 1925, a survey from Aichi noted that "the most difficult problem experienced by Korean workers is obtaining housing," and that "because Japanese do not rent homes to Korean workers, Koreans are compelled to live in hamba or rent rooms in temporary boarding houses" (*geshuku*).[13] In 1927, the Kobe city government noted that high rent was only one problem facing Korean tenants, and that the real problem for Koreans was that "Japanese landlords don't like to lease to Koreans because it's like getting tangled up in barbed-wire."[14] In 1929, the Tokyo government wrote how "home rental [for Koreans] is basically impossible, leading Koreans to use Japanese names to obtain rental."[15] In 1930, the Osaka social bureau noted that the housing problem for Koreans was not reducible to high rent only, but was equally related to the collective decisions by Japanese landlord associations to refuse to rent homes or rooms to Koreans.[16] And in 1933, the ministry of justice produced a voluminous survey on Koreans, including a 56-page section on how the refusal by Japanese landlords to lease to Koreans was leading to crimes of fraud and extortion by Korean tenants.[17] All of these surveys emphasized how the housing problem for Koreans could not be understood properly in terms of high rent exclusively, but had to account for the particular dimension of the refusals by Japanese landlords to lease to Koreans.

The Logic of Housing Discrimination

A closer analysis of the logic and reasoning of landlord refusals to lease to Korean tenants will disclose the operations of a vicious cycle of housing discrimination and tenant insecurity. While landlord refusals to rent to Koreans led the latter to adopt methods of subleasing and living in *geshuku* (boarding houses) and barracks, these very forms and methods of housing themselves only reinforced and reproduced the conditions by which Japanese landlords articulated and put into practice their refusal to rent to Koreans. What needs to be fleshed out, then, is how Japanese landlords articulated these conditions, and how these articulations operated on the practical level of everyday life.

Two statements by Osaka landlords can serve as an entryway into this problem. When asked by the Osaka city government's social section why they refused to lease to Koreans, one landlord said:

> First of all, Koreans don't pay rent. Secondly, they bring in twenty or thirty others to reduce their individual share of the rent. In the process they end up damaging the rooms. . . . As a result, a house that would otherwise have a rental life of ten years is reduced to less than half, to four years or so. Therefore, even if we receive twice the amount in rent per month from Korean tenants, we still won't rent to them. . . . Furthermore, since Koreans are noisy, have bad manners and generally don't keep things clean and sanitary, neighbors don't like it and consequently move out of the neighborhood. This is a big problem for me. For these reasons, I do my best not to rent to Koreans.[18]

Another landlord, responding to the same question in 1930, states:

> It's an unfortunate situation for those people [*ano hitotachi ni wa kinodoku desuga*]. But if you rent houses to Koreans, not only do they ruin the property, but nearby tenants move out of the neighborhood. We've therefore refused to lease to Koreans. But even when they do so, they use Japanese

decoys [*otori*] to obtain leases for them. Furthermore, it's a normal course of action for Koreans to demand eviction fees [*tachinoki-ryō*] from us when we move to evict them. They seem to use this means to move from house to house. These cases are not uncommon.[19]

The refusal to rent to Koreans can be broken down into several categories. First, there is the problem of delinquent rent. Landlords often claimed that Koreans did not pay rent. One Japanese landlord from Kobe is quoted in a survey as saying that he wished Koreans would "respect rental contracts and not be delinquent on rent," while a Kobe city housing corporation (*jūtaku kabushi-kigaisha*) opined that it is difficult "to secure rents from Koreans to do normal business."[20] Indeed, Koreans were often delinquent on their rent, largely due to decreased wages and unemployment. As a Kobe municipal bureau survey noted, this was the cause of rent delinquency by Japanese tenants as well.[21]

The real question, however, is how rent delinquencies by Korean tenants compared with rent delinquencies by Japanese tenants. Osaka statistics show revealing differences. Among the total number of tenants surveyed who were delinquent on their rent, the majority of tenants delinquent on rent were Japanese (54.08 percent). For tenants delinquent on rent for three months or less, 45.9 percent were Korean while 33.4 percent were Japanese; for 6 months to 1 year, 41 percent were Korean while 43 percent were Japanese; between 1.5 years and 3 years, 11 percent were Korean while 18 percent were Japanese.[22] On average, Korean tenants were found to be delinquent on rent for 3.37 months while Japanese were delinquent for 5.43 months.[23] Based on these figures, it can be said that Japanese were generally delinquent on rent more often than Koreans; that the average number of months of delinquent rent was higher for Japanese than for Koreans; and that for delinquent rents lasting over six months, Japanese tenants far outnumbered Korean tenants. By contrast, however, more Koreans than Japanese were found to be delinquent on rent for three months or less. Going by these figures, then, we can conclude that Koreans were indeed found to be delinquent on rent, but generally less often, and for shorter periods of time, than Japanese. Nonetheless, the general tendency by Japanese landlords pointed to the refusal to lease to Koreans, and not to Japanese, on the grounds of delinquent rent.

Three other factors emerge in relation to this logic: security deposits (*shi-kikin*), transfer fees (*kenrikin*), and the number of guarantors (*hoshōnin*), all sof which were conditions for securing leases. As for security deposits, which were intended to cover potential damages to the rental property and delinquent rent, Koreans had to pay higher security deposits than Japanese, despite the fact that Koreans were found to be delinquent on rent less often, and for shorter periods of time, than Japanese. On average, Koreans paid 3.41 months as security deposits (shikikin), whereas Japanese paid 1.84 months.[24] For so-called transfer fees, or fees paid to the landlord for the right to take over rental property from former tenants, 12 percent of Korean tenants had to pay this fee, compared to only 6 percent of Japanese.[25] Lastly, tenants were often required to provide landlords with the names of one or more guarantors who could cover rent payment in the case of delinquency. Seventy-seven percent of all Japanese tenants were required to provide one guarantor, compared to 69 percent for Koreans. By contrast, 23.3 percent of all Japanese tenants required two or more guarantors, whereas 31 percent of Koreans had to provide the same.[26] Korean tenants generally had to provide more guarantors to landlords than Japanese tenants did.

The figures for security deposits, transfer fees, and numbers of guarantors strongly suggest that, despite the fact that Koreans were delinquent on rent less often, and for shorter periods of time, than Japanese, Korean tenants were compelled to bear greater economic burdens than Japanese tenants to secure leases from landlords. We can also surmise that these comparatively higher figures required of Koreans represent the indirect and economic means by which Japanese landlords refused leases to Koreans. At the same time, these figures strongly suggest that the refusals were based less on the grounds of Korean rent delinquencies and more on other factors, irreducible to rent, stemming from the fact that these tenants were Korean and not Japanese.

As the two opening statements from Osaka landlords suggest, a salient reason for refusing leases to Koreans was the potential for communal living in single rooms. It was common in the 1920s and 1930s in Japan to refer to Korean communal living as mure seikatsu, strongly connoting an everyday life or lifestyle fit for swarms or infestations of insects, or, alternatively, herds or packs of wild animals. This image stemmed from the forms of housing Koreans were compelled to adopt: subletting, subleasing, so-called Korean geshuku, and barracks. Japanese landlords especially expressed concern with the first two forms. When, in a Kobe survey in 1927, Japanese landlords, housing corporations, and property management companies were asked why they refused leases to Koreans, and what they wanted from prospective Korean tenants, the most common response referenced Korean communal living. A property management company (kaoku kanrigaisha) stated, "We prohibit communal living and strive to enforce, as much as possible, one family per house [or room]," noting additionally that they prohibited "multiple tenancy" (*tasū no dōkyosha*).[27] Another Kobe housing corporation (*jūtaku kabushiki-gaisha*) wrote that multiple tenancy resulted from the practice of subletting and subleasing single rooms, while another housing corporation complained that "most Koreans do not apply for leases, but rather move into places of previous Korean tenants without signing new leases." This kind of communal living, they complained, led to unsanitary conditions that reduced the value of the property. A housing consignment company (*itaku kabushikigai-sha*) stated that refusals to lease to Koreans stemmed from the fact that "they all live together, dirty the residence and argue a lot," while another housing corporation asked that Korean tenants also try to keep the neighboring areas clean. Based on these comments, the Kobe survey claimed that Koreans "lack etiquette, knowledge of legal matters and hygiene."[28]

As the first Osaka landlord quoted above noted, communal living did have an economic dimension in terms of maintaining and repairing these residences. This landlord claimed that Korean communal living reduced the rental life of houses by more than one half, leading the landlord to conclude that even receiving twice the amount of monthly rent from Koreans would not persuade the landlord to lease to them. At the same time, however, Korean communal living was commonly cited as a problem because it drove out other tenants from the neighborhood—by which they meant Japanese tenants. In other words, landlords justified their refusals to rent to Koreans on the basis of purported Japanese flight: "Since Koreans are noisy, have bad manners and generally don't keep things clean and sanitary, [Japanese] neighbors don't like it and consequently move out of the neighborhood. This is a big problem for me. For these reasons, I do my best not to rent to Koreans." Comments from Kobe housing corporations also made the same argument, leading one housing corporation to state that Korean tenants should "keep all acquaintances and socializing with others in the neighborhood under wraps and secretive."[29] Many Japanese landlords thus refused to rent to Koreans because they either felt or experienced a loss of business with other Japanese tenants in the neighborhood. The important point here, however, is not whether this was in fact true; nor is it a matter of discerning whether Japanese tenants had legitimate reasons to move out, thereby taking away business for Japanese landlords. Rather, the problem is how the presence of Korean tenants produced conditions for Japanese landlords to imagine, assume, and then assert that residential housing markets were a priori national housing markets, i.e, Japanese housing markets. The Japanese quality of residential housing markets, as an object of knowledge, did not precede Korean residents moving in. Rather, it would be more accurate to say that it was produced as an effect of the encounters with Korean tenants, and retrospectively naturalized and transformed into what was considered common sense.

Japanese Proper Names and Korean Evictions

Two final points remain to be mentioned in regard to the reasons for Japanese landlords to refuse leases to Koreans. The first is how Korean tenants obtained leases by using Japanese proper names on lease holding contracts. Increasingly, Japanese landlords had to consider the distinct possibility that Japanese proper names on contracts did not represent or signify Japanese tenants or legal subjects, but rather stood in for so-called swarms of Korean tenants. Landlords were no longer even sure if Japanese tenants were actual tenants, or just decoys—as the Osaka landlord above put it—for large communities of unauthorized Korean tenants.

The question of the use of Japanese proper names, in relation to Korean tenants, is evident in a 1932 round table discussion on "the Korean housing problem" (senjin [sic] jūtaku mondai) by Kobe city officials. One panelist remarked, "If you go to a landlord with a Korean name—you know, like Kan or Yi—you'll almost always be refused the chance to rent. You hear about this problem all the time."[30] A Kobe police officer agreed, saying, "Landlords simply won't rent their rooms out if they hear or see a Korean name. All kinds of problems then emerge when the landlords find out that their tenants are in fact Koreans who used Japanese names in order to get the lease."[31] In the face of housing discrimination, however, the use of Japanese proper names to obtain leases was a tactical necessity for Korean tenants. Indeed, this problem was well-known by Korean tenants, as well as by Japanese tenant union leaders. In a 1936 essay published in Minshū Jihō, "Problems for Koreans in Osaka," Kim S. S., a Korean writes:

> Before our very eyes we are witnessing the most serious problem for Koreans today: the housing problem [jūtaku mondai]. More specifically, it's the problem of securing leases for Korean tenants [shakkanin mondai]. This is a problem that all Koreans experience equally, and with equal urgency. Open your eyes! Is it possible to secure leases with Korean names?! Ha! No way![32]

Another Korean, quoted in an Osaka labor survey, also noted:

> Well, it's all fine and well to say in theory that Koreans are treated equally with Japanese. But, really, that's just mindless babble. Look—Japanese landlords refuse to rent to Korean workers. Evidence of this was found when one Korean worker, who was fluent in Japanese and could pass unsuspected as a Japanese, used a Japanese name. He obtained a lease. Now, the same Korean guy, when he presented himself as a Korean, and used his Korean name—well, forget about it, mission impossible![33]

Since Japanese proper names were used to secure leases, which led to subleasing and *geshuku*, the problem of using Japanese names was related to Korean communal living. By extension, it was also related to the last factor in Japanese landlord decisions to refuse leases to Koreans, namely, the difficulties experienced by Japanese landlords in evicting Korean tenants from houses and rooms. Evictions were legally complex matters involving conciliation court rulings based on the Law on Land and Leased Buildings, as well as court rulings based on civil procedural law (*minji soshōhō*) on the city, regional, and even supreme court levels. Often, however, these cases ended in violent force and physical clashes between landlords, tenants, and police, or else in undecided, chronic disputes between Korean tenant and Japanese landlord. According to the Ministry of Justice, difficulties in evicting Koreans were increasingly becoming reasons for landlords to refuse leases to Koreans. Especially in the early 1930s, countless newspapers, such as the *Osaka Mainichi Shimbun* and the *Kobe Shimbun*, printed scores of articles with headlines, such as the following, which expressed difficulties related to the eviction of Koreans: "Japanese agents [*tesaki*] for Koreans / Landlords in Tears / Koreans demand eviction fees";[34] "Korean Evictions / Towards a Solution to the Problem";[35] "They Just Won't Leave . . . The Eviction Problem of Korean Slums";[36] "Violent Embroglio from Korean Evictions";[37] "The Korean Village that Wouldn't Move / Help from Police";[38] "Wiping Out Koreans from Houses / Korean Habits, Eviction Fees";[39] "Like Vermin and Ticks [*dani*]: Korean Construction Bosses / Landlords Fret over Eviction Fees";[40] "Tenant Tactics of Evil Koreans / Object is Eviction Fees";[41] "Unemployed Japanese and Koreans Brawl with Landlords / Struggles over Forced Eviction."[42]

The foregoing discussion has shown and discussed how, within the general problem of high rent after the 1920 economic crisis, Korean tenants experienced a particular form of the housing crisis in Japan, namely the experience of being refused leases in residential housing markets in Japan. We have seen that this refusal was articulated and justified on grounds that were not simply reducible to high rent or delinquent rent, but were colored and overdetermined by presumptions by Japanese landlords that housing markets in Japan were national markets. Refusals, however, were only one problem confronting Korean tenants. While subletting rooms or living in geshuku or barracks provided Korean tenants with means to overcome refusals from landlords, Korean tenants then had to struggle to maintain these living conditions. These struggles were against the eviction from houses and rooms, and the evacuation from barracks, and also revealed how the force of law was an important factor in determining whether Korean tenants could maintain secure housing.

The Force of Law (I): Struggles over Eviction

To repeat an earlier point, until 1941, landowners and landlords in Japan had the right to terminate lease contracts at any time and were not legally obligated to provide tenants with just reason (seitō no jiyū) for evictions at the time of the eviction notice.[43] This power of eviction was granted to landlords and landowners by the mandate of article 617 of the civil code, and by the Law on Land and Leased Buildings.[44]

In the late 1920s and throughout the 1930s, Japanese tenant unions demanded 30 percent decreases in rent, rent control, the end to mandatory security deposits, an increase in public housing, and especially an end to forced evictions.[45] Korean tenant unions, such as the Higashi Osaka Shakkanin Dōmei and the Higashi Osaka Shakkanin Kumiai Kyōgikai, also demanded 30 percent decreases in rent and fought against the unilateral power of landlords to evict tenants. In terms of fighting eviction, both Japanese and Korean tenants generally had only one tactic, namely the adoption of legal means to obstruct the process of filing for eviction by landlords, thereby delaying the actual day of eviction. Legal means included, for example, filing for the tenant's right to demand repairs of the leased house or room or refusing to sign documents required for the processing of the eviction application by the landlord. Other means included demanding eviction fees (tachinoki-ryō, sometimes called moving fees or iten-ryō) from the landlord after receiving eviction notices and refusing to move out unless these fees were received.[46] However, while courts recognized the common practice and custom of paying and receiving eviction fees as a method of resolving housing disputes, there did not exist, in either the civil code or the Law on Land and Leased Buildings, any legal articles or stipulations on the payment or receipt of eviction fees.[47] Eviction fees were thus paid informally, received through out-of-court settlements between landlord and tenant, and often entailed long and arduous negotiations and battles of attrition.

There were significant differences, however, between Japanese and Korean tenants. For Korean tenants, high rent was not the most immediate and urgent problem. The most urgent obstacle was in securing lease-holding contracts amidst a racist housing market. Koreans demanded basic residential rights (kyojūken) that were necessarily different from Japanese demands for residential rights. As a tactical necessity to secure leases, Korean tenants used Japanese proper names to pass unsuspected by discriminating eyes of landlords. When Japanese landlords discovered this process, however, they often moved to evict Koreans for unauthorized subleasing, a legal claim that fell within the purview of the civil code, or else for crimes of fraud and extortion, which fell within the bounds of Japanese criminal law (keihō). A significant difference between Japanese and Korean tenants thus existed in the conditions and legal execution of eviction. While landlords moved to evict both Japanese and Korean tenants because of rent delinquency, landlords additionally moved to evict Korean tenants for reasons that were irreducible to the problem of rent. This fact must be kept in mind when considering the complexity, violence, and large numbers of housing disputes involving Korean tenants.

General trends of housing disputes involving Koreans in Japan can be gleaned from police and court statistics. In 1924, Japanese higher police records only show three housing disputes related to Korean tenants, all in Osaka. By 1929, however, there were 2,517 incidents and over 5,505 incidents in 1933. After 1933, the numbers decrease significantly: 2,053 incidents in 1,934, 1,858 in 1935, 1,386 in 1936, and 499 in 1937. We can conclude that the peak years of housing disputes involving Koreans came after 1925, and peaked between 1928 and 1933.[48]

As a way to specify the causes of these disputes, table 15 shows the reasons cited by landlords and tenants for petitioning to housing conciliation courts (shakuya chōtei saibanjō). As the survey notes, for all housing disputes involving Koreans in Osaka in 1930 and 1931, 100 percent of the Japanese applicants were landlords, and 100 percent of the Korean applicants were tenants. Seven categories were listed for the reasons for submitting applications: eviction, continuance of lease, rent decrease, rent payment, evacuation from land, payment of renovations, and return of security deposit. Applications for both Korean tenants and Japanese landlords, however, fell overwhelmingly

TABLE 15. Housing Conciliation Cases Involving Korean Tenants, Osaka, 1930–1931

	Japanese Plaintiffs (landlords)		Korean Plaintiffs (tenants)	
Reason	1930	1931	1930	1931
Eviction	52	57	0	0
Continuance of Lease	0	0	67	52
Rent Decrease	0	0	15	2
Rent Payment	9	2	0	0
Evacuation from Land	2	2	0	0
Payment of Renovations	0	0	1	1
Return of Security Deposit	0	0	1	0
Total	63	61	84	55

Source: Shihōsho Chōsa-ka, "Shihōsho Kenkyū Dai-17."

under categories related to the following problems, which I list in the order of greatest frequency: eviction, evacuation of land (i.e., barracks, which will be discussed shortly), payment of renovations, and issues surrounding security deposits.

For Japanese landlords, applications for the eviction of Koreans constituted 82.5 percent of the total in 1930, and 93.4 percent in 1931. By contrast, landlord applications citing delinquent rent only amounted to 14.3 percent in 1930, and only 3.3 percent the following year. In short, Japanese landlords were generally not going to the housing conciliation courts to get back delinquent rent, but to evict Koreans. As for the Korean tenants, 80 percent in 1930 filed applications to continue residing in the houses they currently occupied; in 1931, this figure increased to 94.5 percent. By contrast, Korean applications appealing for decreased rent was 17.9 percent in 1930, and only 3.6 percent in 1931. High rent was clearly not as pressing an issue for Korean tenants as the problem of avoiding eviction and maintaining continuous residence.

That high rent was not necessarily the most common cause of housing disputes for Koreans is corroborated by police statistics from Osaka. Table 16 lists five basic categories by which Osaka higher police categorized the causes of housing disputes involving Korean tenants in 1929 and 1933: delinquent

TABLE 16. Causes of Housing Disputes Reported to the Osaka Higher Police, 1929 and 1933

Causes	1929	1933
Delinquent Rent	917	1,058
Non-payment of Security Deposit	157	NA
Use of Japanese Name	302	646
Use of Japanese Renter	NA	536
Unauthorized Subletting/Occupancy	217	1,727

Sources: 1929 figures from Naimushō Keihōkykoku, Shakai Undō no Jōkyō; 1933 figures from Osaka-fu Tokubetsu Kōtō-ka, "Chōsenjin ni kansuru tōkeiyō, Showa 8 nendō."

rent, non-payment of security deposits, the use of Japanese proper names, the use of Japanese renters, and unauthorized subletting or occupancy. Several points can be gleaned from these figures. In 1929, 917 cases (57.6 percent) were caused by delinquent rent, 302 cases (19 percent) by the use of Japanese proper names, 217 cases (13.6 percent) by unauthorized subletting/occupancy, and 157 cases (9.9 percent) by the non-payment of security deposits. In 1933, there were 1,058 cases (26.7 percent) stemming from delinquent rent, 1,182 cases (29.8 percent) from either the use of Japanese proper names or Japanese renters (to secure leases for Korean tenants), and 1,727 cases (43.5 percent) from unauthorized subletting/occupancy.

These figures suggest several points. First, the problem of security deposits aside, according to police the overwhelming causes of disputes in Osaka fell into three areas: delinquent rent, use of Japanese names or Japanese renters, and unauthorized subletting. Second, while delinquent rent was the cause for more than half of the total disputes in 1929 (57.6 percent), this had decreased significantly by 1933, to 26.6 percent. By 1933, the central and most immediate cause of housing disputes involving Korean tenants was not high rent. Third, this decrease was countered by a significant increase in cases caused by the use of Japanese names, Japanese renters, and unauthorized subletting and occupancy. As we have seen earlier, however, the use of Japanese names or Japanese renters was a practice that was closely connected to unauthorized subletting and unauthorized occupancy. Thus, when combined statistically, these two categories (i.e., use of Japanese proper names and unauthorized subletting and occupancy) constituted nearly one third of the causes of disputes in 1929, and almost three quarters in 1933. This increase should be understood as an index of the difficulties in obtaining housing for Koreans, as well as a sign that high rent was not the most immediate or urgent problem facing Korean tenants.

The same police statistics also reveal the percentage of disputes that were resolved and unresolved. In 1929, 65.6 percent were unresolved and 34.4 percent were resolved. By contrast, in 1933, 37.8 percent went unresolved while 62.2 percent were resolved, an almost symmetrical reversal from 1929. While the precise legal status of resolved and unresolved is unclear in these statistics, it is probable that 'unresolved' did not mean eviction. The extent to which resolved cases ended in eviction, however, can be further specified. Out of the 554 resolved cases in 1929, 78.5 percent resulted in eviction, while 67.6 percent resulted in eviction in 1933. Finally, among the resolved cases, the percentage of evictions in disputes caused by delinquent rent, use of Japanese names, and unauthorized subletting can also be gleaned. As table 17 shows, among resolved cases stemming from delinquent rent, eviction resulted 87.8 percent of the time in 1929, and 50.5 percent of the time in 1933. For the same years, percentages of eviction stemming from the use of Japanese names were 76.9 percent and 77.4 percent. For evictions stemming from unauthorized subletting in 1929 and 1933, the percentages were 59.6 percent and 68.2 percent, respectively.

Judging from these figures (and excluding the category for other, which is statistically negligible), evictions stemming from delinquent rent were high in 1929, with 237 out of 270 resolved cases leading to eviction, but comparatively low in 1933 at 50 percent, with 252 evictions resulting from almost 500 resolved cases. Thus, between these years eviction rates stemming from delinquent rent decreased significantly. By contrast, eviction rates stemming from disputes caused by the use of Japanese names (or Japanese renters), or by unauthorized subletting, were generally very high.

It was difficult, however, for landlords to carry out eviction orders of Koreans. These difficulties mostly appeared between the time landlords applied to courts for eviction notices and the time courts ruled for the enforcement of eviction (kyōsei shikkō). This interim period lasted six months with housing conciliation cases, and three months with civil court cases. Tenants, however, were still considered legal subjects of lease contracts during this interim period and thus fought to delay this period for as long as they could by filing applications demanding the repair of the leased property or the remunera-

TABLE 17. Causes of Eviction of Resolved Housing Disputes, Osaka, 1929 and 1933

Cause of Dispute	Year	Resolved Incidents	Evictions No. (%)
Delinquent Rent	1929	270	237 (87.8%)
	1933	499	252 (50.5%)
Use of Japanese	1929	160	123 (76.9%)
Proper Name	1933	780	604 (77.4%)
Unauthorized	1929	114	68 (59.6%)
Subletting	1933	1,230	839 (68.2%)
Other	1929	10	7 (70%)
	1933	9	8 (88.9%)

Sources: 1929 figures from Naimushō Keihōkykoku, *Shakai Undō no Jōkyō*; 1933 figures from Osaka-fu Tokubetsu Kōtō-ka, "Chōsenjin ni kansuru tōkeiyō, Showa 8 nendō."

tion of costs of repairs made by tenants. Tenants could also refuse to sign necessary legal documents as a tactic to delay the eviction process. Even if landlords could overcome these temporary obstacles, however, there was no guarantee that courts would rule in favor of the landlord and order official notices for forced eviction. Moreover, especially in civil procedural cases, courts could rule to withdraw (*torisage*) or dismiss (*kyakka kikyaku*) cases, or else order an out of court settlement, i.e., private reconciliation. This promised a potentially interminable process—what one Kobe landlord called "an entanglement of barbed wire." Lastly, even if courts did rule in favor of landlords and order official notices for eviction, this did not guarantee the immediate and actual evacuation of the property. Other problems thus emerged even after official court orders for eviction were issued. The process of eviction thus included two distinct periods, the interim period and the period after the issuing of court orders. The period leading up to an eviction, often an uncertain and indefinite time filled with anxiety, fear, loathing, dread and—as we will see—violence.

In the interim period landlords faced particular problems with Korean tenants that were not reducible to rent, and that stemmed from unauthorized subletting and the use of Japanese proper names (or Japanese renters) on lease contracts. As we have already seen, the use of Japanese proper names on leases was usually the precondition for unauthorized subletting. This meant that the proper names on the contracts did not match and represent those persons actually residing in the leased property. This posed an immediate, practical, and, especially, legal obstacle for landlords since processing applications for eviction required the submission of a *kōshō shōsho*, a document from the public notary. The public notary, however, only recognized the signatory of the lease. This document therefore could not, and did not, represent those bodies residing and occupying the leased property. In this sense, the Korean tenants were not represented by the Japanese proper names on the contracts, and were, strictly speaking, beyond the application of the law.

The 1933 survey on Koreans by the justice ministry identified precisely this problem as a reason for the delays in processing applications by landlords wishing to evict Korean tenants.[49] Moreover, in *Problems Relating to Official Orders in Real Estate*, authored by lawyer Tanii Shinzō and published in 1936, this problem was raised in a short chapter, "On the Proper Names of Debtors."[50] Tanii asserted that landlords were facing endless delays in obtaining official court orders for the eviction of tenants, and he also noted (without mentioning Korean tenants explicitly) that this was an especially common problem with tenants in boarding houses. Tanii blamed this problem on the Public Notary Law (*kōshōshō-hō*) and urged the government to change and extend the boundaries of this law to recognize, in addition to the lease-holding signatory, those persons actually occupying leased property, but not represented by the contract's primary signatory.[51] In essence, he recommended making the signatory equivalent to those actually inhabiting a rental property in the eyes of the law to facilitate and expedite the process of eviction and to overcome the problem of how proper names often did not represent those residing in a rental property. The basic point here, however, is that the use of Japanese proper names on lease contracts by Korean tenants presented a major stumbling block for landlords wishing to obtain official court orders for the eviction of Koreans.[52]

Eviction Fees

A second difficulty, which emerged both during and after the interim period, was the problem of eviction fees, or *tachinoki ryō*. These fees, which also went by the name of moving fees or *iten ryō*, were paid by landlords to tenants as the result of private negotiations between the two parties. These payments took place both before or after court orders of eviction. The important point

about these fees is that while Japanese courts commonly recognized the practice and custom of eviction fees, these fees (and their specific amounts) were
neither recognized in, nor stipulated by, any law in Japan. Rather, they were
informal payment agreements between landlords and Japanese or Korean
tenants. Therefore, Japanese courts could not enforce the payment or receipt
of eviction fees legally and could only recommend to the disputing parties
that eviction fees and their amounts be resolved privately, out of court. From
the landlord's perspective, the payment of eviction fees was often considered
more economical than risking further unpaid months of rent. Tenants, however, were in no way obligated legally to receive these payments, and could
and often did refuse them. This was especially true for tenants who did not
have enough money to move elsewhere, or who did not accept the reasons
cited by the landlord for the eviction. Since the receipt of eviction fees was
often interpreted by courts as a sign that tenants recognized the stated conditions of eviction by the landlord as legitimate or accurate, the refusal of eviction fees often signaled a discrediting of the landlords' claims.

From the late 1920s until the mid 1930s, tenants took the initiative to demand the payment of eviction fees. Typical reasons cited for the payment of
eviction fees were high moving costs and insufficient funds to put down security deposits for new leases on homes or rooms. This was especially the
case in the Kansai region, where high security deposits on lease-holding
property continues to this day. These reasons were especially cited by tenants
active in tenant unions (shakkanin kumiai) and tenant associations (shakkanin
dōmei).[53] Both Korean and Japanese tenants used this tactic, but Korean tenants also demanded payments of eviction fees by citing the difficulties in obtaining leases from Japanese landlords. Landlords, however, were not legally
obligated to pay these eviction fees. Moreover, especially in cases of delinquent rent, landlords often could not afford to pay tenants the demanded
eviction fees. In turn, however, tenants often refused to evacuate the property
unless some or all of these fees were paid, thereby creating or prolonging a
dispute. The nature of these disputes over eviction fees is a reflection of the
fact that eviction fees were neither legal nor illegal, but were, more accurately,
a-legal.

Fragmentary statistics on the payment of eviction fees to Korean tenants
exist in Japanese higher police records in Osaka for 1929 and 1933. Table
18 shows the percentage of eviction fees paid and unpaid to Korean tenants
among resolved cases, also noting undecided cases that stemmed from further legal processing in housing conciliation courts (for chōtei shikkō) and

TABLE 18. The Adjudication of Eviction Fees, Osaka 1929 and 1933

	January–September 1929	January–December 1933
Eviction fees paid	405 (73.1%)	446 (17.7%)
Eviction fees unpaid	30 (5.4%)	1,257 (49.9%)
Undecided	119 (21.5%)	815 (32.4%)
Total	554 (100%)	2,518 (100%)

Sources: 1929 figures from Osaka-shi Shakai-bu Chōsa-ka, "Honshi ni okeru chōsen jūtaku mondai"; 1933 figures taken from Osaka-fu Tokubetsu Kōtō-ka, "Chōsenjin ni kansuru tōkeiyō, Showa 8 nendō."
Note: Total represents resolved cases only.

civil procedural courts (for *kyōsei shikkō*). In 1929, eviction fees were paid 73 percent of the time and were unpaid only 5.4 percent of the time. Undecided cases account for 21.5 percent. In 1933, there are significant differences. Eviction fees were only paid 17.7 percent of the time, while almost 50 percent of the time they were unpaid. Moreover, 32.4 percent of the time they were undecided.

Thus, at least in Osaka, the payment of eviction fees to Korean tenants decreased dramatically over the course of four years. One explanation for the decrease in payments is that Osaka landlord federations (*yanushi renmei*) had gained political strength after 1929 and collectively decided not to pay Koreans eviction fees. It was well known that these landlord federations collectively decided not to lease to Koreans; it is likely that they collectively decided not to pay Korean tenants eviction fees as well.[54] At the same time, undecided cases clearly rose between these years, suggesting that resolving disputes through eviction fees was becoming increasingly difficult, requiring judgments or assistance from housing conciliation and civil procedural courts.

On Fraud and Extortion

The last problem related to the eviction of Korean tenants, one that combined the use of Japanese proper names and eviction fees, is that Japanese landlords tried to evict Korean tenants on the grounds of fraud (*sagi*) and extortion (*kyōkatsu*). These charges went beyond the applications of the Law on Leased Land and Buildings and civil law and required the application of Japanese criminal law. For this reason, these cases received wide publicity, particularly in newspaper articles. Especially in Osaka and Kobe, these articles typically described a Japanese landlord who, upon learning that Koreans, and not Japanese, were living in the leased room or house, and upon realizing that he had mistakenly taken the Japanese name on the lease for the actual Korean occupant(s) of the lease-holding property, moved to evict the Korean tenants. Landlords thus yelled out: "Deception! Fraud!" Many Koreans, however, refused to evacuate the property, claiming that, since they had paid security deposits and transfer fees (kenrikin) to the primary lease holder, they had rights to live there. Many also insisted that they would not evacuate the property unless eviction fees were paid and would also threaten landlords with the prospect of housing even more friends of theirs, strongly insinuating that if the landlord thought ten Koreans in one room was an "entanglement of barbed wire," thirty or forty Koreans in one room would be akin to the proverbial death of a thousand cuts. Yet in other articles, Korean tenants threatened to destroy the property unless they received eviction fees. Landlords yelled out: "Extortion!"[55]

To what extent were Koreans actually found guilty of extortion and fraud? There are several well-documented court cases involving evictions of Korean tenants based on these charges. A 1933 justice ministry survey provides eight examples of cases from the Osaka ward court (Osaka-ku saibanjo), Osaka regional court (Osaka chihō saibanjo), and supreme court in which Koreans were charged with the crime of extortion, fraud, or both. In all these cases, the methods and practices by Koreans were the same: using Japanese names (or Japanese renters) to secure leases, refusing to vacate the leased property in the face of landlord demands for eviction, and threatening landlords in one form or another unless eviction fees were paid to the tenant. In one case from July 3, 1926, the Osaka Regional Court found one Korean tenant guilty of extortion after he (a) leased a house in the Sumiyoshi ward of Osaka on January 10, 1926, under the Japanese name of Toyokawa Tsurukichi; (b) refused to vacate the house after the landlord's wife demanded his eviction the day after he moved in (with his Korean friend); and (c) threatened to bring thirty other Korean friends to the home the next day if he did not receive 500 yen in eviction fees. The landlord offered to pay him 100 yen; he agreed and moved out. He then repeated this method in four other cases (two by himself, two with the same Korean friend), all in Osaka between January and April of 1926.[56] In addition to extortion (article 249 of the Criminal Code), he was also charged with the crime of committing concurrent crimes (heigōzai) of the same nature (article 55). He was not charged for fraud, however. Out of the remaining cases mentioned in the 1933 Ministry of Justice report, all of the Korean defendants, except one, were either found guilty of extortion (article 249 of the criminal code), fraud (article 246), or both, as well as of committing concurrent crimes of the same nature (article 55).[57]

Mr. Kim Goes to the Supreme Court

Among the cases of fraud and extortion, one case stands out. This was a case involving the eviction of a Korean tenant in which the supreme court ruled out charges of extortion and fraud made in previous rulings from two different courts. The court provided a detailed argument for its judgment,[58] and though the argument was generally ignored or overlooked at the city and regional levels of the court system, this case warrants a brief discussion.

The case in question began in Nagano prefecture in late 1930 and involved two defendants, Mr. Kim, a Korean construction worker, and Mr. Harayama, a Japanese leader of the Labor-Worker's Party (Rōnō-tō) in Nagano, as well as the leader of the Nagano Tenant's Union (Nagano Shakuchi-Shakkanin Kumiai). The original sentencing, which took place in the Nagano regional court, based its rulings on four incidents of alleged fraud and extortion, all of which took place in Nagano and demonstrated similar, if not identical, practices and methods by Kim and Harayama. After the defendants appealed the original ruling, the next hearing was held at the Tokyo Soshōin court. Here, too, the defendants were found guilty as charged, leading to a second appeal. The case was reviewed a final time by the supreme court in 1932. Essential details from two of the incidents will suffice to provide a clear picture of the case.

On September 13, 1930, a Japanese landlord, Mizusaki Genzō, leased a house in Nagano City to Ueno Harukichi, apparently a Japanese. Ueno claimed that he was an electrician and that his wife was a beautician. The landlord believed this and agreed to lease the house to him. The next day the landlord realized that Ueno was not Japanese or an electrician, but in fact Kim, a Korean construction worker, and immediately demanded their eviction. Kim refused and asked Harayama, the Japanese leader of the Nagano Tenant's Union, to negotiate with the landlord on his behalf. Harayama demanded that the landlord pay Kim 450 yen in eviction fees; the landlord countered with an offer of 110 yen, but Kim refused and demanded ten more yen. The landlord relented, paid 120 yen, and Kim moved out.[59] The landlord, however, claimed that Kim fraudulently deceived him and that he and Harayama extorted 120 yen. Both the Nagano regional court and the Tokyo court found Kim and Harayama guilty of fraud and extortion.

On October 7 of the same year a Japanese landlord, Mr. Yamaguchi, leased a house to a man who claimed his name was Kaneyama. Between the time of the signing of the lease and the actual possession of the house by Kaneyama, the landlord learned that Kaneyama was in fact Kim. Without notifying Kim, the landlord re-leased the house to a third party, a Japanese tenant, and then asked his eldest son, Noboru, to inform Kim that the house had been rented out to someone else and that the lease contract was now moot. Kim immediately notified Harayama again, who telephoned Noboru, saying, "My name is Harayama of the Nagano Tenant's Union. Now, you all have done a really nasty thing [in regards to Mr. Kim]. I and Mr. Kim would like to talk to you about this in person; please come by my house tomorrow." The next day, Noboru paid a visit to Harayama's house, and found Kim there as well. Harayama told Noboru that other Japanese landlords in the area were well acquainted with his past work of defending Korean tenants. "This time, however," Harayama said, "I'm here as an individual and not as a representative of the tenants union. But it only takes one call to get the union down here to negotiate with you and your father, and if that happens, believe me, it's nothing to us to give you one or two whacks on the head to get our point across." Harayama then demanded 70 yen in eviction fees. Noboru agreed to pay the amount, but later claimed that he and his father were fraudulently deceived by Kim and were extorted of 70 yen.[60] In both the Nagano regional court and the Tokyo court, Kim and Harayama were again found guilty as charged. The two remaining incidents involving Kim are essentially the same: Kim secures leases by using fictive Japanese proper names and informs landlords that he has a steady job (e.g., an electrician); Kim is evicted by landlords shortly after the lease is signed; and Harayama negotiates on behalf of Kim for eviction fees. In all the cases, the issue of delinquent rent was never raised as a reason for eviction.

The supreme court judgment on Kim is significant because it dismisses this case on several grounds. Regarding the charge of extortion, the judge overruled past verdicts since the threat expressed by Kim and Harayama, while intimidating, did not immediately threaten the safety or livelihood of the plaintiffs. The overruling of past verdicts of fraud, however, was more complex and involved a discussion of the legalities of the contract. In the judge's opinion, the lease contracts were clearly established and completed in all the cases, and the only question was to determine whether the evictions fell into one of three legal categories: the contract's termination (keiyaku kaijō), withdrawal (torisage), or invalidation (mukō). Eviction based on termination of contract was ruled out since termination was based on proving default on payment. In all cases, the tenant made all of the required payments, including rent. Next, eviction based on the withdrawal of contract was also ruled out since, according to article 96 of the civil code, the withdrawal of contracts was defined in terms of fraud. The judge ruled that this was not a case of fraud, however, and explained his judgment by discussing the problem of contract invalidation. Contract invalidation, which was defined in articles 90 and 94 of the civil code, was also ruled out since invalidation was defined in terms of an error (gonin) of "an element of legal action" (hōritsu koi no yōso). The fact that the landlord mistook Kim as a Japanese, however, did not constitute such an error, but rather an error "in relation to a legal action" (hōritsu koi no enyū). Since lease contracts did not stipulate matters of ethnicity, the landlord's error in mistaking Kim for a Japanese did not constitute an error of an element of legal action, only an error "in relation to a legal action." As such, however, this problem did not fall within the boundaries of contract invalidation, and therefore the charge of fraud was ruled out. In other words, the landlords' "errors in relation to a legal act" fell beyond the civil law.[61]

By ruling out termination, withdrawal, and invalidation of contracts, the judge argued that there was no legal basis upon which any of the plaintiffs could justify the eviction of Kim. Moreover, the judge stated that it was understandable for Kim to ask for eviction fees. The judge, however, could not legally enforce the payment of these fees since no article of any law stipulated the payment or receipt of eviction fees. Thus, while the landlord was shown to have no legal basis for eviction, the tenant also did not have a legal basis to demand eviction fees, however understandable this demand was considered to be. The judge therefore had no other choice except to dismiss the case and recommend to both parties that they settle their disputes privately, out of court. Ultimately, the judge did not make a definitive ruling in favor of one party or the other, and while the judge did overrule past verdicts of extortion and fraud charges, he did not drop the charges completely, but rather ruled for a stay of execution (shikkō yūyo), stipulating that if the defendant repeated similar incidents within three years, a prison term of one year would be enforced.[62]

The least that can be said about this case, and arguably for all housing disputes involving Korean tenants who used Japanese proper names and demanded eviction fees, is that they were full of legal and a-legal ambiguities, especially in cases where rent was not the central problem. At the same time, however, it also begs emphasis that the ambiguities of the supreme court case were only brought to light after the case went through two prior hearings, in two different courts and involved two separate appeals. Previous rulings clearly ignored or overlooked these ambiguities. In the seven other cases documented in the 1933 ministry of justice report, none of these ambiguities were raised in either Osaka ward or Osaka regional courts. If this is any indication of rulings on the level of city and regional courts in other cities, one can surmise that when charged with fraud or extortion, Korean tenants were commonly found guilty as charged and that landlords were generally winning cases for the eviction of Korean tenants. Moreover, as table 19 shows, in Osaka civil lawsuit cases, rulings in favor of Korean defendants (tenants) were almost unheard of. Out of 1,264 cases involving the eviction of Korean tenants in Osaka between 1929 and 1931, only one case ruled in favor of the Korean defendant. By contrast, rulings in favor of landlords were, on average, 47.1 percent. Lastly, when landlords were not winning cases, these statistics show that almost 50 percent of the cases were either withdrawn or dismissed as cases to be reconciled privately out of court.

In short, according to these figures, Koreans were basically always losing eviction cases; Japanese landlords were winning eviction cases almost half the time, and when landlords were not winning, the cases were being sent out of court for private settlement. For Korean tenants, this meant that even if they were not ordered to be evicted, they were equally not given any guarantee of staying on, either, but had to negotiate an already precarious situation. A private settlement only deferred a potential eviction, which meant remaining under the threat of eviction.

It should also be pointed out that an out-of-court settlement essentially meant that the disputing parties had to resolve the dispute on their own. This often led to violence. Newspaper accounts, as well as flyers from Korean tenant unions, write about how Japanese landlords often resorted to violent force, such as the hiring of construction workers to act as muscle men, to forcefully remove Korean tenants from leased houses and rooms. An article from December 10, 1932, of the *Osaka Asahi Shimbun* tells of a landlord who rented a room to a Japanese man, Kitajima, for 17.50 yen; Kitajima, acting as

TABLE 19. Civil Lawsuits for the Eviction of Korean Tenants, Osaka-ku Court, 1929–1931

	1929	1930	1931
(A) Total rulings for cases involving the eviction of Koreans	364	460	440
(B) Rulings in favor of plaintiff (Japanese landlord)	183	227	183
(C) Rulings in favor of defendant (Korean tenant)	1	0	0
(D) Order for out-of-court settlement (Wakai)	87	93	140
(E) Cases dismissed (kyakka kikyaku)	1	7	7
(F) Cases withdrawn (torisage)	86	120	105
(G) Cases appealed (sashimodoshi)	2	0	0
(H) Cases undecided (misai)	4	13	5
Rulings for landlord (%)	50.3	49.3	41.6
Rulings for tenant (%)	0.3	0	0
Out-of-court settlement cases (%)	23.9	20.2	31.8
Withdrawn cases (%)	23.6	26.1	23.9
Other (%)	1.9	4.3	2.7
Total (%)	100	100	100

Source: Shihōsho Chōsa-ka, "Shihōsho Kenkyū Dai-17."

a self-employed housing broker, then subleased the rented room to a Korean man, Pak, for 25 yen and pocketed 7.50 yen per month. Pak subleased part of his own room to fourteen other Korean workers. Together they shared a cramped room, each paying, on average, under 2 yen for rent. When the landlord found out about the fifteen Koreans, he ordered their immediate eviction, but the tenants refused to leave. Thus, on the morning of December 9, while the Koreans were out working, the landlord and six hired construction workers broke into the rented room, collected all of the Korean workers' private belongings inside the room and tossed them out into the street, nailing the door shut as they left. Having heard the news, Pak and the fourteen residents of the room returned later that night, purportedly with two hundred Korean workers, to collect their belongings from the street and attempt to re-enter the rented room. Their re-entrance, however, was blocked by twenty construction workers hired by the landlord, leading to a violent imbroglio leaving many injured.[63]

In response to such incidents, Korean tenant unions distributed flyers protesting the use of hired thugs by landlords to forcefully, but illegally, remove Korean tenants from leased property. One flyer, authored by three tenant associations and two communist Korean labor unions, has the heading, "Osaka Tenant Associations Clash with Landlord Thugs" (yanushi no bōryokudan), and describes how a Japanese landlord, who had unknowingly leased a room to two Koreans, hired forty thugs, known as the "Gang of Three Hundred," to enter the room, forcefully remove the two Korean tenants, and confiscate their private belongings, including futons, kitchen utensils, even their garbage. In short, when legal rulings did not cast Koreans out of their homes and into the streets, physical violence often did.[64]

On the Micropolitics of the Proper Name

Before discussing the how Korean evictions led to micropolitical struggles of homeless Korean populations, reflection is warranted on the relationship between Korean housing struggles to obtain leases and to combat evictions, on the one hand, and the status of the Japanese proper name, on the other. While a more detailed legal analysis of (lease-holding) contracts is beyond the scope of this analysis, it should be clear from the preceding discussion of contract fraud that the precise legalities of the Korean use of Japanese proper names was not without great ambiguities. Indeed, an entire micropolitics of Korean tenants, struggling against the insecurities of the housing market, transformed the status of the Japanese proper name into an insecure territory itself. Arguably the center of the problem of the Japanese proper name is the fact that the subject written into lease-holding contracts existed, but only virtually. These proper names represented a subject, but a subject that was vacant and fictitious. Legally speaking, these proper names thus represented nobody in the juridical sphere of contract law. Indeed, it was ultimately a question beyond the problem of representation within the legal machinery. Rather, the signature of the proper name only disclosed a trace of an alterity, an other-space of an occupying mass of anonymous bodies. The Japanese proper name disclosed nothing but traces of unnamed, uncounted, and unrepresented bodies in a mass form. The Korean housing movements that challenged the stability of the Japanese proper name revealed how the proper name is not about an individual, legal subject, or person, but rather about an anonymous collectivity. Indeed, as Deleuze and Parnet write, "Every proper name is collective."[65] This collectivity did not inhabit a terrain of housing beneath the sign of the proper name, but through the signature of the proper name itself. Moreover, the signature of the proper name was disclosed as a problem of a territory or domain of life and living, a territory or domain formed contingently in and out of struggle. "The proper name is not the constituted mark of a subject, but the constituting mark of a domain, an abode. The [proper name] is not the indication of a person; it is the chancy [contingent] formation of a domain. Abodes have proper names. . . ."[66] It has to be said, finally, that this rendering of the proper name as a collective matter, as a matter of unnamed, uncounted, unrepresented, and occupying mass bodies, was perceived by Japanese landlords and the Japanese legal system as a threat to the social order of the housing markets in Japan. What, however, was the actual threat? How could the threat of absolute territorial insecurity, experienced by Koreans in the housing markets of Japan, be transformed and reversed into something that was perceived to be a threat to a Japanese social order? The answer is that the deployment of the Japanese proper name by Korean tenants, as a discursive strategy to combat territorial insecurity amidst a racist housing market, was perceived as a violation of an implicit social order, one that was subsequently policed and litigated as such.

In other words, the deployment of the Japanese proper name by Korean tenants disclosed a reversal of, and a refusal to abide by, the abjecting logic of the housing markets, which told them, instructed them, and legally stipulated to them that they could not live where they pleased, precisely because they were Korean. The Korean strategy to use Japanese proper names and to speak fluent Japanese was a form of political subjectification that altered the habitation and territorial destination of colonial subjects in Japan. The terrain of this micropolitics was the home, yet the territory was the proper name. The takeover of the territory of the Japanese proper name was thus an inventive political strategy that refused and temporarily reversed the social and colonial order that said: "As Koreans, you cannot live here, you must take a Korean name and nothing else, and you may not call yourself anything else but Korean." And in the same stroke, the appropriation of the Japanese proper name exposed the fiction of the Japanese imperial rhetoric that claimed that all Korean (colonial) subjects were equal before the eyes of the great Japanese emperor. The appropriation of the proper name exposed the fiction of the imperial state sign of assimilation and equality, challenging it with an actively practiced and disruptive principle of equality.[67]

The Force of Law (II): Struggles over Barrack Evacuation

The question that remains is where did evicted Korean tenants go? There are no statistics to answer this, but it is probable that most stayed in the same city, staying with friends or family in geshuku, or subletting other rooms or houses, thereby reproducing the very conditions that often led to their evictions in the first place. Going back home to Korea cannot, of course, be ruled out, yet it is likely that most did not. Similar to unemployed Korean workers, evicted Korean tenants often did not have enough money to travel back to Korea or were compelled to stay in Japan in search of work. Yet, if geshuku or sublet rooms were not viable options, the last resort, and the minimum form of dwelling, was life in barracks.

The problem with barrack living, however, was that only a small percentage of the barracks were constructed on unowned land. The vast majority of barracks were constructed on unused plots of land that were privately owned. As long as these lands were unused, Korean barracks were relatively secure. During the 1920s and 1930s, however, Japanese cities underwent massive urban planning changes, such as suburbanization in cities like Tokyo and Osaka. The passage of the Urban Planning Law of 1919 was one index of the urban transformations that would take place in the 1920s and 1930s.[68] As a result of the expansion of urban planning projects, hitherto unused plots of privately owned land were being increasingly sold off to various city developers. Owners of the lands on which barracks were constructed were consequently compelled to plan for the clearance and demolition of the barracks, as well as for the mass evacuation of Koreans living there. This led to a long series of struggles between barrack residents, landowners, city officials, and the police over evacuation. Housing disputes involving Korean worker-tenants, the difficulties in obtaining leases, and the problem of eviction were thus displaced onto disputes centering around barrack living and new territories of struggle on privately owned vacant lots, public land by river banks, reclaimed land near factories or public works construction sites, public spaces beneath railway tracks, and abandoned buildings. Barrack living, the last resort, did not escape the insecurity of territory faced by Koreans.

It is difficult to determine with any real precision when Korean-related barrack disputes began, but newspaper articles, especially in Osaka and Kobe, covered incidents of barrack evacuations and demolitions as early as 1929.[69]

TABLE 20. Barrack Evacuation Disputes Involving Koreans, 1933–1937

	1933	1934	1935	1936	1937
Tokyo	5	7	13	23	20
Osaka	87	48	23	14	15
Hyogo	11	8	18	12	4
Aichi	2	1	3	2	NA
Other 43 prefectures	9	16	24	24	18
Total	114	81	81	75	57

Source: Naimushō Keihōkykoku, Shakai Undō no Jōkyō, 1933–38.

The higher police also mentioned barrack evacuation disputes in 1929 in its annual Shakai Undō no Jōkyō,[70] and wrote in 1931 that "the unauthorized construction of barracks by Korean workers on public land has become more and more frequent. Supported by leftist cells operating behind the scenes. . . these Koreans have refused to vacate these areas and have disturbed the peace with mass demonstrations of force protesting the orders for the evacuation. . . . [This problem] requires vigilant police surveillance and active intervention."[71]

Newspaper articles and police annuals therefore suggest that the years between 1929 and 1933 marked the beginning point for barrack disputes involving Koreans. Unsurprisingly, the first consistent series of police statistics of Korean-related barrack evacuation disputes appeared in 1933. Table 20 above shows that on a national level, there were 114 such disputes in 1933, 81 disputes in both 1934 and 1935, and 75 and 57 in 1936 and 1937, respectively. More-over, while the highest number of disputes took place in 1933, table 21 shows that in 1935 there were more Korean participants involved in these disputes than in any other year between 1933 and 1937. While there were 1,454 Koreans involved in these disputes in 1933, this figure more than doubled to 3,029 in 1935. The numbers decreased in the following years. Thus, according to these figures, the period of greatest intensity of these disputes probably came between the years 1933 and 1935, in terms of both numbers of disputes and participants. As with housing disputes, moreover, Osaka had the highest number of disputes involving Korean barrack evacuations. Kobe and Tokyo followed.

TABLE 21. Korean Participants in Barrack Evacuation Disputes, 1933–1937

	1933	1934	1935	1936	1937
Tokyo	118	94	37	108	44
Osaka	576	1,613	1,616	254	97
Hyogo	356	502	812	216	60
Aichi	2	1	3	5	NA
Other 43 Prefectures	402	439	561	474	240
Total	1,454	2,649	3,029	1,057	441

Source: Naimushō Keihōkykoku, Shakai Undō no Jōkyō, 1933–38.

The nature of barrack evacuations obviously differed from housing evictions insofar as leased contracts on land (shakuchi) were usually not involved in constructing the barracks. This meant that residents of barracks had little or no legal ground on which to stand in the face of orders for evacuation. None of the cases listed in the higher police annuals or in newspapers disclose which laws were cited to justify the demolition of barracks and the evacuation of Koreans. However, if a supreme court ruling on the demolition and evacuation of barracks occupied by Japanese in Tokyo in 1933 provides any indication, both the Urban Planning Law (tochi keikakuhō) (article 12) and the Law on the Development of Cultivated or Arable Land (kōchi seirihō) (article 17) were commonly cited.[72] In the face of these laws, however, and owing to the fact that the unauthorized construction of barracks on privately owned land left barrack residents devoid of any legal contractual status, there was very little for these residents to do except try to prolong their residence for as long as possible by ignoring notices of evacuation or by physically obstructing the process of evacuations. The latter, however, led to police intervention, violent clashes, and arrests.

A last ditch attempt, so to speak, by many Korean barrack residents was to ask city governments to provide them with "substitute plots of land" (daichi or hōmon daichi kyūkō) on which to construct new barracks. For example, in December 1934 in Kobe's Hayashida Ward, 155 Koreans (33 families) were ordered by the city to evacuate a barracks residence that they had occupied since 1927. According to a higher police report, "Due to the fact that this area is now becoming a zone for the rapid development of residential homes

. . . the City has ordered their immediate evacuation in order to begin the construction of a children's playground."[73] The Korean families in turn demanded that the city government provide them, at the city's expense, with an alternate location.[74] Sometimes this kind of petitioning worked, as in the case of 100 Koreans residing in 45 barracks constructed on unused, city-owned land in Tokyo, known simply to the city government as "Number Three Unreclaimed Land Property." The Koreans refused to leave these barracks for over one year, rejecting any and all orders from the city, including three executive orders of evacuation from the mayor of Tokyo himself. Together with the supporters from the Shiba Unemployed Workers Union (a branch of Zenkyō), the 100 Koreans demanded that the city government change the legal status of the unclaimed property to that of a substitute land, thereby preventing (or at least delaying) the sale of the land to prospective land developers. The city government relented and the Koreans were able to continue living in their barracks.[75]

Most of the time, however, city governments did not relent at all but went on the warpath to clear the sites. This was particularly evident in the Hayashida ward of Kobe, where the land evacuation problem involving Koreans lasted from 1930 to 1936. It is unclear precisely when the 500 Koreans (more than 80 families), first settled into the barracks, which they had constructed beneath an elevated railway line in Hayashida. Beginning in September 1930, however, the railway ministry, backed by the Kobe police, as well as the Hayashida hōmeni'inkai, ordered their immediate evacuation. The families refused, however, claiming that "they had no other place to go and no funds to speak of."[76] The Koreans then asked for legal help from one Kawakami, who was quoted as saying, "The state shows no signs of stopping the evacuation and has not even recognized our appeal. We intend to maintain our position and fight [to remain there]."[77] The protestors lost, however, and the evacuation took place on the morning of October 4, 1930. The only record of what the Koreans had to say about the forced evacuation is found in an interview, conducted by a journalist for the Kobe Shin Nippō newspaper, with a Korean resident of the barracks, known simply as Mr. K. The interview was carried out with Mr. K. as 50 police officers from the Hayashida police department, 9 higher police officers, 10 translators, 50 construction workers employed by the railway ministry, and 10 representatives from the Kobe city court demolished the barracks and organized the permanent evacuation of the 500 Koreans.[78]

Question: What are you going to do about the evacuation?

Mr. K: Well . . . we . . . Do you realize how long and how much effort it took us to construct this living situation for ourselves? I can't believe they're ordering us to evacuate. We don't have any place to go.

Q: Did it occur to you that by constructing these barracks here you were creating problems for others and doing wrong?

Mr. K: Look—Japanese landlords won't rent to us. When we first came here [under the railway tracks] we thought we would only use it as a place to sleep at night. The Railway Ministry didn't say anything about it and recognized our situation completely. Even the police didn't mind then. But all that's changed now and they're ordering us to just pack up and get out of here. But, tell me, how is this different from ordering us to die?!?

Q: How much money would you ideally like to have per day for living expenses?

Mr. K: Well, I suppose maybe fifty to sixty sen. [0.50–0.60 yen][79]

The force of law behind evictions and evacuations expelled Korean tenants from housing markets, even from the fringes of housing markets (in the case of barracks), and severed their relationships to lease-holding private property. Consequently, Korean tenant-workers were compelled to float or simply stagnate in the cities with little or no possessions or commodities except their capacity to work. The expulsion from housing markets increasingly pushed down the cost of the means of subsistence for Korean tenant-workers. The lowering of these costs means, however, that it became less expensive for Koreans to consume the necessary means of subsistence to reproduce one day of their lives. Was this not an important factor in reducing the amount of wages paid to reproduce one day of life?[80]

What has to be considered is how this specific manifestation of the force of law was an indirect, but no less real or crucial, factor in reducing the amount of wages paid to Korean workers in Japan and in maintaining Korean workers in Japan as labor that was cheaper than Japanese workers. During the 1920s and 1930s, daily wages for unskilled Japanese construction workers were, on average, between 1.00 yen and 2.00 yen (100 and 200 sen). For Korean unskilled construction workers, the average was generally 30 to 50 percent lower, and usually between 0.60 yen (60 sen) and 1.30 yen (130 sen). What Mr. K. is saying above is that now that he has lost his barracks, he needs even less money per day to live than the lowest wages earned by unskilled Korean construction workers. Mr. K.'s situation shows that the legal state apparatus and the court system's force of law, in rulings for eviction and evacuation especially, pushed down the cost of means of subsistence for Korean tenant-workers.

Lastly, it is necessary to mention a final problem related to barrack evacuations, namely the payment of evacuation fees to the evacuated residents. The higher police took note of this practice in Osaka: "In an effort to solve the land evacuation problems in the Tenroku area . . . the Osaka Government . . . has agreed to provide evacuation fees of up to 50 yen per person until the end of April 1934 as a method of compromise."[81] In the above example from Kobe, the Kobe city government gave each unmarried individual 15 yen and 30 yen to each family.[82] Yet, payments of evacuation fees decreased as the number of evacuations increased, and as more and more Korean residents began refusing to evacuate barracks unless they were paid evacuation fees. Evacuation fees stopped being paid as a result. As a Kobe city official explained to other city representatives at the 9th Annual Meeting for Welfare Organizations in the Six Major Cities (Roku Daitoshi Shakai Jigyo Kyōgikai), "To evacuate [Korean barracks], the prefectural government has had to spend several thousand yen, an enormous burden and cost. . . . We've therefore begun consultations with the ministry of the interior."[83] The same official then decried indignantly the fact that "[Koreans] refuse to evacuate unless we pay them three to five yen each as 'evacuation fees'! The gall! No doubt, demanding evacuation has become a Korean custom. It's left us completely speechless and dumbfounded."[84] Yet, Mr. K's question still echoes unanswered: how was the evacuation of Korean barrack communities different from ordering the residents to die? As for the life of Mr. K., can there be any doubt that the threat of the outside and the threat of the state were one and the same?

Conclusion: Urban Expropriation and the Proper Name

The history of struggles by Korean tenants in Japan during the 1920s and 1930s strongly suggests that we consider what I would like to call urban expropriation. This was an urban process involving the force of state law that severed tenants from lease-holding property, and that produced a chronically floating mass of surplus populations whose daily costs of subsistence were continually being pushed down. Echoing, but differing from, the experience of agricultural expropriation in colonial Korea, in which direct producers were severed from landed property through state violence and force, the problem of urban expropriation severed tenants from lease holding property through state violence and force. However, the result of urban expropriation was uncannily similar to the expropriation of the farms: the creating of a floating mass of bodies with nothing but their brains and their muscles to sell as a means to live.

Moreover, in the case of Korean tenants in Japan, urban expropriation was tied fundamentally to the problem of housing discrimination and racism and was part of a larger process of segmenting and stratifying the urban residential spaces of surplus populations of proletarians. What we see in the case of Korean tenants is how housing racism spiraled into a vicious cycle with no clear beginning or end: landlord racism against Koreans led the latter to use Japanese proper names to secure lease holding contracts; this led to evictions, which only reproduced the conditions in which Koreans were compelled to repeat the process of using Japanese proper names to secure leases. The legal state apparatus, including the supreme court, was not only unable to stop this cycle, it accelerated and exacerbated it. Moreover, especially since the criminal code was also brought into play in so many cases involving the eviction of Korean tenants, Korean tenants were generally criminalized in the mass media, thereby fueling landlord fears, anxieties, and hatred towards Korean tenants, and legitimating their racism. Urban expropriation was thus closely connected to the criminalization of Korean tenants.

The specific problem of the urban expropriation of Korean tenants, however, turned around the politics of the proper name. The problem to consider is how the strategic use of fictive Japanese proper names by Korean tenants did not represent a legal subject, but rather a vacant subject and an anonymous collectivity of bodies occupying a territory as the result of urban racism in the housing markets. The proper name, in short, was the mark of a radical alterity that the legal system could not account for, sublimate, or legally process, but only expel and criminalize. That this collective and anonymous collectivity could not be legally represented was what the state found most intolerable, for it was a direct challenge—one that was spurred into existence because of housing racism—to a system of private property that only recognizes, cares for, and invests in individualized, legal subjects. As Giorgio Agamben states:

> What the State cannot tolerate in any way . . . is that the singularities form a community without affirming an identity, that humans co-belong without any representable condition of belonging (even in the form of a simple presupposition). . . . For the State, therefore, what is important is never

the singularities as such, but only its inclusion in some identity, whatever identity (but the possibility of the *whatever* itself being taken up without an identity is a threat the State cannot come to terms with).[85]

Urban expropriation was the aggressive expression of this state intolerance, and it reproduced and exacerbated the production of a chronic Korean surplus population toiling in Japan amidst oppressive uncertainties and contingencies in the Japanese labor and housing markets.

5

THE OBSCENE, VIOLENT SUPPLEMENT
OF STATE POWER

....

Korean Welfare and Class Warfare in Interwar Japan

State power itself is split from within and relies on its own obscene spectral underside:
public state apparatuses are always supplemented by their shadowy double,
by a network of publicly disavowed rituals, unwritten rules, institutions,
practices, and so on. . . . So the problem is not simply the marginals who lead
the spectral half-existence of those excluded by the hegemonic symbolic regime; the problem is that this regime itself, in order to survive, has to rely on
a whole gamut of mechanisms whose status is spectral, disavowed, excluded
from the public domain. . . . [T]he opposition between state and civil society
is thoroughly ambivalent.
—Slavoj Žižek, 1999

In February of 1929 in the city of Kawasaki, the largest Korean communist
labor union in Japan, Rōsō, held a mass demonstration against the city's unemployment bureaus, expressing anger and frustration toward an unemployment registration process that many Koreans accused of privileging and
favoring the registration of Japanese unemployed populations over Koreans.[1]
In the spring of 1929, Rōsō was still organizing unemployed Koreans in the
area when a new force appeared on the scene in Kawasaki that competed with
Rōsō to recruit these unemployed Koreans. This was the Korean managed
Sōaikai, a state-funded yet supposedly privately managed "welfare organization specializing in Korean workers" (*chōsenjin senmon shakai jigyō*). According
to Kim Tu-yong, a member of Rōsō, the Sōaikai had succeeded in redirecting unemployed Koreans away from Rōsō and channeling them into the
ranks of the Sōaikai.[2] This time, however, the Sōaikai did not merely solicit
workers while they worked, as they often did in other cities in Japan, but instead went directly to their barracks and waited until the workers, men and
women, returned home. On the afternoon of May 14, 1929, forty-five Sōaikai
members approached a Korean residential area in Tsurumi (near Kawasaki)

and ordered those who were not working that day to register with the Sōaikai. But unlike a similar case in Yamanashi prefecture, in which half of the approached workers agreed to become Sōaikai members, all of the Korean workers in Tsurumi refused the Sōaikai's solicitation. Kim's narration claims that Sōaikai members threatened the workers with steel pipes, picks, and shovels, which immediately brought in 100 Korean resident workers to the showdown to confront the Sōaikai members. An enormous fight erupted just as ten police patrol cars arrived on the scene. Several Sōaikai members tried to flee by car but a group of workers stopped them by surrounding the members' car. Once the group of police patrolmen intervened, the fight subsided, and the Kanagawa prefecture's higher police chief is said to have warned the Sōaikai-Kawasaki branch deputy director to take heed. The Sōaikai deputy director apologized, saying, "I will tell our members not to act so rashly anymore."[3]

Several hours later, however, four large cars with over thirty Sōaikai members pulled into a different Korean barracks residence not far from the Tsurumi area. Workers had still not yet returned home from work, and the Sōaikai members sat in their idle cars while Korean families prepared dinner in the barracks. Just as two workers returned home and started helping with dinner, several Sōaikai members abducted them without warning, forcing them into their cars and driving off to a neighboring residence where they abducted another Korean worker while fending off outraged Korean residents with their picks and pipes. Quickly outnumbered by the alarmed and angered residents, the Sōaikai members hastened to flee the scene by car, forgetting in the process to take one of the Sōaikai members with them and leaving him in the dust to fight, in bloody vain, the furious residents. In less than an hour, over five hundred Korean workers and residents from the area gathered shovels, pipes, and bamboo staves and marched to the Kawasaki Sōaikai branch office with disgusted, surprised, and angry chatter of the living memory of the violent surprise attack by the Sōaikai passing from their lips. Once they arrived, they learned that police officers had already lined up in front of the Sōaikai office to protect it from precisely the possibility (or probability, as the statistician-cops like to say) that was materializing before the very eyes of the police. The Korean residents immediately demanded the release of their three abducted friends. The police refused, but being too few in number to fend off the entire group, they were overwhelmed by the force of hundreds of bodies pressing up against them and chanting and yelling, "Return our captured friends!" The group pushed through the police line, entered the office, destroyed what they could, and forcibly released their three friends. Additional police officers dispatched from Yokohama arrived by car soon afterwards, and the residents, along with their recently liberated friends, ran and scattered. Immediately after the incident six new police boxes (kōban) were constructed near the Korean barracks in Tsurumi and Kawasaki. Shortly thereafter, police arrested over one hundred Koreans said to be affiliated with Rōsō. Fifty Sōaikai members were also arrested, but were soon released.

What became known among Rōsō members as the Kawasaki Sōaikai incident was one of the final catalysts, in December 1929, for Rōsō's decision to dissolve and incorporate into the Japanese Communist Party's main labor union, Zenkyō. Rōsō argued for its dissolution (kaitai) and incorporation (gōdō) into Zenkyō partially on the grounds that it needed to find a better means to defend against what it called "specific forms of repression." In late 1929, at the height of Sōaikai violence and Korean anti-Sōaikai activity, Rōsō published a pamphlet titled, "How should Rōsō Move Forward?" It contained the following key passage:

> Rōsō has encountered specific forms of repression [tokushūteki dan'atsu] by the forces of Japanese Imperialism. This has resulted in the loss of our most important cells. . . . Under the guidance of the Korean Communist Party, these unique forms of repression have only increased. In Japan, therefore, it is necessary to join the Japanese Communist Party and work under its leadership. . . . In order to faithfully represent the interests of the Korean working class in Japan, [Rōsō] will thus abandon completely its ethnic struggle [issai ni minzokuteki tōsō wo hakki shi] and fight for worker hegemony as a leftist labor union.[4]

As of January 1930, however, it was clear that the vast majority of former Rōsō members did not join Zenkyō. Historian Pak Kyung-shik has shown that, while there were over 33,000 Korean members in Rōsō in 1929, the number of Korean members in Zenkyō in 1930 was 2,660, less than one-tenth the number of Rōsō members the previous year. One year later in 1931, the membership rose to 4,500; in 1932, it increased slightly to 4,721, but fell to 3,970 a year later.[5] Former Rōsō members, as well as Korean members in Zenkyō, continued anti-Sōaikai movements and actions well into the 1930s, and as a result the operations of the Sōaikai diminished considerably. This coincided, however, with the meteoric rise to parliamentary fame of Pak Ch'um-gum, the Sōaikai's outspoken vice president. In 1932, Pak Ch'um-gum—a former day worker and ginseng peddler turned commercial entrepreneur and co-founder of the Sōaikai—was elected into the Lower House of the National Diet, becoming the first Korean and colonial subject in Japan to hold a parliamentary position. Precisely when Korean workers in Japan lost their most representative and radical labor union, Rōsō, Pak Ch'um-gum emerged as a parliamentary representative of all Koreans throughout the Japanese Empire.

What is the historical significance of this muddy, bloody, and infamous history of the Sōaikai, this history of Korean-on-Korean violence in Japan, of Koreans exploiting fellow Koreans—and this brief history of Korean parliamentary fame during the Japanese colonial period? Clearly, it is a history that compels us to move well beyond cut-and-dry oppositions between state power and the marginalized, colonial minority. As Žižek points out, the issue today is not simply that state power dominates the marginals, or even that state power partitions the social body by managing those marginals who, while having an economic part in the capitalist commodity economy, have no part in the wider social or political sphere. Rather, attention needs to be drawn to how state power itself is divided internally and along lines that reveal a public face and a disavowed, shadowy, obscene, violent, and supplementary force, one that operates in clandestine ways. What is at stake in analyzing this splitting of state power is the conceptual stability of the binary opposition of state and civil society. In the case of Japan, what many have called Taishō democracy of the 1920s—the heyday of a party politics that claimed to maintain a clear separation between state and civil society—has to be considered, therefore, strictly as an ideological fiction.

In this chapter, therefore, I look at two interrelated problems. First, in looking at the history of the Sōaikai, I show how the police force in post–First World War Japan was reorganized under the slogan, "the massification of the police, and the policification of the masses" (警察の民主化と民主の警察化). This slogan was realized concretely in extending police work to welfare organizations, and was part of a larger strategy of implementing what the Japanese police called preventive policing, or yobō keisatsu. I argue that the notion of the preventive police effectively calls the line between state and civil society into question. Second, however, the history of the Sōaikai reveals that the real significance of this splitting of state power is that it is inextricably bound to a certain public figuration—even idealization—of the ethnic colonial minority called the Korean. This ethnic figuration strove to achieve two things. On the one hand, it worked to displace the reality of class struggles from public consciousness and awareness, even—especially—while the agents of this ethnic figuration were involved in violent class warfare all along. An ideological notion of society and the nation then replaced any thinking of class struggle as a lived experience of everyday life. On the other hand, the ethnic figuration worked to disavow the fact that there never was a coherent ethnic minority, present to itself, to begin with. The figure of the Korean, while criminalizing discursively all Koreans in Japan, thus came to replace any thinking of internal divisions that were tearing Korean populations in Japan apart in economically exploitative and violent ways.

The "Massification of the Police and the Policification of the Masses"

The proper historical background to the work of the Sōaikai exists less in colonial policy per se and more within the larger transformations of the police system of Japan after 1917. Historians of the modern Japanese police system, such as Obinata Sumiō, have shown how the proliferation of mass political and social movements during the years immediately following the end of the First World War compelled a radical reorganization and reconceptualization of the police system in Japan.[6] While the Hibiya Park demonstrations of 1905 and the anti-train fare demonstrations of 1906 alarmed the police in Japan, the real catalysts of police reorganization came in late 1917, with police concerns and fears over the dissemination of Bolshevik thought and practice in Japan. These concerns were further exacerbated by the three subsequent developments: the Rice Riots of 1918; the 1919 Korean independence movements and their proliferating movements within Japan, China, and the United States; and lastly the so-called 1920 reactionary crisis (handō kyōkō), which ended the manufacturing boom of the war years, leading to mass unemployment on an historically unprecedented scale and depth.[7]

The police system was reorganized under the banner of defending what was called society and the nation. As a result, what were variously called "social problems" (shakai mondai), "social crimes" (shakaiteki hanzai), "social accidents" (shakai jiko), and "social uprisings" (shakaiteki bōdō) all fell under the scrutiny of police surveillance and action.[8] Policing became synonymous with maintaining order to better defend and maintain the "peace and order of society" (shakai no annei to jitsujō), as well as to better execute "social purification" (shakai kakusei).[9] Matsui Shigeru, author of several influential treatises on the Japanese police system and one of the most famous police architects of the interwar period, thus argued that the "Era of the Police State" (keisatsu kokka jidai), originally established during the Meiji period, was over, and that a new era of the "national" or "people's police" (kokumin kei-satsu) was needed to take into account a new standard to "defend society."[10] The older era of the police state was based on what Matsui called a "vertical relationship" (tate no kankei) of individual obedience to the government and the police that had since outlived its original raison d'etre. No longer capable of "accounting for the conditions of society," and "failing to establish a horizontal relationship [yoko no kankei] between the government and the people [kokumin]," the older police state was said to be in need of "adjusting [the] vertical and horizontal relationship" to account for the ways in which the "actual conditions of society [were] shifting from the standard of the individual [kojin hon'i] to the standard of society [shakai hon'i], from the consciousness of [individual] rights [kenri] to [social] obligation [gimu]."[11] While the police increasingly were compelled by the constitution to expend their energies protecting the rights of individuals, "the demand today is for the police to focus on society itself, and for individuals to sacrifice their individual rights and their notion of individual obligation for the profit of society [shakai kōeki]."[12] The reorganization of the police during the years immediately following the First World War thus abandoned the notion of the police state and instead followed the banner of the national police, which was said to operate in the name of defending society.

The urgent question, then, was how the new national police should be reorganized into a more horizontal relationship with the masses. For this to succeed, police leaders such as Matsui Shigeru and Maruyama Tsurukichi argued that a double transformation needed to take place that involved a massification of the police (keisatsu no minshūka, or 警察の民衆化) and a policification of the masses (minshū no keisatsuka, or 民衆の警察化). Keisatsu no minshūka to Minshū no keisatsuka was the ubiquitous new police slogan, reiterated across various police treatises, books, and journals such as Keimu Ihō, Keisatsu Geppō, and Keimu Geppō between 1919 and 1925. No longer could the national police exist above the masses in a vertical relationship of separation demanding absolute obedience from the masses; it had to become—as the title of one of Maruyama's books attests—a kind and magnanimous police (yasashii keisatsu), one that existed within the very fabric of the everyday life of the masses. Maruyama wrote that it is not enough "to receive understanding from the masses; the police must take a more active stance towards penetrating into the lives of the masses, to create one harmonious body with the masses."[13] Matsui Shigeru also elaborated on the notion of the "transformation of the police into the masses" in the preface to his book, *Keisatsu Dokuhon* (Police Reader), of 1933. He writes:

> For the maintenance of domestic peace and order, it is crucial that the everyday life of everyone in Japan is never neglected. In addressing red movements, elections, as well as public decency, factories, businesses, fires and disease, the mission of the police administration today must become one with, and never exist apart from, the everyday life of the masses.[14]

In the police journal *Keimu Ihō*, police bureaucrat Tanaka Takeo wrote that the transformation of the masses into the police makes "the entire national body an indirect supplement to the police" [*kokumin zentai wa mina kansetsu ni keisatsu no hojosha de aru*].[15] In Maruyama's words, the masses needed "to be awakened to police themselves,"[16] theoretically leading to the possibility of eradicating the police force. "The social condition in which the police no longer exists," Maruyama wrote, "is the final and ultimate goal of the police itself."[17] Imagining the potential of a society in which the police and the masses fused into one body, Maruyama composed a verse of poetry, which he published in the *Keimu Ihō*:

> Constant vision without form;
> Listening without a voice . . .
> Becoming invisible and silent,
> And from this invisibility and silence,
> Discovering the slightest disturbance of the peace.[18]

The concrete method for realizing the notion of the policification of the masses, and the massification of the police was to establish a police force supplementary to the existing juridical police. Similar to nineteenth-century London and post–First World War New York City, this supplementary police force in Japan engaged in what was called preventive policing. The term preventive police can be traced back to an 1829 essay penned by Edwin Chadwick, an energetic critic of the English Poor Laws and close friend of Jeremy Bentham and John Stuart Mill. The basic idea of Chadwick's concept of the preventive police was that the regular (i.e., juridical) police force would produce enough public knowledge of criminal activity so that "the public at large [would] be converted into a police," and so that "each individual member, by being put on his guard, would perform unconsciously a great portion of the duties of a police officer."[19] In Japan, however, the concept of the preventive police was introduced to the Japanese police in 1917, after high-ranking Japanese police bureaucrats, notably Maruyama Tsurukichi, toured New York City and learned of the concept from Arthur Woods, then commissioner of the New York Police Department. Woods had significantly reorganized the NYPD during the First World War by implementing a social welfare section as part of the police's everyday bureaucracy, and was renowned for his lectures on preventive polic- ing, which he defined as a broadening of police functions to include citizens, especially women, and in particular social work organizations. The broaden- ing of police functions could, he claimed, preempt the outbreak of criminal activity originating in what were deemed "probable" sources of crime among the poor populations, especially in New York City's East End.[20]

In its manifestation in Japan, preventive policing was carried out between two centers of action. First, it included various volunteer groups, youth groups, and what was called giyū keisatsu, literally brave and courageous police, but also an administrative term for voluntary police.[21] The other center of preven- tive policing action comprised social work and welfare organizations. Having learned from Woods in New York, Maruyama Tsurukichi returned to Japan, worked briefly as director of the relief and protection section (kyūgo kachō) in the ministry of the interior, and was then dispatched to the government- general in Korea, where he became the chief of personnel in 1919, the year of the Korean independence movement. Between 1918 and 1919, Maruyama published two lectures on the relationship between the police and social wel- fare organizations, specifying the relationship as one of a "shared control of populations in need, and who tend to commit crimes."[22] The success of the new yobō keisatsu or preventive police, he argued, would depend largely on the extent to which the police could become "one body" with these organi- zations, and on the degree to which the two entities could maintain "close communication,"[23] "eliminate accidents before they throw the social order into chaos, and prevent crimes, even before they break out into the open."[24] Deploying a forensic-entomological metaphor, Maruyama represented the outbreak of crimes as the proliferation of mosquitoes. He contended that the preventive police needed to eliminate not the mosquitoes, but rather, in a "positive and active way," the "stagnant waters" from which the mosquitoes endlessly reproduced. The vast numbers of so-called mosquitoes, he stated, had overwhelmed the juridical police to such a degree that they could only react to crimes, in a "negative and passive way."[25]

Here, a few points bear emphasis. First, the preventive police force was part of the larger movement of reorganizing the police system in Japan. It was a concrete, institutional effect of the massification of the police, and the policification of the masses. In this way, the preventive police were irreducible to either the state police or the masses dwelling in so-called civil society. Rather, it embodied the difference in the binary opposition of the state and civil society; in itself, it was rather neither and both simultaneously. As I will discuss below, however, it was precisely this ambiguous status that allowed for organizations such as the Sōaikai to function as a disavowed police supplement, a disavowal that allowed for the ideological maintenance of this binary opposition itself. Second, the notion of the preventive police has to be understood in terms of an inherent and endemic weakness on the part of the juridical police, a weakness that emerged in reaction to the growing popularity of Bolshevism among the working classes and in response to the deepening of class contradictions and social crisis in Japan after the First World War. This weakness formed the impetus to extend police functions, beyond the boundary of the juridical police, to the masses themselves.[26] Lastly, in none of the writings on the preventive police was there ever a discussion of how the notion of prevention could itself be prevented from unfolding into a notion of preemption. As we will see shortly in the Sōaikai's various activities, there was a clear turn from prevention to violent preemption in 1925, a turn that disclosed ambiguities in the notion of policing authority itself and that revealed a suspension of the difference between constituting law and constituted law—i.e., a moment of what Walter Benjamin called the "ignominy" of police violence in the state of exception.[27] Roughly between 1925 and 1932, the Sōaikai revealed precisely this kind of ignominy, and it was precisely this ignominy that was publicly disavowed by the Sōaikai's co-founder and vice president, Pak Ch'um-gum, once he was elected into the National Diet.

The Sōaikai as Preventive Police

Three years after the Korea independence movement and after the colonial government changed its policy of military rule to cultural rule, Maruyama Tsurukichi worked as a director in the government-general's personnel office in Seoul. He lectured widely on the necessity of close communication between the police and welfare organizations, specifically to document and learn how, in the aftermath of the military suppression of the violent social movements demanding colonial independence, Korean populations "have abandoned the idea of immediate liberation through violence," and "have resorted to the promotion of education, Korean culture and ethnic identity as way to realize Independence gradually."[28]

Koreans now plan for Independence in the future, as a future goal, as part of a larger cultural movement, if not for their children, then for the grandchildren. . . . They have turned to education as the basis for promoting Korean culture . . . but have never lost sight of their original goal of Independence. . . . This is their fundamental tactic regarding education, and it should be stopped and eradicated completely."[29]

Maruyama's concern was two-fold. On the one hand, he argued that military repression would no longer be adequate to account for the social reality of the immediate post-independence movement, namely, that while "peace and order" has been achieved through military suppression, "the thought of Koreans is actually worsening, despite the appearance of peace."[30] In compliance with the shift in colonial rule from military rule to cultural rule, Maruyama acknowledged that "it's impossible to simply erase the ethnic spirit of the Korean masses"; that the state should even consider electing Koreans to parliamentary positions as a means of "conciliation" (kaijū); and that "limited support of minzoku movements is inevitable." This was qualified, however, with the statement that the "police must always ensure that the minzoku movements do not develop into a unified movement."[31] Put differently, colonial governance would only consider supporting minzoku movements so long as they were divided and fragmented. But how could this division and fragmentation be secured, especially in the face of the dissemination of so-called red thought and communism among Koreans and Korean youth in particular? In Maruyama's eyes, this immanent possibility could only exacerbate the original goal of the Koreans of "realizing colonial independence through violence if necessary, even if they disavow the use of violent means."[32] It was this last potential that drove Maruyama to assert the necessity of keeping in reserve the repressive power of the police and military in Korea while simultaneously extending preventive policing through the work of what were called Japanese-Korean harmony programs (naisen yūwa jigyō), also known as "social welfare organizations specializing in Koreans" (chōsenjin senmon shakai jigyō). "Japanese–Korean Harmony [organizations]," Maruyama writes, "form a foundation for the mutual understanding and agreement between the police and the masses. . . . The practices of the [juridical] police will encounter great difficulties in executing its goals without them."[33]

More concretely, as chief of police in Korea, Maruyama secured over 300,000 yen in funds from various sources, including the government-general, the home ministry police bureau, the army, Mitsubishi, and Mitsui, and donated these funds to two Koreans, Yi Ki-dong and Pak Ch'um-gum, who had just established a Korean welfare organization in Tokyo called the Mutual Love Society, or Sōaikai.[34] This was in 1921, barely two years after the outbreak of the Korean independence movements and less than a year after the economic crisis of 1920.[35] With this initial infusion of government funding, the Sōaikai was able to expand beyond its original headquarters in Tokyo to other prefectures in Japan. Over the next two years, the Sōaikai established six branch offices in Nagoya (May 12, 1923); an Osaka branch (May 15, 1923) with headquarters established in Mishima (August 11, 1923) and Izumi (September 23, 1923); Shizuoka prefecture headquarters in Hamamatsu (March 5, 1924); Yamanashi prefecture headquarters in Kōfu City (April 10, 1924);[36] and, in Korea, a headquarters in Pusan (April, 1924) and three branches in Seoul.[37] Then, in 1928, with the support of Maruyama Tsurukichi, the Sōaikai became an official foundation (zaidan hōjin) and received additional funds; and in 1929, the Sōaikai was enlisted, again by Maruyama, as a private social work organization (shisetsu shakai jigyō) in the National Federation of Private Social Work Organizations (Zen Nippon Shisetsu Shakai Jigyō Renmei). By 1929, the Sōaikai boasted a membership of over 16,000 and a net worth of over 420,000 yen. These extensive funds served to support Sōaikai labor exchange facilities for Korean day workers, Sōaikai housing facilities, Sōaikai medical clinics for Korean workers and their families, as well as Sōaikai cultural events, which I will discuss briefly below.

Yet, despite the clear funding for Sōaikai institutional practices, the general status of the Sōaiaki was extremely ambiguous. Financially supported by public institutions such as the government-general, the metropolitan police, and the Bank of Korea, the Sōaikai publicly appeared nonetheless on the nation's largest list of private social work organizations. The ambiguous existence of the Sōaikai, an existence that calls into question any a priori binary opposition between the public and private spheres, was not unknown to the members of the National Federation of Private Social Work Organizations. If anything, it was too well known, and there were ongoing debates on the topic in journals like Shakai Fukuri, or Social Welfare. For example, a roundtable discussion in 1939 among federation leaders, including a Korean listed only as Kim, tried in vain to define the criteria and meaning of the term private social work organization.[38] The discussion focused on the following basic question: If private social work organizations have no other choice but to rely on state subsidies for their existence, how can they be called private social work organizations? Some members, like Mr. Kim, argued that private social work organizations were private, but only "formally" (keishikiteki) and not "in substance" (jittaiteki). Others disagreed, claiming that the criteria of this "formal" quality were ambiguous and probably no different than what constituted "substance." This then justified claims made by others that, ultimately, perhaps there was no real difference between private and public social work organizations. This point only provoked further voices of dissension, however, and nothing was conclusively agreed upon. The members only agreed on three points, namely that the object (taishō) of social work organizations—whether private, public, neither or both—was the relief (kyūsai) and guidance (shidō) of the "propertyless classes" (musansha kaikyū)[39]; that social work organizations must rely on state funding to a certain extent; and that these organizations must "be an ally of the capitalist class" (shakai jigyō wa shihonka kaikyū no mikata de aru).[40]

What begs emphasis here is the extent to which private welfare organizations were understood to function in the service of the capitalist class and in ways that reveal the ambiguities of the binary opposition between state and civil society. With the institutionalization of concepts such as the preventive police and private social welfare organizations, state power no longer could be defined or conceptualized in terms of discrete and unified state apparatuses standing in opposition to, and separate from, the masses dwelling in civil society. This is what confounded the round table discussants on private welfare organizations mentioned above, for they still operated with the assumption of a clear separation and opposition between state and civil society. What they unwittingly put a finger on, however, was the very blurring of this opposition as a new kind of institutional force, one that was based on networks of power that did not exist apart from the masses. Without using these words, the round table discussants essentially discovered a model of state power that deconstructed the base-superstructure and state/civil society paradigm. The Sōaikai—classified as a private social welfare organization, a preventive police organization, and a social work organization specializing in Koreans—was nothing short of an institutional embodiment of the difference that went beyond the binary opposition of state and civil society.

Controlling and Commodifying Surplus Populations through Mutual Love

That the Sōaikai was neither public nor private and both simultaneously is closely related to the institutional pervasiveness of the Sōaikai. This was particularly clear in the way the Sōaikai commodified, disciplined, and managed

Korean surplus populations in Japanese labor markets. Writing in July 1929 shortly after the Kawasaki incident, Kim Tu-yong published an article in the journal *Senki*, denouncing the violence of the Sōaikai. He urged his readers to understand the history and specificities of the Sōaikai's operations and management beyond the immediate grounds of the Kawasaki attack, and to identify its leadership and management as a gang of "rich sub-contractors" working for various public works construction contractors, the Japanese government, and the police.[41] Kim addresses and questions how the Sōaikai, in addition to relying on brute force and violence to recruit new members, gained such momentum and power:

> Why does the Sōaikai have so many members? Let's imagine an unem-
> ployed worker who's just arrived in Japan from Pusan [Korea]. . . . He has
> to find work as soon as possible, but he has no technical skills to speak
> of, and hardly speaks a word of Japanese. So first he goes to the [City or
> Ward] Labor Exchange Office—but he's told to go to the Sōaikai's internal
> labor exchange office instead. If he becomes homeless, the police will tell
> him to go to the Sōaikai, and when, as is often the case, a Korean man sells
> candy on the streets to make ends meet, the police will tell him to stop his
> business and introduce him to the Sōaikai, where he will be surrounded
> by the thought of, and teachings on, "Japanese–Korean Harmony" [*naisen
> yūwa shisō*]. In particular, if he wants to work as a general construction
> worker, or find day work hauling carts or digging in gravel pits, he's told
> by crew bosses or foremen to go to the Sōaikai. To get work through the
> Sōaikai, however, requires that he become a Sōaikai member. . . . All of
> this, of course, in the name of "Japanese–Korean Unity and Amity" [*naisen
> yūgō*].[42]

Kim's depiction of the Sōaikai brings into focus an inter-institutional network that connected the Sōaikai to day labor sub-contractors, public labor exchange offices, and the police. Similar to most social welfare organizations and insti-tutions in Japan, the establishment of the Sōaikai was part of a general de-velopment of social welfare programs in the years of recession that followed in the wake of the manufacturing boom of the First World War. In 1918, the district committee system (*hōmen i'inkai seidō*) was established along with large research institutes into poverty and welfare, such as the Research In-stitute for Poverty Relief (*Kyūsai jigyō chōsakai*) and the Social Welfare Survey Association (*Shakai jigyō chōsakai*). Both of these research institutes pushed for institutional shifts away from older models of welfare based on charity programs (*jizen jigyō*) and toward social welfare (*shakai jigyō*). This shift toward social welfare was further reflected in 1920 with the establishment of the home ministry's new social bureau (*shakai kyoku*), which produced countless surveys and statistics on unemployed and impoverished individuals in need of state-led protection (*hogo*) and relief (*kyūsai*). Moreover, in 1921, the first Labor Exchange Law was passed in Japan, establishing public labor exchange offices across Japan for the purpose of placing unemployed workers with jobs. The establishment of the Sōaikai in December 1921 in Tokyo cannot be understood outside of this wider institutionalization of labor exchanges.

With generous funding from the government-general, the metropolitan police in Tokyo, the Bank of Chōsen, Mitsubishi, and Mitsui, the Sōaikai had its own labor exchange office and worker dormitory facilities, and was considered, in the words of Maruyama Tsurukichi, a "titan of a welfare organization for Koreans." This is to say that the Sōaikai represented a welfare organization for Koreans only, one that functioned outside of, but parallel to, the newly instituted system of labor exchange offices that were managed by city government bureaus under the supervision of the Home Ministry. Another Korean-only welfare organization, the *Naisen Kyōwakai*, headquartered in Osaka and established in 1924, would function in a similar way. Thus, the Sōaikai functioned, first of all, to separate out Korean unemployed workers from Japanese unemployed workers, channeling the former away from city managed labor exchange offices and into the labor exchange offices within so-called Korean welfare organizations. This trend to establish independently managed, Korean welfare organizations found many supporters among the highest ranking city bureaucrats, not only Maruyama Tsurukichi of the Tokyo metropolitan police, but also Hiraga Shu of the Osaka prefectural government, and Sakai Toshio of the Osaka metropolitan government. Each separately argued that the institutionalization of Korean-only welfare organizations, outside of the wider labor exchange system, was necessary, not only to provide relief (*kyūsai*) to impoverished Koreans, but also, in Sakai's words, "to ensure that unemployed Korean workers do not take away jobs from unemployed Japanese workers" through the public labor exchange system, and specifically through the labor exchange offices under the Unemployment Emergency Relief Programs, established in the winter of 1925 in the six major cities.[43]

It also has to be said, however, that the Sōaikai and the Naisen Kyōwakai were only the most publicly well-known Korean welfare organizations.

TABLE 22. Total Assets of Osaka Sōaikai and Naisen Kyōwakai, 1925–1933

Year	Sōaikai	Naisen Kyōwakai
1925	33,000 (yen)	NA (yen)
1926	198,674	200,000
1927	NA	NA
1928	351,640	15,450
1929	326,944	349,912
1930	334,243	259,312
1931	422,799	259,312
1932	422,799	206,762
1933	422,799	209,161

Sources: Sōaikai figures taken from Tokyo-fu, "Tokyo-fu Tōkeisho," 1925–33; Naisen Kyōwakai figures are from Osaka-fu, Osaka-fu Tōkeisho, 1925–33.

Beginning in the early 1920s, hundreds of other independently managed, grass-roots Korean organizations provided informal labor exchanges and housing to poor Koreans in the face of a striking lack of public funding for unemployed Korean workers in Japan. In 1928, the home ministry counted 59 "social welfare organizations with the purpose of providing protection to Koreans residing in Japan," all with membership over 1,000, 57 percent of which were established between 1924 and 1926.[44] By 1931, there were over 450 different Korean organizations categorized by the home ministry under the names of Korean self-help, friendship societies (shinbokkai), or social welfare, and combined these had more 65,000 Korean members. The majority of these organizations (67 percent) had 100 or fewer members; 2.2 percent had membership between 500 and 1,000; and only 1.8 percent had a membership of over 1,000.[45] The Sōaikai was part of this 1.8 percent and was by far the largest organization of them all, followed by the Naisen Kyōwakai in Osaka. What separated these two organizations from other Korean welfare organizations in Japan was the fact that both received state funding to cover expenses to construct labor exchange offices, worker dormitories, and health clinics, as well as night schools for Japanese language instruction (table 22). These two organizations also had in common the political support of Maruyama Tsurukichi, one of the architects of post-war preventive policing in Japan.[46] But whereas the Naisen Kyōwakai was managed directly by the

Osaka prefectural government, making it a government agency, the Sōaikai was not directly affiliated with any prefectural or city government. Despite receiving over 300,000 yen at its inception in 1921 from various government sources, it was never enrolled as a state agency per se. In short, the Sōaikai's institutional status was extremely ambiguous: financially supported by public institutions such as the government-general and the metropolitan police, as well as the Bank of Korea, the Sōaikai publicly appeared nonetheless on the nation's largest list of private social work organizations.

The Sōaikai as Labor Supplier in the Day Labor Market

Existing under the banners of Japanese–Korean harmony and mutual love, the Sōaikai was essentially a highly organized supplier of cheap and temporary Korean labor. Supported, promoted, and utilized by the police, the UERP, and city governments as an institutionalized labor broker (rōdō burōkā) in the day labor market, the Sōaikai made its profits by mediating labor exchanges between Japanese public works sub-contractors and factory foremen in need of temporary and cheap labor, on the one hand, and masses of chronically unemployed Korean workers in the major cities of Japan, on the other. Almost from its establishment in 1921, the Sōaikai maintained a monopoly over Korean day labor in Tokyo. According to Sōaikai statistics from 1922 and the first 4 months of 1923, out of a total of 10,878 Koreans living in Tokyo in 1922, 84 percent or 9,096 Koreans obtained work through the Sōaikai's labor exchange office. Out of the 9,096 finding work through the Sōaikai, 45 percent worked on public works construction sites performing manual labor, 30 percent in commercial and miscellaneous jobs, and 24 percent in small factories. From January to April 1923, this trend continued virtually unchanged, with 80 percent of Koreans employed through the Sōaikai.[47]

The Great Kanto Earthquake, which shook the cities of Tokyo and Yokohama to the ground, and the subsequent Tokyo reconstruction plan, which lasted from 1923 to 1927, further solidified the position of the Sōaikai as a day labor supplier. The earthquake, as is well known, not only burned down much of Tokyo and Yokohama, but also led to the massacre of over 6,000 Koreans, rumored to be vandalizing and rioting in the chaos of the quake's aftermath. Amidst the blood and the ashes of early September 1923, the Sōaikai was first called upon by the police and the army to prevent Koreans from fleeing the burning city by forcibly housing them in newly constructed Sōaikai worker dormitories and barracks in the northeastern part of the city, in Honjo ward. Maruyama Tsurukichi, then the chief of the Tokyo police department, directly ordered Pak Ch'um-gum, the vice president and co-founder of the Sōaikai, to transform these dorms into what he called *shūyūjō*—a term that variously signified a home, camp, asylum, as well as prison—in order to both protect Koreans from further massacres at the hands of vigilante organizations and prevent them from leaving the city and spreading the news of the massacre.[48]

In the following weeks, however, the department of civil engineering, the police, and the army steadily recruited the Sōaikai to provide Korean day workers to begin the daunting task of reconstructing the city. The Japanese army was the first to use Korean workers for various social services after the earthquake, mobilizing 4,000 Koreans in Tokyo, all under Sōaikai supervision, for the purposes of general clean-up and the construction of make-shift barracks.[49] Sōaikai vice president Pak was quick to answer the call, believing that Sōaikai-led work in the city would promote and popularize the organization. Pak and the Sōaikai also immediately began organizing Korean workers, mostly in groups of thirty to forty, to work on construction sites for two months—and without pay.[50] A newspaper headline read: "To Eliminate Japanese Suspicions: Sōaikai Members Clean Streets of Tokyo Without Pay for Two Months."[51] Pak was quoted as saying, "Because there are currently no manifest signs of Korean sincerity [*senjin no seii*], the best way to counter this trend is by providing social services [*shakai hōshi*]."[52] Speaking on behalf of these public works construction sub-contractors, one police bureau representative readily recognized that "now, if Korean workers decide to move into manual labor work for good, there will always be work for them, and they will always be able to make a living from that work."[53]

Two months of unpaid labor for Korean workers paid off for the Sōaikai. In late 1923, Pak Ch'um-gum himself proudly stated:

> Before the earthquake, Japanese wouldn't use the workers [the Sōaikai] sent to construction sites. . . . But now that they're finally being used, feelings between Japanese and Koreans have become much more harmonious. . . . Little interest was given to Koreans workers before, but now employers have taken considerable interest in them. Employers have opened their eyes, and this is a wonderful thing.[54]

By 1924, the reconstruction department of the Tokyo government had enlisted the Sōaikai as a sub-contractor (*ukeyoin gyōsha*), and consistently gave Pak and the Sōaikai some of the largest contracts, typically requiring no fewer than 500 day workers per construction site.[55] Investments and donations from the government-general, the police, the army, and other private corporations poured into Sōaikai coffers, and by late 1924, the Sōaikai had been able to establish branches nationwide, including branches and headquarters in Pusan and Seoul. And while the most profitable times for the Sōaikai came during the reconstruction, even after the completion of the reconstruction in 1927, the Sōaikai still maintained and extended its influence over Korean day workers, most notably in Tokyo, but also in the cities of Nagoya, Shizuoka, Yamanashi, Fukuoka, and Osaka.[56]

The Sōaikai Milieu of Commodification and Intermediary Exploitation

The institutional mechanics of the Sōaikai functioned around three primary areas of financial investment: worker dormitories (shukuhakujō), labor exchange offices (shokugyō shōkaijō), and medical clinics (table 23). Each arm had its own separate functions, but all three worked in a combined way to form a specific milieu of commodifying and exploiting the labor power of Korean surplus populations in the day labor markets in Japanese cities.

The biggest investments, which were at the center of Sōaikai operations, were the worker dormitories. By 1925 in Tokyo, 63,900 yen had been invested in Sōaikai dormitories for Korean workers, an amount far larger than investments in similar dormitories managed by Japanese welfare or charity organizations in Tokyo.[57] The construction of such large housing facilities was justified by the Sōaikai as a means to provide much-needed shelter for Korean tenant-workers facing racist Japanese landlords who either refused to lease to Koreans, or who evicted Korean tenants, casting hundreds and even thousands into a state of homeless limbo (see chapter 5). The Sōaikai thus justified and promoted its dormitories, not only as a sign of so-called mutual love for impoverished and often homeless Koreans, but also as a place of moral reform for Korean workers, a place to cultivate Japanese lifestyles (seikatsu) that would not disrupt Japanese–Korean harmony. As a 1929 Sōaikai pamphlet states:

> As the result of unsympathetic landlords refusing to rent to Koreans, entire Korean families and countless Koreans wasting away on the streets have not found a place to live. Especially with regard to homeless Koreans, their condition is such that if they are left to a life on the streets, they will inevitably fall into misery and endless sorrow, resulting in linguistic and

TABLE 23. Sōaikai Expenses in Tokyo, 1925–1934

Year	Labor exchange	Worker dormitories	Medical clinics
1925	NA	63,900	NA
1926	522	134,488	1,397
1927	NA	NA	NA
1928	NA	49,467	420
1929	40,964	40,964	7,216
1930	40,964	63,460	12,271
1931	40,964	42,273	12,602
1932	40,964	42,273	12,602
1933	40,964	42,273	NA
1934	NA	NA	NA

Source: Tokyo-fu, "Tokyo-fu Tōkeisho," 1925–36.

cultural misunderstandings which are sure to disrupt Japanese–Korean Harmony . . . Most alarmingly, they will fall into a nomadic and wandering lifestyle [furyō seikatsu] which will certainly deteriorate their thoughts and worsen their spirits. Sōaikai worker dormitories have thus been constructed in order to provide relief and a reformed lifestyle for these men, that is, to train them into a Japanese lifestyle.[58]

What was meant by the term Japanese lifestyle was primarily a matter of gaining a certain level of fluency in the Japanese language, an accomplishment the Sōaikai stated was "indispensable for everyday life in Japan," and that would promote the "cultivation of common sense" (jōshiki kan'yō), "spiritual discipline" (seishin shūyō), and "ethical character" (hinsei). Thus, within the housing facilities, Sōaikai housing held night classes for its workers in conversational Japanese, in addition to elementary mathematics and written Korean.[59] It is more likely, however, that Japanese, Korean, and basic mathematics were taught to Korean workers to facilitate and expedite work-related matters on day labor jobs involving Japanese factory bosses or subcontractors, as well as Korean labor brokers and kumigashira, or day labor crew bosses.[60] What the Sōaikai called its educational programs were carried out primarily to prevent any unnecessary disruptions or misunderstandings on work sites, especially when these sites involved dangerous machinery, toxic chemicals, or explosives (e.g., dynamite on tunnel construction sites). In this sense, education through Sōaikai housing was part of a wider, more general effort to maximize worker efficiency on jobs and to reproduce and maintain smooth social relations of production that top Sōaikai representatives mediated in the day labor market.

Every housing facility was divided into large sections, supervised and managed by a *shukuhaku shitsuchō* or housing manager, and several *kumichō*, or group leaders. The housing director, who was permitted to dwell in the Sōaikai dormitories free of charge, had the general job of "ensuring that all the rules pertaining to hygiene, discipline and public morals [*fūki*] were obeyed."[61] His job was also to relay information about employment openings found through the Sōaikai labor exchange offices. This information, however, was not relayed directly to the worker-tenants, but rather to the *kumichō* or group leader.[62] More than the housing director, the kumichō was in constant and direct contact with the Koreans under his command. His basic function was to see that his group was properly registered with the Sōaikai, to gather information about them, to inform his group about daily employment opportunities passed down from the shukuhaku shitsuchō, and most importantly, to escort and supervise Korean workers in groups of ten or fewer on work sites.

Workers staying in Sōaikai dormitories therefore could not go directly to the labor exchange offices for work. Rather, the kumichō would learn of daily jobs for the group of workers he supervised from the housing manager, who had direct connections to the labor exchange office. The labor exchange office dispatched Sōaikai labor brokers all over the city, visiting public works sub-contractors and factory foremen on a daily basis to see if temporary day laborers were needed, and if so, how many. These visitations were usually carried out early in the morning or late in the evening, when work crews had not begun or had already finished their work. From 1921 onward, for example, twenty-three full-time Sōaikai employees, including Sōaikai vice president Pak Ch'um-gum himself, made daily visits to hambagashira or crew bosses on public works sites, factory foremen, and other sub-contractors in and around the city to secure positions for Sōaikai workers.[63] Upon learning how many workers were needed for any particular day, these employees would then return to the Sōaikai labor exchange and contact the shukuhaku shitsuchō and kumichō, both of whom knew, with the most accuracy, how many workers were presently residing in the dorms, and could calculate the precise supply of workers accordingly.[64]

Finally, in their role as overseers and gatherers of knowledge of Sōaikai workers, the shukuhaku shitsuchō and the kumichō also regulated a system of awards and punishments (shōbatsu seidō). Borrowed from the oyakata and hamba systems in the coal mining industry, the shōbatsu system was a practice that promoted worker productivity and efficiency.[65] Awards were given to workers "who displayed exemplary models of benevolence" and "who served the Sōaikai or society in general," while punishments were meted out to "those who corrupt or sully the dignity and respectability of the Sōaikai," and "who violate Sōaikai rules."[66] In a Sōaikai pamphlet, three types of awards and three types of punishment were described, all of which were closely related to the process of obtaining work through the Sōaikai. For awards (shō), the basic award was praise (shōkyō), followed by wage increase (shōkyū), and finally promotion (shōshin), mostly to the level of kumichō. The system of punishments reflected the opposite of the awards: reprimand or rebuke (kenseki), followed by wage decrease (genpō), and finally dismissal from work (menshoku).[67]

The shōbatsu system essentially turned around the problem of wages. In other words, it is impossible to understand Sōaikai worker dormitories or the labor exchange system, without understanding how the Sōaikai managed all of the workers' wages directly. Wages were not paid to individual Sōaikai workers by the factories or construction contractors; rather, as a mediating labor broker in the day labor market, the Sōaikai distributed wages to workers directly. Furthermore, wages were paid out only after a multiplicity of commission fees were subtracted from the formal daily wages, mostly for labor exchange introductions and housing fees.[68] Percentages of formal wages were additionally subtracted for the consumption of everyday necessities. Everyday necessities such as food, clothing, and tobacco were not paid directly by the worker, but were rather advanced to the worker through the Sōaikai's privately operated commissary. The expenses for the goods were then subtracted from their formal wages at the end of month, and often at rates that were double and sometimes triple the market value of the goods. As I have discussed in detail in chapter 3, this practice was pervasive in Japanese coal mines and public works construction work camps, and was not significantly different from the truck system or concession system in the English coal mining industry. The point of this system is that wages were largely paid in the form of everyday necessities, not in money. The Sōaikai called their commission system itaku keiei, a "consignment accounting" plan, and followed this practice not only on its own construction sites, but also within its housing facilities.

In short, the Sōaikai's wage system was consistent with the general practice of what workers called *chūkan sakushu*, or intermediary exploitation. This was a specific wage system, commonly found in the day labor market as well as in the coal mining industry, whereby a multiplicity of fees were subtracted from the formal wages, leaving little, and sometimes nothing left in real wages.[69]

The last aspect of the institutional mechanics of the Sōaikai—what one could call the Sōaikai's operations of biopolitical power—is that it invested in its own private health clinic, offering medical services ranging from general treatment to obstetrics and gynecology.[70] The latter treatments were instituted largely for Korean women, especially in the late 1920s, when the population of both Korean women and children in Japan increased, and when the number of married Korean workers also increased. The Sōaikai was in fact a promoter of creating working class Korean families in Japan, going out of its way to arrange marriages for Korean workers through its "marriage introduction center" (*kekkon baikaijō*).[71] As Yi Ten-jun, a former worker at the Kishiwada cotton factory in Osaka, discloses, however, arranged marriages by the Sōaikai were often a euphemism for an informal business of selling Korean women to the highest bidder. Yi herself was approached by Sōaikai management to marry a Korean man who had offered money to the Sōaikai for the arrangement, but she refused, lying to them that she had already promised to marry a man in Korea. Yet, she speaks of other instances when Korean women were coerced into marrying Korean men under the threat of violence. I quote her at length:

> I saw ghastly things done by the Sōaikai. They weren't simply violent thugs; they were violent thugs working on the side of the companies. Women never stopped crying about the Sōaikai. It's maddening enough that they forced us to give up 50 sen every month from our wages as a "membership fee," but women were also a source of profit [*tane*] for crew bosses. Let me explain. You see, most Korean workers were day workers, mostly single men. So one of these guys would go up to the Sōaikai bosses and say, "Hey, know any available women?" The Sōaikai would then take money from the guy—probably twenty or thirty yen or so—and approach a female worker, always while she was working, too. Then they'd basically force the woman to marry the guy, or they'd make it really difficult for the woman to say no.... If the female worker refused, she risked getting beaten. Actually, we never knew what they'd do to us....

TABLE 24. Day Labor Injuries and Illnesses in Tokyo, November–December 1926

Private Welfare Organizations	Injury	Illness	Total
Sōaikai	31	9	40
Fujimachi	15	5	20
Hamazono Rinjikai	3	11	14
Oshima	3	4	7
Kokuryūkai	0	5	5
Tamahime	3	1	4
Enoyama	5	1	6
Kan'ai	1	2	3
Nichirenshū	1	2	3
Keirenkai	2	0	2
Kyūsegun	1	1	2
Senjū	0	1	1
Uemiya Kyōkai	3	3	6
Other	7	2	9
Total	75	47	122

Source: Tokyo Shiyakusho, "Hiyatoi rōdōsha no shippei shōgai ni kansuru chōsa."

Of course, the company knew what was going on all along. But, you
see, the company couldn't just let all the women go if they got married
because if they did, they'd be short on workers. So they'd tell the women
not to quit even if they got married. Two or three days after a marriage, the
new wife would return to her job—but now she'd wear a tengi hairband
which kept her hair out of her face. This was a sign that she recently married. She'd walk in, we'd see the hairband, and we'd all think silently, "Oh,
look, she got married." I think this was a kind of human trading operation,
you know, selling to the highest bidder. . . . This is why so many women
ran away and escaped from the factories. But since the women were considered an "asset" to the workings of the Sōaikai, those guys would bend
over backwards trying to find the women—and if they caught them, they
gave them a nasty beating.[72]

Thus speaks Yi Ten-jun on marriages at the Sōaikai. What is important
here, however, is not only the violent way heterosexual marriages were a side

business for the Sōaikai, but also the way (forced) marriage reflected a larger concern of the Sōaikai regarding the promotion and stability of Korean working class families. Sōaikai clinics, with their emphasis on obstetrics, gynecology, and child rearing, were inseparable from the way the Sōaikai functioned to reproduce Korean working class families in Japan.

A second reason for consistently investing in these clinics, however, was that Sōaikai workers were typically distributed to some of the most dangerous jobs in the day labor market, often requiring work with explosives on construction sites, with toxic chemicals for sewage systems, or in dangerous gravel pits, and they were frequently injured or ill as a result. For example, as a 1926 Tokyo municipal office survey on the relationship between private welfare organizations and day labor injuries showed, out of 122 injury or illness incidents for day workers, 40 incidents (35 percent) of the total were related to Sōaikai jobs, by far the most numerous among private welfare organizations (table 24). Sōaikai health clinics, therefore, were designed to maintain the health and life of Korean surplus populations, not simply for the sake of their health and welfare, but more fundamentally for the sake of maintaining and ensuring a continual supply of healthy labor power that could be commodified in the day labor market through Sōaikai housing and labor exchange offices.

The Figure of the Korean and the Discourse of Futei Senjin

The institutional work of the Sōaikai was a key nodal point in the Japanese labor markets, through which Korean surplus populations were commonly compelled to pass in order to find erratic and temporary employment. As the quote from Kim Tu-yong expressed, Korean surplus populations did not simply go to the Sōaikai on their own accord, but were rather funneled into the Sōaikai through other institutional and social channels, such as the police, the UERP, and sub-contractors in the public works industry. In thinking about how the Sōaikai commodified the labor power of Korean workers, therefore, it is crucial to understand that the work of the Sōaikai separated Korean surplus populations from their Japanese counterparts, thereby contributing to an ethnic segmentation of the labor markets. This ethnic separation and segmentation was a fundamental social condition for the commodification of Korean labor power.

The problem, however, of separating and segmenting Korean workers from Japanese workers was also accompanied—and ideologically supported—by a figuration of the Korean and by a discourse of the so-called Korean problem. This ideological and discursive production was spearheaded especially by police networks, including preventive police organizations such as the Sōaikai. Indeed, precisely because of the Sōaikai's deep investments in managing Korean workers in Japan, it also became an important—albeit, as we will see, highly contested—point of enunciation for the representation of the Korean in Japan. The figure of the Korean especially revolved around what was called *futei senjin* (不逞鮮人), or the unruly Korean.[73] This was a police discourse that emerged with particular clarity after the Korean Independence Movement, but that increasingly was used to signify radical Korean nationalists, anarchists, and especially Bolsheviks, as an imminent threat to the cohesion and peace of the Japanese nation. The significance of the unruly Korean, however, is that it was deployed in ways that criminalized all Koreans, since, as the police argued, it was difficult to recognize futei senjin, to separate them from Japanese ethnically, and even more difficult to separate futei senjin Koreans from non-futei senjin Koreans. Futei senjin, therefore, became a policing sign that operated less through the identification of Korean lawbreakers, and more through a general misidentification of all Koreans as potential or probable criminals. The figure of the Korean, combined with the sign of the futei senjin, thus allowed the police to target all Koreans in Japan for strict and even violent surveillance, and to carry out and legitimate preventive policing in the name of defending society and the nation from the perceived threat of Koreans as lawbreakers.

The point, however, is that this ethnic figuration of the Korean, of the Korean as a threat to the nation and to society, necessarily implied a representation of Japanese society that was disconnected from the wider process of separating Korean surplus populations from Japanese surplus populations, and unscathed and undivided by class struggles—by either Japanese or Korean working-class movements. Emphasis on Korean ethnicity instead directed attention to what the police called the manifest and "latent" characteristics of Koreans in Japan, a distinction, argued by the police, that was essential for policing not only the visible signs of Korean activities, but also Koreans' supposed inner, secretive, and concealed motivations and schemes. For example, a police report from Nara prefecture in 1940, hysterically titled, "Watch Out, they're here! Futei Senjin!," stated that "Koreans always have an outward appearance, and a concealed, hidden depth. Unless this distinction is recognized, it will be impossible to carry out proper surveillance of Koreans."[74]

This same report also contained another way in which the figuration of the Korean displaced in thought the problem of class struggle. Koreans were represented by the police in ways that promoted what they called "virtuous" Koreans. Here, then, the figure of the Korean did not produce a conception of a homogenized body of Koreans, but rather divided them along a moralizing binary of good and evil. By 1940 this line of thought was already quite established. For example, in a police report from 1922 dealing with recent conditions of Koreans in Japan, police officers were instructed to work closely with certain Koreans deemed "good-natured and virtuous" as a "considerably indirect" method of surveillance over the "hostile emotions, thoughts and antipathies" of radical Koreans. This passage is found in a subsection called "Inspection and Surveillance Methods" (shisatsu torishimari no hōhō):

> It is necessary to monitor the hostile emotions, thoughts and antipathies [hankan, fukai no nen] of these Korean workers . . . through considerably indirect methods [kanari kansetsu shisatsu no hōhō]. This should be done, on the one hand, by tightening police correspondences between the prefectures [in Japan] and the Government General in Korea, and, on the other, by protecting and guiding virtuous and good-natured Koreans [zenryō naru mono ni taishite wa tsutomete kore wo hogo yūdō shi].[75]

The divide-and-conquer strategy implicit in this statement is strongly related to the discourse of protecting (hogo) Koreans. Throughout the 1920s and 1930s the word hogo (保護) was used widely among social welfare institutions to signify practices of providing social and economic relief (kyūsai) to impoverished workers, but in this context the word also carried a semiotic valence that harked back to the years immediately prior to the formal colonialization of Korea, when Japan, having triumphed militarily over Russia between 1904 and 1905, became the protectorate of Korea (hogokuni). The combination of these two uses of hogo increasingly fused into a general policing strategy to place Koreans and Korean workers under constant police surveillance in Japan. This was not done by simply deploying the juridical police force, however, but by extending a police logic and practice of surveillance to social welfare institutions for impoverished Korean workers and, moreover, institutions that could be headed by so-called "virtuous and good Koreans."

It is at this point that the work of the Sōaikai becomes legible, for an important dimension of Sōaikai work was its stated effort "to eradicate" certain populations of Koreans that the Sōaikai variously called thugs (gorotsuki), vagabonds, communists, nationalists, lazy Koreans, professional anti-Japanese Koreans (shokugyōteki hai-nichi senjin), and Koreans who do not show a moderate way of thinking (ontō na shisō). The purpose of this selective targeting was to promote Japanese–Korean harmony and mutual love between Japanese and Koreans, and even to end ethnic discrimination against Koreans in Japan. What was done in the name of ending ethnic discrimination as the ground for Japanese–Korean harmony, however, meant nothing outside of the processes that separated Koreans from Japanese—processes that served to differentiate Korean populations internally to prevent a unified ethnic movement, and ultimately to commodify Korean labor power. What was called Japanese–Korean harmony, moreover, was not to be achieved by addressing the conditions of discrimination, but by eradicating those Korean populations that the Sōaikai criminalized while upholding and disseminating a simplistic image of the pure and innocent Koreans. In 1923, the Sōaikai vice president, Pak Ch'um-gum, enunciated the views of the Sōaikai in the following way:

> Korean workers have wandered into every region of Japan, and their thought has strayed into evil ways. It pains us to think of how they take part in spontaneous acts of violence, curse the Japanese state [literally, to cast a spell over the state], hold grudges against others, plot various crimes . . . and hinder the spirit of the annexation between Japan and Korea.[76]

> That all Koreans are mistakenly considered lazy is the fault of the Korean gorotsuki. These thugs, vagabonds and punks . . . drag down the innocent and pure Koreans [muku senjin], and are known for organizing political groups which threaten factory bosses and foremen. So for the sake of Japanese–Korean relations, they simply must be eradicated and driven out of Japan. If we find any of them, we'll investigate their personal histories, check any criminal records they might have, and give them stern advice. For those who show a resilience to repent, we will contact the government-general or the Pusan police bureau [in Korea] and move to expel these punks and thugs from Japan once and for all.[77]

The confluence of the preventive police and Korean-managed welfare organizations in Japan revealed a concerted political strategy of criminalizing Korean workers selectively and of dividing and conquering Korean worker movements in Japan in the name of the protection, relief, and welfare of Korean workers in Japan. These categories, moreover, often flew under the banner of mutual love, and they made for a discourse that, implicitly and explicitly, critiqued ethnic discrimination against Koreans within Japan. From its institutional inception, the Sōaikai was deeply involved in the criminalization and political repression of those Koreans who resisted the practice of separating out Korean surplus populations from the general working population by forming political alliances outside of the boundaries of Sōaikai work. Sōaikai-led criminalization was not an identification of criminals, but rather a production of knowledge that identified what they considered probable criminals within mass surplus populations as the basis for several interrelated practices: separating Korean workers from Japanese workers, dividing Korean labor movements in Japan, carrying out preemptive violence and political repression on Korean radicals, and, most importantly, commodifying Korean labor power in a smooth and uninterrupted fashion, primarily in the day labor market. Preemptive violence, moreover, was justified publicly by appealing to Japanese–Korean harmony and by producing knowledge of pure and innocent Koreans whose identities would become objects of Sōaikai support, promotion, and idealization. Statements about potential Korean criminals were balanced precariously by a selective production of the ideal Korean in Japan, one whose identity could be produced in order to be valorized positively and supported politically and economically.

This precarious balancing act revealed what could be called the two poles of the Sōaikai. Its negative pole was to criminalize and eliminate Korean class struggles as much as possible by destroying Korean class consciousness, and its positive pole was to idealize and support an ethnic and national consciousness, but only so long as the latter did not threaten to become a unified political consciousness of national liberation or anticolonial struggle. What was called Japanese–Korean harmony was a sign that stood in for an entire series of constant political adjustments that strove to suppress instances of Korean class struggles while promoting a consciousness of Korean ethnic identity and difference, but only up to a certain, critical point. When the latter exceeded this point, and when ethnic consciousness disclosed political struggles for national liberation, Sōaikai violence emerged again as a repressive force. The origins of this precarious, political balancing act, and the violence that accompanied it, can be traced back to the momentous shift in colonial governance in Korea immediately following the 1919 Korean Independence Movement, from so-called military rule (budan seiji) to cultural rule (bunka seiji). At the center of this shift in colonial governance, the government-general overhauled its repressive state apparatuses by reducing (but not eliminating) Japanese military forces in Korea and by implementing a preventive police that could transform the masses into a policing body while garnering more public support for the juridical police. As historian Kan Don-chin has argued, this new combination of police and military power, to which we should add the preventive police, changed the strategy of political repression radically, from a strategy of repressing and targeting Koreans in general to a more selective, discriminating strategy of dividing revolutionary Korean populations from within those populations—in short, a strategy of divide and conquer (bungai tōchi).[78]

The Sōaikai, while operating primarily in Japan and not in Korea, presented a particular form of this general colonial strategy, one that exhibited the negative and positive poles mentioned above. On the one hand, Sōaikai leaders tried to promote, solidify, and elevate their interpretation of Korean identity while also claiming that Koreans were new Japanese (atarashii nipponjin). The Sōaikai did not consider this contradictory; they considered it consistent with Japanese colonial governance after 1919. They would therefore often say that for true Japanese–Korean harmony to exist, Japanese needed to understand the extent to which the Korean ethnos (chōsen minzoku) was different from that of the Japanese in terms of culture, language, customs, and habits, as well as in terms of its long and rich history. Despite their claim that Koreans were new Japanese, they did not suppress notions of Korean identity or difference, but rather promoted them in contradistinction to Japanese for the purpose of harmonizing the relation between Japanese and Koreans. As the Sōaikai leader Pak Ch'um-gum said in a newspaper interview, "The Sōaikai strives exclusively to bridge Japanese and Koreans, and to create harmony between them. Koreans, after all, are new Japanese."[79]

Sōaikai leadership consequently reasoned that creating this bridge required a more robust promotion of "Koreanness." Toward this end, for example, in 1925 the Sōaikai headquarters in Osaka published a two-hundred-page book on the history, economy, and customs of Korea, titled, simply, Chōsen [Korea].[80] As Sōaikai president Yi Ki-dong and other Sōaikai members wrote in the preface, the purpose of the book was to "provide Japanese with an accurate portrait of the conditions of Korea" and to "introduce Japanese to the particular habits and customs of Koreans" in order to advance "Japanese–Korean friendship."[81] In addition to publications such as this, notions of Korean history, customs, culture, and identity were also disseminated in Japan through public cultural events held by the Sōaikai. For example, at the May 1924 opening ceremony of the Sōaikai branch in Nagoya, 1,200 Sōaikai leaders, staff, administrators, and general members (i.e., workers) gathered publicly to speak about the necessity of creating "solidarity among the Korean ethnos," "the need to rely on each other," and even the need for promoting "Korean self-determinism" (Chōsen jiketsu).[82]

The Sōaikai appropriated the Wilsonian discourse of self-determination in order to represent the uniqueness, difference, and identity of Koreans as a unified and undivided ethnos. Solidifying this Korean ethnos, the Sōaikai reasoned, did not weaken but rather strengthened the Japanese Empire:

> We have put our energies into establishing a self help welfare organization [jijūteki hogo kikan] called the Sōaikai. Founded on the spirit of humanistic mutual love [jinrui sōai], co-existence and co-prosperity . . . our mission is to end ethnic discrimination and to promote Japanese–Korean Harmony. Our grand mission, however, is to plan for and promote the spiritual cultivation and economic relief of Korean workers.[83]

This passage, taken from a 1929 Sōaikai pamphlet, deploys the signs of coexistence and co-prosperity, and clearly speaks in the language of Japan's greater East Asian co-prosperity sphere. One of the most important, though often ignored, elements of this imperial language is its insistence on appealing to humanism as a system of imperial reasoning. Moreover, those who invoked this reasoning further strove to justify Japan's imperial project on the basis of a critique of ethnic discrimination so clearly seen and practiced in various forms of European colonialism and imperialism. As the important work of historians Harry Harootunian, Naoki Sakai, and William Haver show in different ways, Japanese fascism and Japanese imperialist expansion and integration did not disclose a detour or derailing of humanism, but rather a reliance on humanist thought.[84] This humanism is traceable to a reasoning that articulated a notion of universal humanity on a presumed basis of irreducible differences between ethnicities and nationalities. Japanese fascism was one possible result of an imperial reasoning that posited irreducible ethnic and national differences as the space through which imperial integration could take place. The presumption of, and insistence on, this difference was the key for envisioning and regulating a multiethnic (or multicultural) empire under the single roof of the Japanese emperor. Rhetorically, it was the emperor's task, therefore, to see that the appearance of these differences be seen without privileging or being partial towards one particularity over another. Thus, the imperial language of humanism deployed the ubiquitous sign of isshi dōjin, or "One Sight, Impartial Benevolence." Isshi dōjin was a key sign through which the appearance of presumed differences of ethnicity and nationality could work harmoniously together for co-existence and co-prosperity.

The Warfare of Welfare: From Prevention to Preemptive Violence

The full extent to which the Sōaikai functioned as a preventive policing organization cannot be appreciated unless we take a brief look into the way the Sōaikai recruited members and challenged Korean workers who refused to become members. The latter trend, moreover, became increasingly common as communist Korean labor unions in Japan, notably Rōsō, widened their field of influence in Japan after 1925. As for recruitment, the Sōaikai was given special permission by the Home Ministry to actively recruit Korean peasants in Korea, even after the government-general and the home ministry collectively agreed to end mass recruitments in Korea after the First World War. While Japanese coal mines, factories, and public works were generally prevented from conducting mass recruitment campaigns for Korean workers in Korea, mass recruitments of peasants were allowed if they became members of the Sōaikai. The Chōson Nippō reported in May 1924, for example, that large groups of Koreans wishing to migrate from Pusan to Japan to work in coal mines could only do so by agreeing to become Sōaikai members.[85]

Frequent trips to Korea for the purpose of recruiting new members, however, often overlapped with trips to Korea for the purpose of settling peasant disputes, often by force. In August 1924, for example, Sōaikai vice president Pak Ch'um-gum and other Sōaikai members crossed the straits to Korea after a Japanese absentee landlord, Tokuda, who lived in Osaka, paid Pak to settle a dispute that Tokuda had been having with Korean peasants in South Cholla province in Korea. More than 8,000 Korean peasants were protesting the state expropriation of over 1,400 chōshō of land on Haido Island (荷衣島), off the southern coast. The peasants had also, since 1923, protested the state sale of the land to Tokuda, who purchased the 1,400 chōshō for the amount of 170,00 yen.[86] By 1924 the peasants had already become tenants on Tokuda's land, and had protested his high interest rates for farm loans and demanded reductions in farming expenses for rice and barley cultivation. In the face of the demands, Tokuda lowered expenses by only 4 percent for rice and 3 percent for barley, which the peasants did not consider enough, leading to another round of protests.[87] It was at this point that Tokuda contacted Pak and the Sōaikai, which had recently began its operations in Osaka in the spring of 1923. On August 8, 1924, Pak and a large group of Sōaikai members were brought in to "quell" the peasants and to "translate the terms of the landlord" to the peasants, while colonial police officers made arrests to protest leaders. An article from the *Keijō Nippō* stated that "because of the Sōaikai's appearance, the peasant strike ended with good prospects for the future."[88]

The interventions by the Sōaikai on Haido Island revealed how the Sōaikai served as a mediating force that displaced and redirected the peasant struggles against the Japanese absentee landlord to struggles against the Sōaikai itself. This pattern of displacing and redirecting peasant and worker struggles and shifting them onto the Sōaikai would be the dominant pattern of Sōaikai strike repressions, especially after the establishment of the Peace Preservation Law of 1925. The Sōaikai, acting as a mediating force to displace the original objects of critique and struggle, intervened in strikes and caused violent fights in response to which the police could subsequently intervene, cite violations of the Peace Preservation Law, and make arrests. Sōaikai violence, made on behalf of landlords, incited counter-violence that paved the way for and legitimated police intervention.

There is no clearer example of this pattern than in the famous Nihon Gakki Kabushikigaisha strike in Hamamatsu city of Shizuoka prefecture, a huge strike lasting from April 26 to August 8, 1926, and led by Nihon Rōdō Kumiai Hyōgikai, the forerunner of Zenkyō. By 1920, Nihon Gakki, a musical instruments factory established in 1897, had lost out to German manufacturers in the international market for musical instruments (especially harmonicas and pianos) and had fired over 60 percent of its labor power, leaving only 351 workers. All of the workers employed at Nihon Gakki were Japanese; none were Korean. By 1925, in the midst of recession, Nihon Gakki again threatened with mass firings and wage cuts.[89] The strikers, protesting against firings and demanding higher wages and wage increases twice a year, had established a vast support network outside the factory, including over 3,000 volunteers, non-union support, and two Korean labor activist supporters from Rōsō, one of whom was a Korean who went by the Japanese name of Tachibana.[90] On May 20, the Sōaikai distributed leaflets around the city of Hamamatsu denouncing Tachibana for participating in the strike. They read:

> Tachibana's actions did not comply with or cherish the principles and spirit of our organization, which we felt needed to be rectified—for

otherwise Japanese would not extend their mutual love towards Koreans. This is our responsibility as Koreans! [Signed,] Japan-Korea Harmony Organization, the Sōaikai.[91]

Rōsō responded with its own flyer:

Regarding the blind violence of the Sōaikai members, we Korean workers do not detest those members. Rather, we detest the rancid black bile that secretly operates behind the scenes of the Sōaikai . . .

Japanese workers! Citizens of Hamamatsu City! Do not confuse all Korean proletarians with the blind actions of the Sōaikai!! Know the truth about the Sōaikai!!

The Sōaikai was established by the Japanese government in the name of 'Japanese–Korean Harmony' . . . and annually receives exorbitant financial subsidies directly from the Home Ministry . . . For what purpose are these massive funds used? We have no idea . . . But what is truly astonishing is that while the Sōaikai organizes violent gangs and thugs, the police authorities not only tacitly but publicly approve of them, even when the Sōaikai carries out illegal operations. . . . Open your eyes! . . . We, Rōsō, demand the eradication of the Sōaikai! Citizens! Do not be led astray by the "Mutual Love" of the Sōaikai! Join us in our fight against the Sōaikai! Support the Nihon Gakki strikers![92]

As Oniwa Shinsuke has documented, the uniqueness of the Nihon Gakki strike lay in the fact that the repression of the strike was not led by the police, but by outside violent gangs (bōryoku-dan). As Oniwa writes, the use of the outside gangs served three simultaneous purposes: (1) to forcefully coerce the strikers to stop striking; (2) to divert the strikers from directly attacking the company, and to create tensions within the strikers in order to make them lose energy; and (3) based on these two points, to bring in the police, après-coup, to make arrests on the grounds the peace had been violated.[93] In this way, as Oniwa writes, "The strike became less a struggle between labor and capital and more a struggle between the strikers and the violent gangs."[94] There were four such gangs, including the Sōaikai, which was contacted and hired by the second son of the company's president.[95] Here, however, Oniwa's important observation, that the violent gangs served to displace the antagonism between labor and capital, has to be supplemented with the additional insight that this displacement was related fundamentally to the ideological figuration, by the Korean-led and police-backed Sōaikai, of the unruly Korean.

4. Anti-Sōaikai flyer by Rōsō, denouncing Sōaikai repression at the Hamamatsu Musical Instruments Strike of 1926.

Just over a month after the Nihon Gakki strike, the Sōaikai shifted gears and no longer waited until strikes broke out to intervene with force; the slide from prevention to preemption had taken place. On June 13, 1926, 70 Sōaikai members broke into and destroyed the Rōsō headquarters in Tokyo, injuring 10 Rōsō members.[96] Then, a day later on June 14, in the neighboring prefecture of Yamanashi, Sōaikai leaders and musclemen confronted 1,000 Korean workers employed as day workers on the Fuji Minobu railroad construction site in Nishihachidai-gun. Thirty Sōaikai members armed with pistols and clubs approached the workers while they were working and made the following announcement: "Membership in the Sōaikai is your duty and an obligation."[97] The newspaper report then claims that approximately half of the workers stopped their work to reply back, "The Sōaikai is meaningless to us . . . Membership fees are collected so that a few directors can get fat,"[98] in reaction to which 15 of the 30 armed Sōaikai members instigated a brawl that escalated into a fight. Three construction workers died from the battle, and 50 workers were injured.[99] Seeing the carnage and fearing death, hundreds of workers, who had until then remained silent, quickly signed up and became Sōaikai members.[100] As a result, the Korean workers in Yamanashi became divided. As a Kōfu City telegraph report writes, "Pro-Sōaikai and Anti-Sōaikai groups emerged from within the one thousand workers."[101]

5. Korean labor union cartoon of Pak Ch'um-gum of the "Sō-gai-kai" (Mutual Harm Society), standing with police before workers, circa 1932.

The Kawasaki Sōaikai incident of 1929, mentioned at the outset of this chapter, brought Sōaikai repressive techniques into the space of everyday life of Korean workers, into the intimate spaces of barrack life itself, where soliciting became kidnapping, where work became coerced, where membership was called a duty, and where workers were beaten and killed in the streets of their own neighborhoods or hamba. Sōaikai strike repressions and aggressive solicitations continued unabated into the early 1930s, but especially after the Kawasaki Incident, anti-Sōaikai movements significantly weakened both the institution and public image of the Sōaikai.[102] While the Sōaikai had a membership in 1932 of 16,080 members, by 1934 it had fallen to less than 7,500 members, and by 1936 membership had dwindled to just over 3,000.[103] Anti-Sōaikai movements remained active at least through 1934, and Korean labor organizations in Japan began calling the Sōaikai the Sōgaikai (相害会), not the mutual love society, but the mutual harm society.[104]

Ethnic Difference, Representation, and Disavowal

Precisely at the height of anti-Sōaikai protests, the Sōaikai's co-founder and vice president, Pak Ch'um-gum, publicly distanced himself from the Sōaikai and succeeded, in 1932, in becoming the first Korean elected to the National Diet as a representative of Tokyo's Fourth Ward in the Lower House.[105] Pak's election campaign, however, was criticized vociferously by Koreans on the left. For example, the Korean sections in the Japanese communist labor union Zenkyō, for its part, extended Rōsō's original critique of the violence of the Sōaikai and maintained anti-Sōaikai and anti-Pak Ch'um-gum slogans on its political agenda. In 1932, just before parliamentary elections, Zenkyō's Chemical Workers Labor Union in Tokyo distributed flyers to non-unionized Korean workers, denouncing Pak Ch'um-gum. "Fight Against Pak Ch'um-gum's Candidacy!" begins the flyer, culminating in the following passage:

Korean Worker Comrades!
Korea has been ravaged by Japanese Imperialism, eaten up and spit out, all our wealth and profits snatched away by the Japanese bourgeoisie. Unable to survive in Korea, we've had to cross over to Tokyo, so far away from our native home, and yet we are given no guarantees for a livelihood here.

In spite of this, Pak Ch'um-gum has offered his services to the Japanese Imperialists, precisely because Korea has become colonized and enslaved. With Maruyama Tsurukichi's support, he has now become a candidate for a seat in the Diet, and is desperately fighting—in the name of Japanese-Korean harmony—to light the way for the expropriation of Manchuria. . . .

However, we do not have to submit one single vote to support the loyal Japanese Imperialist Dog. Compared to the grand Pak, what do we have? Even when we work for low wages, face closed factory doors and toil in temporary work, even if we have families to support, we're looked down on as 'Those Koreans, Koreans' [senjin senjin]. We're sick of it all! Pak gets protection by the Japanese Imperialists while he sits on the soil where the blood of our friends has been spilled! What kind of 'Japanese–Korean Harmony' is this?!

. . . To all Korean workers, form alliances with Japanese worker cells and do not vote for Pak Ch'um-gum. Organize mass action under the leadership of Zenkyō's Chemicals Union and initiate demonstrations calling for the destruction of the bourgeois parliamentary system. Initiate and extend anti-Sōaikai and anti-Pak movements, organize public speeches for this purpose, distribute flyers exposing Pak and create Korean clubs to counter Sōaikai organizations. . . . Form strong alliances with representatives from construction sites and integrate struggles on construction sites with struggles against the election.[106]

In tandem with anti-Pak movements, Korean movements protesting the conditions of the General Election Law (futsū senkyo-hō) emerged soon after

the passage of universal suffrage in 1925. These movements specifically identified conditional, selective, and discriminating legal stipulations, outlined
in the general election law, for Korean populations in Japan. Unlike Koreans
in Korea, or Taiwanese in Taiwan, Koreans in Japan were given the right to
vote after 1925, but only on the condition that they met two basic criteria:
that they were men over the age of 25, and that they could prove continuous residence in Japan for one year. The latter condition in particular was a
problem in a double sense, for not only was the residential condition of one
year for Koreans six months longer than the requirement for Japanese, but,
given landlord racism within Japanese housing markets and the often illegal
enforcement of evictions of Koreans, it was extremely difficult for Koreans to
maintain continuous residence in Japan in the same place for one year, thereby
making it nearly impossible to register as a voter in the general elections.[107]
Furthermore, Korean homelessness, a common condition and omnipresent
possibility faced by thousands of Koreans throughout the 1920s and most
of the 1930s, legally prohibited thousands of Koreans from voting because
they did not have a stable or registered address. Korean workers were acutely
aware of how the difficulties in obtaining secure housing were directly preventing Koreans from voting in Japan. Many Koreans, such as those active in
the Osaka branch of the Worker-Peasant Party (Rōnōtō), therefore protested
the election law's stipulation of one year, continuous residency for Koreans as a condition for voting rights. As a Rōnōtō flyer reads from February
1928:

> The general election is all the rage now. . . . But what are we Korean work-
> ers to do? While we Korean workers have a right to vote, don't be fooled!
> Not all of us in Japan have these rights. Of course, for our brothers in Ko-
> rea, voting is totally out of the question. But here in Japan you can't vote
> even if you're 18 years old, and what's more, you have to live in the same
> place for at least one year. But for us Korean workers, it's difficult to live in
> the same place for over a year. Renting a house [in Japan] is hardly a piece
> of cake! As everyone knows, in order to rent a house, not only is it neces-
> sary to use Japanese proper names [and conceal one's real Korean proper
> name], but when they [landlords] find out you're Korean, they throw you
> out. Living in one place for over a year is nothing short of a dream. . . . .Put
> an end to Restrictions on Residence Now! [ijū seigen wo yamero!][108]

Despite protests against Pak and the Sōaikai, Pak nonetheless succeeded,
in 1932, in becoming the first Korean elected to the National Diet as a repre-

sentative of Tokyo's Fourth Ward in the Lower House. How did Pak fare as a Diet politician? Miserably. His efforts to open the imperial army to Koreans failed; his proposals to keep immigration completely open for Koreans traveling between Korea and Japan (so-called *jiyū tokō*) were rejected; and his proposal to establish universal suffrage in Korea was shot down. All were rejected on the argument that conditions in Korea were not yet ready for such changes.[109] Finally, on the floor of the Diet in 1934, Pak failed to win Diet support against the government's decision to reduce and then end rice imports from Korea and failed also to convince Prime Minister Saito Makoto that this policy was discriminatory. Rice imports from Korea continued to be reduced until the colonial program to increase rice production was ultimately scrapped in 1934.

Pak's sudden rise to parliamentary fame, however, coincided with a general disavowal of the work and history of the Sōaikai. During Pak's time as a parliamentarian, not a word was ever spoken of the practices of the Sōaikai. The same was true for his Diet campaign speeches, such as the fifty-six-page speech from November 1930, titled, "Our State, the New Japan: A Public Complaint to the Ladies and Gentlemen of the Government Describing the Instability and Distress of our Korean Compatriots."[110] Not once in this campaign speech was the work of the Sōaikai mentioned. While Pak could never have succeeded in becoming the first Korean to be elected into the Diet without his close affiliation with the Sōaikai, Pak's campaign and parliamentary politics were based on an active disavowal of the preventive police work of the Sōaikai. Once Pak was elected into parliament, the Sōaikai became a vanishing mediator, replaced by an individualized, ethnic representative of Koreans in the Japanese Empire. In his campaign victory speech, Pak proudly stated, "As a Japanese born in Korea, my standing as a National Diet member is not simply a victory for me personally, but for the twenty million Koreans in Korea."[111] Once Pak could speak as a parliamentarian, he no longer had to speak as a particular representative of the Sōaikai, and therefore no longer had to address the particular class of Korean workers in Japan whom he had once deemed "unruly Koreans" and worthy of "elimination." Pak's parliamentary representation of all Koreans thus rested on what this representation did not, and could not, say about the Sōaikai.

The significance of the ethnic figure of Pak-the-Parliamentarian, therefore, is not that he was simply the first colonial representative in the Japanese state machinery. Rather, his figure was a sign of a disavowed splitting of the state machinery itself, between its public face and the obscene violence on which it covertly relied and depended—institutionally and para-institutionally. The importance of Pak Ch'um-gum is not simply that he was a colonial collaborator, a colonial opportunist, and a colonial exploiter of his fellow countrymen and women. Rather, his collaborations, opportunisms, and exploits were endemic to everyday practices of managing, disciplining, commodifying, and repressing Korean surplus populations in Japan, practices that were publicly disavowed through the splitting of the juridical police and its supplement, the preventive (i.e., preemptive) police. In this regard, the (ethnic) figure of Pak-the-Parliamentarian should not be read as another example of the validity of the binary opposition of civil society versus the state. The figure of Pak rather points to a symbolic undoing, an undoing that also revealed how the figuration of ethnicity, in an avowedly multiethnic empire, ideologically displaced and stood in for the class struggles that could not be eliminated—only repressed and disavowed.

6

AT THE GATES OF UNEMPLOYMENT
....

The Struggles of Unemployed Korean Workers

> Yet in his darkness he is now aware of a radiance that streams inextinguish-
> ably from the gateway of the Law. Now he has not very long to live. Before he
> dies, all his experiences in these longs years gather themselves in his head
> to one point, a question he has not yet asked the doorkeeper . . . "Everyone
> strives to reach the Law," says the man, "so how does it happen that for all
> these many years no one but myself has ever begged for admittance?" The
> doorkeeper recognizes that the man has reached his end, and, to let his failing
> senses catch the words, roars in his ear: "No one else could ever be admitted
> here, since this gate was made only for you. I am now going to shut it."
> —Franz Kafka, *Before the Law*

During the economic recession and depression of the 1920s and early 1930s,
masses of Korean workers, like their Japanese counterparts and comrades,
looked to the state to alleviate the oppressions of employment insecurity. This
turn to the state for minimal employment security had already begun in 1921,
when the Labor Exchange Law was implemented in Japan. The phenomenon
of industrial unemployment, which began most clearly with the end of the
manufacturing boom of the First World War, was clearly not going away. By
the mid-1920s, it was clear to various government ministries, industrial leaders, and especially workers in Japan, that the labor exchange system was inadequate to stem the unemployment throughout Japan. By the mid-1920s,
unemployment had become a chronic, and not a temporary, problem, which
is why the Japanese government, in the winter of 1925, implemented the Unemployment Emergency Relief Programs.

As we have seen already, Korean workers experienced the insecurities of
employment in Japan in extremely severe ways. Often the last to be hired and
the first to be fired in the Japanese factory system, the vast majority of Korean workers were compelled to sell their labor power on a daily basis in the

day labor markets. Institutional forms of power, embodied in Korean-managed and police-supported welfare organizations such as the Sōaikai, sought to alleviate some of the insecurities of employment for Korean workers, but only reproduced forms of intermediary exploitation in the day labor market while simultaneously channeling Korean workers away from the labor exchange system. Moreover, welfare organizations like the Sōaikai operated as supplementary yet publicly disavowed police forces to repress radical Korean worker movements. Masses of Korean workers therefore did not trust these organizations, and by the late 1920s, thousands of Koreans had abandoned them. Korean workers thus increasingly turned to the UERP. The UERP initially appealed to Korean workers because of its publicly stated promise of being open to all workers in Japan, of providing competitive wages irrespective of ethnicity, and especially of rejecting sub-contracting practices that were endemic to the day labor market. While the UERP was often a last ditch attempt to secure employment and a minimal income for Japanese workers, for Korean workers the UERP increasingly became the first place to go for work. For Korean workers, the radical contingencies of commodification and employment in Japan compelled them to become dependent on the UERP.

The problem by 1929, however, was that, despite the UERP's stated openness to all workers in Japan, the UERP was overwhelmed by the vast numbers of unemployed workers and was incapable of registering all workers seeking public aid. Moreover, Japanese workers and Japanese state officials began to complain of the high numbers of Korean workers flocking to the UERP for daily employment. Yet, because the UERP publicly promised openness to all workers, Korean workers could not be turned away automatically on the basis of their ethnicity. As a result, the UERP was compelled to invent specific institutional techniques and criteria to regulate the massive flow of workers yelling and pounding at its gates.

The work of UERP registration was strikingly similar to the work of the doorkeeper in Kafka's parable, *Before the Law*. Appearing open to all, the UERP gates were in fact guarded so that only certain individuals could pass through. Like Kafka's doorkeeper, moreover, the UERP never imparted unto those standing before its gates—often until it was too late—that the door could be closed shut at any moment. The effect of this doorkeeping, however, is not simply that it prevented certain workers from passing through the UERP's gates. Rather, in excluding workers selectively, the function of the UERP doorkeepers created a social and institutional milieu in which workers were compelled to become individualized—marked, coded, registered, and known by the state as individuals—in order to pass through the gates of the UERP. Once inside the UERP, however, workers faced a series of institutional techniques and practices that not only commodified and exploited their labor power, but that reproduced certain forms of job insecurity as the basis for enforcing work discipline. The UERP therefore did not provide unemployment relief so much as it invented an institutional and social milieu for the commodification, exploitation, and disciplinization of labor power on the basis of individuating masses of surplus populations. In this regard, the UERP worked to conceal the class character and class antagonisms of the masses of labor power. How the institutional doorkeeping of the UERP affected and impinged on Korean workers outside the gates of UERP, and how Korean working-class struggles emerged in response to institutional techniques and regulations inside the UERP, are the two specific and interrelated topics of this chapter.

Korean Unemployment in Japan and the Crisis of the Nation

During the height of the economic crisis in 1929 and 1930, the UERP was experiencing an acute crisis in handling a massive flow of Korean labor power. More specifically, this crisis was felt by the UERP and the network of state institutions upon which the UERP executed its various projects to aid the unemployed population, namely, the labor exchange offices on the national, prefectural, city, and city-ward levels, as well as city and prefectural public works departments. This was not new, however, for Koreans had already been using the UERP for employment since 1925, when the UERP was first established in the six major cities during the winter season.[1] As the recession deepened into full blown crisis in late 1929, however, and as thousands of unemployed Japanese workers were lining up at the gates of the UERP, the fact that the Korean percentage in the UERP had, by 1928, climbed to over 50 percent of the total number of registered workers in the UERP did not sit well with Japanese workers or with Japanese policy makers. In 1925, only 11.9 percent of the registered workers in the UERP were Korean; in 1928, however, 19,130 out of a total of 34,388 registered workers, or 55.6 percent, were Korean. In Tokyo, the Korean percentage was just below the national average at 54.7 percent; in Nagoya it was 71.6 percent; Osaka was comparatively low in 1928 with only 21.3 percent, but rose to 52.1 percent the following year.[2]

Around 1928–29, the interior ministry's social bureau began surveys of the conditions in the labor exchange offices to get a sense of the social relations between workers seeking unemployment aid and to prepare for policy changes in the UERP.[3] In these surveys, many Japanese workers, such as one Nakajima Shōichiro, expressed anxiety that they would not be able to register at their nearest labor exchange office because so many Koreans were flooding the offices. Nakajima, age 50, born in Toyohashi city but residing in the Honjo ward of Tokyo, was applying for unemployment registration at the Yotsuya labor exchange office in Tokyo when he described his situation:

> I used to work at a machine factory for three years but the factory closed down. I've since joined the throngs of free laborers. When I'm able to get some work I can usually afford to drink a little . . . but when there's no work I have to cut down on food. I often work at the free workers' lodgings as an assistant to make ends meet. Of course, I used to go to the labor exchange offices, but there were so many Koreans there that I couldn't even get in the door. So I just don't go there anymore and generally wait for jobs on the corner at the Kōtōbashi day labor market, you know, as a tachimbō.[4]

One man, only known as Naitō-san, age 42, originally from Kōfu city in Yamanashi prefecture and also residing in the Honjo ward in Tokyo, disclosed:

> Got a wife but we're living apart. No kids, thank god . . . Until now I'd get jobs as a free worker [jiyū rōdōsha] once every three days or so, but lately, nothing. . . . I used to work in an iron ore factory but became a free worker after the earthquake in '23. I used to earn between 1.00 and 1.30 yen a day. I'd spend 10 sen for breakfast, 10 sen for lunch, 15 sen for dinner and 30 sen for sake and smokes. . . . But there were times when I couldn't afford to eat on the days I didn't work. Friends helped me out, you know. . . . I've tried to find regular work [jōkō no shigoto, i.e., factory work] but found no luck. I've been going to the free labor market everyday as a tachimbō because when I went to the labor exchange offices all the Koreans just pushed me out and I couldn't find work there.[5]

It was not long before policy makers and economists addressed what was increasingly becoming a public debate on the relationship between Korean workers and the UERP. Korean unemployment in Japan was increasingly spoken of as the sign of a general crisis of the Japanese nation. The well-known professor and policy maker Fukuda Tokuzō wrote, "Presently, the unemployment relief programs in the six largest cities of our nation are, in fact, one of the biggest programs for importing unemployment. . . . Our suffering nation of Japan has, on her own volition, successfully been able to gradually increase unemployment by exclusively importing unemployment from Korea."[6] These words were quoted in many sources dealing with unemployment in Japan. For example, a Kyoto municipal office survey on unemployed workers took Fukuda's import metaphor a step further, proclaiming that "In our great city, over sixty percent of the workers flowing in and out of the Kyoto UERP offices are from Korea. Indeed, as far as the unemployment problem is concerned, it is difficult not to regard Japan as *Korea's colony*."[7] A slightly different variation on this theme was also found in the words of Akiyama Fusuke, of the Tokyo regional labor exchange bureau, in an essay titled "Korean Workers and the Unemployment Problem" in the December 1929 edition of *Shakai Seisaku Jihō*: "The unemployment problem in Japan is fundamentally an unemployment problem for Japanese workers; the existence of unemployed Korean workers in Japan is nothing more than an incidental, collateral problem [*fuzui-teki mondai ni suginai*]. . . ."[8] For Akiyama, unemployed Korean workers in Japan represented what Marx called the faux frais of capitalist production—the incidental expenses.[9] Akiyama's bottom line, however, was that providing state relief to unemployed Koreans was ill advised because it would come at the cost and expense of providing aid to unemployed Japanese workers. As the faux frais of capitalist production, he intended to shift the burden of this so-called incidental expense onto anybody except Japanese workers and the Japanese state. This is why Akiyama argued that the key to resolving the Korean unemployment problem in Japan was to "export unemployed Korean workers to Manchuria or Siberia." The entire burden of Korean unemployment in Japan, he argued, should be placed onto the shoulders of the Government General in Seoul, and specifically on the police in Pusan Harbor. Akiyama thus argued for stricter immigration laws for Koreans as a method to solve Korean unemployment in Japan.[10]

Unlike Akiyama, Sakai Toshio of the Osaka-fu social section took a critical stance toward this line of argumentation, but in a way that ultimately corroborated Akiyama's position. What was needed, Sakai argued, was a mode of thinking that challenged "the prevailing attitude towards the control of Korea, which consider[ed] Japanese as number one and Koreans as number two."[11] Sakai thus proposed a new "attitude towards the control of Koreans," one that would treat Korean "imperial subjects" equally alongside their Japanese brethren. Restricted immigration for Koreans only, Sakai argued, contradicted imperial policy, for "while it is said that freedom is granted to all subjects [shinmin] of the Empire to travel wherever they please, restricted migration policies in fact violate the rights of Koreans as Imperial Subjects [teikoku no shimnin toshite no kenri wo shingai suru mono] . . . After all, with the Annexation of Korea . . . Koreans became Imperial nationals [teikoku kokumin]."[12] Sakai thus argued that the problem of Korean unemployment could not be solved through restricted immigration policies. Unlike Akiyama, Sakai recognized that curbing unemployment in the domestic labor market by tightening Korean immigration were merely stop-gap measures. These measures only served to "protect Japanese workers by expelling Korean workers out of the depths of the labor market in Japan." So long as a "safe and comfortable life in Korea" was not guaranteed by the Japanese state for unemployed Koreans returning to Korea, initiatives taken to repatriate unemployed Koreans back to Korea—for example, by providing discounted boat fares back to Korea— were doomed.[13]

By "safe and comfortable," however, Sakai meant an improved economic situation in the Korean countryside, as well as a more developed industrial sector. Sakai thus argued that accelerated industrial development in Korea, led by Japanese capital, was necessary to "absorb unemployed Koreans returning from Japan." He proposed two policies to put this plan into action. The first policy targeted the agrarian sector in Korea, which would "eliminate any last traces of feudal social relations on the farms," while simultaneously "improving the landlord-peasant relationship by offering protective measures at least to Korean landlords" so that they would be "less inclined to exploit the Korean peasants." The second policy outlined the development of Korean commerce and industry through the implementation of public works on a wide scale. This, Sakai said, would aid in absorbing expropriated Korean peasants and unemployed Korean workers repatriating back to Korea from Japan.[14] When Sakai called for changes in the prevailing "attitude towards the control of Korea," he specifically meant an end to discrimination against Koreans and the protection of Korean rights, not by addressing material conditions of discrimination and exploitation in Japan, but rather by expanding and developing Japanese colonialism and imperialism and by exporting Japanese capital to Korea as a means to accelerate Korean industrial development. This is why, in the end, Sakai was unable to provide any concrete measures addressing the specific problems of Korean workers in the Japanese unemployment system. Ultimately, he argued—now in complete agreement with Akiyama— that the best and most immediate method of solving Korean unemployment in Japan was to "export" them to Manchuria or Siberia.[15]

Guarding the Gates of the UERP

The various positions and public policy opinions discussed above help paint a general picture of how Korean unemployment and its relation to the UERP were commonly understood in terms of a national crisis that could only be resolved by expanding Japan's empire and colonial projects and by preventing Koreans from entering the nation through immigration laws and regulations. What is crucial to these approaches to Korean unemployment, however, is that they were silent about the microscopic institutional techniques and practices, implemented by the UERP especially in 1929, for managing the international pool of surplus populations within Japan. For in this year the UERP underwent institutional changes regarding its registration policies, primarily by instituting a system of distributing work books (rōdō techō).[16] With this system, workers had to obtain work books as a necessary precondition for registration. Workers would take their work books to the labor exchange office where they would file for registration, after which they could be told when and where their first day of work would begin.

The new work book registration policy affected unemployed Korean and Japanese workers in significant yet differing ways. First, after the implementation of the work book system, Korean registration in the UERP dropped significantly. As table 25 shows, nationally, the percentage of Koreans registered in the UERP fell from 55.6 percent in 1928 to 38.8 percent in 1929. By 1932 it had fallen to 22.5 percent. The decrease in registered Koreans was particularly acute in Tokyo, where the percentage of registered Koreans had fallen from 54.7 percent in 1928 to 27.6 percent the following year (table 26). This led to many protests by Korean workers against the labor exchange offices and officers of the UERP.

Most of the protests were organized protests demanding equal registration in the UERP. Many Koreans claimed that they were denied registration on the basis of their Korean ethnicity. Thus, for example, 530 Koreans from the Kanto Free Workers Union (Kanto Jiyū Rōdō Kumiai) stormed Shinjuku's labor exchange on October 24, 1930, and protested with the following two slogans: "We refuse to submit the country of birth on registration applications!" and "We demand total registration for all unregistered workers!"[17] These demands had two important effects. First, they put increased pressure on the UERP and the labor exchange offices to provide equal and fair registration to Koreans. For example, unlike Tokyo's UERP, the UERP in Osaka took the demands for equal registration by Koreans very seriously, and maintained an almost

TABLE 25. Registered Workers in UERP

Year	Total	Number of Koreans	Percent Korean
1925	24,417	2,920	11.9
1926	29,971	8,230	27.4
1927	25,331	8,452	33.4
1928	34,388	19,130	55.6
1929	40,115	15,545	38.8
1932	171,489	38,605	22.5
1933	151,062	33,585	22.2
1934	101,658	22,652	22.3

Sources: Kase: "Shigsugyōsha kyūsai kokyō doboku jigyō ni okeru shūrōsha senbetsu hōshiki to chōsenjin tōrokusha," 370; Senzen Nihon no shitsugyō taisaku—kyusaigata kokyou doboku jigyo no rekishitekibunseki, 142.

perfect balance between registered Korean and Japanese workers from 1929 to 1934. In 1929, the percentage of registered Koreans was 52.5 percent; in 1934, it was still over half with 51.5 percent. In this regard, these demands enabled Korean workers to get jobs on construction sites through the UERP. But the demands for fairer registration and for registration for all unregistered workers had a second, extremely deleterious effect—for both Korean and Japanese workers. Namely, it displaced the problem of exploitation, cheap wages, and low revenue onto a terrain of struggle in which registration with the UERP itself was transformed into the primary goal of unemployed workers. More specifically, insofar as registration with the UERP proceeded only on the basis of the individual and not on the basis of class (or ethnicity), the goal for registration became an individual goal, with the movement toward registration an extended process toward the individualization of the worker. This wet the worker's feet, preparing him for the regime of wage labor awaiting him on the other side of the UERP's institutional threshold. As workers clamored at the gates, it was as though the UERP might say, "Be patient. You just might get what you're asking for."

The second point is related to the method of distributing the work books. Japanese obtained their work books from the city ward office (kuyakusho), police stations, district committee (hōmen i'inkai) offices, or directly from the UERP-related labor exchange offices themselves.[18] Koreans, by contrast, had

TABLE 26. Registered Unemployed Workers: Tokyo

Year	Total	Number of Koreans	Percent Korean
1925	15,667	1,369	8.7
1926	12,701	1,472	11.6
1927	8,379	1,687	20.1
1928	19,160	10,496	54.7
1929	22,603	6,235	27.6
1932	45,559	9,215	20.2
1933	43,679	8,010	18.3
1934	34,375	6,425	18.7

Sources: Kase: "Shigsugyōsha kyūsai kokyō doboku jigyō ni okeru shūrōsha senbetsu hōshiki to chōsenjin tōrokusha," 370; Senzen Nihon no shitsugyō taisaku—kyusaigata kokyou doboku jigyo no rekishitekibunseki, 142.

to go to so-called private welfare organizations (shisetsu shakai jigyō dantai) to obtain the work books before heading to the labor exchange offices to register with the UERP.[19] The most prominent of these organizations, however, were the two largest Korean welfare organizations: the Sōaikai, headquartered in Tokyo, which maintained close connections with the police, and the Naisen Kyōwakai (est. 1924), headquartered in Osaka, within the Osaka Government Social Bureau. Both organizations had their own labor exchange offices that were designed exclusively for Korean workers, and that functioned as a parallel system to the general labor exchange offices, first established in 1921 with the Labor Exchange Act. Around 1926–27, however, both organizations began to lose members. To many Korean workers, the UERP was more appealing than so-called Korean welfare organizations because of its insistence on equal wages for Koreans and Japanese, and for its original refusal to employ sub-contractors (this refusal would change, as we will see later). Moreover, at least in the case of the Sōaikai, workers were leaving it in droves because of the organization's right-wing tactics of repressing Korean labor strikes after 1925. The result was that Koreans began leaving these Korean-managed welfare organizations and flocking to the UERP instead.[20]

The UERP, however, did not allow unemployed Korean workers seeking public aid from the UERP to cut their ties so easily with these assimilation organs. Rather, the UERP commonly made it a condition for Korean workers

TABLE 27. Registered Unemployed Workers: Osaka

Year	Total	Number of Koreans	Percent Korean
1925	3,484	1,030	29.5
1926	7,530	4,017	53.3
1927	4,642	1,970	42.4
1928	1,488	317	21.3
1929	12,359	6,452	52.5
1932	26,169	13,307	50.9
1933	29,955	15,613	52.1
1934	20,564	10,593	51.5

Sources: Kase: "Shigsugyōsha kyūsai kokyō doboku jigyō ni okeru shūrōsha senbetsu hōshiki to chōsenjin tōrokusha," 370; Senzen Nihon no shitsugyō taisaku—kyusaigata kokyou doboku jigyo no rekishitekibunseki, 142.

to obtain work books from the Sōaikai and the Naisen Kyōwakai, meaning that registering with the UERP therefore became contingent on obtaining the work books from these welfare and assimilation organs. By using these organizations as the distributors of work books, the UERP was able to channel Korean workers all the more powerfully toward the idea of registering with the UERP on an individual basis. A survey of the UERP by the Tokyo social bureau's labor exchange, published in October of 1929, writes that the "Sōaikai and other Korean social welfare organizations have encouraged Koreans to register [with the UERP] through their offices."[21] Similarly, according to a survey on UERP work books by the Osaka investigations section, as many as 90 percent of the work books distributed by so-called private social welfare organizations came from the Naisen Kyōwakai and the Sōaikai.[22] And as Korean activist Kim Tu-yong wrote in 1929, "Let's imagine an unemployed worker who's just arrived in Japan from Pusan. . . . He has to find work as soon as possible but has no technical skills to speak of and hardly speaks a word of Japanese. So first he goes to the [City or Ward] Labor Exchange Office—but he's immediately told to go to the Sōaikai."[23] Thus, while Korean workers were clearly abandoning the labor exchange offices established and operated by welfare and assimilation organs, registration procedures with the UERP were able to enforce a limited but influential pressure on unemployed Korean workers to maintain relations with them.

Koreans protested against this pressure, demanding that organizations other than the Sōaikai and the Naisen Kyōwakai be permitted to distribute work books to unemployed Korean workers. The Korean-led union, Kōtōbashi Registered Workers Council, for example, which based its political activities and operations within the Kōtōbashi labor exchange office in Tokyo, had numerous clashes with the Sōaikai throughout 1933 in relation to this problem. For example, two different articles from the Shakai Undō Tsūshin reported that the Kōtōbashi Registered Workers Council "has been showing a fierce struggle against the Sōaikai in the Honjo Ward of Tokyo, demanding the 'Absolute Refusal of Registration!' and the 'Refusal of Work Books!'" from the Sōaikai.[24] Also in Tokyo, the director of the Nishi Sugamo Labor Exchange Office in Tokyo noted, in a dossier from 1931, that "squads of Koreans were coming to the labor exchange office protesting that work books were not being distributed fairly," and claiming that "the work books should be distributed through a different mediating organization."[25] Having said this, the director asked that the police be the only administrative office with the authority to distribute work books.[26]

Finally, the work book registration process led to a new problem, namely what came to be called work book hoarding (rōdō techō no shizō). The Osaka survey mentioned above described two types of hoarding. The first type, common among Japanese, had its origin in workers who, having obtained regular employment after registering with the UERP, did not use their work books.[27] This first type was thus less a hoard than an accumulation of unused work books. The second type, "particularly rampant in the case of Koreans," was a method of hoarding work books in which applicants illegally accumulated books originally registered under other workers' names. Alternatively, Korean applicants "lacking Japanese language skills and often ineligible for the work books due to lack of fixed residency, [sought] out and sometimes [paid] others . . . to apply for work books on their behalf."[28] The report notes that the going rate for such deals was ten sen per work book, which meant that for the 3,877 discovered cases of hoarded work books, an estimated total of 387 yen was exchanged between workers.[29] In Tokyo, a similar observation was made by the director of the Nishi Sugamo labor exchange office in 1931. In addition to noting that "countless Korean workers were leading the movement for the fair distribution of work books," the director stated that Koreans had found ways to use work books belonging to others, or to stand in for someone else on a work site by using borrowed or stolen work books.[30] This action was called kaedama, an example of which can be seen in an incident on September 19,

1930, when the foreman of a construction site in Sugamo, in northern Tokyo, discovered that Korean workers were using work books belonging to other workers. The foremen then confiscated the work books and the Korean workers were immediately dismissed from the site.[31] Work book hoarding thus always contained this risk of losing all privileges in the UERP. Nonetheless, the hoarding problem became so common that, beginning in 1930, all workers, Japanese as well as Korean, were required to attach photographs of themselves on the backs of the work books.[32] Asked what he thought about mandatory photographs on work books, one construction foreman from Osaka commented that placing "the worker's photograph on the work book reduces a lot of wasted time from checking to see if a worker on a construction site is legitimate or not."[33] Another foreman added, "It's remarkable how much the work book system has helped expedite investigations into Korean crime."[34] As the foreman's comment makes clear, the hoarding of work books by Koreans was considered criminal and, when discovered, was accompanied by the penalty of work suspension and the confiscation of the work book. What has to be said is that the hoarding of work books was considered criminal because it was anathema to the basic idea that registration had to proceed on the basis of the individual.

In sum, therefore, the implementation of the work book registration system not only functioned to separate unemployed Korean workers from unemployed Japanese workers, but also produced individuals as effects of registration. Registering with the UERP was a mechanical function of marking, coding, stamping, registering, and, most of all, producing labor power in the form of individuals for the purpose of inaugurating them into exploitative regimes of wage labor that the UERP coordinated, specifically (as we will see shortly) in the public works industry. The UERP functioned, therefore, to identify and code un-individualized, de-territorialized, amorphous masses of surplus labor power into individualized, reterritorialized, determinate, and discernible signs of the economy. Deleuze and Guattari would say that this process disclosed a transformation from a neuter/intensive system to a discrete/extensive system.[35] In short, the process of registering and marking prepared the ground for the transformation of labor power, as a pure potentiality, into that which capital cannot directly produce itself, namely labor power as a commodity. In this way, the registration process worked to conceal both the class character of the unemployed workers and the class antagonisms of the surplus populations, the latter of which were banging on the doors of the UERP on a daily basis and in large masses. Moreover, the UERP's reliance

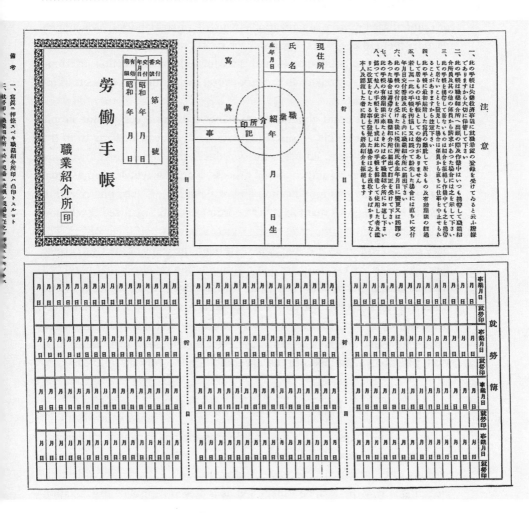

6. Unemployment Emergency Relief Program (UERP) work book.

on ethnic-based welfare organizations to distribute work books, as a supplementary method to guard the gates of the UERP, reveals how the ethnic separation of surplus populations—and the concomitant production of ethnic identity—was closely related to the production of unemployed subjects as individual wage workers.

The important point about the UERP registration process is not simply that it tended to exclude, in discriminatory ways, Korean workers from the unemployment system. Rather, UERP produced individual Korean workers as an effect of a selective registration process, a process whose ultimate goal was to ensure the commodification and exploitation of labor power within specific wage regimes that the UERP coordinated and organized. Exclusion and discrimination at the gates of the UERP were only half the problem. For once Korean workers were able to pass through the gates of the UERP, once they overcame the exclusionary and discriminating practices that regulated the relationship between the UERP and the vast pool of unemployed workers, Korean workers faced an even more insidious and complex series of practices within the UERP. These practices not only exploited and discriminated against Korean workers in specific ways, but also ultimately maintained high levels of employment insecurity as a precondition for work discipline.

Inside the UERP: Inventing the Relative Autonomy of the State

In the previous chapter on the Sōaikai, the important point about state power was that it was internally split between a public face and a disavowed supplementary force on which state power nonetheless relied. This was particularly clear in the way the Sōaikai functioned as a preventive police organization that used violence as a means to repress Korean communist movements while commodifying Korean labor power. As we have already seen, the UERP relied on the Sōaikai as a distributor of UERP work books and therefore was part of a wider policing network that was ultimately committed to the commodification of Korean labor power as cheap and disposable colonial labor. In this sense, the UERP was closely related to the internal splitting of state power between its public face and its disavowed supplementary force. When we turn our analysis to the internal workings of the UERP, however, a different problem of state power emerges. Here the problem is how the relative autonomy of the state is maintained outside of economic processes such as exploitation, but only in order to allow the state to intervene in these processes, and in a form that reacts to changes in class compositions and shifting populations of the labor market.[36] The state is not simply separated from the economic base, floating above it as if it were disconnected from class antagonisms and economic processes of exploitation. Rather, it is separated from the economic base as a precondition for its own intervening function within processes of exploitation itself. The crucial aspect of this functioning, however, is that its form is continually invented in specific situations as a means to ensure the reproduction of capital and the maintenance of class division. As Suzanne De-Brunhoff cogently argues, the problem is to see how "the state has an agency which is both immanent in, but not reducible to, the fundamental relationship of capitalist exploitation. . . . [The] immanence of state action does not imply the suppression of—but actually requires—an external relationship to the movements of capital."[37] The way state power articulates this immanence and separation, however, necessitates an understanding of how "the relative autonomy of the state is never given; it has to be constantly created. . . . [The state] has to ceaselessly redefine and adjust economic boundaries to one another."[38]

The practices of the UERP reveal precisely this kind of constant redefinition and adjustment of economic boundaries. These practices were evident in the way the UERP guarded its gates by requiring unemployed workers, beginning in 1929, to obtain work books as a precondition for registering with the UERP. Within the UERP, however, and in relation to registered workers, two additional practices revealed the extent to which the relative autonomy of the state was invented to maintain the smooth commodification of labor power. First, the UERP produced and enforced institutional distinctions between preferred workers, or registered workers who were institutionally granted consecutive working days, and alternating workers, who were granted only alternating working days, and who therefore had to endure relative job insecurity even within the UERP. Differences in the application of these binary categories of preferred and alternating workers, however, revealed striking differences between the distribution and commodification of registered Korean workers and registered Japanese workers. Second, the UERP also invented and maintained institutional distinctions regarding the form of employment of registered workers. The two distinctions were called direct management and sub-contracted labor. Direct management meant that registered workers could work directly under the authority of the UERP-managed construction sites. Sub-contracted labor meant that registered UERP workers would work under bosses who were sub-contracted by the UERP. Here, too, striking differences emerged in the way these practices affected Japanese and Korean workers. A clear ethnic-based hierarchy emerged out of the ways these distinctions were produced and reproduced by the UERP and its satellite functionaries in the public works industry (e.g., construction site foremen). For Korean workers, especially, these distinctions led to a reproduction of job insecurity within the UERP. Job insecurity, however, was maintained in such a way that work discipline insinuated itself in new and more insidious ways to ensure an uninterrupted process of commodification and exploitation.

Employment Insecurity within the UERP: The Problem of Working Days

Arguably the most important data found in the surveys of the UERP are the statistics on working days obtained through the UERP. Working days were categorized and organized in terms of (1) consecutive workdays and preferred workers (*shitei ninpu*, or, in the vernacular, *kaotsuki* or *mentsuki*), and (2) alternating workdays and alternating workers (*kōtai shūrōsha*). It goes without saying that a worker seeking employment in the UERP would prefer as many consecutive working days as possible, and would therefore desire the status of a preferred worker over alternating worker. However, from the perspective of the labor exchange offices through which the UERP distributed its workers, it was practically impossible of providing consecutive working days to all registered workers. While the labor exchange offices were premised on the idea of unemployment emergency relief, the waves of registered workers far outnumbered the possibility of providing consecutive working days for all workers. To be fair to as many workers as possible, therefore, these offices generally favored alternative working days over consecutive working days. This did not mean, however, that consecutive working days and corresponding preferred workers were abandoned altogether. In large measure, this was due to the fact that construction site foremen, working through public works departments within state, prefectural, and city governments, but employing workers coming out of the UERP and the labor exchange offices, overwhelmingly favored preferred workers over alternating workers. The reason was that the former provided continuous labor on construction sites. Public works departments, which organized the actual plans for constructing the dams, bridges, roads, and other infrastructure, did not favor alternative workers because labor was interrupted by the appearance of new workers on the sites every day.

As Kase has shown, therefore, another way to understand the problem of preferred workers versus alternating workers is to see how this binary opposition expressed institutional conflicts of interest between, on the one hand, the public works departments wishing for the former and, on the other, the UERP-related labor exchange offices wishing for the latter. Kase's point is that, while the UERP itself was always torn between these two positions, the organization tended to compromise and sacrifice the original goal of the UERP as a source of worker relief in favor of an ideology of efficiency dictated by public works departments.[39] Prior to 1929, when the number of workers was fairly limited since the UERP only functioned in the winter season and only in the six major cities, the tension between relief and efficiency was mitigated by giving most workers the status of preferred worker. For example, in 1928, Kyoto's UERP used preferred workers 100 percent of the time. Kobe used them 99 percent of the time, while even Osaka, which had an enormous number of registered workers, used alternating workers only 33 percent of the time.[40] As the number of unemployed workers increased exponentially after 1929, however, and after registration procedures were changed to control and drastically limit the number of registered workers, the UERP had to invent ways to balance the ratio between preferred workers and alternating workers. Since the UERP rules and regulations did not specify a fixed ratio between the two categories, individual labor exchange offices working with the UERP and with individual construction site foremen had no other choice but to make the decisions on their own.[41]

What resulted was a two-step process whereby the labor exchange offices would send, on a given day, all alternating workers to a particular construction site. After a day's work on the site, the construction foremen handpicked which workers he felt should be considered preferred workers for the remaining period of the construction site. The foreman then provided the labor exchange offices with a list of selected workers, and the labor exchange offices in turn contacted those workers with the news that they could work consecutive days on the site and that they no longer had to appear at the labor exchange offices every morning before heading out to the construction site.

Precise data showing the ratio of preferred to alternating workers does not exist in any systematic way, although a report in the journal *Toshi Mondai* (Urban Problems) asserts that, in Tokyo in 1932, preferred workers averaged 24 workdays per month while alternating workers averaged only 8.[42] The best method to address this ratio, however indirect, is to look at the number of working days given to registered workers, as seen in table 28.

What we see is a pattern showing clear differences in working days between Korean and Japanese workers. First, in Osaka, Kyoto, and Tokyo, the percentage of Koreans working 1 to 14 days was consistently higher than the percentage of Japanese. In Osaka, 31.1 percent of Koreans, nearly double the percentage of Japanese workers, secured between 1 and 14 days of work. In Kyoto, 73.2 percent of Koreans worked 1 to 14 days in contrast to 64.5 percent of Japanese; and in Tokyo, those percentages were 93.8 for Koreans and 86 percent for Japanese. In the 10 to 14 day range, Koreans also had higher percentages compared to Japanese.

Second, looking at figures for monthly working days higher than 14, Japanese percentages were consistently higher than Korean percentages. In Osaka, 47 percent of Japanese worked more than 14 days, compared to 32 percent for Koreans. In Kyoto, Japanese and Koreans working more than 14 days was 35.5 percent and 26.7 percent, respectively; and in Tokyo, Japanese percentages were twice as large as Korean percentages (14.1 percent to 6.3 percent). What is particularly striking is how Japanese workers predominated in the over 25 working days category. In Osaka, Japanese and Koreans working more than 14 days was 16.8 percent and 3.4 percent, respectively; in Kyoto, it was 15.6 percent and 3.7 percent; and in Tokyo, 9.3 percent and 2.5 percent.

Finally, there is the difference between Japanese and Korean workers in the category of no workdays. This meant that the worker did not work any days on UERP sites despite the fact that he was registered with the UERP. In all likelihood, these workers registered with the UERP as a kind of back-up system in case other jobs fell through. Having met the basic requirements for registration, these workers, while given permission to work with the UERP, did not have to work through the UERP. Unfortunately, we only have data from Osaka and not from Kyoto or Tokyo, but the difference is stark. Almost 23 percent of Japanese fell into this category while only 8.8 percent of Koreans were in this category. It is not unreasonable to conclude, therefore, that if a Korean worker was able to register with the UERP (which was not easy), the chances were extremely high that he was not registering as a back-up system for regular employment, and that he would probably accept any job given to him by the UERP. Japanese had more flexibility in this regard.

Overall, then, these statistics show that Korean workers worked fewer days through the UERP and likely were granted fewer consecutive working days per month compared to Japanese. In this regard, we follow Kase's conclusion, namely that registered Japanese workers, and not registered Korean workers, tended to be preferentially granted the status of preferred worker and were

TABLE 28. UERP Work Days for Registered Workers in Osaka, Kyoto, and Tokyo, 1932

	Japanese	%	Korean	%
Osaka				
No work days	544	22.9	201	8.8
1–4	83	3.5	94	4.1
5–9	135	5.7	308	13.5
10–14	497	20.9	948	41.6
15–19	319	13.4	471	20.7
20–24	399	16.8	179	7.9
25+	398	16.8	78	3.4
Total	2,375	100	2,279	100
Kyoto				
No work days	NA		NA	
1–4	4	2.8	9	2.6
5–9	14	9.9	26	7.4
10–14	73	51.8	222	63.2
15–19	19	13.5	57	16.2
20–24	9	6.4	24	6.8
25+	22	15.6	13	3.7
Total	141	100	351	100
Tokyo				
No work days	NA		NA	
1–4	2,643	19	695	12.5
5–9	7,103	51	3,487	62.6
10–14	2,222	16	1,045	18.7
15–19	669	4.8	210	3.8
20+	1,290	9.3	137	2.5
Total	13,927	100	5,574	100

Sources: Matsui, *Kyoto ni okeru shitsugyōsha seikatsu jōtai chōsa*, 34–35; Osaka-shi Shakai-bu Rōdō-ka, "Osaka-shi Shitsugyōsha Seikatsu Jōtai Chōsa" in Kase, *Senzen Nihon no shitsugyō taisau*, 151; Tokyo-shi, *Tokyo-shi shitsugyōsha seikatsu jōtai chōsa*, 72–73.

able to work more consecutive days than Koreans.[43] Moreover, and as we will see later, this translated into lower incomes for Korean workers compared to Japanese workers.

What bears emphasis, however, is that the relationship between consecutive working days and alternating working days, itself expressed practically in the relationship between preferred and alternating workers, was a relationship that created lines of alliance, interest, and division among registered workers seeking the most numerous working days possible. It was not simply a matter of obtaining this status that created the divisions, but rather the institutional conditions through which interest in obtaining this status at all were created, improvised on, modified, and touched up here and there by the UERP like a real bricoleur. Yet while this improvisation perhaps modified the ratios between preferred workers and alternating workers, it decidedly did not eliminate this basic relation at its core. Rather, the shifting ratios between these two types gained additional influence over workers because there were no officially fixed levels mandated by the central labor exchange office of the interior ministry's social bureau that stipulated what percentage of workers should be granted preferred status. Rather, it was decided upon by the judgments of UERP bureaucrats and individual foremen hired by the UERP.

The stakes were thus extremely high for those registered workers who were still only considered alternating workers. In this way, then, the relation to the status of preferred workers effected and enforced a kind of internalized work discipline by individual workers on a construction site. While it can be said that Japanese workers tended to be given the status of preferred worker more often compared to Koreans, the more important point is that this status difference existed at all. This difference rippled throughout the entire community of registered workers in the UERP and created compelling conditions for workers to strive for the status of preferred worker. It divided workers even as it compelled workers to be productive and disciplined so that they could be picked to work as many consecutive days as possible. The distinction between preferred and alternating workers was therefore, inevitably, a highly charged political problem as well, one that touched upon the problem of Korean labor power as a colonial labor force.

It is for this reason that the preferred worker status was heavily criticized by all workers, but especially by Koreans, as evidenced by these four brief examples. First, in a report from the *Shakai Undo Tsūshin*, over 200

Korean workers from the petition section from the Korean organization *Zai-na Chōsenjin Shitsugyō Taisaku Kiseidōmeikai* (The Unemployment Policy Regulation Alliance of Koreans in Nagoya) gathered in Nagoya's Tsurumai Park on May 4, 1933. After fiery speeches criticizing the UERP, the crowd stormed the Nagoya city ward office and demanded that "the system of preferred workers be destroyed" in addition to eleven other demands.[44]

Another case comes from the outskirts of Tokyo in 1931, at the Fuchū labor exchange office. According to Toyohara, the director of the Tokyo central labor exchange bureau, 93 registered Korean workers, "showing a stubborn and strong sense of solidarity . . . formed a leftist organization called the *Isshinkai*" and demanded the immediate abolition of the system of preferred workers (*kaotsuki*) and the requirement to employ only registered workers every day.[45]

Also in 1931, Korean and Japanese workers registered with the Fukagawa labor exchange office in Tokyo published a newsletter for unemployed workers, called *Chika Tabi* (Underground Journey), in which the problem of the preferred worker system was criticized. These workers thus made demands to the director of the Fukagawa Labor Exchange to abolish the preferred worker system on the grounds that it "deliberately divides Korean and Japanese workers within the labor exchange."[46]

Finally, we have a detailed dossier from the Nishi Sugamo labor exchange in Tokyo, dated January 1931. "A Report on the current situation of Day Workers with Emphasis on the Nishi Sugamo Labor Exchange Office" was a handwritten dossier, authored by a clearly distraught director of the Nishi Sugamo office and mimeographed and circulated to all labor exchange offices in Tokyo and its environs.[47] In the section "incidents arising among workers," the director writes:

> These incidents stem from the severely restricted number of employment opportunities available through the Labor Exchange office. The UERP has had no other choice except to throw some unemployed workers out into the streets. These incidents between workers stem from feelings of jealousy and frustration in the face of other workers' success in obtaining registration as well as consecutive working days. These feelings, moreover, have led to violent outbreaks among workers. Both Korean and Japanese workers share these feelings of jealousy but Koreans are actually involved in clashes with other workers on this issue.[48]

The director gives three specific cases:

    (a) July 24, 1930: Korean worker beats up Japanese worker. As a penalty, the Korean worker's work book was confiscated and his work days were immediately suspended.

    (b) November 5, 1930: Korean and Japanese workers jointly agree to collectively reject the status of preferred worker [mentsuki] in all cases in which they are granted this status by the UERP.

    (c) December 19, 1930: Korean workers fight against fellow Korean workers who have obtained the status of preferred worker. The latter Koreans, however, decided in the end to reject this status in solidarity with the former Koreans.[49]

These last two cases are particularly noteworthy insofar as they show how the workers were very aware of how the preferred worker system not only divided Japanese and Koreans, but also divided Koreans among themselves. The first case, however, shows how the problem of working days was treated as an institutional privilege that could be taken away as a form of punishment and discipline. The strength of the UERP vis-à-vis registered workers was its capacity to mobilize the fear of not working while simultaneously creating a desire—inextricably connected to the machinery of the UERP's institutional channels themselves—for employment and working days under terms and conditions set by the UERP and, by extension, by the public works department of the interior ministry's social bureau.

Work Discipline in the UERP: Differences between
Direct Management and Sub-Contracting

At the center of these terms and conditions was the enormous problem of how to manage the public works construction sites where registered UERP workers found employment. For the UERP, basing its operations in the labor exchange offices but simultaneously working in close conjunction with the interior ministry's public works department, did not merely send its registered workers to public works construction sites, but also managed many of those sites as well. The problem, however, was whether the UERP would directly manage the construction sites or instead hire private subcontractors.

Prior to 1925, public works offices within city and regional governments carried out their construction projects by contracting out to sub-contractors.

Sub-contractors were responsible for innumerable basic jobs of the construction project, at the center of which was supplying day workers. Moreover, sub-contractors hiring day workers often housed the latter in temporary or cheap lodging, gave them cash loans at interest, lent workers tools, and, in exceptionally rare cases, covered medical costs in cases of injury or death. All of these aspects combined into a unique economy unto itself centering around the sub-contractor's methods of wage payment and wage skimming, or pin-hane, a process in which fixed percentages of workers' wages were taken by sub-contractors. The more complex the division of labor and the network of primary and secondary sub-contractors, the more the real wages fell below the nominal wage. At the same time, pinhane was a source of income for sub-contractors, who relied on that income to the same degree workers despised it as a method of devouring their wages. Considered by many a pre-modern, feudal remnant, the sub-contracting system was the object of much social criticism.[50]

For this reason, the establishment of the UERP in 1925 made it a matter of policy to abandon the sub-contracting system and to manage workers directly through city and prefectural public works bureaus (chokuei jigyō hōshiki). These bureaus, which until 1925 had no experience in directly managing the everyday life of day workers, now faced the daunting task of executing the basic jobs sub-contractors had once done. When the UERP was initially established in 1925 it proudly touted its rejection of the sub-contracting system in favor of direct management. And early in the UERP's institutional history, it considered direct management an excellent opportunity for Korean day workers. For example, in a twelve-page survey of Korean workers in Osaka by the Osaka regional labor exchange bureau, UERP specialists explained the benefits of direct management especially for Korean workers:[51]

> Section 6. Winter Unemployment Relief Programs and the Welfare of Korean Workers
>
> The public relief programs established in the three cities [Osaka, Kyoto, Kobe] have done much more than merely provide relief to day workers by alleviating the duress of unemployment. Originally, public organizations which provided unemployment relief to workers relied upon and entrusted sub-contractors to directly supply workers, control worker efficiency, supervise construction sites, and pay workers their wages on their own. It would have been nearly impossible for the relief programs to directly manage these functions anyway. All of this has changed, however, and

we are now fully confident that we will be able to make an easy transition from the system of sub-contracting to direct management. Not only is this a great boon for workers, but it is also a major innovation for the public relief programs. The welfare of workers can be seen, in particular, in the following points:

1. The elimination of the wage problem of intermediary exploitation. With the new system of direct management, wages will be paid directly, every day, by the UERP through the Labor Exchange Offices.
2. The program under direct management will fix minimum wages. There may be some slight differences depending on ability, but by and large they will be the same. Also, workers under direct management are better off than workers working under sub-contractors insofar as wages in the former will be increased in the case of overtime work. Finally, differences in wages will not be based on the distinction between Japanese and Korean workers.[52]

There were difficulties, however, in completely abandoning the sub-contracting system in favor of direct management. Kase discusses four areas that were especially challenging to the direct management system. First, there was the problem of the procurement and management of tools. Prior to the establishment of the UERP in 1925, public works bureaus did not have to purchase tools for construction sites nor involve themselves in the lending of tools to workers; sub-contractors owned their own tools, which they lent to workers at the construction site. In cases where the worker damaged or destroyed the tools, the sub-contractors took the expenses out of the workers' wages through pinhane. The UERP's rejection of the sub-contracting system now meant that the public works bureaus themselves were responsible for purchasing the tools, lending the tools to the workers, and managing and penalizing workers for damages to tools. Costs of replacing tools in cases of theft were also the public works bureaus' new responsibility.

Second, public works bureaus were now responsible for meeting medical costs stemming from work-related injuries and death. While sub-contractors were able to evade responsibility for paying for medical costs for worker injuries, the UERP's rejection of the sub-contracting system placed this burden onto the shoulders of the public works bureaus themselves. Also, in cases of death, the latter were required to cover funeral and burial expenses. In 1931 and within the national road improvement construction sites alone, medical and funeral costs stemming from 29 deaths, 150 critical injuries, and 1,820 minor injuries were the public works bureaus' responsibility.[53]

Third, workers increasingly demanded that if available employment opportunities were publicized and posted, the bureaus take full responsibility for guaranteeing the availability of those jobs, even on days when bad weather prevented work. By contrast, in the sub-contracting system, work was invariably stopped in cases of bad weather. Sub-contractors would often advance money to workers on off-days and get back its full amount plus a fixed percentage of interest by subtracting the sum from the worker's wages on payday, usually at the end of the month. The direct management system, however, could not replicate this process and had to sustain vociferous demands by workers to give work on days when work was theoretically guaranteed but practically impossible for an assortment of reasons, including bad weather. Increasingly it became clear that the public works bureaus and the UERP could not afford to keep these guarantees.

Fourth, the system of direct management was held responsible for determining worker wages, resulting in conflict. Wages had to be kept below the average wages found in the so-called free labor market, but could not be completely fixed, either, given the diversity of forms of work within construction sites. Wages for so-called light work could not be the same as so-called heavy and relatively dangerous work, such as jobs in dams or sewage systems. This did not ease the task of determining the precise wages for individual workers, and strikes and protests demanding wage increases were not uncommon, especially among Koreans. Moreover, an additional problem lay in negotiating standards for overtime pay, which in the past was done by the sub-contractors.[54]

These problems, coupled with the economic austerity measures enforced by the ruling Minseitō party, presented considerable challenges to the UERP. For during the acute depression years between 1929 and 1931, a central problem was the challenge of balancing radically reduced finances for public works construction sites while simultaneously providing relief for unemployed workers flooding the UERP offices. The UERP simply could not meet the costs to maintain a complete direct management system.[55] As a result, not only did the UERP rethink its previous anti-sub-contracting position, it began to incorporate the sub-contracting system into the heart of the UERP. In fact, as Kase has shown, the UERP was already heading in this direction as early as 1926 and 1927.[56] The 1929 austerity measures, however, tipped the scale in the direction of a reversion back to the sub-contractor system. Sub-contractors were now, through a kind of institutional loophole, *sewa-yaku* or assistants. An example of this shift or reversion can be seen in Nagoya in 1926, where sub-contractors within the UERP were used as assistants in the form of hambagashira to house and provide labor exchanges for Korean workers, who constituted over 70 percent of the registered workers.[57] This example is particularly germane to this discussion because it reveals how and in what capacity the UERP compromised its general principles by using sub-contractors as so-called assistants, and how this practice combined with the commodification of Korean labor power within the UERP. In other words, the UERP's so-called direct management system was in fact supplemented by the sub-contracting system that already existed in the labor market. This dismayed many Koreans, who in particular were attracted to the UERP precisely because of its ostensible commitment to so-called direct management, its rejection of the sub-contracting system, and its refusal to base differences in wages on ethnicity. By 1929, however, the UERP was using the vast sub-contracting system in addition to directly managing its various projects.

Especially in Tokyo, Koreans led mass protests against the reversion and inclusion of the sub-contracting system through the backdoor of the UERP. For example, according to the director of the Nishi Sugamo labor exchange office in 1931, angry Korean workers, storming the labor exchange offices, argued that they were discriminated against because the jobs they were given through the UERP were all under the authority of sub-contractors. As the director writes: "December 22, 1930: Violent incident inside the office involving Korean workers. They demanded the fairer distribution of work books and also protested that it was not fair that Korean workers were sent exclusively to construction sites operated by sub-contractors."[58] Other incidents under the category of "Incidents arising between workers and sub-contractors" were described as conflicts "involving complaints of harsh treatment from sub-contractors who managed construction sites, complaints against wage reductions," and finally demands that the labor exchange offices pay the medical expenses of injured workers since "the sub-contractors were indifferent to the injuries and did not pay." Additionally, three specific examples were given, all of which involved Korean workers:

> August 17, 1930: Korean workers band together to demand sub-contractors to give them rest breaks.

October 8, 1930: Sub-contractors refuse to use Korean workers who were
appointed by the labor exchange office.

January 4, 1931: Korean workers leave work site, claiming they are sick and
tired of working on sub-contractor's site.[59]

Precisely at the same time that these problems were plaguing the Nishi
Sugamo labor exchange office in Tokyo, the Tokyo regional labor exchange
bureau began coordinating what would become the first UERP-funded, inter-
prefectural unemployed worker mobilization plan. Unemployed workers in
Tokyo were mobilized to be sent to Yamanashi prefecture, Tokyo's neighbor
to the west, to work on national road 8. The work was slated to commence
in the winter of 1930. Tokyo's labor exchange offices (including the belea-
guered Nishi Sugamo office), sent half of the workers needed to complete the
road construction; Yamanashi's government supplied the remaining workers
from its own labor exchange offices, and also provided local sub-contractors
to manage three sections of the construction.[60] Eventually, a total of 4,204
workers were used, out of which 1,776 or 42.2 percent were Korean. Section
three of the construction site employed 1,109 of the 1,776 Koreans, or 62.4
percent (see table 29).

What followed shortly after the construction began were two large labor
strikes and a sub-contracting nightmare for all parties involved, but especially
for the Korean workers in section three, all of whom were housed in nineteen
hamba operated by nineteen Japanese sub-contractors. Their lodgings were
separated not just from Japanese workers but also from Yamanashi-based Korean workers.[61]

The first strike began in section three on November 8, 1930, when a large
group of Korean workers started a protest, claiming that sub-contractors in
Yamanashi were breaking the agreement, made to the workers by Tokyo labor
exchange offices, that wages would fall between 1.10 and 2.00 yen. Upon ar-
riving in Yamanashi, however, all of the workers only received 1.10. They thus
demanded 1.40 yen but were flatly denied. This protest, however, inspired
Japanese workers in section one to protest low wages as well. Both Koreans
in section three and Japanese in section one, however, were flatly rejected by
the sub-contractors, and as a result, 35 Koreans and 122 Japanese decided
to quit and return to Tokyo.[62] Enough workers remained, however, for the
construction site to keep going into early December, when a second strike
broke out. The primary sub-contractor for section three, Kobayashi Jûtaro,
reduced the wages of 200 workers from 1.00 yen to 0.70 sen, a decrease of

TABLE 29. Japanese and Korean Workers on the Yamanashi No. 8 Site

Construction Section:	I		II		III		Total	
	Jpn.	Kor.	Jpn.	Kor.	Jpn.	Kor.	Jpn.	Kor.
Yamanashi Workers	674	305	403	111	206	783	1,283	1,199
Tokyo UERP Workers (total)	693	196	45	55	407	326	1145	577
a. Tokyo-shi Labor Exchange	331	137	33	40	267	181	631	358
b. Tokyo-fu Labor Exchange	362	59	12	15	140	145	514	219
Total number	1,367	501	448	166	613	1,109	2,428	1,776
Total percent	73.2	26.8	73	27	35.6	64.4	57.8	42.2

Source: Tokyo Chihō Shokugyō Shōkai Jimukyoku, "Yamanashi-ken kokudō 8-gōsen kaishu kōji rōdō idō keika tenmatsu, Rōdō idō dai-3 shū," 129–35.

30 percent. This led 800 Koreans to immediately protest the wage decrease and to stop working, pleading angrily that the prefecture broke its promise to pay 1.20 yen for wages.[63] The sub-contrator, Kobayashi, rejected the demand, defensively arguing that "sub-contractors have the right to freely determine the employment and working conditions for all workers who are not part of the Yamanashi prefecture UERP [i.e., from Tokyo]."[64]

Thirty-three workers in section one walked out in sympathy, and many in section two did the same. The sub-contractors then went on the attack. On December 9, 100 Koreans in section three were fired;[65] on December 11, an announcement was made that wages for 700 Korean workers in section three would be cut; then on December 13, 700 Koreans in section three were fired.[66] Finally, on December 19, Kobayashi announced the complete stoppage of construction in section three, citing bad weather as the reason.[67] In response, on January 12, 1931, 60 Korean workers formerly employed in section three formed the Yamanashi branch of Nihon Doboku Kenchiku Rōdō Kumiai (Japan Public Works Labor Union) and demanded: (1) the immediate end to wage differences based on ethnicity; (2) an eight-hour workday and full coverage of unemployment insurance by the government; and (3) liberation of Korea and happiness for all Koreans.[68] Kobayashi, now fearing a prolonged walkout and facing pressure by members of two parties in the Yamanashi prefectural parliament to end the strike, decided to raise wages to 0.85 sen, but only on the condition that workers wishing to continue into the spring sign a "Written Worker Oath" (Rōdō Seiyakusho).[69]

The written oath, reprinted in its entirety in the official account of the Yamanashi road 8 construction by the Tokyo regional labor exchange office, was composed between February 19, 1931 and March 5, 1931, by fifteen public office holders, including the governor of Yamanashi prefecture, Hirata Yūichi.[70] The opening line of the oath concisely stated its purpose: "In light of the frequent outbreaks of worker uprisings, the sub-contractors of the Yamanashi prefecture number eight national road construction have concluded that an excellent method to prevent similar outbreaks in the future is to require all workers to sign the following oath upon obtaining employment."[71] Following this, the representative from the Tokyo regional labor exchange office re-stated the purpose of the oath vis-à-vis unemployed workers from Tokyo's UERP offices currently employed on the construction site. The most important points of the oath were as follows:

Section One: Matters Relating to Discipline [kiritsu kankei]
  1. To always obey, without question, the orders of the sub-contractor or the prefecture-appointed supervisor
  2. To execute one's work with loyalty and devotion [chūjitsu ni]
  3. To never organize factions, conspirators or initiate mass action [taishū kōdō]

Section Two: Methods of Work and Wage Calculations
  ... In the case differences of opinion arise between a worker and the sub-contractor in relation to the calculation of said wages, we will respect the decision [hantei] of the prefecture's appointed supervisor. The decision must be obeyed absolutely ...

Section Three: Payment of Wages and Accumulated Fees
  ... A minimum of five yen will be taken out of the worker's wages at the end of the month or on the 15th of the month for travel costs (for Tokyo workers)

Section Four: Hamba and Lodging
  1. Fees for lodging in the sub-contractor operated hamba will cost each worker 35 sen
  2. Bedding and other lodging fees will cost 6 sen

Section Five: In case of Illness and Injury
  1. In cases of injury, travel fees will be waived, medical costs will be covered and 20 sen daily will be given until the worker has healed

Section Six: Firings [kaikō]

1. . . . The sub-contractor has the authority to lay off the total number of workers on the construction site or fire individual workers whenever the progress of the construction site requires a decrease in workers, or whenever the sub-contractor feels it is necessary . . . .

2. Layoffs will be announced one week in advance. The released worker is not permitted to object to the appointed day and must leave the construction site on that day.

3. If any points stipulated on this oath are violated the worker will be released immediately . . . .[72]

Unfortunately, the 1933 report from the Tokyo regional labor exchange office does not recount the extent to which the oath was effectively deployed for the duration of the construction period in Yamanashi. The report did, however, quote a Tokyo representative saying that he specifically wanted Korean workers to participate in signing the oath in the next round of transporting workers from Tokyo to Yamanashi. A representative from Yamanashi's Dōrō Shuji Gishi agreed to this, however, only if their numbers were halved.[73] Indeed, the report stated that, "sub-contractors as well as the prefecture in general has become wary of using Korean workers and has tried to evade dealing with them."[74]

The fact, however, that similar written oaths were deployed by other sub-contractors on different construction sites in different prefectures around the same time reveals the extent to which written oaths were deployed for disciplining unemployed workers on UERP-related construction sites. One last example, again involving striking Korean workers, dates from July 1931, just a few months after the completion of the Yamanashi construction. Some 90 Korean workers struck at a UERP sub-contracted construction project in western Tokyo in Fuchū, on a gravel pit construction site on the banks of the Tama river. Among other demands, the Korean workers requested increased wages (from 1.00 yen to 1.50 yen), the elimination of the system of preferred workers, and the immediate payment of 60 percent of back wages.[75] The back wages were paid, but the workers were told that if the strike continued into the next day, their UERP registration would be immediately suspended. Three Korean activists were arrested; one was jailed.[76] Simultaneously, the interior ministry's construction bureau held an emergency meeting on the Fuchū strike, and outlined the need to "use the police departments to enforce the signing of written oaths in order to register workers [in the UERP], to mobilize and transport to Fuchū registered workers from other labor exchange offices, and to judiciously select serious and dutiful registered workers from among the workers in Fuchū."[77] These plans were then put into action and realized on August 19, when registration was only granted to the Korean workers who signed the written oath composed by the construction bureau. The oath read as follows:

1. We agree to dutifully obey the orders of the sub-contractor and labor exchange officer
2. We agree not to incite actions or debates among workers
3. We agree not to leave the construction site without permission
4. We agree not to incite unrest among other workers through the spreading of one's beliefs
5. We accept dismissal from the job after three absences
6. Violating any of the above promises will disqualify us from registration with this construction site.[78]

The function of the oath was to commit each worker to a regimen of discipline while working under sub-contractors for the UERP. It is worth repeating that the oath was a product of the UERP's integration, through the backdoor, of the sub-contracting system as a supplement to its official policy of direct management. Moreover, failure to abide by the oath meant being released from the UERP—in which case it did not even matter if one was a preferred worker or an alternating worker. For registration in toto was threatened to be taken away if the oath was not signed. At the same time, it has to be said that while the disciplining aspects of the worker oath stemmed from the incorporation of the sub-contracting system into the heart of the UERP, this incorporation itself has to be understood as an effect of the difference between preferred workers and alternating workers, that is, as an effect of the problem of the insecurity of employment. The fear immanent to the insecurity of employment, embodied in the difference between preferred and alternating workers, was the precondition and not the result of work discipline. In other words, the social tensions and economic pressures effected by the difference between preferred and alternating workers were mechanically and institutionally raised up to economic pressures, only now on a different level with different social tensions and forms of compulsion, manifested in the difference between direct management and the sub-contracting system.

Inside and outside the UERP

Both the insecurity of employment and work discipline were thus enforced through the workings of invented binary oppositions such as alternating versus preferred worker. Moreover, these binaries were implanted within Japanese and Korean communities to maintain larger, ethnic oppositions. The important point, however, is that the UERP was not only fueled by each set of binary oppositions, but also embodied in practice a series of relays between sets of binary oppositions invented by the UERP to manage surplus populations. Each set played a different function and created lines of alliance, interest, and division among the workers who were attached to them. This is why state bureaus and offices became distraught when workers attacked each set of binary oppositions. They became lines of flight and lines of refusal. When this happened, the relays between the sets themselves were cut and held in suspense; the relays lost their meaning. When the relays worked, however, when each set was able to remain sturdy and functional, then work discipline on UERP construction sites was effective: construction sites were completed, profits were made, and wages were distributed among workers.

Table 30 shows the differences in levels of income obtained by registered workers in the UERP in 1932 in Osaka, Kyoto, and Tokyo. What we can see is that the 30 yen income range was the dividing line between Koreans and Japanese. In Osaka, 18.8 percent of Japanese workers earned 30 yen or more while only 3.2 percent of Koreans earned the same; in Kyoto, Japanese and Korean workers earning more than 30 yen was 12.1 percent and 1.7 percent, respectively; and in Tokyo, it was 8.1 percent and 1.8 percent. Inversely, for the 1 to 30 yen range, Koreans consistently had higher percentages than Japanese.

Similar trends in income levels between Japanese and Korean workers can be seen in incomes obtained by registered Japanese and Korean workers immediately prior to entering the UERP. Looking at table 31, we see that within the general category of industry (kōgyō), the clear dividing line between incomes between Japanese and Koreans was the 30 yen range. Japanese with incomes of 30 yen or more made up 75 percent, compared to 34.4 percent for Koreans. Lastly, while 27.4 percent of Koreans earned between 10 and 20 yen, only 7.1 percent of Japanese earned the same.

Looking now at the incomes for construction as well as day labor, the same income differences are visible in even stronger contrast. Again, the cut-off line was the 30 yen range. On the high-end, the percentage of Japanese earning incomes over 30 yen was 66.6 percent in construction and 65.1 percent in

TABLE 30. Income Obtained from UERP in Osaka, Kyoto, and Tokyo, 1932

Wage (yen)	Japanese	%	Korean	%
Osaka				
No income	544	22.9	201	8.8
Under 10	204	8.6	391	17.2
10–20	685	28.6	1,354	59.4
20–30	495	20.8	259	11.4
30–40	260	10.9	67	2.9
40–50	150	6.3	7	0.3
Over 50	37	1.6	0	0
Total	2,375	100	2,279	100
Kyoto				
Under 10	24	17	52	14.8
10–20	79	56	261	74.4
20–30	21	14.9	32	9.1
Over 30	17	12.1	6	1.7
Total	141	100	351	100
Tokyo				
Under 10	7,747	55.6	3,184	57.1
10–20	4,122	30	1,948	34.9
20–30	930	6.7	340	6.1
30–40	688	4.9	79	1.4
40–50	347	2.5	20	0.4
Over 50	93	0.7	3	0
Total	13,927	100	5,574	100

Sources: Matsui, *Kyoto ni okeru shitsugyōsha seikatsu jōtai chōsa*, 34–35; Tokyo-shi, *Tokyo-shi shitsugyōsha seikatsu jōtai chōsa*, 72–73; Osaka-shi Shakai-bu Rōdō-ka, "Osaka-shi Shitsugyōsha Seikatsu Jōtai Chōsa," in Kase, *Senzen Nihon no shitsugyō taisaku*, 151.
Note: The overlap of wages (1–10, 10–20, etc.) is reproduced here as in the original.

TABLE 31. Monthly Income Immediately Prior to UERP Registration, Osaka 1932

Wage (yen)	Japanese		Korean	
	No.	%	No.	%
General Industry				
No income	22	1.5	6	0.4
1–10	35	2.4	37	2.7
10–20	102	7.1	379	27.4
20–30	200	14	487	35.2
30–40	217	15.2	246	17.8
40–50	351	24.5	148	10.7
Over 50	505	35.3	82	5.9
Total	1,432	100	1,385	100
Construction				
No income	2	0.8	5	0.5
1–10	5	2	33	3.3
10–20	24	9.8	339	33.9
20–30	51	20.7	401	40.1
30–40	51	20.7	148	14.8
40–50	60	24.4	50	5
Over 50	53	21.5	25	2.5
Total	246	100	1,001	100
Day Labor				
No income	1	2.3	0	0
1–10	0	0	54	9.7
10–20	4	9.3	243	43.7
20–30	10	23.3	156	28.1
30–40	9	20.9	53	9.5
40–50	11	25.6	38	6.8
Over 50	8	18.6	12	2.2
Total	43	100	556	100

Source: Osaka-shi Shakai-bu Rōdō-ka, "Osaka-shi Shitsugyōsha Seikatsu Jōtai Chōsa," 29–78, 185–219.
Note: The overlap of wages (1–10, 10–20, etc.) is reproduced here as in the original.

day labor. Korean percentages for the same, respectively, were 22.3 percent and 18.5 percent. By contrast, Korean percentages for incomes between 1 and 30 yen were 77.3 percent in construction and 81.5 percent in day labor; Japanese percentages for the same were both less than half the Korean figures at 32.5 percent and 32.6 percent. Again, the differences in the 10 to 20 yen range and the over 50 yen are stark.

The income statistics for workers prior to entering the UERP and after entering the UERP strongly suggest three general points. First, differences between Japanese and Korean income levels tended to fall around the 30 yen income level. Compared to Korean workers, Japanese workers by and large tended to earn incomes higher than 30 yen both within, as well as outside, the UERP. By contrast, for the 1 to 30 yen range, Korean workers consistently had higher percentages than Japanese, both within and outside the UERP. Second, the incomes obtained in the UERP for both Japanese and Koreans generally did not represent a radical increase or decrease in income compared to incomes from prior employment. Third, incomes obtained in the UERP tended to replicate the ratios, found outside the UERP, between Japanese and Korean workers for particular income brackets. What is clear is that there were no reversals in ratios between Koreans and Japanese; rather, these ratios tended to be consistently maintained.[79]

The point of this comparison between pre-UERP incomes and UERP incomes is that, from the perspective of Koreans and in terms of income, nothing was lost or gained by registering with the UERP. From the viewpoint of Korean workers in Japan, the UERP was almost identical to the so-called free labor market. This, no doubt, was one reason why so many Korean protests were made against the UERP and the labor exchange offices. What, then, was the meaning of so-called unemployment emergency relief? We have shown that there was no relief given to Koreans by the UERP and that, if there was any meaning at all attached to the idea of relief from the UERP, it was the struggle against the UERP's idea of relief. For the UERP only reproduced job insecurity and the basic conditions for the exploitation of Korean labor power as cheap, colonial labor. In this sense, the UERP did not exist outside of its purpose as a state machine possessing a specific, mechanical function, namely to pore over and sift through the mass of un-individuated workers, to identify and mark them, to strategically select, permit, or deny admission to the UERP—in short, to create as many opportunities to individualize as many unemployed workers as possible by registering them with state apparatuses in order to promote, regulate, and enforce a life indebted to wage labor and the state.

In this book I have tried to narrate a history of the search for work and to document some of the most pervasive, repetitive, and entrenched contingencies of this search experienced by Korean workers in Japan during the interwar period. I wanted to show how many of the most urgent political and social movements by Korean workers in Japan were formed against and in reaction to these contingencies. But I also wanted to reveal the historical emergence of lines of fragmentation within Korean surplus populations, lines that fell across institutionalized borders and regulations in the labor markets, across ambiguous tenant-landlord and labor boss-worker relations, and across the divides between the so-called employed population and the so-called unemployed population. Most importantly, I wanted to bring to light the specific nature of Korean-led protests and strikes in Japan, and to emphasize that, while the conditions surrounding their struggles were often unique to Koreans, especially in regard to the problem of racism, they also revealed common problems that all workers inevitably must confront—namely, the unavoidable contingencies inherent in the process of commodifying labor power. The problem here, however, is that state apparatuses tried in all kinds of ways to disavow this common ground, for example, by blaming various problems on Koreans themselves (as if unemployment was a problem of innate Korean laziness), or else by individualizing the process of commodification to such a degree that the shared experience between workers was lost amidst bureaucratic red tape. In short, state apparatuses tried to disavow the commonness between Korean and Japanese workers through individuating tactics, divide and conquer strategies, and through efforts to essentially create competition between Korean and Japanese workers, as well as among Korean workers themselves.

Perhaps the most important discovery that I made by going through various archival materials is the extent to which Korean workers were continually funneled into the day labor market. It is as if all of the long detours on the many roads toward work in Japan ultimately led to an epicenter of day labor, in which the most basic and carnal quality of selling labor power as a commodity in a capitalist economy was laid naked and bare in the most brutal and unpredictable fashion. No doubt, there were Korean workers who toiled in small- and medium-sized factories, but the vast majority of Korean workers could not maintain job security in those factories owing to a confluence of economic rationalizing and racism. This is to say that Korean day workers served as a reserve army for these factories; the unpredictable and oppressive conditions of the small factory system existed precisely because the day labor market was always so full. At the same time, and going against a certain historiography of labor studies, I wanted to highlight the conditions of the day labor market more than the conditions of the factories, largely because the former has been ignored with such historiographical persistence. This is because, in part, the day labor market is considered an informal economy, which, for the historian, means very few documents are available for analysis. In fact, however, this was not the case once I turned my historian's gaze to sources that usually fall outside of the purview of the labor historian. Sources regarding welfare, unemployment, and especially police matters all dealt with matters of the day labor market explicitly. The day labor market was not as informal as it seemed at first blush; it was highly integrated into some of the highest levels of government. Similarly, it would be a mistake to relegate the social management of day workers in Japan to remnants of pre-modern feudalism (e.g., the oyakata system), as if these practices were historical aberrations in the heyday of modernity in Japan. Rather, these remnants were preserved in ways that corresponded with—and indeed supported—some of the highest and most developed sectors of capitalist and imperialist economy in Japan.

What especially interested me in the analysis of Korean proletarians in the day labor market was the institutional and social networks they were compelled to use for labor introductions, housing, and subsistence. No doubt, these were networks of power that worked on the populations and bodies of living Korean labor. But I quickly realized that power was not a precise analytic category to describe the real functions and operations of these institutional networks. For ultimately they were used to maintain and exploit Korean labor as cheaply as possible, and for this reason I found myself moving away from a reliance on Foucault's notion of power. This is why I commonly referred to this network as a network of commodification, or as a milieu of commodification. Once I realized that various institutional sites had connections with each other, and that they all worked in one way or another to maintain surplus populations for the purpose of commodifying and exploiting labor power as cheaply as possible, there was only one question to pursue: How was Korean labor power transformed into that which capital cannot produce directly on its own—that is, labor power as a commodity?

In addition, how can we characterize this transformation? This was the question that allowed me to hear the many voices of the Korean workers in Japan, voices that declared and announced that low wages were hardly the only problems in their lives. In fact, low wages often seemed secondary compared to the radical insecurity of trying to find a job in Japan. What increasingly became clear to me, then, was that the contingency of exchange was none other than the basic precondition for the low wages that Koreans workers received in Japan. Korean poverty existed because of their insecurity of existence. Poverty, therefore, has to be understood within the continuum of the process of transforming labor power into a commodity, but especially in terms of the contingent discontinuities of that continuous process. If there is a rhythm to the commodification of labor power, it is that it is continually discontinuous; the rhythm reveals a continuity of discontinuity. Put differently, the commodification of labor power is bound to both contingency and repetition.[1]

Contingencies of Commodification

There are other reasons for focusing on the experience of contingency by sellers of labor power in the search for work in capitalist commodity economies. Not only has it been pointed out that contingent labor is now a permanent aspect of contemporary capitalism and its neoliberal policies and ethos, but the problem of contingency has also figured prominently in contemporary critiques of representation and identity politics. For example, the problem of contingency has been foregrounded in discussions by Judith Butler, Ernesto Laclau, and Slavoj Žižek in their co-authored book, Contingency, Hegemony, Universality: Contemporary Dialogues on the Left. Among the many important lessons that can be drawn from these dialogues, perhaps one of the most important is that contemporary critical theory needs to find a way to break through the impasses of constructing critiques of capitalist society after the postmodern critique of essentialism. The critique of essentialism, as is now well known, has been pursued by various strains of postmodern theory, and it is arguable that it has been led by an emphasis on the concept of contingency. It is now (or rather, still) commonplace to speak of contingent or plural formations of political identity that deconstruct the ontologies of presence that are so often naturalized ideologically in capitalist society. Yet, as Slavoj Žižek has argued, this reliance on the concept of contingency for the critique of essentialism tends to assume, more often than not, that contingency is opposed to the historical problem of capitalist society. Arguing against this assumption, Žižek thus writes, "Against the postmodern political theory which tends increasingly to prohibit the very reference to capitalism as 'essentialist', one should assert that the plural contingency of postmodern struggles and the totality of Capital are not opposed. . . . Today's capitalism, rather, provides the very background and terrain for the emergence of shifting-dispersed-contingent-ironic-and so on, political subjectivities."[2]

How should the relationship between capitalism and contingency be understood more specifically? There is already a substantial body of work that has begun to pursue this problem in greater detail. In an older text, for example, Žižek has argued that dialectical materialism cannot be thought about properly without taking into consideration the problem of contingency as it relates to the repressed origin of capitalist societies in the process of so-called primitive accumulation.[3] Claude Meillassoux, Suzanne DeBrunhoff, and Karatani Kojin have also all emphasized, in their diverse ways, the centrality of the problem of contingency in the process of capitalist exchange.[4] Finally, the late writings by Louis Althusser offer important reflections on the theoretical and political stakes in thinking about the problem of contingency in the sale and purchase of labor power in Marx's *Capital*. For Althusser, this reading of Marx sets the tone for a larger demonstration of constructing an alternative lineage of materialism, one that moves away from the *telos* of necessity and toward a thinking of what Althusser called the "becoming-necessary of contingent encounters." He called this an "aleatory materialism," or a materialism of the contingent encounter.[5]

In this book I have specified the materialism of the encounter in terms of the contingency that inheres in the position of selling labor power as a commodity. As a further theoretical specification of this problem, it is perhaps useful to make special mention of the work of the Japanese Marxist economist, Uno Kōzō, who discussed how the process of commodifying labor power always contains within it what he called a *muri* (無理).[6] The word *muri*, as every speaker of Japanese knows, is a very common, everyday word. Transliterally, the individual characters mean (and I'm simplifying greatly) *nothingness* (無) and *reason* (理), which, when combined, might suggest something like an evacuation of reason, or an ungrounded and abyssal limit of thought. But in everyday Japanese speech, no one uses muri to express the ungrounded and abyssal limit of thought. It's generally used as a common noun, or else as a mundane transitive verb. As a noun, it indicates the impossibility of a specific situation, or that which is unreasonable, unjustifiable, unwarrantable, unnatural, and excessive. It is usually articulated by a speaker as an emphatic denial or rejection to a question, as in, "Will you work today?"—"Muri!" ("No way!") As a transitive verb, it generally indicates an action that is carried out with force, and is commonly used by a speaker to tell someone to not do something with force, or to not over do something, as in, muri shinaide (or more strongly, muri suru na!), which, depending on the intensity of the articulation, could mean something light like, "Yo, take it easy," or the more urgent, "Don't force it!" In other words, it is strongly associated with a position of opposition and negation.

These everyday nuances of opposition and negation are implicit in Uno Kōzō's use of the word muri. More specifically, however, as contemporary theoretician and historian Nagahara Yutaka has emphasized, Uno primarily used the word muri to describe two interrelated problems. First, muri describes capital's fundamental angst, its Achilles heal, its most vulnerable weakness and impotence. For what the process of commodifying labor power inescapably discloses is that, fundamentally, capital can never produce labor power as a commodity, and must therefore rely on state power to expropriate, by the force of violence, direct producers in the process of so-called primitive accumulation. This process of expropriation then creates a mass of surplus populations compelled to encounter the process of commodifying labor power at capital's most exteriorized extremities. Here at this extremity, in the pores of capitalist society, and often at the furthest strata of the surplus populations, the boundaries of the inside and outside of the capitalist commodity economy are suspended, however briefly, in the commodifying process of labor power. Second, these boundaries are suspended because of an inescapable contingency disclosed in the process of exchange. As Nagahara has argued, the word muri in Uno's text thus discloses, on the one hand, the fundamentally social tensions immanent to the force of expropriation, carried out by the capitalist state at the furthest extremities of the commodity economy, and, on the other, the sudden appearance of contingency in the sale and purchase of labor power as a commodity. I have tried to expand on these insights by Uno and Nagahara by emphasizing the relationship between contingency and what Marx called the virtual pauper, and also by considering how state power, including its many publicly disavowed supplementary organizations, maintains the contingencies immanent to commodification as a precondition for the exploitation of surplus populations.[7]

In the history of Korean surplus populations discussed in this book, the basic and ongoing precondition of the contingencies of commodification was the experience, by thousands and thousands of Koreans, of becoming severed from landed property in colonial Korea. The institution of a system of private property, carried out through the cadastral survey in Korea from 1910 to 1917, and subsequently accelerated through the implementation of the program to increase rice production, were the two basic processes that led to the immiseration and expropriation of thousands of Korean peasants in the southernmost provinces of Korea. This was the ongoing precondition of their experience of contingency within the precarious day labor markets in Japan, where Korean free workers were compelled to sell their labor power with no guarantees on a daily basis. Their appearance in Japan as a surplus population was an effect of the violence of the colonial state's inscription of private property and capitalist agricultural production in Korea.

State Power and Surplus Populations

State power has appeared in different forms, and with different functions, throughout this book. Yet all of them were related, in one way or another, to the maintenance of the contingency of exchange that inheres in the position of having to sell labor power as a commodity in order to live. Compelled to ensure the smooth commodification of labor power on the one hand, they also worked to maintain the contingencies of exchange and commodification as a precondition for the exploitation of labor power. The important point is how this contingency is maintained by these forms of state power. The experience of Korean proletarians in Japan shows us that it is a selective and discriminating process, one that integrates or registers flows of labor power as individual subjects on the one hand, while rejecting, abjecting, and expelling flows of labor power on the other hand. The effect of this, I have argued, is that surplus populations become stratified, segmented, and divided internally, often along ethnic lines, but also within particular ethnicities. What begs particular emphasis, however, is the way the stratification of the surplus populations is inextricably tied to the institutional maintenance of the contingencies of commodification that serve as the basic condition for exploitation. This problem was particularly visible in the work of the UERP and the preventive police work of the Sōaikai, the Korean welfare organization that was supported by the police.

The Sōaikai, however, leads us to understand how state power is split internally, between a public face and a disavowed and supplementary form of violence on which the public face of state power nonetheless relies. I have focused on this problem in this book for two reasons. First, it allows us to see how the margin was itself divided and split as a result of the splitting of state power. The politics surrounding Pak Ch'um-gum's election in 1932, as the first Korean to be elected into the National Diet, testifies to this problem. Second, it allows us to trace not only the microphysics of power, but more specifically how microphysical forms of power are tied to the commodification of labor power, and ultimately to the exploitation of the working class. It is true that the Sōaikai was closely associated with forms of power that were concerned with the *bios* or life of Korean populations, to forms of power that tried to make Korean populations live on while simultaneously abandoning their deaths. But an important point is that biopolitical power targeted the life of Korean populations as a means to ensure the continual commodification of labor power and to maintain the insecurity of employment as a precondition for exploitation. In itself, therefore, Foucault's notion of biopolitical power must be criticized for its inability to account for the profound relationship between the process of transforming labor power into a commodity and the dissemination of microphysical forms of modern power and their attendant forms of knowledge. More specifically, Foucault's notion of biopolitical power should not be reducible simply to the life of populations. It is rather a problem of the living labor power of surplus populations and the capacity and potential to work and transform reality that inheres in the materiality of living labor.[8]

The UERP also revealed important aspects of how state apparatuses maintain the contingencies of exchange that are experienced by surplus populations. First of all, it has to be said that the category of the unemployed was produced institutionally through various mechanisms internal to the state apparatus of the UERP, as well as through the external gate-guarding function of the UERP. The UERP ultimately did not provide relief to the masses of surplus populations knocking upon the doors of the UERP. Rather, it maintained and reproduced the contingencies inherent in the process of exchange as a precondition for the commodification and exploitation of labor. It should come as no surprise, therefore, that Japanese policy makers of the UERP closely followed the thesis on unemployment by William Beveridge, who argued for "palliating" the problem of unemployment, and who famously wrote, in 1909, that since unemployment was "as necessary to [the industrial system] as are capital and labour," the pressing task for governments was to invent ways not to eliminate unemployment, but rather to maintain an "irreducible minimum of unemployment."[9] Perverting and disavowing Marx's insights on the relative surplus populations as a social phenomenon that is produced cyclically and periodically as an endemic problem of industry, Beveridge argued that a "sheer surplus" could be maintained through labor exchanges in order to "squeeze out" the inefficient from the ranks of the surplus populations, and to discipline the remaining others for work in "newly created industries" in Britain or in the colonies.[10] The policy makers of Japan's UERP were particularly apt pupils of Beveridge's policies, though the important twist to the story of unemployment in Japan was that the maintenance of the "irreducible minimum of unemployment" was tied to an institutionalized separation and policing of the relative surplus populations in terms of those who were considered natives (naichijin) and those who were considered foreigners (gaichijin), the latter of which meant essentially colonial populations.

That chronically unemployed and semi-employed Korean day workers experienced the bureaucratic machinery of the UERP in ways that diverged from how Japanese workers experienced it should not, however, blind us to a general point about the place of the unemployed masses in a capitalist commodity economy, and about what Claude Meillassoux has called the "unique proletarian risk." This is a risk that the proletariat experiences especially in its forms of existence in (and as) the relative surplus population. What is the real significance of the relative surplus population, as a category of analysis? As an effect of two, ongoing historical processes—expropriation through primitive accumulation and exploitation within capitalist production processes—the surplus population creates the basic social conditions for the reproduction of capitalist social relations, and indeed for the entire capitalist mode of production. The reason is that its existence marks a space of separation between owners of labor power and owners of capital that is the sine qua non of the commodification of labor power. The problem of (institutionalized) racism and discrimination, for example, should therefore be approached in ways that are critical of how this separation becomes targeted by institutional forms of power that stratify and segment surplus populations. Certain surplus populations experience the separation in different ways, and in different distances from capital. This is the reason Marx specified the relative surplus population in terms of differing strata of the industrial reserve army. The point, however, is not simply that certain strata of the surplus population are at the bottom while some are not. Nor is the ultimate point that certain strata experience the contingencies of exchange more severely or acutely than other strata. Rather, these various and particular historical stratifications conceal and hide the common and universal condition of members of the proletariat having to sell their labor power as a commodity on the market, but with no guarantees of exchange. In other words, while the surplus population is organized (and often managed) in terms of particular strata, these strata conceal what is universal and common to all labor power, namely the unique proletarian risk.

The surplus population is important for an additional reason. It reveals the work of a law of populations peculiar to capitalist commodity economies, one that continually places owners of labor power in a position of disadvantage and inequality compared to owners of money and capital. Critical knowledge of the way the production (and maintenance) of the surplus population reproduces capitalist social relations is therefore central to an overall critical knowledge of the capitalist mode of production itself. This critical knowledge can and must be used politically to expose how capitalist social relations are necessarily exploitative—not only of surplus labor time, but also of the precarious social position in which owners of labor power are thrown in the process of commodification. This critical knowledge can foster the creation of political alliances of solidarity and cooperation between employed and unemployed workers, an alliance that holds the potential of exposing and challenging the real violence of capitalism that persists beneath the surface appearance of the supply and demand of labor. As Marx wrote:

> The industrial reserve army, during the periods of stagnation and average prosperity, weighs down the active army of workers; during the periods of over-production and feverish activity, it puts a curb on their pretensions. The relative surplus population is therefore the background against which the law of the demand and supply of labour does its work. . . . The movement of the law of supply and demand of labour on this basis completes the despotism of capital. Thus as soon as the workers learn the secret of why it happens that the more they work, the more alien wealth they produce, and that the more the productivity of their labour increases, the more does their very function as a means for the valorization of capital become precarious; as soon as they discover that the degree of intensity of the competition amongst themselves depends wholly on the pressure of the relative surplus population; as soon as, by setting up trade unions, etc.,

they try to organize planned co-operation between the employed and the unemployed in order to obviate or to weaken the ruinous effects of this natural law of capitalist production on their class. So soon does capital and its sycophant, political economy, cry out at the infringement of the 'eternal' and so to speak 'sacred' law of supply and demand. Every combination between employed and unemployed disturbs the 'pure' action of this law. But on the other hand, as soon as (in the colonies, for example) adverse circumstances prevent the creation of an industrial reserve army, and with it the absolute dependence of the working class upon the capitalist class, capital, along with its platitudinous Sancho Panza, rebels against the 'sacred' law of supply and demand, and tries to make up for its inadequacies by forcible means.[11]

Here Marx mentions in passing that trade unions are one form of social and political organization through which the cooperation between the employed and unemployed can become actualized. What needs to be explored further, however, is how trade unionism has also often worked against this form of cooperation, and in ways, moreover, that often overlap with problems of racism, particularism, and social exclusion. For example, that the majority of Korean workers in Japan were so-called free workers toiling in and around the day labor market had a significant impact on the relationship between Korean labor unions and Japanese trade union movements. For the problem here was that the latter privileged trade unions within the factory system. Here in the factories, if the problem of the contingency of exchange was discussed at all, it was reduced to the problem of sudden firings, i.e., unemployment. The prevailing problem for the majority of Korean workers, however, was not only in maintaining or extending job security, but of securing a job in the first place. Both Korean and Japanese day worker unions thus suffered beneath the hegemony of the trade union movements, but for Korean day workers especially, this meant that the politics of Korean labor unions commonly went unheard within the trade union movements. Partially for this reason, the largest Korean communist labor union in Japan between 1925 and 1930, Rōsō, announced in April of 1927 that it would break from the Japanese labor union movement and carry out independent struggles, claiming that the object and place of struggles were fundamentally different from the struggles taking place in the Japanese trade union movements. In this sense, the contingencies experienced by Korean free workers had a significant impact on the way Korean labor unions related to Japanese labor unions.[12] Rōsō's call to carry out independent struggles draws attention to the peculiar circumstances of Korean free workers. These workers were not toiling in factories, but were rather rejected and abjected from the factory system. They formed a surplus population outside the immediate process of production, yet were nonetheless compelled to search for wage labor as a surplus population amidst the most unpredictable conditions found in the day labor market. What we learn from the history of Korean struggles in the day labor market is that categorical differences such as the active and inactive labor forces, productive and unproductive labor, the worker and the pauper, or the employed and unemployed are essentially inadequate analytical categories. These categories, however, were not only maintained and reproduced in discourses of the social sciences and political economy in Japan, but also in practical organizations within labor movements, often at the expense of neglecting the specific politics of entire strata of surplus populations. In analyzing the historical conditions of contingency and uncertainty confronted by Korean surplus populations in Japan, however, these binary divisions do not help sharpen historical analysis, and in fact impede precise historical analysis.

The State of Emergency

> The tradition of the oppressed teaches us that the 'state of emergency' in which we live is not the exception but the rule. We must attain to a conception of history that is in keeping with this insight. Then we shall clearly realize that it is our task to bring about a real state of emergency.
>
> —Walter Benjamin, *Illuminations*, 257

I have argued in this book that the concept of the proletariat must be revitalized in relation to the concepts of contingency and social surplus. This, in turn, has demanded an attentiveness to the materiality of proletarian praxis in the contingent present, of the historicity of political praxis and its materiality in the often agonizing yet inevitable passing of the here and now. For Korean proletarians, the problem of political praxis was always tied to specific situations and milieus that were inseparable from the contingencies immanent to the process of commodification, a process, moreover, that was infused with institutionalized forms of racism and the racialization of labor. Korean workers' political practices did not survive beyond these contingencies, nor did they precede them.

I have tried in this book to remain faithful to this contingent history of Korean political praxis in Japan and to the struggles disclosed in their aleatory encounters within the process of commodification. To paraphrase Benjamin, this history teaches us that the state of emergency in which Korean proletarians lived, searched for work, and labored erratically and irregularly amidst acutely contingent conditions of social existence, was not the exception but the rule. It was this naked fact that drove so many of them to bring about a real state of emergency, to articulate and improve their position in the struggles against colonial domination, capitalist exploitation, and fascism in Japan, and to alert various guardians of the Japanese empire, its critics, and even its future historians, that capitalist exploitation and fascism were neither an inexorable progression of history nor a historical norm.

This history of Korean proletarians teaches us that if we are to attain to a conception of history in a capitalist world, it must be one that is not reducible to a notion of inevitable progress or development, but rather to the sudden, unpredictable and contingent failures of any capitalist progress or development whatsoever. What we learn is that if capitalist exploitation and fascism were ever a historical norm, this was so only insofar as they were, and continue to be, policed and guarded effects of a compulsive, possessive, and obsessive practice of disavowing the necessarily contingent nature of history in a capitalist commodity world.

This is to say that Korean proletarian struggles in Japan made history, but they did not make it simply as they pleased. While they were often subjects in history, they were not a subject of history. For they did not always make history under self-selected circumstances, but under circumstances that existed contingently (necessarily so), circumstances that were transmitted from a past whose origins were not only possibly unknown to them, but ultimately irrelevant for what they had to do in the present. The necessity of challenging and overturning presently existing circumstances, which marked a series of historical reversals by Korean proletarian struggles in Japan, did not exist apart from the way these circumstances necessarily appeared before Korean workers contingently in the present. Yet, it is precisely through these reversals that their struggles appeared in Japan as a multiplicity of social and political contingents to be reckoned with. These multiple and important historical reversals, however ephemeral and fleeting they might have been, need to be accounted for in the calculus of historical inquiry.

APPENDIX 1

....

Korean Self-help and Social Work Organizations in Japan
(by prefecture and with membership over 1,000)

Prefecture and Name of Organization	Date of Establishment (Y/M/D)	Summary and Translation of Statement of Purpose	Organization, Activities, and Programs
AICHI			
a. Sōaikai Aichi-ken Honbun (branches in six wards)	1923.5.12	Protection (*hogo*) of Koreans in Aichi prefecture	Labor exchange; boarding; help with travel; aid to ill and injured; aid; night school; lectures; newspaper
GIFU			
a. Zenjukai	1927.4.4	Stabilize everyday life of Koreans and support their social place in Japan	Labor introductions for unemployed Korean workers
FUKUOKA			
a. Wakamatsu Naisen Yūwakai	1926.8	Labor exchange; conciliation between labor and capital; Japanese–Korean harmony	Labor exchange; housing facilities; counseling; expatriation and repatriation help
b. Kōyūka	1922.7	Promote cooperation and welfare of workers at the Kaijima Corporate coal mine	Assistance, relief, and medical care for injured coal miners; maternity clinic; marriage service

Prefecture and Name of Organization	Date of Establishment (Y/M/D)	Summary and Translation of Statement of Purpose	Organization, Activities, and Programs
FUKUOKA, *continued*			
c. Hōtokukai	1926.5	Education, training, advancement of social standing; Japanese–Korean harmony and friendship	NA
d. Maruyama Gakuin	1922.9.11	Korean education	Labor exchange; boarding; housing supply; cultivation of harmony
HIROSHIMA			
a. Nissen Rōdō Kyōkai	1924.10.1	Japanese–Korean harmony and relief	Labor exchange; boarding; dining hall; labor supplier; sub-contractors
b. Hiroshima Senyūkai	1924.5.6	Advancement of Korean education; mutual aid for members	Night school; labor exchange; hygiene section
HYOGO			
a. Hyogo-ken Naisen Kyōkai (Foundation)	1925.3.9	Promotion of Japanese–Korean harmony; assistance and protection of Koreans in Japan	Housing; labor exchange; night school; lectures; publications
b. Naisen Kyōjukai	1926.5.1	Support mutual help between Japanese and Koreans; offer protection to Koreans in Japan; develop thought and everyday life for Koreans	Labor exchange; dining halls; boarding
c. Naisen Dōaikai	1926.3.31	Advance Korean education; mutual aid for Koreans; promote spirit of mutual love, co-prosperity, and friendship (*shinboku*) between Japanese and Koreans	School for uneducated Koreans workers; classes in Japanese language; boarding

Prefecture and Name of Organization	Date of Establishment (Y/M/D)	Summary and Translation of Statement of Purpose	Organization, Activities, and Programs
HYOGO, *continued*			
d. Senjinrō(dō) Yūwagōkai	1924.12.9	Promote mutual aid among Korean workers	NA
e. Senjin Dōshidan	1924.8.25	Promote mutual aid among Korean workers	NA
f. Hyogo Senjin Seinenkai	1924.12.14	Promote mutual aid for Korean youth and proper conduct (*shūyō*)	NA
g. Uri Sōgokai	1925.5.1	Mutual aid for Koreans in Japan	NA
h. Kobe Chōsen Rōdō Dōmeikai	1925.3.29	Advance the social standing of Korean workers	NA
i. Miyazumi Kōshinkai	1925.8.22	Advance education of members; promote friendship (*shinboku*)	NA
j. Kyūsankai	1925.10.20	Organize and form solidarity among Korean packing workers at the Kawasaki Shipping Factory	NA
k. Kobe Chōsen Seinenkai	1923	Education for Korean elementary students; proper conduct (*shūyō*), guidance, and enlightenment of Korean youth; aid for Korean families; promotion of family-related activities	Offices for proper conduct; leisure activities; housewives; children; labor; surveys; section for movement to reform Korean women's clothing
KANAGAWA			
a. Kanagawa-ken Naisen Kyōkai	1921.2.25	Promotion and research of Japanese–Korean harmony	Boarding; labor exchange; dining halls; night school; lectures; publications; medical clinic; assistance and protection (*kyūgo*)

Prefecture and Name of Organization	Date of Establishment (Y/M/D)	Summary and Translation of Statement of Purpose	Organization, Activities, and Programs
KUMAMOTO			
a. Kumamoto-ken Naisen Shinwakai	1926.12.1	Promotion of mutual love between Japanese and Koreans based on spirit of general social co-prosperity	Free boarding; labor exchange; counseling; poor relief
KYOTO			
a. Kyoto Kyōjukai	1920.5.1	NA	Boarding; labor exchange; aid to sick and injured
b. Sōaikai Kyoto Honbu	1926.4.1	Assistance for, education of, Koreans; promote Japanese–Korean harmony and eliminate ethnic discrimination	Boarding; labor exchange
OKAYAMA			
a. Nissen Rōdōrenmei Kyōkai	NA	Japanese–Korean harmony	NA
NARA			
a. Nara Shinbokukai	1924.2.12	Japanese–Korean harmony	NA
NAGANO			
a. Dōshikai	1926.3.15	Advance Japanese–Korean harmony, mutual friendship and interests based on spirit of co-prosperity	Labor exchange; boarding; counseling; enlightenment and cultivation
b. Kyōzaikai	1926.9.15	Provide relief to Korean workers from the perspective of human co-prosperity	Labor exchange; marriage introductions; housing introductions; boarding

Prefecture and Name of Organization	Date of Establishment (Y/M/D)	Summary and Translation of Statement of Purpose	Organization, Activities, and Programs
NAGANO, *continued*			
c. Nanshin Nissen Rōdōkai	1927.8.10	Japanese–Korean worker harmony	NA
d. Dōshikai	1926.12.1	Advance Japanese–Korean harmony, mutual friendship and interests based on spirit of co-prosperity	NA
OSAKA			
a. Naisen Kyōwakai	1924.5	Protection for Koreans; enlighten Koreans; stabilize and develop everyday life of Koreans; realize Japanese–Korean harmony	Boarding; labor exchange offices; free medical clinics; night school; general housing; job placement center (*jusanjo*)
b. Sōaikai Osaka Honbu	1923.5.15	Same as above	Boarding; general housing; labor exchange office
c. Sōaikai Izumi Honbu	1925.8.1	Same as above	Same as above
SHIZUOKA			
a. Sōaikai Shizuoka-ken Honbu	1924.3.5	Promotion of Japanese–Korean harmony based on spirit of mutual ethnic love; elimination of ethnic discrimination based on proper public conduct; establishment of co-prosperity, freedom, and equality and the reform of Korean thought; stabilize everyday life of Koreans	Labor exchange; boarding; dining halls; housing supply; aid; lectures; leisure clubs

Prefecture and Name of Organization	Date of Establishment (Y/M/D)	Summary and Translation of Statement of Purpose	Organization, Activities, and Programs
TOKYO			
a. Sōaikai Sōhonbu	1921.12.23	Thorough practice of Japanese–Korean harmony based on mutual love between ethnicities; provide aid (kyūsai) to Koreans in Japan; improve welfare and happiness for Koreans	Free boarding; free labor exchange office; free medical clinics; counseling center; night school for workers; Sunday classes; housing for students in need; Sôai shrine
b. Ryokkōsha	1924.9.20	Guidance for struggling Korean students in Japan; assistance (sewa) to Korean workers	Boarding; labor exchange; dining hall; financial aid to students; lectures to promote enlightened thought
c. Zainichi Chōsenjin Rōdō Isshinkai	1925.8.14	Co-prosperity (kyōzai kyōei) for Korean workers	Boarding; labor exchange; free worker medical clinic; dining hall
d. Nogata Jōairyō	1928.9.20	Promote social solidarity and equality; house struggling Korean students	Counseling for working students; labor exchange; lectures; clubs
e. Jitankai	1924.5.25	NA	NA
f. Ichizen Rōdōkai	1924.8.1	NA	NA
g. Kōninsha	1920.8.27	Promote camaraderie among Korean and Japanese	Counseling for elementary, junior high, high school, and college students; general counseling
h. Minzoku Keiaikai	1925.4	NA	NA
i. Tōshōkai	1925.12.15	NA	NA
j. Tokyo Chōsen Shônendan	1927.11.20	Japanese–Korean harmony	NA

Prefecture and Name of Organization	Date of Establishment (Y/M/D)	Summary and Translation of Statement of Purpose	Organization, Activities, and Programs
TOKYO, *continued*			
k. Chōsen Bukkyōkai	1919.6	Cooperation between Japanese and Koreans; develop Korean culture	NA
l. Jōdōshu Rōdō Kyōsaikai	1912.5.1	Protection, rectification, guidance, and enlightenment of workers; welfare programs (*fukushi jigyō* and *rinpo jigyō*)	Boarding; dining halls; labor exchange office
TOYAMA			
a. Shaden Jūgyōsha Kyōgankai	1927.4.15	Raise the education of workers; promote peace, amity, industriousness, and thrift (*kinken*); reform improper conduct; cultivate proper hygiene; accelerate mutual interest, profit, and happiness	Insurance; mediations for Japanese–Korean labor strikes
b. Senjin Rōdōgō Shukujo	1926.11.18	Provide free boarding rooms to immigrant Korean workers who cannot find housing in Japan; provide employment to extremely poor Koreans	NA
c. Fushiki Minyu Sōgokai	1927.5.11	Protection and help based on spirit of general social co-prosperity	Free boarding; labor exchange
WAKAYAMA			
a. Naisen Yūwakyōdōkai	1927.4.29	Promote friendship and harmony between Japanese and Koreans	Program to develop character; counseling; labor exchange

Prefecture and Name of Organization	Date of Establishment (Y/M/D)	Summary and Translation of Statement of Purpose	Organization, Activities, and Programs
WAKAYAMA, *continued*			
b. Nissen Yūwa Rōdōkyōkai	NA	Mutual help, guidance, and relief to members; free labor exchange	NA
YAMAGUCHI			
a. Onoda Rinpokai	1927.4.10	Japanese–Korean harmony	Labor exchange; relief; conduct reform
b. Naisen Kyōwakai	1925.4	Promote mutual friendship between Japanese and Koreans; provide free labor introductions	Labor exchange; medical clinic; free boarding; food supply; relief
c. Shōwakan	1928.5	Japanese–Korean harmony	Labor exchange; housing supply; education; counseling; emergency medical care
d. Tetsudō Hoyūin Shimonoseki Hosenkai	1923.11.1	Guidance and protection of Koreans	Labor exchange; free boarding; dining hall
e. Nissen Shinwakai	1924.3.10	Total harmony between Japanese and Koreans	Counseling; labor exchange; supplier of Korean workers (*chōsenjin rōdōsha ninpu kyōkyū*)
f. Chōsen Rōdōsha Hodōjo	1928.2	Korean worker employment; boarding; counseling	Labor exchange
g. Nissen Yūwakai	1916.12	Promote spirit of thrift through savings organizations; provide labor introductions	Labor exchange; lectures; relief and savings

Prefecture and Name of Organization	Date of Establishment (Y/M/D)	Summary and Translation of Statement of Purpose	Organization, Activities, and Programs
YAMANASHI			
a. Sōaikai Yamanashi Honbu	1924.4.10	Promotion of mutual love based on spirit of general social co-prosperity	Labor exchange; boarding; dining halls; mediations of disputes (*funsō chōtei*)

Source: Hogo-ka, "Naichi zaiju senjin hogo wo mokuteki to suru shakai jigyo dantai-cho," May 1928.

APPENDIX 2

....

A Timeline of Anti-Sōaikai Activity

1921   • Sōaikai headquarters is established in Tokyo. Within three years branches established in Yamanashi, Shizuoka, Kyoto, Osaka, and Fukuoka prefectures in Japan, and in Seoul and Pusan in Korea.

1922   • Korean anarchist group, Kokuyūkai, led by Pak Yol (Boku Retsu), established in November.

1923   • "Korean Massacre" following the September 1, 1923 Kanto earthquake; Sōaikai called upon by Army to control Korean populations; Japanese anarchist, Osugi Sakae, is assasinated in days following earthquake.
      • Sōaikai receives massive funding from the Government-General, the Bank of Korea, the Home Ministry, Mitsubishi, and Mitsui.
      • Sōaikai vs. 450 Korean factory strikers. Nara prefecture. December 19.

1924   • Sōaikai vs. 8,000 Korean peasant strikers (First Intervention). Haido Island, S. Cholla, Korea. August.

1925   • Peace Preservation Law enacted.
      • Korean communist labor union, Zainichi Chōsen Rōdō Sōdōmei (Rōsō), established in Japan.

1926   • Sōaikai violence against Rōsō, Osaka. April 27.
      • Sōaikai vs. Nihon Rōdō Kumiai Hyōgikai strikers. Nihon Gakki factory, Hamamatsu City, Shizuoka Prefecture. April–August.
      • Sōaikai violence against Rōsō. Rōsō headquarters, Tokyo. June 13.
      • Sōaikai violence against 1,000 Korean workers. Fuji Minobu Railway Construction site, Yamanashi prefecture. June 15.
      • Rōsō publishes anti-Sōaikai article in *Musansha Shimbun*, June 19.

• Rōsō distribution of anti-Sōaikai flyers, August, following Nihon Gakki strike.

1927 • Chōsen Rōdō Kumiai established.

1928 • Sōaikai granted foundation status (*zaidan hōjin*); former colonial police chief Maruyama Tsurukichi assumes directorship of Sōaikai; Pak-Ch'um-gum and Yi Ki-dong remain as vice president and president.
     • Korean communists publish article on Sōaikai spies in *Musansha Shimbun*, February 5.
     • Sōaikai vs. Korean peasant strikers and Rōnō-tō. (Second intervention.) Haido Island, S. Cholla, Korea. March.
     • Critique of Sōaikai involvement in Haido strike, published in *Musansha Shimbun*, March 5.
     • Zenkoku rōdō kumiai and Jiyūrengō (including Korean anarchists) publish anti-Sōaikai article in *Jiyūrengō Shimbun*, April 10.
     • Korean communists publish anti-Sōaikai article in *Musansha Shimbun*, April 10.

1929 • Sōaikai vs. Korean factory strikers. Mie prefecture, February.
     • Sōaikai violence against and kidnapping of Korean Rōsō members. Kawasaki, Kanagawa prefecture, May.
     • Rōsō dissolves and merges with Nihon Rōdō Kumiai Zenkoku Kyōgikai (Zenkyō).
     • Korean Communists publish article in *Musansha Shimbun*, calling for destruction of Sōaikai, May 21.
     • Tokyo Chōsen Rōdō Kumiai publishes anti-Sōaikai article in *Musansha Shimbun*, calling the Sōaikai a terrorist organization, May 26.
     • Tokyo Chōsen Rōdō Kumiai writes anti-Sōaikai flyer, published in *Musansha Shimbun*, June 9, and in *Shakai Undō Tsūshin*, June 10.
     • Kim Tu-yong writes and publishes anti-Sōaikai essay in *Senki*, July, exposing Sōaikai violence in Kawasaki.
     • Korean communists form Victims of Sōaikai Violence group and publish anti-Sōaikai article in *Musansha Shimbun*, August 20.

1930 • Sōaikai vs. Korean factory strike. Kishiwada Cotton factory, Osaka.
     • Korean anarchists publish anti-Sōaikai article in *Jiyurengō Shimbun*, March 1.
     • Sōaikai vs. 80 Korean factory strikers, Dai-Ichi Seitan Glass factory, Tokyo. November.

- Sōaikai co-founder and vice president Pak Ch'um-gum publishes speech, On the Problem of Repatriating Koreans in Manchuria.
- Pak Ch'um-gum publishes speech, Our State, New Japan: A Public Complaint to . . . the Government describing the Instability and Distress of our Korean Compatiots, November.
- Critique of Sōaikai's involvement in Dai-Ichi glass factory strike published in Shakai Undō Tsūshin, November 15 and February 3.

1932
- Sōaikai vs. Korean and Japanese coal miners' strike. Aso Coal Mine, Fukuoka.
- Sōaikai housing and labor exchange programs start to crumple, losing significant popular support and membership.
- Sōaikai co-founder and vice president Pak Ch'um-gum becomes first Korean in Japan publicly elected to National Diet (Lower House, representing Fourth Ward of Tokyo), February.
- Korean anarchists publish anti-Sōaikai article in Jiyūrengō Shimbun, March 14.
- Zenkyō Chemical Workers Union distributes anti-Sōaikai and anti-Pak Ch'um-gum election campaign flyers in Tokyo.
- Nihon Heimin Bijutsuka Dōmei Tokyo branch distributes anti-Sōaikai flyers, calling the Sōaikai the "Sō-gai-kai," or Mutual Harm Association, May 1.

1933
- Violent clash between Sōaikai and Zenkyō Construction workers Union, Tokyo, January 19.
- Sōaikai violence against Koreans members of the Toyohashi Gōdō Rōdō Kumiai (labor union). December 1932 and January 21.
- Toyohashi Gōdō Rōdō Kumiai distributes anti-Sōaikai pamphlets and flyers in Toyohashi and Nagoya, March.

1934
- Sōaikai begins shutting down its housing and labor exchange facilities.

1941
- Sōaikai closes and donates remaining assets of 130,000 yen to the Kyōwakai. By 1945, the Kyōwakai would mobilize over two million Korean workers for the war effort.

NOTES

....

Introduction: The Proletarian Gamble

1 See Koh, Ekkyō: Chōsenjin, watashi no kiroku.

2 Ibid., 83.

3 Ibid., 96–97.

4 Susan Strange, Casino Capitalism, quoted in Jean Comaroff and John Comaroff, "Millennial Capitalism," 296–97.

5 Althusser, "The Underground Current of the Materialism of the Encounter," in Philosophy of the Encounter, 163–207.

6 See Kathleen Barker and Kathleen Christensen, eds., Contingent Work: American Employment Relations in Transition. See also the New York Times article, "Temporary Workers Are on the Rise in Factories," July 3, 1993.

7 Grace Chang, Disposable Domestics: Immigrant Women Workers in the Global Economy, 1–21, 155–90.

8 Martin Kopple, "U.S. Rulers Wrangle over New Immigration 'Reform' Bill," The Militant 7, no. 22, June 4, 2007.

9 See Bergström and Storrie, Contingent Employment in Europe and the United States. See also Jamie Peck, Workplace: The Social Regulation of Labor Markets, 1–152.

10 Zhang, Strangers in the City, 23–46.

11 Fureeta is an abbreviated Japanese word that borrows from the German frei arbeiter, or free worker.

12 Sismondi, "Nouveaux principes d'economie politique," quoted in DeBrunhoff, The State, Capital and Economic Policy, 16.

13 Rancière, Nights of Labor, 31.

14 Ibid., 147.

15 Marx, Grundrisse, 604.

16 Ibid., my emphasis.

17 See Balibar, "In Search of the Proletariat: The Notion of Class Politics in Marx," in Masses, Classes, Ideas: Studies on Politics and Philosophy before and after Marx, 125–50; Rancière, Nights of Labor, vii–xii, 3–163; and "Marx's Labor," in The Philosopher and His Poor, 57–124.

18 Marx, "So-called Primitive Accumulation," part 8, Capital.

19 For this approach to so-called primitive accumulation, see Perelman, *The Invention of Capitalism*; and also Read, *The Micropolitics of Capital*, chapters 1 and 2.

20 Marx writes, "[If] a surplus population of workers is a necessary product of accumulation or of the development of wealth on a capitalist basis, this surplus population also becomes, conversely, the lever of capitalist accumulation, indeed it becomes a condition for the existence of the capitalist mode of production. It creates a mass of human material always ready for exploitation by capital in the interests of capital's own changing valorization requirements. . . . Effects become causes in their turn, and the various vicissitudes of the whole process, which always reproduces its own conditions, take on the form of periodicity." *Capital*, 784–85.

21 The English language historiography on Japanese factories goes back to the heyday of modernization theory during the Cold War, when Japan's rapid recovery after the Second World War was hailed by mainstream social scientists as a model for development. The first influential book on Japanese factories was James Abegglen, *The Japanese Factory: Aspects of its Social Organization* (1958). For more recent monographs on Japanese factories, see A. Gordon, *The Evolution of Labor Relations in Japan: Heavy Industry, 1853–1955*; Hazama, *The History of Labour Management in Japan*; Garon, *The State and Labor in Modern Japan*; Large, *Organized Workers and Socialist Politics in Interwar Japan*. For a trenchant critique of modernization theory and its implementation in the field of Japan studies, see Harootunian, *The Empire's New Clothes: Paradigm Lost, and Regained*.

22 There are, of course, exceptions to this general characterization. Histories of the Japanese textile industry, and the cotton spinning factories in particular, have focused on the recruitment factory girls, a practice that connected the rural countryside in Japan to the cotton mills in cities like Osaka. In this way, these analyses have drawn attention to the social and institutional relations of power and violence on the unpredictable roads toward commodification and exploitation. They therefore reveal how institutional power becomes entangled in the problem of exploitation within the factory system. See Hunter, *Women and the Labour Market in Japan's Industrializing Economy*. On day labor in Japan, see Gill, *Men of Uncertainty*, 1–36; Fowler, *San'ya Blues*; Amakyōtō, *Yararetara Yarikaese*, parts 1 and 2; and Imagawa, *Gendai Kiminkō*, 9–18, 121–60.

23 See Pak, *Zainichi Chōsenjin Undō-shi 8–15 kaihōzen*; Iwamura, *Zainichi chōsenjin to nihon rōdōsha kaikyū*; Weiner, *Race and Migration in Imperial Japan*.

24 For a concise elaboration of the critique of this kind of assumed experience of a putatively unified and coherent minority, see Joan W. Scott, "Experience," in *Feminists Theorize the Political*, edited by Butler and Scott.

25 Even a short list of the significant surveys from the interwar period amply demonstrates the frequency of the trope of "The Korean Problem." "On the Korean Problem," published in August 1923, was penned by a top executive of the Social

Section of the Osaka Metropolitan Government. In 1924, the Survey Section of the Osaka City social bureau produced "The Korean Worker Problem." In 1925, the Aichi prefectural government published a survey on Korean day workers in and around Nagoya city, called "The Korean Problem." In 1928, the Criminal Investigation Bureau of the Ministry of Justice released two surveys, one called "The Korean Problem," and another called "Present Conditions of Japanese Social Movements: The Korean Problem." Long dossiers on the "Korean Problem" were also published annually, from 1928 to the end of the Second World War, by the Police Bureau of the Home Ministry, in their "Conditions of Social Movements." In 1929, a journal of social policy, *Shakai Seisaku Jippō*, published a survey called "Korean Workers and the Unemployment Problem." In 1930, the Osaka journal, *Dai-Osaka*, printed "Koreans in Osaka and the Housing Problem," while the Osaka City government published "The Korean Housing Problem in Osaka." In 1931, Osaka City Social Bureau published an updated version of its original 1924 survey titled "The Korean Worker Problem." In 1934, the *Kōsaikai*, a private welfare organization, wrote a three-part survey called "Welfare Organizations and the Korean Problem," and in 1936, the Japanese–Korean Harmony Survey Association, or the *Naisen Yūwa Jigyō Chōsakai*, printed, under the auspices of the Osaka government, "The Problem of Korean Residents in Japan and Its Policies." Lastly, we cannot forget the 1940 survey, from the Police Bureau of the Nara prefecture, hysterically titled, "Watch out, They're Here: Lawless Koreans!"

26 An influential critique of positivist methods of the social and human sciences is Laclau and Mouffe, *Hegemony and Socialist Strategy*. See especially chapter 3, "Beyond the Positivity of the Social: Antagonisms and Hegemony," 93–148.

27 In English, see Weiner, *Race and Migration*.

28 Pak, *ZCKSS*.

29 The Ohara Shakai Mondai Kenkyūjō also has an excellent and useful website: http://oohara.mt.tama.hosei.ac.jp.

1. Uncontrollable Colonial Surplus

1 Marx, *Capital*, 935.

2 On the colonial cadastral survey in Korea, see Gragert, *Landownership under Colonial Rule*; in Japanese, see Asada, *Kyūshokuminchi Nihonjin Daitochi Shoyūron*, 67–166.

3 Gragert, ibid., chapter 6. Land taxes in Korea were around 1.3 percent of the assessed land values; by comparison, tax rates in Meiji Japan were around 3 percent. In Japan, high land taxes were exacted as a means for the young Meiji state to garner a substantial cash flow it would eventually channel toward investing in industrial and military developments. Land taxes in Korea, however, were kept low to attract Japanese finance and monopoly capital investments in agricultural development, primarily for the purposes of the Program to Increase Rice Production, which lasted from 1920 to 1934.

4 Kim, "The Landlord system and the agricultural economy during the Japanese Occupation period," in *Landlords, Peasants and Intellectuals in Modern Korea*, edited by Pang Kie-chung, Michael D. Shin, Yong-sop Kim, chapter 4, 131–74.

5 Large, *Organized Workers and Socialist Politics in Interwar Japan*, 18.

6 Oshima, *Nihon Kyōkōshi-ron*, vol. 2, 5.

7 Shōkō daijin kanbō tōkei-ka, *Chingin tōkeihyō*, February 1930.

8 Oshima, *Nihon Kyōkōshi-ron*, vol. 2, 46.

9 Ibid., 47; Large, *Organized Workers and Socialist Politics in Interwar Japan*, 19. Between 1914 and 1919, the demand for higher wages was consistently the most common among workers. In 1914, out of 7,904 strikes, 4,105 included demands for higher wages; in 1919, out of 63,137 strikes, 53,130 included demands for higher wages (Oshima, *Nihon Kyōkōshi-ron*, vol. 2, 47).

10 For Korean migration before and around 1910, see Weiner, *Race and Migration*. In Japanese, see Kan, *Zainichi' kara no shiza*, especially the chapter, "Zainichi chōsenjin tokōshi," 182–252.

11 The remaining 200 were in glass factories. The category of other contains 700 sawyers, 500 rope and nail manufacturers, and 500 wood burners. In an article from the *Manshu Nichi Nichi* newspaper from July 7, 1917, 21 factories and coal mines were listed as having recruited Korean workers. Those factories were the Chūgoku iron foundary; Amagasaki Kishimoto iron works; Osaka Innoshima iron works; Monji railway; Harima Zōsenjo ship manufacturing; Dairi glass manufacturing; Osaka Sakuragawa glass manufacturing; Hokkaido Fuji paper manufacturing; Kurashiki cotton spinning; Fukushima cotton spinning; Settsu cotton spinning; Tōyō cotton spinning; Osaka Yamamoto cotton spinning; and Toyohashi silk. Coal mines listed were Kumashiro coal; Yubari coal; Hokkaido Mitsubishi coal; Fukuoka-ken Yamada coal; Fukuoka-ken Arairi coal; Kameyama coal; and Dai Nippon kōgyō kaisha. For the names of other factories and coal mines recruiting Korean workers during the war years, see Nishinarita, *Zainichi chōsenjin no 'sekai' to 'teikoku' kokka*, 83–90.

12 Hunter, *Women and the Labour Market in Japan's Industrializing Economy*.

13 Ibid. See also Faison, *Producing Female Textile Workers in Imperial Japan*.

14 On industrial paternalism, see Andrew Gordon, *The Evolution of Labor Relations in Japan*; on the relation between paternalism and labor movements in heavy industry, see Large, *Organized Workers and Socialist Politics in Interwar Japan*; on the rise of temporary labor in heavy industry, see Hazama, *The History of Labour Management in Japan*, especially chapter 7.

15 *Chōsen Ihō*, October 1917.

16 Kokka Gakkai Zasshi, "Chōsenjin no inyū."

17 Naimushō Keihōkyoku Hōan-ka, *Chōsenjin Gaikyō (Dai ni)*, May 1918, reprinted in Pak, *ZCKSS*, vol. 1, 61–80.

18 Hokkaido Tankō Kisen Kabushikigaisha, "Hokutan 50 nenshi Kōhon," quoted in Hokkaido Kaitaku Kinenkan, "Hokkaido ni okeru Tankō no Hatten to Rōdōsha," 85–86.

19 In April 1913, the Chōsen Sōtokufu Keimu Sōkanbu issued a police notice, "Naichi ni okeru jigyo ni jūji suru shokkō rōdōsha boshū torishimari ni kansuru ken," in which it stated that recruitments of more than ten Korean workers required police permission. On September 1, 1917, the same bureau issued "Chōsenjin rōdōsha boshū torishimarikata no ken" (Regulations on the recruitment of Korean workers); and in October 1917, issued "Naichiyuki senjin rōdōsha ni kansuru tsūchō" (Notice on Korean workers bound for Japan).

20 *Kawaboku Shimpō*, September 9–14, 1917.

21 Ibid.

22 *Fukuoka Nichi Nichi Shimbun*, November 27, 1917.

23 Sōtokufu Keimu Hōan-bu, "Rōdōsha Boshū Torishimai ni tsuite," printed in *Keijō Nippō*, January 30, 1918.

24 *Chōsen Ihō*, October 1917, 123.

25 Part four of *Osaka Mainichi Shimbun*, August 17, 1917.

26 *Fukuoka Nichi Nichi Shimbun*, November 27, 1917.

27 *Manshū Nichi Nichi Shimbun*, July 7, 1917.

28 *Keijō Nippō*, August 9, 1917.

29 *Fukuoka Nichi Nichi Shimbun*, August 12, 1917.

30 *Naichi Zairyū Chōsenjin no saikin ni okeru ippan jōkyō*, Naimushō Keihōkyoku, December 1922 in *Tokkō Keisatsu Kankei Shiryō Shūsei*, edited by Tomio Ogino, 85.

31 Chapter 6, which deals with the historical relationship between the Unemployment Emergency Relief Program and Korean workers, explores in greater detail the reasons for and methods of enforcing this ethnic distinction institutionally.

32 *Osaka Asahi Shimbun*, December 1, 1918.

33 *Taishō Nichi Nichi Shimbun*, May 19, 1920; *Osaka Mainichi Shimbun*, June 9, 1920 and August 8, 1920.

34 *Osaka Asahi Shimbun*, June 9, 1920.

35 *Keijō Nippō*, November 26, 1918.

36 *Osaka Asahi Shimbun*, December 1, 1918.

37 Printed in the *Keijō Nippō*, January 31, 1918. See also Naimushō Keihōkyoku, "Chōsenjin rodosha no boshu ni kansuru ken."

38 *Osaka Mainichi Shimbun*, April 15, 1919.

39 *Chōsen Ihō*, October 1917, 124.

40 Ibid.

41 *Hokkaido Hō*, July 3 (evening edition), 1917, quoted in Hokkaido Kaitaku Kinenkan, "Hokkaido ni okeru Tankō no Hatten to Rōdōsha," 87. Strikes revealing similar problems found in the *Yubari* coal mine in Hokkaido appeared with greater frequency. A July 26, 1918 article from the *Tokyo Nichi Nichi Shimbun* describes the sudden appearance of these clashes in the months of June and July, noting six other similar incidents including one at the *Nihon Hokkaido Yubari* coal mine. Historian Pak Kyung-shik has further documented ten other factory- or mine-related strikes involving recruited Korean workers between 1917 and 1919. See his *Zainichi Chōsenjin Undō-shi 8–15 kaihōzen*, 62–63.

42 *Chōsen Ihō*, October 1917. These sorts of recruiting problems eventually led the Japanese government to introduce a new recruiting ordinance in 1925 that brought recruiting practices under stricter surveillance and control by the police. Interestingly, many of the basic tenets of the new ordinance repeated many of the recruiting practices that were already standard practices in the case of recruiting Koreans. For example, the new ordinance required that "(1) When the recruiting agent proposes to begin work he must report beforehand to the police authority within whose jurisdiction the recruiting area lies. (2) When the agent proposes to depart with the recruited persons, he must report to the police authority at least three days prior to his departure. (3) When he intends to stop overnight with the recruited persons . . . he must report this to the police authority." See Shunzo Yoshisaka (then Director of Factory Inspection, Bureau of Social Affairs, Home Ministry), "Labour Recruiting in Japan and its Control." See also Hunter, *Women and the Labour Market in Japan's Industrializing Economy*, chapter 7.

43 *Otaru Shimbun*, July 28, 1919, quoted in Hokkaido Kaitaku Kinenkan, "Hokkaido ni okeru Tankō no Hatten to Rōdōsha," 85–86.

44 "Hokkaido ni okeru chōsenjin rōdōsha" in *Shakai Seisaku Jippō*, Tokyo, October 1930, 99.

45 *Chōsen Ihō*, October 1917. Mandatory savings plans for recruited workers were also reported at the *Kōdai Tankō* coal mine in Fukuoka. There we see that 6 yen is theoretically supposed to be sent home every two months, but in fact 3 yen are first automatically deducted by the company for the purposes of "medical, emergency and shipping costs of various kinds," meaning that only 3 yen every two months, or 1.50 yen per month, are sent back to Korea. In comparison, a whopping 10 yen per month were put aside as savings. See *Fukuoka Nichi Nichi Shimbun*, November 27, 1917.

46 *Chōsen Ihō*, October 1917.

47 Naimusho Keihōkyoku, "Naichi zairyū chōsenjin no saikin ni okeru ippan jōkyō," 9, in *Tokkō Keisatsu Kankei Shiryō Shūsei*, vol. 12, edited by Tomio Ogino, 85. This section is called "On the Relationship between Korean Workers and Japanese Workers."

48 Cumings, *Korea's Place in the Sun: A Modern History*.

49 Chōsen Sōtokufu Keimu-sōkan, "Ordinance 3, Chōsenjin no ryokō torishimari ni kansuru ken," April 1919; Naimusho Keihōkyoku, "Ordinance 660, Chōsen dokuritsu ni kanshi gaikoku senpaku ni taishi chūihō no ken," April 1919.

50 The debates surrounding free travel and the rhetoric of the empire will be discussed in more detail in the next chapter.

51 Suh, *Documents of Korean Communism, 1918–1948*.

52 On the origins of the Japanese Communist Party, see Dirlik, *The Origins of Chinese Communism*. On Sun Yat-sen and Korean independence movements, see Suh, *Documents of Korean Communism, 1918–1948*.

53 Chōsen Sōtokufu Keimukyoku Tokyo Shuchōin, "Zaikyō Chōsenjin Gaiyō," May 1924. See also Nomura, "Chōsen Rōdō Dōmei ni tsuite."

54 Nomura, "Chōsen Rōdō Dōmei ni tsuite," 76. It should be noted, too, that the Osaka branch of the Nihon Rōdō Sōdōmei was instrumental in providing funds for the establishment of the Osaka Korean Labor Federation.

55 Naimushō Keihōkyoku, "Chōsenjin no shisatsu torishimari ni kansuru ken."

56 For example, of particular concern to the police in Kanagawa prefecture in July 1918 were Koreans entering Japanese ports after traveling on boats from Shanghai that had secretly traveled to Honolulu, where Korean activists carried out fund-raising campaigns for the independence movement. In this way, money raised in the United States then found its way to Korean student activists in Tokyo. Police in Kanagawa were instructed to send these Koreans back to Korea under police protection and the Immigrant Protection Law (Imin hogo-hō, established in 1897). See Ordinance 20, Home Ministry, "Beikoku mikkō no chōsenjin torishimari ni kansuru ken imei tsūchō," July 6, 1918.

57 Naimushō Keihōkyoku, "Ordinance 3, Chōsenjin rōdōsha boshū ni kansuru ken," May 14, 1923.

58 Taishō Nichi Nichi Shimbun, May 19, 1920.

2. Colonial Surplus, Virtual Pauper

1 Sismondi, "Nouveaux principes d'economie politique," quoted in DeBrunhoff, The State, Capital and Economic Policy, 16.

2 The contemporary critic and philosopher, Karatani Kojin, takes particular note of this insight of Marx's: "[I]t is perhaps only Marx who shared this interest in approaching [exchange] from the standpoint of selling. . . . In Marx . . . for a commodity to be a synthesis of use value and exchange value, a 'leap' must be made as a rite of passage. Both classical economics and Hegel interpreted this phenomenon from the wrong direction, beginning from the result and not with the conditions of this exchange." See his Architecture as Metaphor: Language, Number, Money, 117.

3 Marx, Grundrisse, 604.

4 Sakai Toshio, "Chōsenjin Rōdōsha Mondai," Shakai Jigyō Kenkyū, May 1931.

5 On the rice riots of 1918, see Lewis, Rioters and Citizens.

6 Asada, Nihon teikokushigu to kyū shokuminchi jinushisei, esp. 67–166.

7 Gragert, Landowernship under Colonial Rule, 112–15.

8 These figures are from Kim Yong-sop, "The Landlord System and the Agricultural Economy during the Japanese Occupation Period," in Landlords, Peasants and Intellectuals in Modern Korea, Pang, Shin, and Kim, eds., 170.

9 Ibid., 152.

10 These figures are from Shin, Peasant Protest and Social Change in Colonial Korea, chapter 4.

11 A small percentage of this population was composed of students who came to Japan to study. The highest percentage of Korean students was in 1918, with 6.63 percent. After that, while their numbers grew absolutely, the percentage fell, from 4 percent in 1922 to less than 2 percent between 1930 and 1937. Previous occupations in small commercial businesses, or else as wage workers in Korea, only constituted small percentages. For example, in Kobe in 1926, Koreans involved in commerce accounted for between 6 and 10 percent; for wage workers, it was less than 2 percent. In Tokyo in 1929, Koreans involved in commerce or wage labor in Korea accounted for 5 to 6 percent, and 2.5 percent, respectively. These figures are from Kobe shiyaskuho, "Zaikō Hantō minzoku no genjō," September 1927; Tokyo-fu shakai-ka shakai chōsa shiryo (Dai 7 gō), "Zaikyō chōsenjin rōdōsha no genjō," 1929. The Kobe survey lists 27 previous occupations for single Korean workers in Japan, and 18 for Korean workers in households. The Tokyo survey lists 20 and 27 for the same categories.

12 Osaka-shi Shakai-bu Chōsa-ka, "Chōsenjin Rōdōsha Mondai," 1924.

13 Kobe Shiyaskuho, September 1927.

14 Tokyo-fu shakai-ka shakai chōsa shiryo (Dai 7 gō), 1929.

15 Osaka-shi Shakai-bu Rōdō-ka, "Osaka-shi Shitsugyōsha Seikatsu Jōtai Chōsa," 1933.

16 Kyoto-shi shakai-ka, "Shinai zaiju chōsen shusshinsha ni kansuru chōsa," 1937; Hyōgō-ken gakumubu shakai-ka, "Chōsenjin no seikatsu jōtai," 1937.

17 On the historical significance of the 1920 crisis in Japan, see Murakami, *Nihon ni okeru Gendai Shihonshugi no Keisei: Senkanki Nihon Shihonshugi no Kōzō*, chapter 2; and also Oshima, *Nihon Kyōkōshi-ron*, esp. chapter 2.

18 Uno, *Kyōkōron*; Ouchi, *Nōgyo Kyōkō*.

19 Naimushō Keihōkyoku Hōanka, "Chōsenjin Gaikyo Daisan," 1920; Naimushō Keihōkyoku, *Shakai Undō no jōkyō*, 1935.

20 See table 5 in the present volume.

21 Osaka-shi Shakai-bu chōsa-ka, *Chōsenjin Rōdōsha Mondai*, reprinted in Pak, *ZCKSS*, vol. 1, 351. Also quoted in a different translation in Weiner, *Race and Migration in Imperial Japan*, 58.

22 Shihōshō Keijikyoku, "Naichi ni okeru chōsenjin to sono hanzai ni oite."

23 For example, average wages in Osaka's glass factories were 1.50 yen for Japanese and 1.00 for Koreans; in rubber, 1.50 for Japanese and 1.10 for Koreans. In Kyoto's metals, 1.50 yen for Japanese and 1.20 for Koreans; in chemicals, 2.00 yen for Japanese, 1.30 for Koreans; in ceramics, 1.80 for Japanese, and 1.30 for Koreans. See Naimushō Shakaikyoku (Dai-Ichibu), "Chōsenjin rōdōsha ni kansuru jōkyō," July 1924. For a more detailed analysis of Korean wages and worker conditions in small- and medium-sized factories, see Ha, *Kanjin Nihon Imin Shakai Keizaishi*, esp. chapters 2 and 3. Another important point is the relationship between the expansion of the small- and family-sized factories during the recession, the use of

colonial workers, and the stratification of the surplus population along large-scale factories and small- and medium-sized factories.

24 Matsumura, "Nihon teikokushugika ni okeru shokuminchi rōdōsha," 139.

25 Sakai, "Chōsenjin Rōdōsha Mondai." It was common, for example, that Korean factory workers would be laid off at the end of the year, in the winter, right before the annual bonuses were paid to the regularly employed workers.

26 Kyongsang Namdo Keisatsu-bu, "Naichi dekasagi senjin rodosha jōtai chōsa."

27 Kyoto-shi Kyōiku-bu Shakai-ka, "Kyoto-shi ni okeru hiyatoi rodosha ni kansuru chosa," 28.

28 Osaka-shi Shakai-bu Chōsa-ka, "Hiyatoi Rōdōsha Mondai," 6.

29 As various surveys noted, the day labor market in Japan had historical roots going back to the development of public works construction projects in the major cities during the Tokugawa period, and especially in the city of Edo. Ninpu has strong connections to the Tokugawa period word ninsoku, which designated non-manufacturing, unskilled, manual labor for these public works projects. As I will discuss in greater detail later in the book, especially in chapter 4, the close connection between ninpu and public works construction workers was maintained throughout the interwar period.

30 Tokyo-shi Shakaikyoku, "Jiyū rōdōsha ni kansuru chōsa," 1923, 3.

31 Osaka-shi Shakai-bu Chōsa-ka, "Hiyatoi Rōdōsha Mondai," 1.

32 On the history of modern Japanese urban planning, see Sorensen, The Making of Urban Japan.

33 Kyoto-shi Kyōiku-bu Shakai-ka, "Kyoto-shi ni okeru hiyatoi rōdōsha ni kansuru chosa," 19.

34 Shihōshō Keijikyoku, "Naichi ni okeru chōsenjin to sono hanzai ni oite."

35 Tonomura, Zainichi Chōsenjin shakai no rekishiteki Kenkyū, 89–90.

36 Osaka-shi Shakai-bu Rōdō-ka, "Osaka-shi Shitsugyōsha Seikatsu Jōtai Chōsa," 178–251.

37 Ibid.

38 Keisho Namdo Keisatsu-bu, "Naichi dekasagi senjin [sic] rōdōsha jōtai chōsa"; Tokyo-fu shakai-ka, shakai chōsa shiryō dai 7 go, "Zaikyō chōsenjin rōdōsha no genjō"; Kobe Shiyakusho, "Zaikō Hantō minzoku no genjō"; Osaka-fu Gakumu-bu Shakai-ka, "Zaisaka Chōsenjin Seikatsu jōtai," 1933.

39 Keihōkyoku Hōanka, "Taisho 14 nen chu ni okeru chōsenjin no jōkyō." Other specific demands were: (1) establishment of an 8-hour working day and a 48-hour working week; (2) establishment of a minimum wage; (3) eradication of what were called evil laws (akuhō); (4) institution of rest days for May Day demonstrations; and (5) cooperation for economic actions.

40 Zai-Nihon Chōsenjin Rōdō Sōdōmei, "Zai-Nihon Chōsen Rōdō Sōdōmei Dai 3 Kai Taikai: Senden, Kōryō, Kisoku," reprinted in Zainichi Chōsenjinshi Kenkyū 1 (December 1977): 95–102.

41 In 1929, Rōsō dissolved under the pressure of police repression and joined with the National Conference of Japanese Labor Unions (Nihon Rōdō Kumiai Zankoku Kyōgikai; or Zenkyō). This is addressed in more detail in chapter 5.

3. Intermediary Exploitation

1 Shihōshō Keijikyoku, "Chōsenjin Mondai."

2 On the history of modern Japanese urban planning, see Sorenson, The Making of Urban Japan, esp. chapter 3. The 1919 city planning system had five main parts: a land use zoning system; a new building code that provided detailed regulations for zoning; a building-line system to control growth in the urban fringe; a system for designating public facilities; and a land readjustment system.

3 Doboku Kōgyō Kyōkai, Nihon doboku kensetsugyōshi, 140.

4 Japan Statistical Association, Historical Statistics of Japan, 218–19.

5 Doboku Kōgyō Kyōkai, Nihon doboku kensetsugyōshi, 958–66.

6 Japan Statistical Association, Historical Statistics of Japan, 536–37.

7 Doboku Kōgyō Kyōkai, Nihon doboku kensetsugyōshi, 951.

8 Ibid., 145.

9 Tokyo Shiyakusho, "Jiyū Rōdō ni kansuru chōsa," 19–20. Also mentioned are bridge building, water works, sewage systems, and telephone and telegraph construction, 61–64.

10 Osaka-shi Shakai-bu Chōsa-ka, "Hiyatoi Rōdōsha Mondai," 18–26.

11 Osaka-shi Shakai-bu Chōsa-ka, "Chōsenjin Rōdōsha Mondai," 351, 376.

12 Tokyo-shi Shakaikyoku, Tokyo-shi Shakaikyoku Nenpō, 1929 nendō, 78.

13 Ibid.

14 Tokyo Shiyakusho, "Jiyū Rōdō ni kansuru chōsa," 19–20.

15 Ibid., 17.

16 Ibid., 27.

17 Ibid., 20.

18 Osaka-shi Shakai-bu Chōsa-ka, "Hiyatoi Rōdōsha Mondai," 29–30.

19 Tokyo Shiyakusho, "Hiyatoi rōdōsha no shippei shōgai ni kansuru chōsa," 13–14.

20 Ibid., 14.

21 Ibid., 24–29.

22 Kyoto-shi Kyōiku-bu Shakai-ka, "Kyoto-shi ni okeru hiyatoi rōdōsha ni kansuru chōsa," 19.

23 Chuo Shokugyō Shōkai Jimukyoku, "Tokyo-fuka zairyu chōsenjin rōdōsha ni kansuru chōsa" in Pak, ZCKSS, vol. 1, 435.

24 Ibid., 351–52.

25 Tokyo Shiyakusho, "Hiyatoi rōdōsha no shippei shōgai ni kansuru chōsa," 67.

26 On the social regulation of labor power as a commodity, see Peck, Workplace, 23–45.

27 Labor exchange offices were originally created in 1921, with the Labor Exchange Law. As I show in chapter 6, the UERP was an extremely complex institutional machinery that not only maintained the distinction between skilled and unskilled labor in terms of ethnicity, but also created other institutional micro-criteria that separated unemployed Korean and Japanese workers. The discussion of Korean welfare begins in chapter 5, with an exploration of changes in the police system, and the introduction of what was called preventive policing. A fuller treatment of one particularly notorious Korean welfare organization, the Mutual Love Association, is found in chapter 5.

28 During the Tokugawa period, oyakata or oyabun (親分) were master craftsmen who housed, trained, and attended to the everyday lives of their apprentices (kokata, 子方, or kobun, 子分) in a tight social relationship that endured for so long because of the authority granted to the oyakata by the apprentice. In other words, it was the master–slave dialectic translated into Japan and into a social system that has been described by post–Second World War anthropologists as a fictive kinship structure. See Bennett and Ishino, *Paternalism in the Japanese Economy*, esp. chapters 3–5. In Japanese, see Fujimoto, "The Nature of the Feudalistic Boss-system"; and Oyama, "Labor Organization and [the] Oyakata System in the Japanese Mining Industry." *Kōnan Keizaigaku Ronshū* 4, no. 3 (Feb. 1964). On *ninsoku yoseba* and the penal system, see Botsman, *Punishment and Power in the Making of Modern Japan*.

29 Harootunian, *Overcome by Modernity*.

30 On the truck system in England, see Hilton, *The Truck System, Including a History of the British Truck Acts, 1465–1960*.

31 Hilton, "The British Truck-System in the Nineteenth Century," 237–56.

32 Kyoto-shi Kyōiku-bu Shakai-ka, "Kyoto-shi ni okeru hiyatoi rōdōsha ni kansuru chosa," 43.

33 Kyoto-shi Shakai-ka, "Shinai zaiju chōsen shusshinsha ni kansuru chōsa" in Pak, ZCKSS, vol. 3, 1165.

34 Ibid. As we will see in the final chapter of this book, conditions stemming from low wages and the hamba-fees were exacerbated by the limited number of days many workers—especially Korean workers—were permitted to work through the state unemployment relief programs. All three dimensions—low wages, hamba-fees, and limited working days—reinforced each other in a general system of control over day workers. Yet there were challenging limitations to this system that took on specific forms of protest and struggle for day workers, the most vociferous of whom were Korean.

35 Tokyo city officials created no less than five subcategories to further specify the labor broker: (a) *junsui ninpu ukeyogyōsha*, or pure worker supplier, who lived with workers in worker dorms, and who was colloquially called a shadow construction worker or *mōrō ninpu*; (b) *Doboku kenchiku ukeyogyōsha (kengyō)*, or public works subcontractors operating side businesses, usually found in the Yamanote area;

(c) *Chihō-yuki ninpu kuchi-ire gyōsha*, or subcontractors specializing in construction workers from distant (more or less agricultural-based) regions; (d) *Kugaku Rōdōsha Shōkaijo*, a labor exchange office operated by subcontractors specializing in recruiting students, especially in the Kanda area of Tokyo; and (e) *Amiko jōninpu* subcontractors who recruited female workers for the fishing industry. See, Tokyo Shiyakusho, *Jiyū Rōdō ni kansuru chōsa*, 1923, 69–72. In the Kansai region, labor brokers were often called *ninpu kyōkyū gyōsha*, literally worker supplier, while in Kyoto the more specific term *Doboku kenchiku kyōkyū gyōsha*, or public works supplier, was used. In day labor markets in contemporary Japan, the term *tehainin* is also used.

36 Aichi-ken, *Senjin Mondai*.

37 Tokyo Chihō Shokugyō Shōkai Jimukyoku, "Doboku, Bōseki, Kōfu toshiteno senjinrōdōsha," reprinted in Pak Kyung-shik, ed., "Nihon Shokuminchika no zainichi chōsenjin no jōkyō," 24. The 1924 survey of Korean workers in Tokyo similarly states, "The majority of Koreans find work either through veteran Korean workers . . . or else through Japanese construction worker suppliers, sub-sub-contractors or labor brokers." Chuo Shokugyō Shōkai Jimukyoku, "Tokyo-fuka zairyu chōsenjin rōdōsha ni kansuru chōsa" in Pak, *zcкss*, vol. 1, 439.

38 Osaka-shi Shakai-bu Chōsa-ka, "Chōsenjin Rōdōsha Mondai," 375.

39 Often, however, these distinctions were fluid. For example, it was often the case that the *tehaishi* or labor broker was also a *kumigashira* or crew boss of day workers. This was particularly apparent in regard to the organization of Korean day workers by Korean labor brokers and kumigashira. The Korean tehaishi-kumigashira were hired by Japanese *oyakata* because they not only knew where Korean day workers lived and resided, and could therefore supply Korean day workers to Japanese oyakata easier than Japanese labor brokers could; but also because they knew and understood the Japanese language, thereby allowing Japanese oyakata to have their work commands and orders translated into Korean to the day workers, the majority of whom could not speak, read, or write Japanese. In this capacity, the Korean tehaishi-kumigashira were indispensable for the smooth functioning of construction work. At the same time, it was often the case that the oyakata themselves were sub-contractors; here, too, it is difficult to make absolute distinctions between them.

40 Tokyo Shiyakusho, "Jiyū Rōdō ni kansuru chosa," 75.

41 Ibid. The names for these contracts varied from city to city but all of them signified the same indirect relationship between day worker and primary employer. In Kyoto, for example, the term *Rōmu Kyōkyū Keiyaku* was used.

42 Tokyo Chihō Shokugyō Shōkai Jimukyoku. "Doboku, Bōseki, Kōfu toshiteno senjinrōdōsha," 22–42.

43 Tokyo Shiyakusho, "Jiyū Rōdō ni kansuru chosa," 75.

44 Kyoto-shi Kyōiku-bu Shakai-ka, "Kyoto-shi ni okeru hiyatoi rōdōsha ni kansuru chōsa," 61–64.

45 "Each level of sub-contractors wants to maximize his profits but cannot pinch prices off of the materials for the construction site, in other words, from the non-labor expenses. The reason is that the prices of these materials are strictly outlined in the contract with the immediate superior or boss. Therefore, the only place to go to extract a surplus is from human labor. It is not far-fetched to say that the basis upon which these sub-contractors and the *oyakata* system operate is a process of exploitation pure and simple." Kyoto-shi Kyōiku-bu Shakai-ka, "Kyoto-shi ni okeru hiyatoi rōdōsha ni kansuru chosa," 53–54.

46 Kyoto-shi Kyōiku-bu Shakai-ka, "Kyoto-shi ni okeru hiyatoi rōdōsha ni kansuru chosa," 48–49.

47 Osaka-shi Shakai-bu Chōsa-ka, "Hiyatoi Rōdōsha Mondai," 139.

48 Kyoto-shi Kyōiku-bu Shakai-ka, "Kyoto-shi ni okeru hiyatoi rōdōsha ni kansuru chosa," 48–49.

49 Ibid.

50 Ibid., 54–55.

51 Tokyo Shiyakusho, "Jiyu Rōdō ni kansuru chōsa," 47.

52 Osaka-shi Shakai-bu Chōsa-ka, "Hiyatoi Rōdōsha Mondai," 137.

53 Kyoto-shi Kyōiku-bu Shakai-ka, "Kyoto-shi ni okeru hiyatoi rōdōsha ni kansuru chosa," 61.

54 Tokyo Shiyakusho, "Jiyu Rōdō ni kansuru chōsa," 51.

55 Naimusho Keihōkyoku, *Shakai Undō no Jōkyō*, 1925, 1927, 1930.

56 Naimushō Keihōkyoku Hōanka, "Taisho 14 nen chu ni okeru chōsenjin no jōkyō," in Pak, *zckss*, vol. 1, 180.

57 Pak, Kyung-shik, *Zainichi Chōsenjin Undō-shi 8–15 kaihōzen*, 238–39.

58 *Shakai Undō no Tsūshin*, August 23, 1930.

59 Takai, 57.

60 *Shakai Undō no Tsūshin*, August 23, 1930.

61 Ibid.

62 Takai, "Sanshin Doko Sogi no gen'in," 58.

63 Ibid.

64 Ibid., 59–61.

65 Ibid.

66 Ibid.

67 Hirabayashi, "Sanshin Tetsudo Sōgi ni tsuite."

68 Takai, "Sanshin Doko Sogi no gen'in," 61.

69 *Shakai Undō no Tsūshin*, August 3, 1930.

70 Hirabayashi, "Sanshin Tetsudo Sōgi ni tsuite."

71 *Shakai Undō no Tsūshin*, August 3, 1930. The other demands were: (1) the payment of wages on the promised payday; (2) 10 percent increase in total construction funds; (3) for injuries, the immediate payment of medical expenses on the day or the incident and, for deaths, payment of pensions to the family of the deceased; (4) payment of 30,000 yen to the kumigashira for damages; (5) responsibility of

covering damages by the primary employer; (6) supply of everyday staple goods, sold at the hamba commissary, at normal market prices; and (7) payment of wages accruing during the period of the strike.

72   *Shakai Undō no Tsūshin*, August 23, 1930.

73   Ibid.

74   Ibid. The Sanshin railway strike is perhaps just as famous for the violent police repression as it is for the victory won by the Korean workers. Many have argued that the violent tactics used by the police were only outdone by the violence that pervaded the equally notorious strike by Japanese workers at the Hamamatsu Gakki factory in Shizuoka—where, as I discuss in chapter 5—the company hired the police-supported, Korean-led assimilation organization, the Sōaikai, to destroy the strikers headquarters and to kidnap a communist Korean activist. While the Sōaikai was not directly involved in the repression of the strikers at Sanshin, it would play an increasingly important role in repressing Korean workers in Aichi prefecture after 1930. For details on the violence at Sanshin, see Hirabayashi, "Sanshin Tetsudo Sōgi ni tsuite," and Ohara, *Higashi Sangawa Toyohashi Chihō Shakai Undō Zenshi*, 1966, 27–35.

75   The precise number of arrests was 314, and the charge was violating the Peace Preservation Act. Naimushō Shakai-bu, *Shakai Undō no Jōkyō*, 1930, 1170–73.

76   Zai-Nihon Chōsen Rōdō Sōdōmei (hereon cited as Rōsō in notes), "Zai-Nihon Chōsen Rōdō Sōdōmei Dai 3 Kai Taikai: Senden, Kōryō, Kisoku."

77   Choi, "Zai-Nihon Chōsen Rōdō Undō no saikin no Hatten."

78   Naimushō Keihōkyoku Hōanka, "Taisho 14 nen chu ni okeru chōsenjin no jōkyō," reprinted in Pak, *ZCKSS*, vol. 1, 215.

79   Pak, *Zainichi Chōsenjin Undō-shi 8–15 kaihōzen*, 128. The Shinganhoe eventually established a Tokyo branch in May 1927, which worked closely with Rōsō and the Chōsen Seinen Dōmei (Tokyo Korean Youth Federation). The Korean Communist Party, originally established in April 1925, also established a branch in Japan in February 1927. Ibid., 131.

80   Rōsō, 96–97; Choi, "Zai-Nihon Chōsen Rōdō Undō no saikin no Hatten," 46. From 1925 to 1929, Rōsō worked closely with various Japanese labor unions, notably Nihon Rōdō Sōdōmei, Nihon Rōdō Kumiai Hyōgikai (the left-wing splinter union of Nihon Rōdō Sōdōmei that would become, in 1928, the Nihon Rōdō Kumiai Zenkoku Kyōgikai or Zenkyō), and the Japanese Worker-Peasant Party (Rōnōtō).

81   Choi, "Zai-Nihon Chōsen Rōdō Undō no saikin no Hatten," 45–46.

82   Ibid.

83   Ibid.

84   Ibid., 44.

85   Ibid. Available statistics from 1926, 1928, 1935, and 1937 on Korean workers' occupations before they moved to Tokyo, Kobe, Osaka, and Kyoto show that about 80 percent of workers were previously peasant farmers and 3 percent were industrial laborers.

86 *Rōsō* 97. For example, the main trade unions under the umbrella of the Nihon Rōdō Kumiai Hyōgikai (eventually Zenkyō in April 1928) operated in large-scale factories in the metal, transportation, electrical, chemical, and publishing industries. See Sumiya, *Nihon Rōdō undōshi*; and Watabe, *Nihon rōdō kumiai undōshi: Nihon rōdōkumiai zenkoku kyōgikai wo chūshin toshite*.

87 Choi, "Zai-Nihon Chōsen Rōdō Undō no saikin no Hatten," 45.

88 *Rōsō*, 97.

4. Urban Expropriation

1 *Osaka Jūtaku Nenpō*, 1925, 9–21.

2 In Osaka, for example, the housing vacancy rate fell from 8.4 percent in 1914 (17,902 vacancies out of 214,154 housing units for a population of 1,424,596 in Osaka) to 0.15 percent in 1919 (341 vacancies out of 223,417 housing units for a population of 1,583,650). Only in 1925, after the Osaka city government expanded its jurisdiction to become greater Osaka, and after new housing construction increased in these newly acquired wards, did the overall vacancy rate in Osaka rise to 3.9 percent. Seven years later, in 1932, it rose further to 5.4 percent, nearly matching the 1915 vacancy rate (5.5 percent). *Osaka Jūtaku Nenpō*, 1926, 131–34.

3 An Osaka report, for example, analyzed the extent to which tenant incomes were spent on rent, and found that for tenants whose income was below 30 yen, rent consumed as much as 90 percent of their income; for tenants who earned below 40 yen, rent consumed 85 percent; for tenants who earned below 50 yen, rent consumed 73 percent; and for tenants who earned below 60 yen, rent consumed 47.1 percent. Only with incomes between 140 and 200 yen did the percentage fall under 20 percent. The same journal provided rent statistics for three different types of landowners in Osaka from 1928–1938: large (over 50 units), medium (between 30 and 50 units), and small (under 30 units). Rent in all three categories did not fall more than 6 percent, whereas wages in the cotton, glass, and day labor industries during the same years fell 32 percent, 12 percent, and 20 percent, respectively. Osaka-shi Shakai-bu Chōsa-ka, *Hokuku Dai 240*, 21; and Nihon rōdō undō shiryō i'inkai, *Nihon rōdō undō shiryō, Dai-10Kan, Tōkei-Ren*, 279–80.

4 *Osaka Jūtaku Nenpō*, 1927, 22.

5 Ibid.

6 For example, while there were only 17 land companies in Osaka in 1917, there were 63 companies in 1919. The same report also noted how stocks in these land companies (three in particular) had in some cases doubled during these two years. *Osakashi Jutaku Nenpo*, 1926, 131–34. Stocks of three land companies between 1917 and 1919 are listed: the Shioka land company, whose stock rose from 60 yen in 1917 to 170 yen in 1919; the Izuo land company, whose stock rose from 118 to 180 yen; and the Osaka Minato land company, whose stock rose from 119 to 215 yen. The *Osaka Jūtaku Nenpō* showed that between 1914 and 1921 rents almost doubled because

of frenzied land speculation, rising from 100 to 194 yen in that time. See Osaka-shi Shakai-bu Chōsa-ka, "Osaka-shi Shakai-bu Chōsa-ka rōdō chōsa hōkoku dai 35," 14. Seki Hajime, the mayor of Osaka and renowned urban planner, noted in his *Jutaku Mondai to Toshi Keikaku* (1923) that the total capital of land companies in 1913 amounted to 5 million yen, and by 1919, land companies had amassed 111,400,000 yen. Deeply concerned by the rampant land speculating practices of these monopolies, Seki Hajime wrote disparagingly that "in the interest of making a quick profit, and without a thought for the future, [the land holding companies] have erected housing . . . in an increasingly disorderly condition. . . . As land values and housing rents increase, they construct new housing units as they please." Quoted in Hanes, *The City as Subject*, 199.

7 Suzuki, *Shakuchi-shakuyahō no kenkyū*, 108–60. In this sense, as Suzuki has argued, these laws did not differ significantly in essence from the Law Concerning the Protection of Buildings, passed in 1910, which provided the rising industrial capitalist classes with more lease holding protection against the older landowning classes. Suzuki shows how both laws were effects of a compromise between landowners and the newer industrial classes. For example, while landowners were now prevented from exploiting short-term leases on land to increase rent on high turnover—thereby protecting industrial and manufacturing investments on leased land and buildings (e.g., factories)—landowners were nonetheless allowed to increase rent as they pleased. The Leased Land and Leased Buildings Law thus worked to protect investments on leased land and leased buildings, but not resident tenant rights, per se. This is evident, Suzuki claims, in the clause that states that while lease contracts must end with the destruction of leased buildings, owners of leased land or buildings have the legal option to sell and collect on their investments (vol. 1, 108–35). The point is that residential tenant protection was considered secondary to the protection of tenants who invested in leased land and buildings.

8 Rent controls were only initiated nationwide in Japan in 1941, with the revision of the Leased Land and Leased Buildings Law.

9 The Leased Land and Leased Buildings Law only differed from the civil law's articles on lease termination by extending the time between the notification of the lease termination and the eviction of property to six months. According to section 7, subsection 3, the civil law stipulates three months for the termination of leases. See *Civil Code of Japan*, 136–41. The revision of the Leased Land and Leased Buildings Law in 1941 did not eliminate this basic power of landlords, and only added the ambiguous clause, in article 1.2, that it was necessary to provide "just reason" (*seitō no jiyū*) for termination of leases.

10 In 1929, Japanese higher police listed 10 major tenant unions covering 111 branch cells. Out of this figure, tenant unions categorized as left wing were the most numerous, with 57 cells. Most of these cells were under the organizational umbrella of the Worker-Labor Party, or Rōnō-tō (Naimushō Shakai-bu, *Shakai Undō no Jōkyō*,

1929). See *Shakkanin*, the official newspaper for the Osaka Shakkanin Dōmei, and also *Osaka Jūtaku Nenpō*, 1925, 15–31.

11 Higashi Osaka Shakkanin Kumiai Honbu, flyer, probably from 1929.

12 The supposed logic of this refusal to rent to Koreans is analyzed in greater detail in the third section of this chapter.

13 Aichi-ken, reprinted in *ZCSK* 11 (March 1983): 80, 82.

14 Kobe Shiyakusho, "Zaikō Hantō minzoku no genjō," 198.

15 Tokyo-fu, *Zainichi chōsenjin rōdōsha no genjō*, 1929, 104.

16 These landlord associations, the survey notes, were formed by landowners in reaction to Japanese and Korean tenant unions, according to Osaka-shi Shakai-bu Chōsa-ka, "Honshi ni okeru chōsen jūtaku mondai," reprinted in Pak, *ZCKSS*, vol. 2, 1194. Higher police note the rise of landlord associations in December 1929 in the Kansai area (Naimushō Shakai-bu, *Shakai Undō no Jōkyō*, 1929, 1034–35); the *Osaka Asahi Shimbun* notes the same emergence in November 1929. The 1934 *Osaka Jūtaku Nenpō* notes 13 landlord associations formed between 1925 and 1929.

17 Shihōsho Chōsa-ka. "Shihōsho Kenkyū Dai-17," 52–60 and 210–58.

18 Osaka-shi Shakai-bu Chōsa-ka, "Chōsenjin Rōdōsha Mondai," 380.

19 Osaka-shi Shakai-bu Chōsa-ka, "Honshi ni okeru chōsen jūtaku mondai," 1196.

20 Kobe Shiyakusho, "Zaikō Hantō minzoku no genjō," 202.

21 Ibid. A 1930 Osaka survey thus found that, among 729 Koreans who were delinquent on their rent, 32.4 percent had not paid rent for 3 months or less; 52.4 percent had not paid between 6 months and one year; 8.1 percent for eighteen months; 4.7 percent had not paid between 2 and 2.5 years; and 2.5 percent had not paid for 3 years or more. See Osaka-shi Shakai-bu Chōsa-ka, "Honshi ni okeru chōsen jūtaku mondai," 1197.

22 Osaka-shi Shakai-bu Chōsa-ka, "Honshi ni okeru chōsen jūtaku mondai," 1197.

23 Osaka-shi Shakai-bu, *Honshi ni okeru furyō jūtakuchiku chōsa*, 1939.

24 Ibid.

25 Ibid.

26 Ibid.

27 Kobe Shiyakusho, "Zaikō Hantō minzoku no genjō," 1927.

28 Ibid.

29 Ibid.

30 *Kobe Mata Shin Nippō*, August 2, 1932.

31 Ibid.

32 Kim, "Zaisaka chōsenjin no shōmondai," *Minshū Jihō*, January 12, 1936.

33 Osaka-shi Shakai-bu Chōsa-ka, "Chōsenjin Rōdōsha Mondai," 380. Lastly, in a tenant union pamphlet from 1931, "How must we fight landlords?," author Mutō Unjuro, a Japanese lawyer and tenant rights advocate, notes that in Nagoya it was common to find signs on the doors of real estate offices stating, "Rooms for rent— Except to Koreans." He then asks, "If Japanese landlords refuse to rent to Koreans because they notice the tenant's Korean name, what other choice do Koreans have

other than using pseudonyms or other names [in order to secure housing]?" See Unjuro, *Ikani yanushi wo tatakau beki ka*, 193–95.

34 *Osaka Mainichi Shimbun*, October 4, 1928, 7.

35 Ibid., August 6, 1929, 2.

36 Ibid., September 12, 1932, 7.

37 Ibid., March 14 (evening edition), 1932, 2.

38 *Kobe Shimbun*, May 5, 1931, 4.

39 Ibid., June 6 (evening edition), 1931, 2.

40 Ibid., June 1, 1932, 4.

41 Ibid., August 31 (evening edition), 1932, 2.

42 *Akahata*, June 11, 1933, 4.

43 As noted earlier, this applied only to tenants who signed leases with unspecified rental periods. This, however, was the most common type of lease for residential buildings.

44 Landlords could file for eviction using either law. The only difference between these laws, in terms of eviction (*kaoku akewatashi*, or *tachinoki*), was the legally stipulated period of time given to tenants between the moment of the eviction notice and the actual eviction. If the landlord filed for eviction under the civil law, tenants had three months, starting from the day of the eviction notice, before they were required to evacuate the property; for evictions filed under the Law for Leased Buildings, the time was six months. At the end of the interim period, courts would then issue official orders (*kyōsei shikkō*) for forced evictions. The landlord or housing manager (*kanrinin*) would then take this order to the tenants to oversee the evacuation of the property.

45 Naimushō Shakai-bu, *Shakai Undō no Jōkyō*. Other demands included the revision of the Law on Leased Land and Leased Buildings, the end to increased taxes on rental property, and the securing of housing management rights by tenants (*kanriken*). See *Osaka Jūtaku Nenpō*, 1927–32, as well as Osaka shakai undō kyōkai, *Osaka Shakai Rōdō Undōshi*, Dai-2, 1584–91.

46 For a detailed account of using legal means to fight against and delay evictions, see Muto, *Yanushi to ikani tatakau beki ka?*, chapters 4, 5, 8, 15, and 18.

47 Suzuki, *Shakuchi-shakuyahō no kenkyū*, vol. 1, chapter 3.

48 1924 figures are from Naimushō Keihōkyoku Hōanka, "Taisho 14 nenchū ni okeru zairyu chōsenjin no jōkyō"; the rest are from Naimushō Shakai-bu, *Shakai Undō no Jōkyō*, 1929–37. Most of these disputes took place in Osaka. In Osaka in 1929, police statistics show 1,610 incidents, more than half of the national total, and 4,046 incidents in 1933, almost 75 percent of the national total. Figures for other prefectures for 1929 and 1933 include: Tokyo, from 255 to 405; Kanagawa, from 31 to 50; Aichi, from 231 to 271; Hyōgo, from 148 to 611; and in the remaining prefectures, from 242 to 275. These police statistics show slight statistical differences with the national total. Similar to the national trend, the number of

incidents decreased in Osaka after 1933: 1,673 in 1934, 1,109 in 1935, 825 in 1936, and 91 in 1937.

49 Shihōsho, Shihō no kenkyū, 58, 254.

50 Tanii, Fudōsan kyōsei shikkō no shōmondai, 505–41.

51 Ibid., 536–38. On a variation on this theme, Tanii also discusses how this problem emerges in cases where the person represented by the signatory on the lease flees and subleases the home or room to third parties. In the 1933 Ministry of Justice survey on Koreans, this specific problem is also mentioned as another obstacle for landlords applying for official court orders (kyōsei shikkō) for the eviction of Korean tenants. See also Shihōsho, Shihō no kenkyū, 254.

52 So far as I can tell, Tanii's recommendation to change the public notary law was not put into effect. However, this problem raises a potentially important clue as to why, for example, the Osaka government carried out a survey of Koreans in 1932 to determine how many Koreans were using Japanese proper names. The survey found that out of 11,088 Koreans surveyed in 26 locations in Osaka, 747, or 6.3 percent, used Japanese proper names at one point. See Osaka-shi Shakai-bu Chōsa-ka, "Honshi ni okeru chōsen jūtaku mondai," 75.

53 For example, Muto Unjuro, a tenant union activist lawyer, advocated this tactic for these reasons. See Muto, "On Moving and Eviction Fees" (Itenryō no hanashi), chapter 18.

54 Osaka-shi Shakai-bu Chōsa-ka, "Honshi ni okeru chōsen jūtaku mondai," 1194.

55 As an example of Koreans demanding eviction fees (in this case, the equivalent of 10 months rent) from landlords after bringing in more Korean tenants (10, in this case), see the article from January 24, 1933 in Kobe Shimbun, 8. A similar story is found on page 4 of the June 1, 1932 edition of the same newspaper.

56 Shihōsho, Shihō no kenkyū, 218–21.

57 Ibid., 218–53.

58 Interestingly, the 1933 Ministry of Justice survey excised the section from the Supreme Court ruling in which the argument was made for the dismissal of the charges of extortion and fraud. The excised section can be found, however, in the 1932 edition of the Supreme Court's book of criminal cases (Daishin'in Keiji Hanreishū). The reason for the excision is clear. The author of the report, Miki Imaji, energetically supported court rulings that found Koreans guilty of extortion, yet criticized courts for not finding all of the Koreans guilty of fraud as well. The excised passage was removed because it provided a strong argument for the dismissal of both crimes of extortion and fraud.

59 Daishin'in Keiji Hanreishū, 655–56.

60 Ibid., 657–58.

61 The judge further noted that the problem of "errors in relation to legal actions" were found in cases of forgery (zahitsu) and cited a Tokyo regional court case from 1920 in which it was ruled that mistaking a signature as authentic did not constitute

an error of a legal action, but only an error in relation to a legal action (e.g., sale and purchase), and therefore fell beyond the boundaries of civil law. The judge thus ruled out invalidation of contracts on this basis, arguing additionally that the charge of fraud could not be proven. Article 246 of the criminal code defines fraud as follows: "Every person who has deceived another person and thereby defrauded such person of property shall be punished with penal servitude not exceeding ten years." Ibid., 201.

62 *Daishin'in Keiji Hanreishū*, 662–64.

63 *Osaka Asahi Shimbun*, December 10, 1932, cited in *Osaka Jūtaku Nenpō*, 1932, 35. Another case of a similar nature is found in an article from March 14, 1933, on page 2 of the evening edition of the *Osaka Mainichi Shimbun*. In this case, the landlord employed four acquaintances (two drivers, an 18-year-old boy, and a 63-year-old construction worker) to forcefully remove two Korean tenants from a leased room.

64 *Shakai Undō no Tsūshin*, July 6, 1928. Since no official eviction order had been issued, this last incident theoretically revealed a case of breaking and entering, as well as petty theft. Even if an eviction had been issued, however, this action still would have broken the law, given that confiscating private necessities, such as bedding or eating utensils, was not legally permitted in cases of eviction. The flyer thus urged tenants, both Japanese and Korean, to become vigilant against illegal actions of landlords and their use of hired thugs.

65 Deleuze and Parnet, *Dialogues*, 143.

66 Deleuze and Guattari, *A Thousand Plateaus*, 316.

67 See Rancière, *Disagreement*, esp. chapter 2, "Wrong: Politics and Police."

68 On Osaka's urban transformations, see Hanes, *The City as Subject*. On Tokyo's, see Sorensen, *The Making of Urban Japan*, esp. chapters 3 and 4. In addition to Tokyo's suburbanization, the city also underwent vast urban changes due to reconstruction following the 1923 earthquake.

69 For example, see *Osaka Mainichi Shimbun*, November 1 (evening edition), 1929, 2, which tells of the demolition of 62 barracks for 341 Korean residents (221 men and 120 women) for the construction of an airfield. The *Kobe Shimbun* records on May 5, 1931 the demolition of 6 or 7 Korean-managed barracks and vegetable fields for the purpose of land development. On the demolition of eighty barracks and the evacuation of 300 Korean families, see *Kobe Shimbun*, November 5, 1931, 4.

70 Naimushō Shakai-bu, *Shakai Undō no Jōkyō*, 1929, 1202.

71 Ibid., 1931, 1159.

72 *Daishin Minji Hanreishū*, 1979–2011.

73 *Tokkō Geppō*, December 1934 in ZCKS, vol. 3, 238. There were many examples just like this in Osaka, as well, where modern urban planning was firmly underway by 1925. As Jeffrey Hanes discusses in his biography of Osaka Mayor Seki Hajime, planner of a "Garden City" for workers, the outskirts of Osaka were often slated for

new urban plans, mostly for small residential areas, parks, playgrounds, athletic grounds, and gardens.

74 From at least 1927 on this was a common demand in Kobe. See Kobe Shiyakusho, "Zaikō Hantō minzoku no genjō."

75 Naimushō Shakai-bu, *Shakai Undō no Jōkyō*, 1932, 1532–33. Another example dealing with substitute lands is from Tokyo's Fukagawa Ward. On September 17, 1933, 27 Koreans were ordered by the Tokyo finance department to evacuate the land. On September 18, 10 police officers disguised as construction workers forcefully demolished the barracks, leading to an immediate confrontation with the Koreans from the barracks and their friends and supporters from the Taisho Ashikinen. As a result, the demolition was ceased, and the Koreans petitioned the city for substitute land (*hōmon daichi kyūkō*). See Naimushō Shakai-bu, *Shakai Undō no Jōkyō*, 1933, 1627–29.

76 *Kobe Shin Nippō*, September 24, 1930.

77 Ibid., October 1, 1930.

78 Ibid., October 5, 1930.

79 Ibid., October 4, 1930.

80 This problem has been overlooked in the historiography on Koreans in Japan, especially by historian Ha Myung-sen. His argument in sum is that because Korean wages were generally 30 to 50 percent lower than Japanese wages, Koreans were unable to pay for rent individually and were compelled to share rooms and houses to compensate for the restrictions posed by low wages. Ha thus argues that the phenomenon of Korean communal living (which, he calls, following Japanese government discourse, Korean *mure* or swarms) can be explained by the way Korean immigrants in Japan "actively" and "positively" "adapted to the demand, found in the lowest strata of the labor market in Japan, for cheap labor." He thus calls this an "adaptive process."

The problem with Ha's analysis, however, is that rather than attempting to show how low Korean wages might have resulted from various historical factors within Japan, he presupposes the wage levels of Koreans in Japan and treats them as fixed. Second, he offers no real analysis of housing racism, and he fails to mention the problem of state power within the housing market. As I am suggesting here, however, a proper understanding of Korean wages in Japan is impossible without a serious consideration of the state apparatus. By enforcing evictions and evacuations, the legal system was a crucial factor in pushing down the means of subsistence of Korean tenant-workers and therefore must be considered a factor in both reducing Korean wages, as well as in maintaining cheap wages.

81 Naimushō Shakai-bu, *Shakai Undō no Jōkyō*, 1933, 1629.

82 Ibid. On October 5, 20 yen is reported, and on October 6, 30 yen.

83 Nagoya-shi Shakai-bu, "Dai-9-kai roku daitoshi shakai jigyō kyōgikai gijiroku," 37.

84 Ibid., 38.

85 Agamben, *The Coming Community*, 1–2, quoted in Haver, *The Body of This Death*, 146.

5. *State Power*

1 Kim Tu-yong, 78–79. For news on the demonstrations, see *Nihon Shakai Undō Tsūshin*, February 9, 1929, 3.

2 Ibid.

3 Ibid.

4 Naimushō Keihōkyoku, *Shakai Undō no Jōkyō*, 1930, 1124.

5 For further readings on Rōsō's merge with Zenkyō, see Zainihon Chōsen Rōdō Sōdōmei in *Shakai Undō Tsūshin*, January 13, 1930, Year in Review edition, 104–7; also, Kim, Jin-toku. "Zainihon Chōsen Rōdō Sōdōmei ni tsuite no ichi kōsai"; Pak Kyung-shik, *Zainichi Chōsenjin Undo-shi*: 8–15 *kaihōzen*, 215–24; Imamura, *Zainichi chōsenjin to nihon rōdōsha kaikyū*, 178–97.

6 Obinata, *Keisatsu no shakaishi*, especially chapters 2 and 3. Obviously, there were many significant changes to the police system between 1868 and the end of the First World War, many of which overlap with themes raised in this chapter. Of particular interest are the changes between military police and civil police in the Japanese colonies. See the research on the colonial police in Taiwan by Ching-chih Chen, "Police and Community Control Systems in the Empire," in Myers and Peattie, eds., *The Japanese Colonial Empire, 1895–1945*; Lee, "Modernity, Legality and Power"; Tipton, *The Japanese Police State*; and Mitchell, *Thought Control in Prewar Japan*.

7 Obinata, *Keisatsu no shakaishi*, 93–120. For further information see Lewis's book, *Rioters and Citizens*.

8 Obinata, *Keisatsu no shakaishi*, 109–10.

9 Maruyama, "Keisatsu to Shakai Kyūsai," 164.

10 Matsui, *Keisatsu Dokuhon*, 1.

11 Ibid., 171.

12 Ibid.

13 Maruyama, *Yasashii Keisatsuron*, 104.

14 Matsui, *Keisatsu Dokuhon*, 1.

15 Tanaka, "Keisatsu no minshūka to minshū no keisatsuka," 15.

16 Maruyama, *Yasashii Keisatsuron*, 109.

17 Maruyama, "Keisatsu to Shakai Jigyō," 2.

18 Maruyama, *Yasashii Keisatsuron*, 109.

19 Chadwick, "Preventive Police," 278. Chadwick's influence on the regulation of the poor is discussed in Dean's article, "A Genealogy of the Government of Poverty."

20 Cahalane, *Police Practice and Procedure*, introduction by Arthur Woods, iii–iv and 1–6. Woods is also well known for implementing a long-lasting series of athletic events for children of families on various forms of public welfare. This was also considered an integral part of preventive policing.

21 Obinata, *Keisatsu no shakaishi*, 115–20. As Obinata has shown in greater detail, the national police (*kokumin keisatsu*), in its effort to transform the masses into a police force through preventive policing, also enlisted youth groups, fire fighter organizations, veterans' associations, and other groups to unite for the purpose of self-defense (*jiei*) and self-policing (*jikei*). The *jikeidan*, of course, became infamous for its central role in executing the murders of over 6,000 Koreans in the immediate, chaotic aftermath of the Kanto earthquake on September 1, 1923. On the Korean massacre of 1923 and the jikeidan, see Kang, T. S., *Gendai-shi Shiryō*, in particular chapter 3, "Keishichō oyobi kaku keisatsu kannai ni okeru ryūdō jōkyō." In English, see Weiner, *Origins of the Korean Community*, esp. 83–84.

22 Maruyama, "Keisatsu to Shakai Jigyō," 8.

23 Ibid., 9.

24 Ibid., 164.

25 Maruyama, "Kindai shakai jigyō no sūsei," 43.

26 As Rancière writes in *Disagreement*, 28: "The petty police is just a particular form of a more general order that arranges that tangible reality in which bodies are distributed in community. It is the weakness and not the strength of this order in certain states that inflates the petty police to the point of putting it in charge of the whole set of police functions. The evolution of Western societies reveals *a contrario* that the policeman is one element in a social mechanism linking medicine, welfare, and culture."

27 As Benjamin writes, "the 'law' of the police really marks the point at which the state, whether from impotence or because of the immanent connections within any legal system, can no longer guarantee through the legal system the empirical ends that it desires at any price. . . . Unlike law, which acknowledges in the 'decision' determined by place and time a metaphysical category that gives it a claim to critical evaluation, a consideration of the police institution encounters nothing essential at all. Its power is formless, like its nowhere tangible, all-pervasive, ghostly presence in . . . democracies where their existence . . . bears witness to the greatest conceivable degeneration of violence." Benjamin, "Critique of Violence," in *Reflections*, 286–87.

28 Maruyama, "Chōsen no chian no genjō oyobi shōrai," 6–7.

29 Ibid., 7.

30 Ibid., 1.

31 Ibid., 21.

32 Ibid., 6–7.

33 Maruyama, "Keimu Danpen [Ni]," 42.

34 Maruyama, "Chōsenjin dantai Sōaikai," in *Nanajūnen tokoro dokoro*, 85–94.

35 The establishment of the Sōaikai's private labor exchange office also coincided with the passage of Japan's first Labor Exchange Law of 1921. This would prove to be significant, especially during the Shōwa crisis of 1930, when the Sōaikai, at least in Tokyo, was used as a supplementary labor exchange office for the UERP.

36 Hogo-ka, "Naichi zaiju senjin hogo wo mokuteki to suru shakai jigyo dantai-cho."

37 The Sōaikai branch in Pusan is listed in Chuo Shokugyō Shōkai Jimukyoku, "Tokyo-fuka zairyu chōsenjin rōdōsha ni kansuru chōsa" by the Central Labor Exchange, 1924, in Pak, ZCKSS, vol. 1, 442. As far as funding to the individual branches, a report by the Chōsen Shisō Tsūshin states that in 1926, 9,430 yen went to Osaka, 1,500 yen to Kyoto, 8,840 yen to Aichi, 3,000 to Shizuoka, and 2,870 to Yamanashi. By comparison, Sōaikai headquarters in Tokyo amassed 51,000 yen. See Chōsen Shisō Tsūshin, November 22, 1927, 5; and Naimushō Keihōkyoku, Shakai Undō no Jōkyō, 1931, 1145.

38 See the essays, "Shisetsu shakai jigyō no hōkō tenkō," "shiei shakai jigyō keiei mondai ni tsuite," "Shiei shakai jigyō keieinan non konpon gei'in," "Shieishakai jigyō keiei mondai," in the journal, Shakai Fukuri, 5–27.

39 "Shiei shakai jigyō zadankai," in Shakai Fukuri, March 1930, 15.

40 Ibid., 27.

41 Kim, "Kawasaki ranto jiken no shinsō."

42 Ibid., 77–78.

43 Sakai, "Chōsenjin Rōdōsha Mondai," 130–31. As is shown in more detail in the next chapter dealing with the micropolitics of the UERP, these kinds of statements were common in the early 1920s. For example, the influential unemployment policy researcher, Fukuda Tokuzō, wrote that the UERP was "importing unemployment from Korea" and exacerbating the conditions for unemployed Japanese workers. Bureaucrats in Kyoto went so far as to say that the UERP was a Korean colony. This consequently led to various discussions to regulate Korean migration to Japan, or else to create institutional mechanisms that could provide unemployment relief to Koreans without threatening the position of unemployed Japanese workers. The point here is that these arguments were deployed and used to divide and separate Korean surplus populations from Japanese surplus populations through the institutionalization of Korean-only welfare organizations, such as the Sōaikai and the Naisen Kyōwakai.

44 See appendix 1 for a complete list and description of each organization.

45 Osaka had the highest numbers of these organizations with 134, followed by Tokyo (62), Aichi (38), Fukuoka (36), Yamaguchi (25), and Hyogo (23). Osaka also had the highest number of members, with 23,000, followed by Tokyo (15,106). However, Tokyo and Wakayama prefectures had the highest percentages of Koreans enlisted in Korean welfare or self-help organizations, with 49 percent and 66 percent, respectively. See Naimushō Keihōkyoku, Shakai undo no jokyo, 1931.

46 For Maruyama's connections to the Naisen Kyōwakai, see the journal Shakai Jigyō no Kenkyū, 100.

47 Sōaikai Sōhonbu, "Sōaikai Jigyō Kōgai," in Ringhoffer, "Sōaikai—Chōsenjin dōka dantai no ayumi," 58.

48 Maruyama, Nanajūnen tokoro dokoro, 88–89. Three days after the earthquake, at the height of the "Korean massacre," there was a systematic effort by the state and

local police and the government-general in Korea to control the information about the events following the earthquake. Six notable actions taken were: (1) the complete ban on travel between Japan and Korea on September 3; (2) the *Imperial Ordinance for the Preservation of Public Order*, September 7, which prohibited any publications of materials deemed injurious to the public order; (3) the confiscation by the government-general in Seoul and the ministry of communications in Japan of all telegrams containing "information injurious to public order"; (4) the confiscation of all Japanese newspapers by the government-general in Korea; (5) the creation of internment centers for Koreans in and around the southern port city of Pusan, where commercial and passenger shipping lines to and from Korea were the busiest; and (6) Tokyo metropolitan police department orders to policemen to prevent Koreans from leaving Tokyo. The suppression of information was not simply about printed information, but about population control as well. See Weiner, *The Origins of the Korean Community in Japan*, 83–84.

49 *Keijō Nippō*, September 24, 1923, 2. This information was also documented in a 1926 Tokyo Ward Office publication on the earthquake. See Tokyo Shiyakusho, *Tokyo Shinsai-roku*, 1926, 933.

50 *Keijō Nippō*, December 19, 1923.

51 *Keijō Nippō*, September 14, 1923, 2.

52 Ibid.

53 Ibid. These services included cleaning ashes off the streets of Tokyo, as well as collecting human corpses.

54 *Keijō Nippō*, "Daishisai de kyūgōshita zaikyōnai senjin. . . . Senjin ni yoi insho wow o kizami tsuketa" [Assimilation through the Earthquake . . . Koreans Make Good Impression], December 19, 1923. See also *Keijō Nippō*, "Zaikyō senjin man-zoku: yonen no rōdōshak majime ni hataraku / yatoinushi to no aida ni wa na-midagumashii bidan mo aru" [Satisfaction with Koreans in Tokyo / 4,000 Workers Serious about Work / Relations with Employers, Some Even Remarkable], October 31, 1923.

55 *Keijō Nippō*, December 5 (evening edition), 1924; see also Chūō Shokugyō Shōkai Jimukyoku, "Tokyo-fuka zairyu chōsenjin rōdōsha ni kansuru chōsa," 429–44, reprinted in Pak, *zcκss*, vol. 1.

56 In 1927, 90 percent of Sōaikai work in Tokyo went to public works; in 1930, 35 percent; in 1931, 72.7 percent; and in 1932, 67.5 percent. By comparison, with the exception of 1929, when factory labor constituted 74 percent of Sōaikai labor exchanges, work to factories generally did not go over 35 percent. See Tokyo-fu, "Tokyo-fu Tōkeishō," 1925–33. In Osaka and Nagoya, the Sōaikai tended to place more workers in factory-related jobs, especially in cotton factories employing female Korean workers. See Ringhoffer, "Sōaikai—Chōsenjin dōka dantai no ayumi," 58–59; and Nishinarita, *Zainichi chōsenjin no 'sekai' to 'teikoku' kokka*, 177–79.

57 Compared to the 63,900 yen invested in the Sōaikai's worker dormitory number one, the next largest investment in similar dorms in Tokyo was by the *Kokuryū*

worker dorm in Kojimachi (established in 1923), with 25,000 yen. Moreover, according to a 1927 survey of shelters and worker dorms in Tokyo, 10 out of 14 did not exceed values of 10,000 yen. In terms of size, the Sōaikai's was also by far the largest, capable of housing five hundred workers and covering a site of 1,770 tsubo (1 tsubo = 3.954 sq. yards. Therefore, 1,770 tsubo = 6,998.58 sq. yards). By comparison, the Kokuryū dorm only housed 258 workers and covered a site of 400 tsubo. Municipal Office of Tokyo, Statistical Bureau, 666–67, 696–97.

58   Zaidan Hōjin Sōaikai-kan, "Zaidan Hōjin Sōaikaikan Jigyō Yōran," 13–14.

59   Ibid., 17–18; and Sōaikai Sōhonbu, "Jigyō shisetsu no yōran."

60   According to a Tokyo survey from 1924, 91.1 percent of Koreans in Japan were illiterate in the Korean language or did not have any schooling experience. In 1940, 60.3 percent were illiterate in Korean. Historian Tonomura Masaru has found that between 1926 and 1938, approximately 20 to 60 percent of Koreans in Japan did not understand the Japanese language (171). It is probable that the Sōaikai's concern with teaching Japanese (and Korean) to Korean workers was similar to the concern of the Naisen Kyōwakai in Osaka, which published its own Japanese language handbook for Korean workers that provided translations not only of words but of entire phrases that were said to be commonly used on the job, such as "I am a day worker." (See chapter 6, note 31.)

61   Sōaikai-kan, "Zaidan Hōjin Sōaikaikan Jigyō Yōran," 28.

62   *Keijō Nippō*, July 17, 1926, 1.

63   Sōaikai-kan, "Zaidan Hōjin Sōaikaikan Jigyō Yōran," 15.

64   Ibid. This, furthermore, is the reason the Sōaikai made it mandatory that workers maintain continuous residence in the Sōaikai dorms. Not only did it prevent "nomadic and roving" Koreans, who had not yet registered with the Sōaikai housing facilities, from obtaining employment through the labor exchange offices before the Sōaikai's own worker-tenants, but also it served as a means to count the supply of workers on any given day.

65   For details on the awards and punishment system in the coal mining industry, see Oyama Shikidarō, *Kōgyō rōdō to oyakata seidō*, 89–105.

66   Sōaikai-kan, "Zaidan Hōjin Sōaikaikan Jigyō Yōran," 26.

67   Ibid.

68   In 1925, the Tokyo Government Statistics list two kinds of Sōaikai housing fees at its number one worker dormitory: free and 5 sen. In 1926, housing was completely free for all, but in 1927 free lodging was stopped. Lodgers were then charged 10 sen. From 1928 to 1933, however, the fees increased to 15 sen. Tokyo-fu, "Tokyo-fu Tōkeishō," 1924–36.

69   It should also be mentioned that an additional percentage—what many Korean workers critical of the Sōaikai sarcastically called tokens of mutual love—was taken off of their formal wages through a mandatory savings plan, or what the Sōaikai called a savings promotion plan (*chokin shōrei keikaku*). The additional importance of the savings plans was that Sōaikai workers could not collect on their savings

until fixed terms came to an end, a policy that prevented worker desertion. This was a practice that the Sōaikai copied from mandatory savings plans for female cotton workers in Japanese cotton factories.

70 Sōaikai-kan, "Zaidan Hōjin Sōaikaikan Jigyō Yōran," 16. On biopolitical power, see Foucault, "Society must be Defended."

71 Zaidan Hōjin Sōaikai-kan, "Zaidan Hōjin Sōaikaikan Jigyō Yōran," 20–21.

72 Quoted in Kim and Pan Son-hi, Kaze no Dōki: Zainichi Chōsenjin Jokō no Seikatsu to Rekishii, 159–60.

73 As is well known, the term "senjin" was an abbreviated signifier for a Korean person, or "chōsenjin," and is comparable to "nigger," "kike," "chink," "spik," "honky," etc.

74 Nara-ken Keisatsu-bu, Keisatsu sōshō dai 45. Iru zo! Futei senjin, April 1940, 2–3.

75 Naimushō Keihōkyoku, "Chōsenjin Kinjō Gaiyō," January 1922, in Pak, ZCKSS, vol. 1, 126. Police reports unanimously conclude that the most urgent and disconcerting emotion and thought among Koreans were not only thoughts of independence but also feelings being anti-Japanese (hainichi-teki shisō). The same police report from January 1922 thus mentions, as another indirect method of surveillance and control, the strategic use of three laws to specifically suppress the proliferation of written anti-Japanese thoughts: the Chian Keisatsu-hō (enacted in Meiji 33); the Newspaper Law (Meiji 42); and the Publishing Law (Meiji 26). These three laws together combined to define the basic parameters of the "Genron Tōsei" policy.

76 Zaidan Hōjin Sōaikai-kan, "Zaidan Hōjin Sōaikaikan Jigyō Yōran," 3–4.

77 Interview with Pak Ch'um-gum, Osaka Mainichi Shimbun, April 28, 1923.

78 Kan, Don-chin, Nihon no chōsen shihai seisaku-shi no kenkyū, 5–6.

79 Interview with Pak Ch'um-gum, Keijō Nippō, February 15, 1928, 2.

80 Sōaikai Osaka Honbu Bunka-bu, Chōsen, 1925.

81 Ibid., 7.

82 Tōa Jiron, "Nagoya Sōaikai harusetsu taikaiki," 47–49.

83 Zaidan Hōjin Sōaikai-kan, "Zaidan Hōjin Sōaikaikan Jigyō Yōran," 2–3.

84 See Harootunian, Overcome by Modernity, especially the author's discussions of humanist philosopher Miki Kiyoshi; Sakai, Translation and Subjectivity, especially on philosopher Watsuji Tetsuo and Tanabe Hajime's Shu no Ronri; and Haver, The Body of This Death, especially chapter 2 on the thought of philosopher Nishida Kitaro.

85 Chōson Nippō, May 17, 1924, quoted in Tonomura, 31. It is also mentioned in the Sōaikai Sōhonbu from 1923 that the Sōaikai carried out mass recruitments in Korea.

86 Keijō Nippō, August 6, 1924.

87 Ibid. The peasants also demanded that Tokuda cover expenses for the establishment of schools, the establishment of boat lanes and boat travel (presumably to the mainland), the construction of five reservoirs, and the renovation of levees and embankments. All were rejected as well.

88 These good future prospects manifestly did not happen, however, for the same problem erupted on a more violent scale—now involving pistol-wielding Sōaikai members—four years later in March 1928, and on the same island of Haido. By then, however, the peasants had established a peasant union with connections with the Labor-Peasant Party (Rōnō-tō) in Osaka and were demanding landed property rights (tochi shoyūken) and further decreases in farming expenses. The same absentee landlord from Osaka, Tokuda, refused again, and again called upon the services of Pak and the Sōaikai, for a fee of 6,000 yen, to cross the straits with Sōaikai musclemen and put down the peasant strikers for a second time. According to a Rōdō-Nōmin Shimbun article from March 24, 1928, a major protest on March 22 involving 500 to 600 peasants demanding decreases in farming expenses was put down by pistol wielding Sōaikai members acting in concert with colonial police from the island. Sōaikai members were quoted as shouting, "This is an order from the government-general!" The peasants chanted back, "Sōaikai—get off the island!! Go back to Japan!!" For related news on the ongoing battle on Haidō island, see also the article in Musansha Shimbun, March 5, 1928, "Chōsen Kosaku Sōgi . . . Teki wa Nihon no Fuzai Jinushi." See also the pamphlet in Musansha Shimbun, "Chōsen Haidō Tochi Shoyūken, Haidō dōmei sōritsu taikai," from May 10, 1928, in (Ohara collection, T1–2).

89 Oniwa, Hamamatsu Nihon Gakki Sogi no Kenkyū, 1926 4.26–8.8, 64.

90 Ibid., 109.

91 Leaflet by the Sōaikai, May 21, 1926, reprinted in ibid., 331. In a Nihon Gakki internal dossier, "On the Progress of the Walk-Out," it is noted that Tachibana was eventually arrested (ibid., 349).

92 Rōsō flyer titled, "On the Company Organization, the Sōaikai: Rōsō speaks out to the Citizens of Hamamatsu City." Source is preserved at the Ohara Institute of Social Problems in the "Nihon Gakki Sōgi" documents. Also reprinted in ibid., 330–31.

93 Ibid., 118.

94 Ibid., 117.

95 Yūkan Nippō, May 21, 1926, quoted in ibid., 138.

96 Musansha Shimbun, June 19, 1926.

97 Yamanashi Nichi Nichi Shimbun, June 15, 1926.

98 Ibid.

99 Telegraph report from Kōfu City (capital of Yamanashi prefecture), June 14, 1926, reprinted in Meiji-Taisho-Shōwa Shimbun Kenkyukai, Shimbun Shūsei Taishō-hen Nenshi: Taishō15nendō han, 424–25.

100 Ibid.

101 Ibid. For an excellent overview of Korean workers in Yamanashi prefecture, as well as of the Sōaikai's short history there, see Kim, Kō, "Yamanashi ni okeru zainichi chōsenjin no keisei to jōkyō—1920 nendai."

102 Even the Ministry of Justice was aware of the bad publicity the Sōaikai was receiving, writing in 1928 that the Sōaikai was "the biggest pro-Japanese organization in Japan whose activities may have to be curbed as a result of all the publicity it has received lately." Shihōshō Keijikyoku, *Chōsenjin Mondai*, 1928.

103 Ringhoffer, "Sōaikai—Chōsenjin dōka dantai no ayumi," 69.

104 Nihon Heimin Bijutsuka Dōmei Tokyo-shibu, *Mokchū Unbok*. Anti-Sōaikai movements gained momentum through five other major incidents: (1) Sōaikai suppression of a Korean construction worker strike in Mie prefecture, February 1929 (see *Shakai Undō no Tsūshin*, February 9, 1929); (2) Sōaikai suppression of the massive strike at the Kishiwada Cotton factory, 1930 (see Kim and Pan, *Kaze no Dōki*); (3) Sōaikai suppression of the coal miners' strike at the Aso Coal Mine in Fukuoka prefecture (see Smith, "The 1932 Aso Coal Strike"); (4) violent struggles between the Sōaikai and a Zenkyō-affiliated construction workers' union in Tokyo, December 1932 (see *Tokkō Geppō*, January 1933, 59); and (5) violent struggles between members of the Sōaikai's Toyohashi headquarters and the *Toyohashi Gōdō Rōdō Kumiai* in Aichi prefecture, December 1932 (see *Tokkō Geppō*, January 1933, 60).

105 Historian Oguma Eiichi has additionally shown that for Korean Sōaikai members, the number of Koreans meeting the criteria to vote was extremely low. While the Sōaikai energetically supported Pak's Diet bid, less than 1.5 percent of the Koreans in the Sōaikai were actually able to cast their ballots on election day. Oguma and Matsuda have also made separate but similar claims in their analyses of Pak's elections. Both point out, for example, the degree and extent to which Pak's victory was greatly aided by Maruyama, who helped manage Pak's campaign. See Oguma, "Chōsen umare no nipponjin," 46; and Matsuda, "Maruyama Tsurukichi no chōsen dokuritsu undō ninshiki."

106 Zenkyō Nihon Kagaku Rōdō Kumiai Tokyo Shibu, "Pak Ch'um-gum no Rikkoho to tatakae." The precise date is unknown, but it is most likely late 1931 or early 1932.

107 For a detailed discussion of Korean tenants and housing discrimination, see chapter 4.

108 Rōdō-Nōmintō Osaka-fu shi-bu rengōkai, February 5, 1928, 31–32. This same flyer also describes how it is a struggle to find employers who will allow Korean workers to take time off from work to vote. Voting often meant sacrificing a day's wages in a labor market in which a day of work could never be taken for granted. Lastly, the linguistic problem of ballots was also identified as a problem facing Korean voters who could not read Japanese well. The slogans were: (1) Put an end to restrictions on residence! (2) Recognize Korean language on ballots! (3) Stop the persecution of Koreans! (4) Stop the repression of Koreans! and (5) Down with the Reactionary Tanaka Cabinet!

109 These points are drawn from historian Oguma Eiji's analysis of transcriptions taken from debates on the floor of parliament in which Pak participated. See Oguma,

"Chōsen umare no nipponjin: Chōsenjin Shūingiin, Pak Ch'um-gum," 45–51. For another detailed and excellent discussion of Pak's election, see Matsuda, "Pak Ch'um-gum ron: sono senkyō undō to gikai katsudō wo chūshin toshite."

110 Pak, Ch'um-gum, *Warera no kokka shin-nippon.*

111 Quoted in Oguma, "Chōsen umare no nipponjin: Chōsenjin Shūingiin, Pak Ch'um-gum," 47.

6. At the Gates of Unemployment

1 Kase, *Senzen Nihon no shitsugyō taisaku.*

2 Kase, "Shigsugyōsha kyūsai kokyō doboku jigyō ni okeru shūrōsha senbetsu hōshiki to chōsenjin tōrokusha," 370.

3 Shakai-kyoku, "Hisoka: shitsugyō ni kansuru chōsa," 55–61.

4 Ibid., 55. Tachinbō is a colloquial term literally meaning "guy standing around." Its usage, however, signifies a day worker, and it is particularly used in the Tokyo and the Kanto areas. In Osaka, for example, the term *ankō*—literally an angler fish (i.e., a fish that waits for the bait to come around)—is widely used.

5 Ibid., 58.

6 Quoted in Sakai, "Chōsenjin Rōdōsha Mondai," 193–94.

7 Kyoto Shiyakusho Shakai-ka, "Kyoto-shi ni okeru shitsugyōsha seikatsu jōtai chōsa," 1933, 15.

8 Akiyama, "Chōsenjin rōdōsha to shitsugyō mondai," 116–17.

9 Marx, *Capital,* 797. "Pauperism is the hospital of the active labor-army and the dead weight of the industrial reserve army. Its production is included in that of the relative surplus population, its necessity is implied by their necessity; along with the surplus population, pauperism forms a condition of capitalist production, and the capitalist development of wealth. It forms part of the *faux frais* of capitalist production: but capital usually knows how to transfer these from its own shoulders to those of the working class and the petty bourgeoisie."

10 Akiyama, "Chōsenjin rōdōsha to shitsugyō mondai," 116. In fact, however, immigration measures had already been debated and put into effect—although they were relatively ineffectual in keeping Koreans out of Japan. Already in July of 1928, the Ministry of the Interior revised its May 1923 immigration policy regarding Korean workers and required all workers to contact the Pusan police prior to departing Korea with employment channels in Japan already established. Also added was the requirement that prevented the migration to Japan of all workers who did not possess 10 yen or more in addition to the cost of the boat fare to Japan. So called free migration (*jiyō tokō*) was suspended many times during the 1920s and 1930s. During the time Akiyama was writing, in 1929, migration policy in Pusan rejected thousands of Japan-bound Korean workers on the basis of several points, the most important of which were: (1) lack of place of employment in Japan; (2) lack of knowledge of Japanese language; and (3) lack of sufficient

funds. The problem was that the number of Koreans legally migrating to Japan everyday was on average 500 people over the daily number of Koreans repatriating back to Korea. Because of this, Akiyama said that the number of those repatriating was "like a single hair amidst nine cows"—in other words, a drop in a bucket.

11 Sakai, "Chōsenjin Rōdōsha Mondai," 194.

12 Ibid., 193–94.

13 Ibid.

14 Ibid.

15 Ibid., 197–98. These arguments by Sakai should also remind us that Japan's imperial expansion into Manchuria, spearheaded by Japanese financial capital, was fundamentally related to domestic problems of unemployment and immigration. On the role of Japanese finance capital in Manchuria and its specific effects on Korean migrant workers, see Park, *Two Dreams in One Bed*, esp. chapter 1, "The Politics of Osmosis: Korean Migration and the Japanese Empire," and chapter 2, "Between Nation and Market."

16 Work books were government-issued documents that unemployed workers received through institutions such as the UERP, the police, and the district committee system (*hōmen i'inkai*). Those in possession of a work book would take them to the UERP office to get stamped for each day of work obtained through the UERP. The work book could only be used by the individually registered worker.

17 *Tokkō Geppō*, November 1930, 179.

18 Osaka-shi Shakai-bu Chosa-ka, "Rōdō Techō ni tsuite," May 1930, 8.

19 Ibid., 8, 17.

20 For example, while 12,436 Korean workers applied for employment introductions from the Sōaikai's labor exchange office in Tokyo in 1928, in the following year only 788 workers applied—a drop of 11,548. In 1930, only 913 workers applied to the Sōaikai. As for the Naisen Kyōwakai, while there were 14,836 applicants to its labor exchange office in 1926, by 1929 there were only 5,574 applicants. Those numbers would dwindle steadily between 1929 and 1938. Osaka-fu, *Osaka-fu Tōkeisho*, 1924–38.

21 Naimushō Shakaikyoku Shokugyō-ka, "Showa 3-nendo Shitsugyo Kyusai Jigyo Gaiyo," 12.

22 Osaka-shi Shakai-bu Chōsa-ka, "Rōdō Techō ni tsuite," May 1930, 17. According to this survey in Osaka, private social welfare organizations accounted for 34.8 percent of the total number of work books distributed. Twenty percent came from the *hōmen i'inkai*; 19 percent from the police; 4 percent from the city ward office; 11.1 percent from labor exchange offices; and 10.5 percent from other sources.

23 Kim Tu-yong, "Kawasaki ranto jiken no shinsō," 77–78.

24 *Shakai Undō Tsūshin*, September 18, 1933, 3. Another article on September 27 notes that so successful was the Kōtōbashi Registered Workers Council fight against the Sōaikai that the Korean Free Workers Union (Chōsen Jiyō Rōdō

Kumiai) dissolved and entered the Workers Council "in order to fight against the reactionary Sōaikai in the Honjo and Fukagawa wards in Tokyo." See also *Tokkō Geppō*, September 1933, 789. This higher police report notes that this union was also able to overcome differences between Leninists and anarchists among the registered workers at the Kōtōbashi labor exchange office and was working to extend a mass movement through the labor exchange offices that similarly overcame factional differences.

25 Nishi Sugamo Shokugyō Shokaijō, "Nishi Sugamo-cho Shokugyo Shokaijo ni okeru Hiyatoi Rōdō Shōkai Genjō," 295–96. My emphasis. They specifically cite the *Kenkoku Chūō Shi-in* as one possible mediating organization. The point is that these Korean workers were protesting against having to go to the assimilation organs as the only place to obtain these work books.

26 Ibid.

27 Osaka-shi Shakai-bu Chōsa-ka, "Rōdō Techō ni tsuite," 16.

28 Ibid., 16–17.

29 Ibid., 18.

30 Nishi Sugamo Shokugyō Shokaijō, "Nishi Sugamo-cho Shokugyo Shokaijo ni okeru Hiyatoi Rōdō Shōkai Genjō," 295–96.

31 Ibid. Another index of the how Korean work book hoarding was considered a problem is that, in 1933, the labor section of the Osaka city social bureau compiled, published, and distributed a book of everyday Japanese words and phrases to Korean workers residing in Osaka. The book was titled *Phrase and Word Book for Korean Labor in Japan*. On the first two pages of the collection, the following sentences were published under the heading "work book": "Bring your own work book with you every morning," "Do not lend your work book to anyone else," and "Your work book is no good." See Osaka-shi Shakai-bu Rōdō-ka. "Naisen Rōdō Yōgoshu," 1–2.

32 Osaka-shi Shakai-bu Chōsa-ka, "Rōdō Techō ni tsuite," 15–16. Also, workers were required to pay for the cost of developing the photographs themselves, as an article in *Shakai Undō Tsūshin* (May 10, 1933) makes clear. An organization of unemployed Korean workers in Nagoya, *Zai-na Chōsenjin Shitsugyō Taisaku Kiseidōmeikai*, gathering on May 4, 1933, in protest against various aspects of the UERP, specifically noted that they opposed the mandatory fees for work book photographs.

33 Osaka-shi Shakai-bu Chōsa-ka, "Rōdō Techō ni tsuite," 19–22.

34 Ibid.

35 See Deleuze and Guattari, *Anti-Oedipus*, 18–19; and *A Thousand Plateaus*, 149–66.

36 On the concept of the relative autonomy of the state, see Althusser, *For Marx*, 89–128; and Poulantzas, *Political Power and Social Classes*, 271–73.

37 DeBrunhoff, *The State, Capital and Economic Policy*, 5.

38 Ibid., 110, 118.

39 Kase, "Shigsugyōsha kyūsai kokyō doboku jigyō ni okeru shūrōsha senbetsu hōshiki to chōsenjin tōrokusha," 361–93; *Senzen Nihon no shitsugyō taisaku*, 133–76.

40 Ibid., 144.

41 Ibid. In fact, these decisions operated through even finer distinctions. For example, the category of alternating workers can be further broken down into three categories: (1) Those receiving advance notice for their work days and the location; (2) Those receiving notice today for work tomorrow, decided by a number ticket system; and (3) Those who did not receive any notice whatsoever for work today or for tomorrow, but who showed up everyday at the labor exchange offices hoping for employment. The public works department and its related construction foremen, however, could not know far in advance how many workers it would need for a particular day on the construction site since conditions changed everyday. Therefore, when the public works department did ask the UERP for alternating workers, it usually asked for types (2) or (3) since this gave them the most flexibility. From the perspective of the UERP and the labor exchange offices, however, type (3) was the most burdensome because they were the most numerous as well as the most politically active among the unemployed workers.

42 Miura, "Hiyatoi rōdōsha no shitsugyō taisaku ni tsuite," 500.

43 Kase, *Senzen Nihon no shitsugyō taisaku*, 151. See also Kase's essay, "Shigsugyōsha kyūsai kokyō doboku jigyō ni okeru shūrōsha senbetsu hōshiki to chōsenjin tōrokusha," 361–99.

44 *Shakai Undō Tsūshin*, May 10, 11, and 18, 1933. Of the eleven other demands, the most important were demands for: (1) Minimum wage of 1.30 yen; (2) the lifting of specific requirements to obtain work books (such as Japanese language exams, registration from the police, and fees for photographs for the work books); (3) the covering of transportation costs by the UERP; (4) the end of wage discrimination; (5) the building of Korean housing; and (6) the requirement that half the total employees working in UERP offices and Labor Exchange offices are Korean, to represent the number of unemployed Koreans.

45 The other significant demands included: (1) the immediate increase of wages from 1.00 yen to 1.50 yen; (2) reduction of working hours and a mandate of two hours of rest time instead of one hour; (3) payment of wages to registered workers on rain days.

46 *Chika Tabi*, published in Tokyo by the "Fukagawa Shokaijonai Chika Tabi Shimbunsha Hakko," October 27, 1931. The Korean workers involved here were predominantly unemployed worker-activists in the Union of Unemployed Workers of the communist union, Zenkyō. For an outstanding essay on the relationship between unemployed Korean workers and this union, see Kadoki, "Zenkyō—shitsugyōsha dōmeika chōsenjin undō," 28–43, in which he also refers to *Chika Tabi*. See also Matsunaga, "Kantō jiyū rōdōsha kumiai to zainichi chōsenjin rōdōsha," 46–69.

47 Nishi Sugamo Shokugyō Shokaijō, "Nishi Sugamo-cho Shokugyo Shokaijo ni okeru Hiyatoi Rōdō Shōkai Genjō." The dossier is divided into seven sections:

1. Incidents arising between workers and the labor exchange office (7)
2. Incidents arising between sub-contracting construction sites and workers (14)
3. Incidents arising between direct management sites and workers (8)
4. Incidents arising among workers (9)
5. Incidents stemming from the distribution of agitation propaganda (6)
6. Incidents stemming from fraudulent actions or schemes, including those involving work books (11)
7. Incidents stemming from injuries on the job (8)

Parts of this document can be found reprinted in the Toshimakushi Hensan Iinkai Hensan, *Toshimakushi: Shiryōhen* 4, 1181–86. The complete document can be found at the Tokyo-to Kōbunshokan (*shozō shiryō*), call number 324.C8.13, vol. 24, "Shokugyō-ka Zakken," and includes information from two other labor exchange offices (Shinagawa and Meguro) that deal with Korean activists.

48 Ibid.

49 Ibid.

50 For a more detailed discussion of intermediary exploitation, *pinhane*, and day labor, see chapter 3 of this book.

51 Osaka Chihō Shokugyō Shōkaijimukyoku, "*Chōsenjin Rōdōsha Chōsa*," in Pak, zckss, vol. 2, 1930, 1164–76.

52 Ibid., 1176.

53 Kase, *Senzen Nihon no shitsugyō taisaku*, 90–91.

54 Ibid., 92.

55 Ibid., see esp. chapter 5, section 3, "Chokuei jigyō hōshiki no nanten," 88–94.

56 Ibid., 92–93.

57 Nagoya Rōdō Shōkaijo, "*Dai ni-kai Nagoya-shi Shitsugyō Kyūsai jigyō shikō gaikyō*," 1927, 17, quoted in ibid., 93.

58 Nishi Sugamo Shokugyō Shōkaijō, "Nishi Sugamo-cho Shokugyo Shōkaijo ni okeru Hiyatoi Rōdō Shōkai Genjō," 295–96.

59 Ibid.

60 Tokyo Chihō Shokugyō Shōkai Jimukyoku, "Yamanashi-ken kokudō 8-gōsen kaishu kōji rōdō idō keika tenmatsu, Rōdō idō dai-3 shū." Nishi Sugamo sent 15 Japanese and 37 Koreans (129). This is the official report of the entire construction plan, including the most important minutes from meetings between Tokyo and Yamanashi governments and subcontractors. Much else has been written about this famous worker mobilization plan (and its miserable failure). For an excellent insider recounting of how the Yamanashi plan came about, see the memoirs of Toyohara (director of the Tokyo Central Labor Exchange Bureau), *Kokuei no Shokugyō Shōkai Jigyō*, 235–73. For a general account of the relationship between the Yamanashi plan and the UERP, see Kase, *Senzen Nihon no shitsugyō taisaku*, 195–238.

61 Tokyo Chihō Shokugyō Shōkai Jimukyoku, "Yamanashi-ken kokudō 8-gōsen kaishu kōji rōdō idō keika tenmatsu, Rōdō idō dai-3 shū," 15, 120–22.

62 Ibid.

63 *Yamanashi Nichi Nichi Shimbun*, December 3, 1931, quoted in Kim, "Zenkyō Doken Yamanashi Shibu to Chōsenjin Rōdōsha (I): Higashi Hachi dai Jiyū rōdō kumiai— Zenkyō Doken Yamanashi Shibu kessei," in *Zainichi Chōsenjinshi Kenkyū* 16 (October 1986): 68.

64 Ibid. Also cited in Toyohara, *Kokuei no Shokugyō Shōkai Jigyō*, 242. Recounts a conversation between himself and the main sub-contractor in charge of section three of the construction site, Jūtaro Kobayashi. The discussion centered around the problem of how to determine the ratio between Korean and Japanese workers to be sent from Tokyo to Yamanashi; these problems were compounded with problems of how to separate and house Japanese and Korean workers. Kobayashi, impatient and fed up, blurts out, "I've heard all that talk about radical Koreans from sub-contractors a hundred times over. But, listen, I'm telling you, we can rectify that problem with education. Sub-contractors never tire of saying that Korean workers are difficult. But for me—hey, I welcome Korean workers. So don't hesitate: send them over." Toyohara replied, "Using Koreans is generally not something to request. . . . Recently, Korean workers are radicalizing and falling into extremely bad ways; they are no longer docile as before. You may regret asking for them, you know." On pages 252–53, Toyohara writes that after the strikes in January 1931, however, Kobayashi plead the Yamanashi prefectural government not to send Korean workers from Tokyo to Yamanashi for the next phase of the construction. In response to this, Toyohara writes, "Now Kobayashi was eating his old words about Koreans and now knows how hard it is to control them." Toyohara also seems to derive pleasure by calling Kobayashi "a Yamanashi country bumpkin."

65 *Yamanashi Nichi Nichi Shimbun*, December 10, 1930.

66 Ibid., December 13, 1930.

67 Ibid., December 20, 1930.

68 *Shakai Undō no Jōkyō*, quoted in Kim, Kō, "Zenkyō Doken Yamanashi Shibu to Chōsenjin Rōdōsha (I): Higashi hachi dai jiyū rōdō kumiai-Zenkyō doken Yamanashi shibu keisei," 72. See also the essay by Umeda, "Nihon Rōdō Kumiai Zenkoku Kyōgikai to zainichi chōsenjin rōdōsha," 250.

69 Tokyo Chihō Shokugyō Shōkai Jimukyoku, "Yamanashi-ken kokudō 8-gōsen kaishu kōji rōdō idō keika tenmatsu, Rōdō idō dai-3 shū," 78–87.

70 Ibid., 83. The others included one representative from the Yamanashi Dōrō Shuji Gishi; one representative from the Tokyo-fu social section; one from the Tokyo-fu social welfare programs; one from the Tokyo-fu labor exchange office; one from the Tokyo-shi labor exchange office; one from the Tokyo-shi labor exchange office and two representatives from the labor relations section (*rōmukei*); one from the Tokyo-shi technical labor exchange office (*gijutsu rōdō shokugyō shōkaijo*); one from

the Tokyo central labor exchange office; and, finally, four representatives from the primary architect of the entire unemployed worker mobilization plan, the Tokyo regional labor exchange bureau.

71 Ibid., 78.

72 Ibid., 78–81.

73 Ibid., 84.

74 Ibid., 87–88. In the final report on the entire construction plan, published by the Tokyo regional labor exchange bureau in July 1933, the authors reflect on what had become a financial, social, and political debacle. The basic causes, in their view, were: "(a.) the use of workers untrained in tunnel construction in mountains; (b.) the use of sub-contractors; (c.) a distortion of the meaning of 'relief' of the UERP; (d.) lack of skilled workers with technical knowledge . . . ; and (e.) the presence of politically radical Koreans . . . ."

75 Toyohara, *Kokuei no Shokugyō Shōkai Jigyō*, 261–64.

76 *Shakai Undō Tsūshin*, September 20, 1931. Toyohara describes in his memoirs what he said to the Korean workers: "There's absolutely no reason why we should register you jerks since you all detest working anyway. *Kue yō ga kue nakarō ga shitta koto dewanai* [Whether you eat or starve, I really don't care], so if you're so hungry, why don't you go drink up the water from the Tama River" (269).

77 Toyohara, *Kokuei no Shokugyō Shōkai Jigyō*, 268.

78 Ibid., 271.

79 Obviously, the problem of wages in the UERP is at the center of these statistics. The trouble is that there are no systematic wage statistics by occupation that also show differences in wages, if any, between Koreans and Japanese. The 1932 statistics from Osaka, for example, only records income levels and not wages. What we do know very generally about wage levels in the UERP, as Kase has shown in his book on the UERP, is that, while in principle wages were fixed below the average price of labor power in the general labor market, in practice these wages tended to be higher than the average wages in the minkan labor market, especially after 1930. For the reasons, see Kase, *Senzen Nihon no shitsugyō taisaku*, 152–62.

Epilogue

1 I have argued this point in more detail in an article. See Kawashima, "Capital's Dice-box Shaking: The Contingent Commodifications of Labor Power."

2 Žižek, "Class Struggle or Postmodernism? Yes, please!," in *Contingency, Hegemony, Universality*, Butler, Laclau, and Žižek, 108.

3 Žižek, *Sublime Object of Ideology*, chapter 1.

4 See Meillassoux, *Maidens, Meal and Money*, 89–144; DeBrunhoff, *The State, Capital and Economic Policy*, 5–36, 101–22; and Karatani, *Architecture as Metaphor*, chapters 14–17, and 19.

5 Althusser, *Philosophy of the Encounter*. "In untold passages, Marx—this is certainly no accident—explains that the capitalist mode of production arose from the '*encounter*' between 'the owners of money' and the proletarian stripped of everything but his labor power. 'It so happens' that this encounter took place, and 'took hold', which means that it did not come undone as soon as it came about, but *lasted*, and became an accomplished fact. . . . What matters about this conception is . . . *the aleatory character of the 'taking-hold' of this encounter, which gives rise to an accomplished fact* whose laws it is possible to state" (197; original emphasis).

6 Deep thanks go to professors Katsuhiko Endo and Yutaka Nagahara for introducing me to the work of Uno Kōzō. See Uno, *Keizai Genron*, 134–35. In English, see Uno's book, *Theory of a Purely Capitalist Society*; and Uno's short article, "The Essence of Capital," 929–30.

7 I have presented this argument in greater detail in Kawashima, "Capital's Dice-box Shaking: The Contingent Commodifications of Labor Power." I owe much thanks also to Yutaka Nagahara, whose essay, "Ronri no Ronriteki Rinkai: jissen e no 'ronri' teki tsuigite," 51–89, has been extremely illuminating.

8 For a similar criticism of Foucault's notion of biopolitical power, see Paolo Virno, *A Grammar of the Multitude*, 81–84.

9 Quoted in Garraty, *Unemployment in History*, 138–39. See also Beveridge's book, *Unemployment: A Problem of Industry*.

10 Garraty, 138–39. After the publication of *Unemployment: A Problem of Industry*, Beveridge was soon appointed by Winston Churchill as the first director of Britain's newly established labor exchange system of 1909.

11 Marx, *Capital*, 794–95.

12 See Zai-Nihon Chōsen Rōdō Sōdōmei (heretofore Rōsō), "Zai-Nihon Chōsen Rōdō Sōdōmei Dai 3 Kai Taikai: Senden, Kōryō, Kisoku"; and Choi, "Zai-Nihon Chōsen Rōdō Undō no saikin no Hatten."

BIBLIOGRAPHY

....

Primary sources

NEWSPAPERS

Akahata. Tokyo, 1933.
Fukuoka Nichi Nichi Shimbun. Fukuoka, 1917.
Kawaboku Shinpō. (Publication origin unavailable), 1917.
Hokkaido-ho. Hokkaido, 1917.
Keijō Nippō. Seoul, 1917–28.
Kobe Mata Shin Nippō. Kobe, 1932.
Kobe Shimbun. Kobe, 1931–32.
Kobe Shin Nippō. Kobe, 1930–32.
Manshū Nichi Nichi Shimbun. (Publication origin unavailable), 1917.
Meiji-Taisho-Shōwa Shimbun Kenkyukai. *Shimbun Shūsei Taishō-hen Nenshi: Taishō15nendō han* [Newspaper Collections from the Taisho Period: 1926]. Tokyo: Meiji-Taisho-Shōwa Shimbun Kenkyūkai, 1983.
Minshū Jihō. Tokyo, 1936.
Musansha Shimbun. Tokyo, 1926–29.
Osaka Asahi Shimbun. Osaka, 1918–32.
Osaka Mainichi Shimbun. Osaka, 1917–33.
Taishō Nichi Nichi Shimbun. Tokyo, 1920.
Yamanashi Nichi Nichi Shimbun. Yamanashi, 1926–31.

JOURNALS AND ARTICLES IN JOURNALS

Akiyama, Fusuke. "Chōsenjin rōdōsha to shitsugyō mondai" [Korean Workers and the Problem of Unemployment]. *Shakai Seisaku Jihō.* Tokyo: December 1929.
Choi, Un-kyo. "Zai-Nihon Chōsen Rōdō Undō no saikin no Hatten" [Recent Developments in Korean Labor Movements in Japan]. *Rōdōsha* (September 1927): 41–49.
Chōsen Ihō. Seoul, 1917.
Chōsen Shisō Tsushin [Bulletin of Korean Thought]. Seoul, 1927.
Daishin'in Keiji Hanreishū 1, no. 11. Tokyo, 1932.
Daishin Minji Hanreishū 2, no. 12. Tokyo, 1933.

Hoso Kōron [Journal of the Legal Profession]. Tokyo, 1926.

Igazaki, Akitatsu. "Shiei shakai jigyō keieinan non konpon ge'in" [Fundamental Causes of Difficulties in Private Social Welfare Programs]. Shakai Fukuri (March, 1930): 11–13.

Keimu Ihō [Police Bulletin]. Seoul, 1923.

Kim, Tu-yong. "Kawasaki ranto jiken no shinsō" [The Truth about the Kawasaki Disturbance Incident]. Senki. Tokyo, July 1929.

Kokka Gakkai Zasshi. "Chōsenjin no inyū" [Migration of Koreans]. 31, no. 8 (August 1918): 1275.

Miura, Katsumi. "Hiyatoi rōdōsha no shitsugyō taisaku ni tsuite" [On Unemployment Policies for Day Workers]. Toshi Mondai [Urban Problems], Osaka, October 1932.

Osaka Jūtaku Nenpō [Annual of Osaka Housing]. Tokyo, 1925–34.

Osake, Eizō. "Shiei shakai jigyō keiei mondai ni tsuite" [On Problems of Private Social Welfare Program Management]. Shakai Fukuri. (March, 1930): 8–11.

Sakai, Toshio. "Chōsenjin Rōdōsha Mondai" [The Problem of Korean Workers]. Shakai Jigyō Kenkyū (May–July 1931): May: 83–101; June: 115–36; July: 184–93.

Sakamaki, Kenzō. "Shisetsu shakai jigyō no hōkō tenkō" [Changes in the Direction of Private Social Welfare Programs]. Shakai Fukuri (March, 1930): 5–8.

Shakai Fukuri. "Shiei shakai jigyō zadankai" [Roundtable Discussion on Private Social Welfare Programs]. (March, 1930): 13–27.

Shakai Jigyō [Social Welfare Programs]. Tokyo, 1925.

Shakai Jigyō no Kenkyū [Research on Welfare Programs]. Tokyo, June 25, 1924.

Shakai Seisaku Jiho [Bulletin of Social Policy]. Tokyo, 1929.

Shunzo Yoshisaka. "Labour Recruiting in Japan and its Control." International Labour Review (October 1925): 484–99.

Takai, Eigo. "Sanshin Doko Sogi no gen'in" [Causes of the Sanshin Construction Strike]. Kyozai [Solidarity] 6, no. 9 (September 1930): 57–61.

Tanaka, Takeo. "Keisatsu no minshūka to minshū no keisatsuka" [The Massification of the Police and the Policification of the Police]. Keimu Ihō [Police Bulletin]. (February 15, 1923): 15.

Tōa Jiron. "Nagoya Sōaikai harusetsu taikaiki" [The Nagoya Sōaikai Spring Convention]. 2, no. 5 (May 1924): 47–53.

Tokkō Geppō [Monthly of Higher Police]. Tokyo: Naimushō Keihōkyoku, 1930, 1933, 1934, 1937.

NATIONAL GOVERNMENT SOURCES

Chōsen Sōtokufu Keimu-sōkan, "Chōsenjin no ryokō torishimari ni kansuru ken" [Matters Concerning Arrests of Korean Vacation Travelers]. Tokyo, April 1919.

Chōsen Sōtokufu Keimukyoku Tokyo Shuchōin. "Chōsen Keisatsu Gaiyō" [Outline of Police in Korea]. Tokyo, 1925.

———. "Zaikyō Chōsenjin Gaiyō." Tokyo, May 1924.

Chūō Shokugyō Shōkai Jimukyoku. "Tokyo-fuka zairyu chōsenjin rōdōsha ni kansuru chōsa" [Survey of Korean Workers under the Tokyo Government]. Tokyo, 1924.

————. "Hiyatoi Rōdōsha Gaikyō" [Overview of Day Workers]. Tokyo, May 1932.

Civil Code of Japan, The. Translated by W. J. Sebald. Kobe: J. L. Thompson and Co, Ltd., 1934.

Hogo-ka. "Naichi zaiju senjin hogo wo mokuteki to suru shakai jigyo dantai-cho" [Survey of Social Welfare Programs Whose Purpose Is the Welfare of Koreans Residing in Japan]. May 1928. Ito Monjo collection. Shakai Kagaku Kenkyujo archive 145, Tokyo University.

Naimushō Keihōkyoku. "Chōsenjin rōdōsha no boshū ni kansuru ken" [Regarding the Recruitment of Korean Workers]. Tokyo, December 12, 1918.

————. "Ordinance 660, Chōsen dokuritsu ni kanshi gaikoku senpaku ni taishi chūihō no ken" [Ordinance 660, Warnings Regarding Incidents Related to Korean Independence and Involving Foreign Vessels]. Tokyo, April 1919.

————. "Chōsenjin no shisatsu torishimari ni kansuru ken" [Matters Involving the Surveillance and Arrest of Koreans]. Tokyo, November 17, 1920.

————. "Chōsenjin Kinjō Gaiyō" [Summary of Recent Koreans]. Tokyo, January 1922.

————. "Kokugai zaiju chōsenjin jokyo" [Conditions of Koreans outside Japan]. Tokyo, May 5, 1922.

————. "Naichi zairyū chōsenjin no saikin ni okeru ippan jōkyō" [Recent and General Conditions of Koreans in Japan]. Tokyo, December 1922.

————. "Ordinance 3, Chōsenjin rōdōsha boshū ni kansuru ken" [Regarding the Recruitment of Korean Workers]. Tokyo, May 14, 1923.

————. Shakai Undō no Jōkyō [Conditions of Social Movements]. Tokyo, 1928–41.

Naimushō Keihōkyoku Hōanka. "Chōsenjin Gaikyo Daisan" [Third Summary of Koreans]. Tokyo, June 1920.

————. "Taisho 14 nen chu ni okeru chōsenjin no jōkyō" [Conditions of Koreans in the Fourteenth Year of Taishō]. Tokyo, December 1925.

————. Chōsenjin Gaikyō (Dai ni) [Summary of Koreans (Part Two)]. Tokyo, May 1918.

Naimushō Shakai-bu. Rodo Jihō [Bulletin of Labor]. Tokyo.

Naimushō Shakaikyoku (Dai-Ichibu). "Chōsenjin rōdōsha ni kansuru jōkyō." Tokyo, July 1924.

Naimushō Shakaikyoku Shakai-bu. "Hisoka: Shitsugyo Jokyo Suitei Geppo-chu chosenjin ni kansuru chosa" [Classified: Mid-month Estimations of Conditions of the Unemployed in Regards to Koreans]. Tokyo, September 1929.

————. "Shitsugyō Jōkyō Suitei Geppō Gaiyō" [Monthly Outline of Estimated Conditions of the Unemployed]. Tokyo, September 1929.

————. "Shōwa 3 nendō shitsugyo kyūsai jigyō gaiyo" [Overview of Unemployment Relief in 1928]. Tokyo, October 1929.

————. "Shitsugyō Jōkyō Suitei Geppō Gaiyō Ji-Shōwa 4-nendō 9-gatsu tatsu Shōwa 8-nendō 8-gatsu" [Monthly Outline of Estimated Unemployed from September 1929 to August 1932]. Tokyo, 1933.

Naimushō Shakaikyoku Shokugyō-ka. "Showa 3-nendo Shitsugyo Kyusai Jigyo Gaiyo" [Outline of Unemployment Relief in 1928]. Tokyo, October 1929.

Shakai-kyoku. "Hisoka: shitsugyō ni kansuru chōsa" [Classified: Surveys Regarding Unemployment]. Tokyo: Kyōchōkai, 1929.

Shihōsho. Shihō no kenkyū. 58, 254.

Shihōsho Chōsa-ka. "Shihōsho Kenkyū Dai-17" [Justice Ministry Research no. 17]. Tokyo, March 1933.

Shihōshō Keijikyoku. "Naichi ni okeru chōsenjin to sono hanzai ni oite" [Koreans in Japan and Their Crimes]. Shihō Kenkyū [Thought Research], no. 5 (December 1927).

———. "Naichi ni okeru chōsenjin to sono hanzai ni tsuite" [On the Crimes of Koreans in Japan]. Tokyo, 1927.

———. "Chōsenjin Mondai" [The Korean Problem]. 1928. Reprinted in Pak, ZCKSS 1, 245–53.

CITY AND PREFECTURE GOVERNMENT SOURCES

Aichi-ken. Senjin Mondai [The Korean Problem]. Nagoya, 1925.

Hyōgō-ken gakumubu shakai-ka, "Chōsenjin no seikatsu jōtai" [Conditions of Korean Living]. Kobe, 1937.

Keisho namdo Keisatsu-bu. "Naichi dekasagi senjin [sic] rōdōsha jōtai chōsa" [Survey of Migrant Korean Workers to Japan]. January 1928.

Kobe-shi Shakai-ka. "Chōsenjin no seikatsu jotai chosa" [Survey of Lifestyles of Koreans]. Kobe, 1936.

Kobe Shiyakusho. "Zaikō Hantō minzoku no genjō" [Present Conditions of the Korean Ethnos in Kobe]. Kobe, 1927.

Kyongsang Namdo Keisatsu-bu. "Naichi dekasagi senjin rodosha jōtai chōsa" [Survey of the Conditions of Migrant Korean Workers to Japan]. 1928.

Kyoto-shi Kyōiku-bu Shakai-ka. "Kyoto-shi ni okeru hiyatoi rōdōsha ni kansuru chōsa" [Survey Related to Day Workers in Kyoto]. Kyoto, 1931.

Kyoto-shi Shakai-ka. "Shinai zaiju chōsen shusshinsha ni kansuru chōsa" [Survey Related to Native Koreans Residing in Kyoto]. Kyoto, 1937.

Kyoto Shiyakusho Shakai-ka. "Kyoto-shi ni okeru shitsugyōsha seikatsu jōtai chōsa" [Survey on Living Conditions of the Unemployed in the City of Kyoto]. Kyoto: Kyoto Shiyakusho Shakai-ka, March 31, 1933.

Municipal Office of Tokyo, Statistical Bureau. "Annual Statistics of the City of Tokyo." 1927–36.

Nagoya-shi Shakai-bu. "Dai-9-kai roku daitoshi shakai jigyō kyōgikai gijiroku" [Minutes from the Ninth Annual Conference of Social Welfare Organizations in the Six Largest Cities]. Nagoya, May 1935.

Nagoya rōdō shōkaijo. "Dai-ni-kai Nagoya-shi shitsugyō kyūsai jigyō shi gaikyō" [Summary of the Second Meeting of the History of Unemployment Relief Programs in Nagoya City]. Nagoya, 1927.

Nara-ken Keisatsu-bu. *Keisatsu sōshō dai 45. Iru zo! Futei senjin* [Police Investigations no. 45, Watch Out, They're Here! Lawless Koreans]. Nara, April 1940.

Nishi Sugamo Shokugyō Shokaijō. "Nishi Sugamo-cho Shokugyo Shokaijo ni okeru Hiyatoi Rōdō Shōkai Genjō" [Present Conditions of Day Worker Introductions at the Nishi Sugamo Labor Introduction Office]. Tokyo, 1931.

Osaka-fu. *Osaka-fu Tōkeisho* [Statistics from the Osaka Metropolitan Government]. Osaka, 1925–38.

Osaka-fu Gakumu-bu Shakai-ka. "Zaisaka Chōsenjin Seikatsu jotai" [Lifestyle Conditions of Koreans in Osaka]. Osaka, 1933.

Osaka-fu Naisen Yūwa Jigyō Chōsakai. "Zaiju chōsenjin mondai to sono taisaku" [The Korean Problem in Japan and Its Policies]. Osaka, 1936.

Osaka-fu Tokubetsu Kōtō-ka. "Chōsenjin ni kansuru tōkeiyō, Showa 8 nendō" [Statistics Related to Koreans]. Osaka, 1933.

Osaka-shi Shakai-bu. *Honshi ni okeru furyō jūtakuchiku chōsa* [Survey of Poor Housing Conditions in Osaka]. Osaka, 1939.

Osaka-shi Shakai-bu Chōsa-ka. "Kōjo Rōdō Kōyo Kankei" [Matters Related to Regular Factory Labor]. Osaka, 1923.

———. "Chōsenjin Rōdōsha Mondai" [The Problem of Korean Workers]. Osaka, 1924.

———. "Hiyatoi Rōdōsha Mondai" [The Problem of Day Workers]. Osaka, March 1924.

———. "Dai-ikkai rōdō tōkei jicchi chōsa gaiyō" [Number One Labor Statistics Survey Outline]. Osaka, October 1924.

———. "Garasu Seizō Jigyōsha no rōdō to seikatsu" [Glass Manufacturing Workers and Their Lifestyles]. Osaka, 1925.

———. "Rōdō chōsa hōkoku dai 35." Osaka, 1925.

———. "Barakku iju chōsenjin no rōdō to seikatsu" [Work and Lifestyle of Koreans Residing in Barracks]. Osaka, January 1927.

———. "Rōdō Techō ni tsuite" [On Work Books]. Osaka, May 1930.

———. "Honshi ni okeru chōsen jūtaku mondai" [Problems of Korean Housing in Osaka]. Osaka, July 1930.

———. *Hōkoku Dai 240* [Report no. 240]. Osaka. (Publication date unavailable).

———. "Hon-shi ni okeru chōsenjin kōjō rōdōsha" [Korean Factory Workers in Osaka]. Osaka, 1931.

———. "Zaisaka chōsenjin no seikatsu jōtai" [Conditions of Korean Lifestyle in Osaka]. Osaka, 1932.

Osaka-shi Shakai-bu Rōdō-ka. "Naisen Rōdō Yōgoshu" [Collection of Terms and Words for Korean Workers in Japan]. Osaka, May 1933.

———. "Osaka-shi Shitsugyōsha Seikatsu Jōtai Chōsa" [Survey of Living Conditions of the Unemployed in Osaka]. Osaka, 1933.

Tokyo Chihō Shokugyō Shōkai Jimukyoku. "Doboku, Bōseki, Kōfu toshiteno senjinrōdōsha" [Korean Construction Workers, Cotton Workers, and Coal Miners]. Tokyo, January 1925.

————. "Yamanashi-ken kokudō 8-gōsen kaishu kōji rōdō idō keika tenmatsu, Rōdō idō dai-3 shū" [The Yamanashi Prefecture National Highway Number 8 Construction's Labor Migration Process, the Third Week of Labor Migration]. Tokyo, July 1933.

Tokyo-fu. "Tokyo-fu Tōkeisho" [Statistics from Tokyo Metropolitan Government]. Tokyo, 1924–36.

————. Zainichi chōsenjin rōdōsha no genjō [Conditions of Korean Workers in Japan]. Tokyo, 1929.

Tokyo-fu Shakai-ka. "Zaikyō chōsenjin rōdōsha no genjō" [Current Conditions of Korean Workers in Tokyo]. Tokyo, 1929, 1936.

Tokyo-shi. Tokyo-shi tōkeisho [Statistics from the City of Tokyo]. Tokyo, 1924–33.

————. Tokyo-shi shitsugyōsha seikatsu jōtai chōsa [Survey of Lifestyle Conditions of Unemployed Workers in Tokyo]. Tokyo, 1933.

Tokyo-shi Shakaikyoku. Tokyo-shi Shakaikyoku Nenpō, 1928 Nendō [1928 Annual of the Tokyo City Social Office], 1929.

————. Tokyo-shi Shakaikyoku Nenpō, 1929 nendō [1929 Annual of the Tokyo City Social Office]. Tokyo, 1930.

————. "Jiyū rōdōsha ni kansuru chōsa" [Survey Regarding Free Workers]. Tokyo, 1923.

Tokyo Shisetsu Shakai Jigyo Renmei. "Dai-Ikkai Shakai Jigyō Hōkōkusho" [Review of the First Social Welfare Program Day]. Tokyo, November 1933.

Tokyo Shiyakusho. "Jiyu Rōdō ni kansuru chōsa" [Survey of Free Workers]. Tokyo, 1923.

————. "Hiyatoi rōdōsha no shippei shōgai ni kansuru chōsa" [Survey of Illnesses and Injuries of Day Workers]. Tokyo, July 1927.

————. Tokyo Shinsai-roku [Record of the Tokyo Earthquake]. Tokyo, 1926.

————. "Showa 5–6 ryōnendo Hiyatoi rōdōsha shitsugyō kyūsai jigyō gaisetsu" [Overview of Day Worker Unemployment Relief Programs in 1930 and 1931]. Tokyo, March 1932.

UNION-RELATED SOURCES

Chika Tabi [Underground Journey]. Tokyo: Fukagawa Shōkaijo Chika Tabi Shimbunsha Hakkō, 1931.

Higashi Osaka Shakkajin Kumiai Honbu [East Osaka Tenants Union Headquarters]. Flier. Osaka, 1929.

Mutō, Unjuro. Yanushi to ikani tatakau beki ka? [How Must We Fight Landlords?]. Tokyo: Shakkajinsha, 1931.

Nihon Heimin Bijutsuka Dōmei Tokyo-shibu. Mokchū Unbok. Tokyo, May 1, 1932.

Nihon rōdō undō shiryō i'inkai [The Committee on Materials Concerning Japan's Labor Movements]. Nihon rōdō undō shiryō, Dai-10Kan, Tōkei-Ren [Documents of Japanese Labor Movements, Volume 10, Statistics Edition]. Tokyo: Tokyo University Press, 1960.

Osaka shakai undō kyōkai [The Association for Social Movements in Osaka]. *Osaka Shakai Rōdō Undōshi, Dai-2* [A History of Social Movements in Osaka]. Tokyo: Osaka Shakai Undō Kyōkai, 1989.

Osaka Shakkanin Dōmei. *Shakkanin* 1 (January 1928): 1–40.

———. *Shakkanin* 5 (May 1928): 3–38.

Rōdō-Nōmintō Osaka-fu shi-bu rengōkai. February 5, 1928. Reprinted in *Nihon Shakai Undō Shiryō (Genshiryō-hen): Musanseitō Shiryō—Rōdō-Nōmintō* [Documents on Japan's Social Movements (Primary Materials Edition): Materials from Proletarian Parties—Rōdō-Nōmintō]. Vol. 5. Tokyo: Hōsei Daigaku Ohara Shakai Mondai Kenkyūjo, 1987, 31–32.

Shakai Undō Tsūshin [Bulletin of Social Movements]. Tokyo, 1928–37.

Zai-Nihon Chōsen Rōdō Sōdōmei (Rōsō) [Federation of Korean Labor in Japan]. "Zai-Nihon Chōsen Rōdō Sōdōmei Dai 3 Kai Taikai: Senden, Kōryō, Kisoku," [The Third Convention for the Federation of Korean Labor in Japan: Propaganda, Party Lines, Regulations]. Tokyo, April 20, 1927. Reprinted in *Zainichi Chōsen Kenkyū*, vol. 1. Tokyo, December 1977, 95–102.

Zenkyō Nihon Kagaku Rōdō Kumiai Tokyo Shibu [Zenkyō Tokyo Branch of Japan's Chemical Labor]. "Pak Ch'um-gum no Rikkoho to tatakae" [The Struggle against Pak Ch'um-gum's Election to the National Diet]. Tokyo, 1932. Ohara Institute for Social Research, pre-war archives, T1–3.

OTHER

Beveridge, William H. *Unemployment: A Problem of Industry.* London: Longmans, Green and Co., 1930.

Cahalane, Cornelius F. *Police Practice and Procedure.* New York: E. P. Dutton, 1914.

Chadwick, Edwin. "Preventive Police." *London Review,* 1829.

———. *An article on the principles and progress of the Poor law amendment act; and also on the nature of the central control and improved local administration introduced by that statute.* London: C. Knight, 1837.

Doboku Kōgyō Kyōkai. *Nihon doboku kensetsugyōshi* [A History of Japan's Construction Industry]. Tokyo: Doboku Kōgyō Kyōkai, 1971.

Hokkaido Kaitaku Kinenkan. "Hokkaido ni okeru Tankō no Hatten to Rōdōsha" [Workers and the Development of Coal in Hokkaido]. Sapporo: The Historical Museum of Hokkaido, 1978.

Hokkaido Tankō Kisen Kabsuhikigaisha. "Hokutan 50 nenshi kohon" [Publications of Fifty Years at Hokutan]. Tokyo, 1938.

International Labor Office. *Industrial Labour in Japan.* Geneva: International Labour Office, 1933.

Maruyama, Tsurukichi. "Keisatsu to Shakai Jigyō" [The Police and Social Welfare Programs]. In *Jikyoku Kōenshū.* Part 2. Tokyo: Keisatsu Kōshūjo Gakuyūkai, 1919.

———. "Chōsen no chian no genjō oyobi shōrai" [Law and Order in Korea, Its Present Conditions and Future]. Lecture. Seoul: Chōsen Sōtokufu, April 20, 1922.

———. "Keisatsu to Shakai Kyūsai" [The Police and Social Relief Programs]. In *Zaisen yonen yūyōhan*. Tokyo: Matsuyamabō, 1924.

———. "Keimu Danpen [Ni]" [Notes on Policing, Part 2]. In *Zaisen yonen yūyōhan*. Tokyo: Matsuyamabō, 1924.

———. *Yasashii Keisatsuron* [Theory of the Magnanimous Police]. Tokyo: Shinseisha, 1935.

———. "Kindai shakai jigyō no sūsei" [Trends in Modern Social Welfare Programs]. In *Zaisen yonen yūyōhan*. Tokyo: Matsuyamabō, 1924.

———. *Nanajūnen tokoro dokoro* [Reflections on Seventy Years]. Tokyo: Nanjunen Tokoro Dokoro, 1955.

Matsui, Shigeru. *Keisatsu Dokuhon* [Police Reader]. Tokyo: Nihon Hyōronsha, 1933.

———. *Kyoto ni okeru shitsugyōsha seikatsu jōtai chōsa* [Lifestyle Conditions of the Unemployed in Kyoto]. Tokyo, 1933.

Ozawa, Yusaku. *Kindai Minshū no Kiroku* [Records of Modern Masses]. Vol. 10. Tokyo: Shinjinbutsu Oraisha, 1979.

Pak, Ch'um-gum. *Warera Kokka Shin-Nippon: Chōsen dōhō no fuan to kinkyu o nobete chōya shoken ni sō* [Our State, Nuovo Japan: A Public Complaint to the Ladies and Gentlemen of the Government Describing the Instability and Distress of Our Korean Compatriots]. Tokyo: Pak Ch'um-gum Jimusho, November 1930.

———. "Chōsen umare no Pak Ch'um-gum yori" [From Korean-born Pak Ch'um gum], *Koki Kinenshi: Maruyama Sensei koki shukugakai-kan* [Seventieth Anniversary: Maruyama Sensei Seventieth-Anniversary Celebration]. Tokyo, 1955.

Pak, Kyung-shik. *Zainichi Chōsenjin Kankei Shiryō Shūsei* [*ZCKSS*] [Collection of Primary Materials Related to Koreans in Japan]. Vols. 1–5. Tokyo: Sanichi Shobo, 1975.

———. *Zainichi Chōsenjin Undō-shi 8–15 kaihōzen* [A History of Movements by Resident Koreans in Japan: Pre-liberation]. Tokyo: San-Ichi Shobō, 1979.

———. "Nihon Shokuminchika no zainichi chōsenjin no jōkyō" [Conditions of Koreans in Japan under Japanese Colonialism]. *Chōsen Mondai Shiryō Sosho* [Series of Primary Materials on the Korean Problem]. Vol. 12. Tokyo: Ajia Mondai Kenkyujo, 1990.

Seki, Hajime. *Jūtaku Mondai to Toshi Keikaku* [The Housing Problem and Urban Planning]. Kyoto: Fubunto Shobo, 1923.

Sōaikai Osaka Honbu Bunka-bu. *Chōsen* [Korea]. Osaka: Sōaikai Osaka Honbu Bunka-bu, May 1925.

Sōaikai Sōhonbu. "Jigyō shisetsu no yōran" [Summary of Project Facilities]. Tokyo: Sōaikai Sōhonbu, January 1926.

Tanii, Shinzō. *Fudōsan kyōsei shikkō no shōmondai* [Problems Relating to Official Orders of Real Estate]. Tokyo: Ganmatsuto Shoten, 1936.

Toyohara, Matao. *Kokuei no Shokugyō Shōkai Jigyō* [Nationally Managed Labor Introduction Programs]. Tokyo: Toyohara Matao, 1941.

Yoshisaka, Shunzo. "Labour Recruiting in Japan and its Control." *International Labour Review* 4 (October 1925): 484–99.

Zaidan Hōjin Sōaikai-kan. "Zaidan Hōjin Sōaikaikan Jigyō Yōran" [Overview of the Programs of the Sōaikai Foundation]. Tokyo: Zaidan Hōjin Sōaikai-kan, April 1929.

Secondary Sources

Abegglen, James. *The Japanese Factory: Aspects of its Social Organization*. Glencoe: The Free Press, 1958.

Agamben, Giorgio. *The Coming Community*. Translated by Michael Hardt. Minneapolis: University of Minnesota Press, 1993.

Althusser, Louis. *For Marx*. London: Verso Press, 1969.

———. *Filosofía y marxismo: Entrievista por Fernanda Navarro*. Mexico City: Siglo XXI Editores, 1988.

———. *Tetsugaku ni tsuite* [On Philosophy]. Translated by Hitoshi Imamura. Tokyo: Chikuma Shobo, 1995.

———. *Machiavelli and Us*. Translated by Gregory Elliot. London: Verso, 1999.

———. *Philosophy of the Encounter: Later Writings, 1978–87*. London: Verso, 2006.

Amakyōtō, San'ya Gentōi-henshūiinkaihen. *Yararetara Yarikaese: Jitsuroku Amagasaki, San'ya kaihō tōsō* [Yararetara Yarikaese: True Accounts of Liberation Struggles of Amagasaki and San'ya]. Tokyo: Tabata Shoin, 1974.

Asada, Kyōji. *Nihon teikokushigu to kyū shokuminchi jinushisei* [Japanese Imperialism and Colonial Landlordism]. Tokyo: Ochanomizu Shobo, 1968.

———. *Kyūshokuminchi Nihonjin Daitochi Shoyūron* [Theory of Large-scale Japanese Land Possession in the Original Colonies]. Tokyo: Nogyo Sogo Kenkyujo, 1968.

Balibar, Etienne. *Masses, Classes, Ideas: Studies on Politics and Philosophy before and after Marx*. New York: Routledge, 1994.

Balibar, Etienne, and Immanuel Wallerstein. *Race, Class, Nation: Ambiguous Identities*. London: Verso, 1991.

Barker, Kathleen, and Kathleen Christensen, eds. *Contingent Work: American Employment Relations in Transition*. Ithaca, N.Y.: Cornell University Press, 1998.

Bennett, John W., and Iwao Ishino. *Paternalism in the Japanese Economy: Anthropological Studies of Oyabun-Kobun Patterns*. Minneapolis: University of Minnesota Press, 1963.

Benjamin, Walter. *Illuminations: Essays and Reflections*. New York: Schocken Books, 1968.

———. *Reflections: Essays, Aphorisms, Autobiographical Writings*. Edited by Peter Demetz. New York: Harcourt Brace Janovich, 1978.

Bensaïd, Daniel. *Marx for Our Times: Adventures and Misadventures of a Critique*. Translated by Gregory Elliot. London: Verso, 2002.

Berberoglu, Berch, ed. *Labor and Capital in the Age of Globalization: The Labor Process and the Changing Nature of Work in the Global Economy*. Lanham: Rowman and Littlefield Publishers, 2002.

Bergström, Ola, and Donald Storrie, eds. *Contingent Employment in Europe and the United States*. Cheltenham: Edward Algar, 2003.

Botsman, Daniel. *Punishment and Power in the Making of Modern Japan*. Princeton, N.J.: Princeton University Press, 2005.

Brosnan, Peter, David Rea, and Moira Wilson. "Labor Market Segmentation and the State: the New Zealand Experience." *Cambridge Journal of Economics* 19 (1995): 667–96.

Brown, Wendy. *States of Injury: Power and Freedom in Late Modernity*. Princeton, N.J.: Princeton University Press, 1995.

Butler, Judith, Ernesto Laclau, and Slavoj Žižek. *Contingency, Hegemony, Universality: Contemporary Dialogues on the Left*. London: Verso, 2000.

Butler, Judith, and Joan W. Scott, eds. *Feminists Theorize the Political*. London: Routledge, 1992.

Callari, Antonio, and D. F. Ruccio. *Postmodern Materialism and the Future of Marxist Theory*. Hanover: Wesleyan University Press, 1996.

Chang, Grace. *Disposable Domestics: Immigrant Women Workers in the Global Economy*. Cambridge: South End Press, 2000.

Ching, Leo. *Becoming Japanese: Colonial Taiwan and the Politics of Identity Formation*. Berkeley: University of California Press, 2001.

Clarke, Simon. *Marx's Theory of Crisis*. New York: St. Martin's Press, 1994.

Comaroof, Jean, and John Comaroff. "Millenial Capitalism: First Thoughts on a Second Coming." *Public Culture* 12, no. 2 (2000): 291–343.

Cumings, Bruce. *Korea's Place in the Sun: A Modern History*. New York: W. N. Norton and Company, 1997.

Dean, Mitchell. "A Genealogy of the Government of Poverty." *Economy and Society* 21, no. 3 (August 1992): 215–51.

DeBrunhoff, Suzanne. *The State, Capital and Economic Policy*. Translated by Mike Sonenscher. London: Pluto Press, 1978.

Deleuze, Gilles, and Claire Parnet. *Dialogues*. Translated by Hugh Tomlison and Barbara Habberjam. New York: Columbia University Press, 1987.

Deleuze, Gilles, and Felix Guattari. *A Thousand Plateaus: Capitalism and Schizophrenia*. Translated by Brian Massumi. Minneapolis: University of Minnesota Press, 1987.

———. *Anti-Oedipus: Capitalism and Schizophrenia*. Translated by Robert Hurley et al. Minneapolis: University of Minnesota Press, 1992.

Dirlik, Arif. *The Origins of Chinese Communism*. New York: Oxford University Press, 1989.

Engels, Friedrich. *The Condition of the Working Class in England*. Oxford: Oxford University Press, 1993.

Faison, Elyssa. "Producing Female Textile Workers in Imperial Japan." Ph.D. diss., University of California, Los Angeles, 2001.

Foucault, Michel. *Discipline and Punish: The Birth of the Prison*. New York: Vintage, 1979.

———. *"Society Must Be Defended": Lectures at the College de France, 1975–76*. Translated by David Macey. New York: Picador Press, 2003.

Fowler, Edward. *San'ya Blues: Laboring Life in Contemporary Tokyo.* Ithaca: Cornell University Press, 1996.

Fujimoto, Takeshi. "Kumigashira oyakata seido no honshitsu: Hikindaiteki koyō keitai no ichi bunseki" [The Essence of the Kumigashire–Oyakata System: An Analysis of Anti-modern Employment Forms]. *Shakaigaku Hyōron* 2, no. 4 (1952): 155–73.

Garon, Sheldon. *The State and Labor in Modern Japan.* Berkeley: University of California Press, 1987.

———. *Molding Japanese Minds: The State in Everyday Life.* Princeton, N.J.: Princeton University Press, 1997.

Garraty, John A. *Unemployment in History: Economic Thought and Public Policy.* New York: Harper Colophon Books, 1978.

Gibson-Graham, J. K., Stephen Resnick, and Richard Wolff. *Re/presenting Class: Essays in Postmodern Marxism.* Durham, N.C.: Duke University Press, 2001.

Gibson-Graham, J. K. *The End of Capitalism [As We Knew It]: A Feminist Critique of Political Economy.* Oxford: Blackwell, 1996.

Gill, Tom. *Men of Uncertainty.* Albany, N.Y.: SUNY Press, 2001.

Gordon, Andrew. *The Evolution of Labor Relations in Japan: Heavy Industry, 1853–1955.* Cambridge, Mass.: Harvard University Press, 1985.

Gordon, David M., R. Edwards, and M. Reich. *Segmented Work, Divided Workers: The Historical Transformation of Labor in the United States.* Cambridge: Cambridge University Press, 1982.

Gragert, Edwin H. *Landownership under Colonial Rule: Korea's Japanese Experience, 1900–1935.* Honolulu: University of Hawaii Press, 1994.

Ha, Myung-sen. *Kanjin Nihon Imin Shakai Keizaishi: Senzenhen* [Social Economic History of Korean Immigrants in Japan: Prewar Edition]. Tokyo: Meiseki Shoten, 1997.

Hanes, Geoffrey. *The City as Subject: Seki Hajime and the Reinvention of Modern Osaka.* Berkeley: University of California Press, 2002.

Harootunian, Harry. *History's Disquiet: Modernity, Cultural Practice and the Question of Everyday Life.* New York: Columbia University Press, 2000.

———. *Overcome by Modernity: History, Culture and Community in Interwar Japan.* Princeton, N.J.: Princeton University Press, 2000.

———. *The Empire's New Clothes: Paradigm Lost, and Regained.* Chicago: Prickly Press, 2006.

Hastings, Sally. *Neighborhood and Nation in Tokyo, 1905–1937.* Pittsburgh, Pa.: University of Pittsburgh Press, 1995.

Haver, William. *The Body of This Death: Historicity and Sociality in the Time of AIDS.* Stanford, Calif.: Stanford University Press, 1996.

Hazama, Hiroshi. *The History of Labour Management in Japan.* Translated by Mari Sako and Eri Sako. New York: St. Martin's Press, 1997.

Higuchi, Yuichi. "Zainichi Chōsenjin ni taisuru jūtaku sabetsu" [Housing Discrimination against Koreans in Japan]. *Zainichi Chōsenjinshi Kenkyū* 2 (June 1978): 70–79.

————. Kyōwakai: Senzenka chōsenjin tōsei soshiki no kenkyū [Kyōwakai: Studies of the Korean Control Organization of the Prewar Period]. Tokyo: Shakai Hyoronsha, 1986.

Hilton, George Woodman. "The British Truck-System in the Nineteenth Century." Journal of Political Economy 65, no. 3 (June 1957): 237–56.

————. The Truck System: Including a History of the British Truck Acts, 1465–1960. Cambridge: W. Heffner and Sons, 1960.

Hirabayashi, Hisae. "Sanshin Tetsudo Sōgi ni tsuite" [On the Sanshin Railway Strike]. Zainichi Chōsenjinshi Kenkyū 1 (December 1977): 9–24.

Humphries, Jane, and Jill Rubery. "The reconstitution of the supply side of the labour market: the relative autonomy of social reproduction." Cambridge Journal of Economics 8 (1984): 331–46.

Hunter, Janet. Women and the Labour Market in Japan's Industrializing Economy: The Textile Industry Before the Pacific War. London: Routledge Curzon, 2003.

Imagawa, Isao. Gendai Kiminkō. Tokyo: Tabata Shoten, 1987.

Iwamura, Toshio. Zainichi chōsenjin to nihon rōdōsha kaikyū [Koreans in Japan and Japan's Working Class]. Tokyo: Azakura Shobo, 1982.

Ishida, Yorifusa. Nihon Kindai Toshi Keikakushi Kenkyū [Research on Modern Japanese Urban Planning]. Tokyo: Kashiwa Shōbo, 1987.

Japan Statistical Association. Historical Statistics of Japan. Vol. 2. Tokyo: Nihon Tōkei kyōkai, 1987.

Kadoki, Shoichi. "Zenkyō—shitsugyōsha dōmeika chōsenjin undō" [Zenkyō—Social Movements of Koreans in the Unemployed Federation]. Zainichi Chōsenjinshi Kenkyū 9 (December 1981).

Kan, Don-chin. Nihon no chōsen shihai seisaku-shi no kenkyū: 1920 nendai wo chūshin toshite [Policy Studies of Japan's Domination over Korea: The 1920s]. Tokyo: Tokyo University Press, 1979.

Kan, Je-on. Zainichi' kara no shiza [Views from a Resident Korean]. Tokyo: Shinkansha, 1996.

Kang, T. S. Gendai-shi Shiryō [6], Kanto Daishinsai to Chōsenjin [Contemporary Documents (6), Koreans and the Great Kanto Earthquake]. Tokyo: Misuzu Shobo, 1963.

Karatani, Kojin. Architecture as Metaphor: Language, Number, Money. Translated by Sabu Kohso. Cambridge, Mass.: MIT Press, 1995.

Kase, Kazutoshi. "Shigsugyōsha kyūsai kokyō doboku jigyō ni okeru shūrōsha senbetsu hōshiki to chōsenjin tōrokusha" [Workers Selection and Registered Koreans in the Unemployment Relief Public Works Program]. In Senkanki Nihon no Taigai Keizai Kankei [On Interwar Japan's Overseas Economy], edited by Kaichiro Oishi. Tokyo: Nihon Keizai Hyôronsha, 1992.

————. Senzen Nihon no shitsugyō taisaku—kyusaigata kokyou doboku jigyo no rekishitekibunseki [Japan's Prewar Unemployment Policy: A Historical Analysis of Relief-type Public Works Programs]. Tokyo: Nihon Keizai Hyoronsha, 1998.

————. "Unemployment Policy in Prewar Japan: How Progressive Was Japanese Social Policy?" *Social Science Japan Journal* 7, no. 2 (2004): 199–221.

Kawai, Kazuō. *Chōsen ni okeru sanmai zoshoku keikaku* [The Program to Increase Rice Production in Korea] Tokyo: Miraisha, 1986.

Kawashima, Ken C. "Capital's Dice-box Shaking: The Contingent Commodifications of Labor Power." *Rethinking Marxism* 17, no. 4 (October 2005): 609–26.

————. "Contingent Commodifications: Micropolitics of Recession and the Colonial Conditions of Korean Labor Power in Japan between the Two World Wars," Ph.D. diss., New York University, 2003.

Kawashima, Takagi. *Doken Ukeyo Keiyakuron* [Theory of Contracts for Construction Subcontractors]. Tokyo: Nihon Hyōronsha, 1950.

Kim, Cham-jon, and Pan Son-hi. *Kaze no Dōki: Zainichi Chōsenjin Jokō no Seikatsu to Rekishii* [Female Korean Factory Workers in Japan: Their History and Everyday Life]. Tokyo: Tabata Press, 1977.

Kim, Jin-toku. "Zainihon Chōsen Rōdō Sōdōmei ni tsuite no ichi kōsai." Translated from Korean to Japanese by Tonomura Masaru. *Zainichi Chōsenjinshi Kenkyū* 26 (September 1996): 74–98.

Kim, Kō. "Zenkyō Doken Yamanashi Shibu to Chōsenjin Rōdōsha (I): Higashi hachi dai jiyū rōdō kumiai-Zenkyō doken Yamanashi shibu keisei" [Zenkyō Construction Yamanashi Branch and Korean Workers: The Formation of the Higashi Hachidai Free Workers Union of Zenkyō's Yamanashi Branch Construction Union]. *Zainichi Chōsenjinshi Kenkyū* 16 (October 1986): 59–77.

————. "Yamanashi ni okeru zainichi chōsenjin no keisei to jōkyō—1920 nendai" [The formation and conditions of resident Koreans in Yamanashi in the 1920s]. *Zainichi Chōsenjinshi Kenkyū* 11 (March 1983): 1–22.

Kim, Santei. *Ame no Doboku: Zainichi chōsenjin doboku no seikatsushi* [The Rain of Construction Workers: The History of Korean Construction Workers and Their Lives in Japan]. Tokyo: Tabata Shoten, 1979.

Kim, Te-yop. *Konichi Chōsenjin no Shogen* [Testimonies of Koreans Who Resisted Japan]. Tokyo: Funi Shuppan, 1984.

Koh, Joon-sok. *Ekkyō: Chōsenjin watashi no kiroku* [Border Crossings: Accounts as a Korean] Tokyo: Shakaihyōronsha, 1977.

Laclau, Ernesto, and Chantal Mouffe. *Hegemony and Socialist Strategy: Towards a Radical Democratic Politics*. London: Verso, 1985.

Laplanche, Jean, and J. B. Pontalis. *The Language of Psychoanalysis*. Translated by Donald Nicholson-Smith. New York: Norton Publishers, 1973.

Large, Stephen. *Organized Workers and Socialist Politics in Interwar Japan*. Cambridge: Cambridge University Press, 1981.

Lee, Chulwoo. "Modernity, Legality and Power." *Colonial Modernity in Korea*. Edited by Gi-wook Shin and Michael Robinson. Cambridge, Mass.: Harvard University Press, 1999.

Lewis, Michael Lawrence. *Rioters and Citizens: Mass Protest in Imperial Japan*. Berkeley: University of California Press, 1990.

Lowe, Lisa. *Immigrant Acts: On Asian American Cultural Politics*. Durham, N.C.: Duke University Press, 1996.

Marx, Karl. *Theories of Surplus Value*. 3 vols. Moscow: Progress Publishers, 1971.

———. *Capital*. Vol. 1. Translated by Ben Fowkes. New York: Penguin Books, 1990.

———. *The 18th Brumaire of Louis Bonaparte*. New York: International Publishers, 1990.

———. *Grundrisse*. Translated by Martin Nicolaus. New York: Penguin Books, 1993.

Massumi, Brian, et al. *The Politics of Everyday Fear*. Minneapolis: University of Minnesota, 1993.

Matsuda, Toshihiko. "Maruyama Tsurukichi no chōsen dokuritsu undō ninshiki: 'Bunka Seiji' no shokuminchi keisatsu kanryō" [Maruyama Tsurukichi's Recognition of Korea's Independence Movement: Colonial Police Bureaucracy of 'Cultural Rule']. *Chōsen Minzoku Undō-shi Kenkyū* [Historical Studies of Korean Ethnic Movements] 8 (April 1992).

———. "Pak Ch'um-gum ron: sono senkyō undō to gikai katsudō wo chūshin toshite" [On Pak Ch'um-gum: Focusing on His Election Campaign and Diet Activities]. *Zainichi Chōsenjinshi Kenkyū* 18 (October 1988): 13–49.

Matsumoto, Takenori. *Shokuminchi Kenryoku to Chōsen Nōmin* [Colonial Power and Korean Peasants]. Tokyo: Shakai Hyoronsha, 1998.

Matsumura, Takaō. "Nihon teikokushugika ni okeru shokuminchi rōdōsha: zainichi chōsenjin, chūgokujin rōdōsha wo chūshin ni shite" [On Colonial Workers under Japanese Imperialism: On Chinese Workers and Korean Resident Workers in Japan]. *Keizaigaku nenpō* 10 (1966).

Matsunaga, Yoichi. "Kantō jiyū rōdōsha kumiai to zainichi chōsenjin rōdōsha" [The Kanto Free Workers Union and Korean Workers in Japan]. *Zainichi Chōsenjinshi Kenkyū* 1 (December 1977).

Meillassoux, Claude. *Maidens, Meal and Money: Capitalism and the Domestic Economy*. Cambridge: Cambridge University Press, 1991.

Mitchell, Richard. *Thought Control in Prewar Japan*. Ithaca, N.Y.: Cornell University Press, 1983.

Mizuno, Naoki. "Chōsen Sōtokufu no 'Naichi' Tokō Kanri Seisaku: 1910 Nendai no rōdōsha boshū torishimari" [The Policy of Sōtokufu 'Naichi' Migration Control of the Sotokufu: Labor Recruitment Policing in the 1910s]. *Zainichi Chōsenjinshi Kenkyū* 22 (September 1992).

Morris, Meaghan, and Brett de Bary. *'Race' Panic and the Memory of Migration*. Traces, Hong Kong: Hong Kong University Press, 2001.

Morse, Robert. *The Peripheral Worker*. New York: Columbia University Press, 1969.

Murakami, Kazumitsu. *Nihon ni okeru Gendai Shihonshugi no Keisei: Senkanki Nihon Shihonshugi no Kōzō* [The Formation of Contemporary Capitalism in Japan: Structures of Capitalism During Interwar Japan]. Tokyo: Sekaishoin, 1999.

Myers, Ramon, and Mark Peattie, eds. *The Japanese Colonial Empire, 1895–1945*. Princeton, N.J.: Princeton University Press, 1983.

Nagahara, Yutaka. "Demarcated Markets of Cultures and Porous Boundaries of the Nation: 1920s–1952." Paper delivered at New York University, April 16, 1999.

———. "Shōhin sekai to shihon no 'kioku'" [The World of Commodities and the 'Memory' of Capital]. *Hihyō Kukan* 22 (1999).

———. " 'Shihon no ronrigaku' no rekishi kijutsu" ['The Logic of Capital' and Its Historical Conjuring Description]. *Hihyō Kūkan* 20 (1999).

———. "Ronri no Ronriteki Rinkai: jissen e no 'ronri' teki tsuigite" [The Logical Limits of Logic: Splicings towards Practice]. In *Shijō keizai no shinwa to sono henkaku*. Tokyo: Hōsei University Press, 2003.

Nakamura, Takafusa, and Odaka Konosuke. *Nihon Keizaishi 6: Niju Kozo* [Japanese Economic History Volume 6: Dual Structure]. Tokyo: Iwanami Press, 1997.

Negri, Antonio. *The Politics of Subversion: A Manifesto for the Twenty-First Century*. Translated by James Newell. Oxford: Polity Press, 1989.

Nishinarita, Yutaka. *Zainichi chōsenjin no 'sekai' to 'teikoku' kokka* [The 'World' of Koreans in Japan and the 'Imperial' State]. Tokyo: Tokyo University Press, 1997.

Nomura, Akemi. "Chōsen Rōdō Dōmei ni tsuite." In *Zainichi Chōsenjinshi Kenkyū* 5 (December 1979): 74–80.

Obinata, Sumio. *Keisatsu no shakaishi* [Social History of the Police]. Tokyo: Iwanami Shinchō, 1993.

Ogino, Tomio, ed. *Tokkō Keisatsu Kankei Shiryō Shūsei*, vol. 12. Tokyo: Funi Shuppansha, 1999.

Oguma, Eiji. "Chōsen umare no nipponjin: Chōsenjin Shūingiin, Pak Ch'um-gum" [Korean Born Japanese: The Korean Parliamentarian, Pak Ch'um-gum]. *Korean Minority Kenkyū* 1 (1998): 31–59.

Ohara, Yokichi. *Higashi Sangawa Toyohashi Chihō Shakai Undō Zenshi* [A prehistory to the social movements in the Higashi Sangawa Toyohashi region]. Toyohashi: publisher unknown, 1966.

Oishi, Kaichiro, et al. *Nihon Teikokushugi Dai-Ichi Taisenki* [Japanese Imperialism During the First World War Period]. Tokyo: Tokyo University Press, 1997.

———. *Senkanki nihon no taigai keizai kankei* [On Interwar Japan's Overseas Economy]. Tokyo: Nihon Keizai Hyronsha, 1992.

Oniwa, Shinsuke. *Hamamatsu Nihon Gakki Sogi no Kenkyū, 1926 4.26–8.8* [Studies of the Hamamatsu Nihon Gakki Strike, April 26–August 8, 1926]. Tokyo: Gogatsusha, 1980.

Oshima, Kiyoshi. *Nihon Kyōkōshi-ron* [Theory of Crisis in Japan]. 2 vols. Tokyo: Tokyo University Press, 1955.

Ouchi, Tsutomu. *Nōgyo Kyōkō* [Agricultural Crisis]. Tokyo: Tokyo University Press, 1955.

———. *Ouchi Tsutomu Keizaigaku Taikei Dai 7-kan Nihon Keizairon-jō* [Ouchi Tsutomu Economic System, vol. 7, part 1. Theory of Japanese Economics]. Tokyo: Tokyo University Press, 2000.

Oyama, Shikitaro. *Kōgyō rōdō to oyakata seidō* [The Oyakata System and Industrial Labor]. Tokyo: Yūhikaku, 1964.

———. "Kumigashira oyakata seido no honshitsu: Hikindaiteki koyō keitai no ichi bunseki" [The Essence of the Kumigashira-Oyakata System: An Analysis of Anti-modern Employment Forms]. *Shakaigaku Hyōron* 2, no. 4 (1952): 155–73.

Pak, Kyung-shik. *Zainichi Chōsenjin Undo-shi: 8–15 kaihōzen* [History of Korean Social Movements in Japan prior to the Liberation of August 15, 1945]. Tokyo: Sanichi Shobo, 1979.

Pang, Kie-chung, Michael D. Shin, Yong-sop Kim, eds. *Landlords, Peasants and Intellectuals in Modern Korea*. Ithaca, N.Y.: Cornell East Asian Series, 2005.

Park, Hyun Ok. *Two Dreams in One Bed: Empire, Social Life, and the Origins of the North Korean Revolution in Manchuria*. Durham, N.C.: Duke University Press, 2005.

Parker, Robert E. "The Global Economy and Changes in the Nature of Contingent Work." In *Labor and Capital in the age of Globalization: The Labor Process and the Changing Nature of Work in the Global Economy*, ed. Berch Berberoglu. Lanham, Md.: Rowman and Littlefield, 2002.

Peck, Jamie. *Workplace: The Social Regulation of Labor Markets*. New York: Guilford Press, 1996.

Peck, Jamie, and Nik Theodore. "Contingent Chicago: Restructuring the Spaces of Temporary Work." *International Journal of Urban and Regional Research* 25, no. 3 (September 2001): 471–96.

Perelman, Michael. *The Invention of Capitalism: Classical Political Economy and the Secret of Primitive Accumulation*. Durham, N.C.: Duke University Press, 2000.

Piven, Frances Fox, and Richard Cloward. *Regulating the Poor: The Functions of Public Welfare*. New York: Vintage, 1971.

Poulantzas, Nicos. *Political Power and Social Classes*. London: Verso Press, 1987.

Rancière, Jacques. *Nights of Labor: The Workers' Dream in Nineteenth-Century France*. Translated by John Drury. Philadelphia, Pa.: Temple University Press, 1989.

———. *Disagreement: Politics and Philosophy*. Translated by Julie Rose. Minneapolis: University of Minnesota Press, 1999.

———. *The Philosopher and His Poor*. Translated by John Drury et al. Edited by Andrew Parker. Durham, N.C.: Duke University Press, 2003.

Read, Jason. *The Micropolitics of Capital: Marx and the Prehistory of the Present*. Albany: State University of New York Press, 2003.

Ringhoffer, Mafred. "Sōaikai—Chōsenjin dōka dantai no ayumi" [Sōaikai: Tracing the Korean Assimilation Organization]. *Zainichi Chōsenjinshi Kenkyū* 9 (December 1981): 45–69.

Russell, Kevin. "An Analysis of Contingent Labor." *Review of Radical Political Economics* 23, no. 1 (1991): 208–25.

Sakai, Naoki. *Translation and Subjectivity*. Minneapolis: University of Minnesota Press, 1997.

Shin, Gi-Wook. *Peasant Protest and Social Change in Colonial Korea.* Seattle: University of Washington Press, 1996.

Smith, Donald. "The 1932 Aso Coal Strike: Korean-Japanese Solidarity and Conflict." *Korean Studies* 20 (1996): 94–122.

Song, Jesook. "Shifting Technologies: Neoliberalization of the Welfare State in South Korea, 1997–2001." Ph.D. diss., University of Illinois, Urbana-Champaign, 2003.

Sorensen, Andre. *The Making of Urban Japan: Cities and Planning from Edo to the Twenty-First Century.* London: Routledge, 2002.

Sprinker, Michael. *Ghostly Demarcations: A Symposium on Jacques Derrida's Specters of Marx.* London: Verso, 1999.

Strange, Susan. *Casino Capitalism.* London: Blackwell Press, 1986.

Sugihara, Kaoru, and Kingo Tamai. *Taisho Osaka Suramu* [Taisho Osaka Slum]. Tokyo: Shinhyoron, 1996.

Suh, Dae-Sook. *Documents of Korean Communism, 1918–1948.* Princeton, N.J.: Princeton University Press, 1970.

Sumiya, Mikio. *Nihon Rōdō Undōshi* [A History of Labor Movements in Japan]. Tokyo: Tokyo University Press, 1969.

———. *Nihon Shihonshugi to Rodo Mondai* [Capitalism in Japan and the Labor Problem]. Tokyo: Tokyo University Press, 1971.

Suzuki, Rokuya. *Shakuchi-shakuyahō no kenkyū* [Studies on the Law of Leased Land and Leased Buildings]. Vols. 2. Tokyo: Minpō Ronbunshū, 1984.

Takanashi, Akira. *Kensestsu sangyō no rōshi kankei* [On Labor-Capital Relations of the Construction Industry]. Tokyo: Toyou Keizaishinpōsha, 1978.

Tamura, Yukiō. "Naimushō Keihōkyoku Chōsa ni yoru chōsenjin jinkō (I)" [Korean Populations According to Surveys by the Ministry of Interior's Police Bureau, Part 1]. *Keizai to Keizaigaku* 46 (February 1981): 51–93.

———. "Naimushō Keihōkyoku Chōsa ni yoru chōsenjin jinko (III)" [Korean Populations According to Surveys by the Ministry of Interior's Police Bureau, Part 3]. *Keizai to Keizaigaku* 48 (January 1982): 23–63.

———. "Naimushō Keihōkyoku Chōsa ni yoru chōsenjin jinkō (V)" [Korean Populations According to Surveys by the Ministry of Interior's Police Bureau, Part 5]. *Keizai to Keizaigaku* 49 (March 1982): 43–94.

Theodore, Nik. "Political Economies of Day Labor: Regulation and Restructuring of Chicago's Contingent Labor Markets." *Urban Studies* 40, no. 9 (August 2003): 1811–29.

Tipton, Elise. *The Japanese Police State: The Tokkō in Interwar Japan.* Sydney: Allen and Unwin, 1990.

Tonomura, Masaru. *Zainichi Chōsenjin shakai no rekishiteki Kenkyū* [Historical Studies on Korean Residents in Japan and Their Society]. Tokyo: Rokuin Shobo, 2004.

Toshimakushi Hensan Iinkai Hensan. *Toshimakushi: Shiryōhen* 4. Tokyo: Toshimakushi-hen, Showa 57, 1983.

Umeda, Toshihide. "Nihon Rōdō Kumiai Zenkoku Kyōgikai to zainichi chōsenjin rōdōsha: Yamanashi-ken Doken rōdōsha sōgi wo tōjite" [Nihon Rōdō Kumiai Zenkoku Kyōgikai and Korean Workers in Japan: Through the Lens of Construction Worker Strikes in the Yamanashi Prefecture]. In Rōdō Undōshi Kenkyū, nos. 55, 56 (September 20, 1974).

Uno, Kōzō. Shihonron Kenkyū [Studies of Das Kapital]. 4 vols. Tokyo: Chikuma Shobo, 1967.

———. Keizai Genron [Fundamental Principles of the Economy]. Vol. 1. Tokyo: Iwanami Shoten, 1973.

———. Kyōkōron [Theory of Crisis]. In Uno Kōzō Chosakushū [Complete Works of Uno Kōzō], vol. 5. Tokyo: Iwanami Shoten, 1974.

———. Uno Kōzō Chosakushu [Collected Works of Uno Kōzō]. 10 vols. Tokyo: Iwanami Shoten, 1974.

———. Theory of a Purely Capitalist Society. Translated by Thomas Sekine. Sussex, UK: Harvester Press, 1980.

———. "The Essence of Capital." In Sources of Japanese Tradition: 1868–1945. New York: Columbia University Press, 2003.

Virilio, Paul. Speed and Politics. Translated by Mark Polizzotti. New York: Semiotext(e) Foreign Agents Series, 1986.

———. L'insécurité du territoire. Paris: Galilee, 1993.

Virno, Paolo. A Grammar of the Multitude: For an Analysis of Contemporary Forms of Life. Translated by Isabella Bertoletti, James Cascaito, and Andrea Casson. Los Angeles: Semiotext(e), 2004.

Watabe, Tetsu. Nihon rōdō kumiai undōshi: Nihon rōdō kumiai zenkoku kyōgikai wo chūshin toshite [A History of Labor Union Movements in Japan: On Nihon rōdō kumiai zenkoku kyōgikai]. Tokyo: Aoki Shoten, 1954.

Weiner, Michael. Race and Migration in Imperial Japan. London: Routledge, 1994.

———. The Origins of the Korean Community in Japan. Atlantic Highlands: New Jersey Humanities International, Inc., 1989.

Yoshida, Kyūichi. Nihon Shakai jigyō no rekishi [A History of Social Welfare Movements in Japan]. Tokyo: Keisō Shobo, 1987.

Zhang, Li. Strangers in the City: Reconfigurations of Space, Power, and Social Networks within China's Floating Population. Stanford, Calif.: Stanford University Press, 2001.

Žižek, Slavoj. The Sublime Object of Ideology. London: Verso, 1989.

———. "The Parallax View." New Left Review 25 (January–February 2004): 121–34.

———. "Class Struggle or Postmodernism? Yes, please!" In Contingency, Hegemony, Universality: Contemporary Dialogues on the Left, Judith Butler, Ernesto Laclau, and Slavoj Žižek. London: Verso, 2000.

INDEX

Agamben, Giorgio, 128

Agriculture, 127, 219; crisis in Korea, 47–49; immiseration of, 4, 50, 53, 65, 67

Aichi prefecture, 78, 84, 108, 217, 233n25, 244n74

Akiyama, Fusuke, 173–74, 260–61n10

Althusser, Louis, 1, 5, 207

Anarchism or anarchists, 40, 41, 44, 154, 227, 228, 229

Banks. *See* Financial institutions

Barracks, 14, 75, 88, 95, 99, 101, 105, 145–46; demolition of, 250n69, 251n75; evacuation, 122–27; Sōaikai soliciting at, 130–32, 164. *See also* Hamba

Benjamin, Walter, 138, 214, 215, 253n27

Beveridge, William, 210–11

Boarding houses. *See* Barracks; Hamba

Bolsheviks or Bolshevism, 40, 41, 134, 138

"Built environment," 61, 67

Capital: finance, 6, 21, 48, 54; industrial, 7, 15; labor and, 12, 81–82, 91, 162, 180, 206, 207, 211; Japanese, 174, 261n15; Marx on, 8, 11, 25, 46, 212–13, 232n20, 260n9; state power and, 183, 208

Capitalism or capitalist: chance concept and, 4–5, 21–22, 45; class and, 65, 91, 141, 213, 246n7; commodity economies and, 5, 7–8, 11, 46, 133, 205–6, 208, 211–12; contingency and, 6–7, 206–7; exchange process and, 45–46, 75, 208;

exploitation and, 10–11, 14, 22, 183, 211, 215, 232n20; in Japan, 10–11, 13, 23, 29, 53–54; Korean agriculture and, 48, 209; origins, 46; production, 9–10, 12, 25, 173, 211–13, 232n20; society, 206–8, 260n9, 267n5; workers and, 34, 41. *See also* Capital; Commodity; Marx, Karl

Chadwick, Edwin, 136

China, 6, 134

Choi, Un-kyo, 91–92

Cholla province, Korea, 26, 49, 50, 160, 227, 228

Class: antagonisms, 171, 180, 183; contradictions, 138; politics, 22, 68; struggles, 10, 41, 43, 65, 93, 133, 154, 157, 168, 171. *See also* Working class

Coal mines, 28–29, 32, 33, 37, 54, 75, 160, 217, 229; in England, 76, 150; Hokkaido, 38–39, 234n11

Colonialism: identity and, 158; independence, 138–39, 157; Japanese government, 26, 32, 34, 39, 133, 139; in Korea, 11, 13, 21, 28, 47–49, 127, 184, 209, 225; Korean workers and, 2, 8, 21, 43, 92; labor, 182, 188, 203; Pak Ch'um-gum's role in, 17, 133, 167–68; police, 144, 161, 228, 258n88; surplus populations, 26–28, 43–44, 45, 54, 65, 211

Colonial surplus, 26–28, 43–44, 45, 54, 65

Ken C. Kawashima is an associate professor of East Asian studies
at the University of Toronto.

· ·

Library of Congress Cataloging-in-Publication Data
Kawashima, Ken C. (Ken Chester)
The proletarian gamble : Korean workers in interwar Japan /
Ken C. Kawashima.
p. cm.—(Asia-Pacific)
Includes bibliographical references and index.
ISBN 978-0-8223-4399-8 (cloth : alk. paper)—
ISBN 978-0-8223-4417-9 (pbk. : alk. paper) 1. Koreans—
Employment—Japan—History—20th century. 2. Korea—Emigration
and immigration—History—20th century. 3. Japan—Emigration and
immigration—History—20th century. 4. Labor supply—Japan—
History—20th century. 5. Japan—Employees—Supply and demand—
History—20th century. I. Title. II. Series: Asia-Pacific.
DS832.7.K6K399 2009
331.6'251905209041—dc22   2008051092